Philosophical Papers

I

Philosophical Papers

Volume I

DAVID LEWIS

New York   Oxford
OXFORD UNIVERSITY PRESS
1983

Library of Congress Cataloging in Publication Data

Lewis, David, 1941–
Philosophical papers.

Includes index.
1. Philosophy—Addresses, essays, lectures.
I. Title.
B29.L49 1982   110   82-22551
ISBN 0-19-503203-9 (v. 1)
ISBN 0-19-503204-7 (pbk. : v. 1)

Printing (last digit):   9 8 7 6 5 4 3

Printed in the United States of America

Contents

Acknowledgments

I thank the editors and publishers who have kindly granted permission to reprint the essays that appear in this volume. The places of first publication are as follows.

"Holes," *Australasian Journal of Philosophy* 48 (1970):206–12.

"Anselm and Actuality," *Noûs* 4 (1970): 175–88.

"Counterpart Theory and Quantified Modal Logic," *Journal of Philosophy* 65 (1968): 113–26.

"Counterparts of Persons and Their Bodies," *Journal of Philsophy* 68 (1971): 203–11.

"Survival and Identity," in Amelie O. Rorty, ed., *The Identities of Persons* (University of California Press, 1976) 17–40.

"How to Define Theoretical Terms," *Journal of Philosophy* 67 (1970): 427–46.

"An Argument for the Identity Theory," *Journal of Philosophy* 63 (1966): 17–25; with additional material from David M. Rosenthal, ed., *Materialism and the Mind-Body Problem* (Prentice-Hall, Inc., 1971) 162 and 164–65.

"Radical Interpretation," *Synthese* 23 (1974): 331–44. Copyright © 1974 by D. Reidel Publishing Company, Dordrecht, Holland.

"Mad Pain and Martian Pain," in Ned Block, ed., *Readings in the Philosophy of Psychology*, Volume I (Harvard University Press, 1980) 216–22.

"Attitudes *De Dicto* and *De Se*," *The Philosophical Review* 88 (1979): 513–43.

"Languages and Language," in Keith Gunderson, ed., *Minnesota Studies in the Philosophy of Science*, Volume VII (University of Minnesota Press, 1975) 3–35.

"General Semantics," *Synthese* 22 (1970): 18–67. Copyright © 1970 by D. Reidel Publishing Company, Dordrecht, Holland.

"Scorekeeping in a Language Game," *Journal of Philosophical Logic* 8 (1979): 339–59. Copyright © 1979 by D. Reidel Publishing Company, Dordrecht, Holland.

"'Tensions," reprinted by permission of New York University Press from *Semantics and Philosophy* edited by Milton K. Munitz and Peter K. Unger. Copyright © 1974 by New York University.

"Truth in Fiction," *American Philosophical Quarterly* 15 (1978): 37–46.

Introduction

The fifteen papers in this volume were originally published from 1966 to 1980. Here, misprints apart, they are reprinted in their original form.[1] For the most part, I stand by what I said. Where I do not, or where additions seemed urgently needed, I have left the paper as it was but appended new postscripts.

The papers in this volume deal with topics in ontology, in philosophy of mind, and in philosophy of language. Papers on counterfactuals, causation, and related matters will appear in a sequel. I have left out papers which are rejoinders, or which are of primarily technical interest, or which overlap too much with the papers I have included.

I should have liked to be a piecemeal, unsystematic philosopher, offering independent proposals on a variety of topics. It was not to be. I succumbed too often to the temptation to presuppose my views on one topic when writing on another. Most notably, my realism toward unactualized possibles shows up in nearly every paper in the book. Sometimes the argument requires it, as in " 'Tensions"; sometimes my principal point could just as well have been put neutrally, as when I allude to other worlds in "Mad Pain and Martian Pain." But many cases fall in between. If I did not take properties as sets of possible individuals, for instance, I could still defend the thesis of "Attitudes *De Dicto* and *De Se*" that properties are

---

[1] With the exception of "An Argument for the Identity Theory," which incorporates notes added on the occasion of an earlier reprinting.

the appropriate objects of attitudes; but I could no longer support this thesis by drawing an analogy between self-location with respect to the entire population of logical space and with respect to the population of the actual world. I hope the sceptical reader will consider breaking up the package and taking the parts that suit him, but I have not done all I could have done to make his task easy. For, after all, my principal interest has not been to proselytize but to figure out what I should believe.

The reader in search of knock-down arguments in favor of my theories will go away disappointed. Whether or not it would be nice to knock disagreeing philosophers down by sheer force of argument,[2] it cannot be done. Philosophical theories are never refuted conclusively. (Or hardly ever. Gödel and Gettier may have done it.) The theory survives its refutation—at a price. Argle has said what we accomplish in philosophical argument: we measure the price.[3] Perhaps that is something we can settle more or less conclusively. But when all is said and done, and all the tricky arguments and distinctions and counterexamples have been discovered, presumably we will still face the question which prices are worth paying, which theories are on balance credible, which are the unacceptably counterintuitive consequences and which are the acceptably counterintuitive ones. On this question we may still differ. And if all is indeed said and done, there will be no hope of discovering still further arguments to settle our differences.

It might be otherwise if, as some philosophers seem to think, we had a sharp line between "linguistic intuition," which must be taken as unchallengeable evidence, and philosophical theory, which must at all costs fit this evidence. If that were so, conclusive refutations would be dismayingly abundant. But, whatever may be said for foundationalism in other subjects, this foundationalist theory of philosophical knowledge seems ill-founded in the extreme. Our "intuitions" are simply opinions; our philosophical theories are the same. Some are commonsensical, some are sophisticated; some are particular, some general; some are more firmly held, some less. But they are all opinions, and a reasonable goal for a philosopher is to bring them into equilibrium. Our common task is to find out what equilibria there are that can withstand examination, but it remains for each of us to come to rest at one or another of them. If we lose our moorings in everyday common sense, our fault is not that we ignore part of our evidence. Rather, the trouble is that we settle for a very inadequate equilibrium. If our official theories disagree with what we cannot help thinking outside the philosophy room, then no real equilibrium has been reached. Unless we are doubleplusgood doublethinkers, it will not last. And it should not last, for it is safe to say that in such a case we will believe a great deal that is false.

---

[2] It would not be nice, of course. Robert Nozick has drawn attention to our strange way of talking about philosophical argument as if its goal were to subjugate the minds of our esteemed colleagues, and to escape their efforts to do likewise unto us. See his *Philosophical Explanations* (Harvard University Press, 1981), pages 4–5.

[3] See the conclusion of "Holes" (in this volume).

Once the menu of well-worked-out theories is before us, philosophy is a matter of opinion. Is that to say that there is no truth to be had? Or that the truth is of our own making, and different ones of us can make it differently? Not at all! If you say flatly that there is no god, and I say that there are countless gods but none of them are our worldmates,[4] then it may be that neither of us is making any mistake of method. We may each be bringing our opinions to equilibrium in the most careful possible way, taking account of all the arguments, distinctions, and counterexamples. But one of us, at least, is making a mistake of fact. Which one is wrong depends on what there is.

So much for method. Let me briefly list some recurring themes that unify the papers in this volume, thus frustrating my hope of philosophizing piecemeal.

Extreme modal realism, according to which there are many unactualized possible individuals, and according to which the actual individuals do not differ in kind from the unactualized ones.

Exploitation of the analogies between space, time, and modality.

Materialism, according to which physical science will, if successful, describe our world completely.

A broadly functionalist[5] theory of mind, according to which mental states *qua* mental are realizers of roles specified in commonsense psychology.

Integration of formal semantics into a broader account of our use of language in social interaction.

Refusal to take language as a starting point in the analysis of thought and of modality.

I thank all those who have helped me to think about the matters discussed in these papers. Those who have helped me most are listed in the footnotes to the papers and the postscripts. Also I thank the University of California at Los Angeles;

---

[4]As Peter Forrest has pointed out, I am perhaps the most extreme polytheist going. If, as I suppose, a being does not have to satisfy some inconsistent description to be a god, then I take the number of the gods to be at least $\beth_2$. Unlike most polytheists, however, I think of this world we live in as entirely godless.

[5]I do not know whether I am, strictly speaking, a functionalist. For I reject at least two main planks in the platform. (1) I reject the individualistic thesis that someone is in pain, say, if and only if he is in a state that occupies the role of pain *for him, then.* I think it also matters what role his state plays in others of his kind. (2) I reject the thesis that "pain" rigidly designates a state shared by all who are in pain. Rather, it nonrigidly designates the state that occupies the role of pain in the particular kind under consideration. Indeed there is a state common to all who are in pain—"being in pain," I call it—but it is not pain, and it does not itself occupy the role of pain. In the terminology of "How To Define Theoretical Terms" (in this volume), it is a "diagonalized sense."

Princeton University; Victoria University of Wellington and the New Zealand-United States Educational Foundation; and all those institutions that have given me opportunities to try these papers out on critical audiences.

Princeton   D. L.
November 1981

Philosophical Papers

I

Ontology

Holes

with Stephanie Lewis

Argle. I believe in nothing but concrete material objects.

Bargle. There are many of your opinions I applaud; but one of your less pleasing characteristics is your fondness for the doctrines of nominalism and materialism. Every time you get started on any such topic, I know we are in for a long argument. Where shall we start this time : numbers, colors, lengths, sets, force-fields, sensations, or what?

Argle. Fictions all! I've thought hard about every one of them.

Bargle. A long evening's work. Before we start, let me find you a snack. Will you have some crackers and cheese?

Argle. Thank you. What splendid Gruyère!

Bargle You know, there are remarkably many holes in this piece.

Argle. There are.

Bargle. Got you!

Bargle. You admit there are many holes in that piece of cheese. Therefore, there are some holes in it. Therefore, there are some holes. In other words, holes exist. But holes are not made of matter; to the contrary, they result from the absence of matter.

Argle. I did say that there are holes in the cheese; but that is not to imply that there are holes.

Bargle. However not? If you say that there are A's that are B's, you are committed logically to the conclusion that there are A's.

Argle. When *I* say that there are holes in something, I mean nothing more nor less than that it is perforated. The synonymous shape-predicates ' . . . is perforated' and 'there are holes in . . .' —just like any other shape-predicate, say ' . . . is a dodecahedron'—may truly be predicated of pieces of cheese, without any implication that perforation is due to the presence of occult, immaterial entities. I am sorry my innocent predicate confuses you by sounding like an idiom of existential quantification, so that you think that inferences involving it are valid when they are not. But I have my reasons. You, given a perforated piece of cheese and believing as you do that it is perforated because it contains immaterial entities called holes, employ an idiom of existential quantification to say falsely 'There are holes in it.' Agreeable fellow that I am, I wish to have a sentence that sounds like yours and that is true exactly when you falsely suppose your existential quantification over immaterial things to be true. That way we could talk about the cheese without philosophizing, if only you'd let me. You and I would understand our sentences differently, but the difference wouldn't interfere with our conversation until you start drawing conclusions which follow from your false sentence but not from my homonymous true sentence.[1]

Bargle. Oh, very well. But behold: there are as many holes in my piece of cheese as in yours. Do you agree?

Argle. I'll take your word for it without even counting: there are as many holes in mine as in yours. But what I mean by that is that either both pieces are singly-perforated, or both are doubly-perforated, or both are triply-perforated, and so on.

Bargle. What a lot of different shape-predicates you know! How ever did you find time to learn them all? And what does 'and so on' mean?[2]

Argle. Let me just say that the two pieces are equally-perforated. Now I have used only one two-place predicate.

Bargle. Unless I singly-perforate each of these crackers, how will you say that there are as many holes in my cheese as crackers on my plate? Be so kind as not to invent another predicate on the spot. I am quite prepared to go on until you have told me about all the predicates you have up your sleeve. I have a good imagination, and plenty of time.

Argle. Oh, dear . . . (ponders)

Argle. I was wrong. There *are* holes.

Bargle. You recant?

Argle. No. Holes are material objects.

Bargle. I expected that sooner. You are thinking, doubtless, that every hole is

[1] *Cf.* W. V. Quine, "On What There Is," *From a Logical Point of View*, 2nd ed. (Cambridge, Mass: Harvard University Press, 1961), p. 13.

[2] *Cf.* Donald Davidson, "Theories of Meaning and Learnable Languages," in Y. Bar-Hillel, *Logic, Methodology and Philosophy of Science, Proceedings of the* 1964 *International Congress* (Amsterdam, 1965), pp. 383–94.

filled with matter: silver amalgam, air, interstellar gas, luminiferous ether or whatever it may be.

Argle. No. Perhaps there are no truly empty holes; but I cannot deny that there might be.

Bargle. How can something utterly devoid of matter be made of matter?

Argle. You're looking for the matter in the wrong place. (I mean to say, that's what you would be doing if there were any such things as places, which there aren't.) The matter isn't inside the hole. It would be absurd to say it was: nobody wants to say that holes are inside themselves. The matter surrounds the hole. The lining of a hole, you agree, is a material object. For every hole there is a hole-lining; for every hole-lining there is a hole. I say the hole-lining *is* the hole.

Bargle. Didn't you say that the hole-lining surrounds the hole? Things don't surround themselves.

Argle. Holes do. In my language, 'surrounds' said of a hole (described as such) means 'is identical with.' 'Surrounds' said of other things means just what you think it means.

Bargle. Doesn't it bother you that your dictionary must have two entries under 'surrounds' where mine has only one?

Argle. A little, but not much. I'm used to putting up with such things.

Bargle. Such *whats?*

Argle. Such dictionary entries. They're made of dried ink, you recall.

Bargle. Oh. I suppose you'll also say that ' . . . is in . . . ' or ' . . . is through . . . ' said of a hole means ' . . . is part of . . . '.

Argle. Exactly so, Bargle.

Bargle. Then do you still say that 'There are holes in the cheese' contains an unanalyzed shape-predicate synonymous with ' . . . is perforated'?

Argle. No; it is an existential quantification, as you think it is. It means that there exist material objects such that they are holes and they are parts of the piece of cheese.

Bargle. But we wouldn't say, would we, that a hole is made out of cheese?

Argle. No; but the fact that we wouldn't say it doesn't mean it isn't true. We wouldn't have occasion to say, unless philosophizing, that these walls are perpendicular to the floor; but they are. Anyhow we *do* say that caves are holes in the ground and that some of them are made out of limestone.

Bargle. Take this paper-towel roller. Spin it on a lathe. The hole-lining spins. Surely you'd never say the hole spins?

Argle. Why not?

Bargle. Even though the hole might continue to be entirely filled with a dowel that didn't spin or move at all?

Argle. What difference does that make?

Bargle. None, really. But now I have you: take a toilet-paper roller, put it inside the paper-towel roller, and spin it the other way. The big hole spins clockwise. The little hole spins counter-clockwise. But the little hole is part of the big hole, so it spins clockwise along with the rest of the big hole. So if holes can spin, as you think, the little hole turns out to be spinning in both directions at once, which is absurd.

Argle. I see why you might think that the little hole is part of the big hole, but you can't expect me to agree. The little hole is inside the big hole, but that's all. Hence I have no reason to say that the little hole is spinning clockwise.

Bargle. Consider a thin-walled hole with a gallon of water inside. The volume of the hole is at least a gallon, whereas the volume of the hole-lining is much less. If the hole is the hole-lining, then whatever was true of one would have to be true of the other. They could not differ in volume.

Argle. For 'hole' read 'bottle;' for 'hole-lining' also read 'bottle.' You have the same paradox. Holes, like bottles, have volume—or, as I'd rather say, are voluminous or equi-voluminous with other things—in two different senses. There's the volume of the hole or bottle itself, and there's the volume of the largest chunk of fluid which could be put inside the hole or bottle without compression. For holes, as for bottles, contextual clues permit us to keep track of which we mean.

Bargle. What is the volume of the hole itself? How much of the cheese do you include as part of one of these holes? And how do you decide? Arbitrarily, that's how. Don't try saying you include as little of the cheese as possible, for however much you include, you could have included less.

Argle. What we call a single hole is really many hole-linings. Some include more of the cheese, some include less. Therefore I need not decide, arbitrarily or otherwise, how much cheese is part of the hole. Many different decisions are equally correct.

Bargle. How can a single hole be identical with many hole-linings that are not identical with one another?

Argle. Really there are many different holes, and each is identical with a different hole-lining. But all these different holes are the same hole.

Bargle. You contradict yourself. Don't you mean to say that they all *surround* the same hole—where by 'surround' I mean 'surround,' not 'be identical with'?

Argle. Not at all. I would contradict myself if I said that two different holes were identical. But I didn't; what I said was that they were the same hole. Two holes are the same hole when they have a common part that is itself a hole.

Bargle. You agreed before that there were as many holes in my cheese as crackers on my plate. Are there still?

Argle. Yes; there are two of each left.

Bargle. Two crackers, to be sure, but how can you say there are two holes?

Argle. Thus: there is a hole, and there is another hole that is not the same hole, and every hole in the cheese is the same hole as one or the other.

Bargle. Be so kind as to say 'co-perforated,' not 'same,' and stop pretending to talk about identity when you are not. I understand you now: co-perforation is supposed to be an equivalence relation among hole-linings, and when you say there are two holes you are trying to say that there are two non-identical co-perforation-classes of hole-linings. Really you identify holes not with hole-linings but with *classes* of hole-linings.

Argle. I would if I could, but I can't. No; holes are hole-linings; but when I speak of them as holes, I find it convenient to use 'same' meaning 'co-perforated' wherever a man of your persuasion would use 'same' meaning 'identical.' You know my reason for this trickery: my sentences about sameness of holes will be true just when you wrongly suppose your like-sounding sentences to be. The same goes for sentences about number of holes, since we both analyze these in terms of sameness.[3]

Bargle. You still haven't told me how you say there are as many holes in my cheese as crackers on my plate, without also saying how many there are.

Argle. Here goes. There exist three things X, Y, and Z. X is part of the sum of the crackers, Y is part of the cheese, and Z is part of Y. Every maximal connected part of Y is a hole, and every hole in the cheese is the same hole as some maximal connected part of Y. X overlaps each of the crackers and Z overlaps each maximal connected part of Y. Everything which is either the intersection of X and a cracker or the intersection of Z and some maximal connected part of Y is the same size as any other such thing. X is the same size as Z.[4]

Bargle. Your devices won't work because co-perforation is not an equivalence relation. *Any* two overlapping parts of my cheese have a common part that is a hole-lining, though in most cases the hole-lining is entirely filled with cheese. To be co-perforated is therefore nothing more than to overlap, and overlapping is no equivalence relation. The result is that although, as you say, you can find two hole-linings in this cheese that are not co-perforated, you can find another one that is co-perforated with both of them.

Argle. If you were right that a hole made of cheese sould be entirely filled with the same kind of cheese, you could find far more than two non-co-perforated hole-linings; and there would be no such thing as cheese without holes in it. But you are wrong. A hole is a hole not just by virtue of its own shape but also by virtue of the way it contrasts with the matter inside it and around it. The same is true of other shape-predicates; I wouldn't say that any part of the cheese is a dodecahedron, though I admit that there are parts—parts that do not contrast with their surroundings—that are *shaped like* dodecahedra.

[3] *Cf.* Quine's maxim of identification of indiscernibles in "Identity, Ostension, and Hypostasis," *From a Logical Point of View,* p. 71; P.T. Geach, "Identity," *Review of Metaphysics* 21 (1967): 3–12.
[4] This translation adapts a device from Nelson Goodman and W. V. Quine, "Steps toward a Constructive Nominalism," *Journal of Symbolic Logic* 12 (1947): 109–10.

Bargle. Consider the paper-towel roller. How many holes?

Argle. One. You know what I mean: many, but they're all the same.

Bargle. I think you must say there are at least two. The left half and the right half are not the same hole. They have no common part, so no common part that is a hole.

Argle. They're not holes, they're two parts of a hole.

Bargle. Why aren't they holes themselves? They are singly-perforated and they are made of matter unlike the matter inside them. If I cut them apart you'd have to say they were holes?

Argle. Yes.

Bargle. You admit that a hole can be a proper part of a bigger—say, thicker-skinned—hole?

Argle. Yes.

Bargle. You admit that they are shaped like holes?

Argle. Yes, but they aren't holes. I can't say why they aren't. I know which things are holes, but I can't give you a definition. But why should I? You already know what hole-linings are. I say the two halves of the roller are only parts of a hole because I—like you—would say they are only parts of a hole-lining. What isn't a hole-lining isn't a hole.

Bargle. In that case, I admit that co-perforation may be an equivalence relation at least among singly-perforated hole-linings.

Argle. All holes are singly-perforated. A doubly-perforated thing has two holes in it that are not the same hole.

Bargle. Are you sure? Take the paper-towel roller and punch a little hole in its side. Now you have a hole in a hole-lining. You'd have to say you have a hole in a hole. You have a little hole which is part of a big hole; the big hole is not singly-perforated; and the little hole and the big hole are the same hole, since the little hole is a common part of each.

Argle. I think not. You speak of *the* big hole; but what we have are two big holes, not the same, laid end to end. There is also the little hole, not the same as either big hole, which overlaps them both. Of course we sometimes call something a hole, in a derivative sense, if it is a connected sum of holes. Any decent cave consists of many holes that are not the same hole, so I must have been speaking in this derivative sense when I said that caves are holes.

Bargle. What peculiar things you are driven to say when philosophy corrupts your mind! Tell me the truth: would you have dreamt for a moment of saying there were two big holes rather than one if you were not suffering under the influence of a philosophical theory?

Argle. No; I fear I would have remained ignorant.

Bargle. I see that I can never hope to refute you, since I no sooner reduce your position to absurdity than you embrace the absurdity.

Argle. Not absurdity; disagreement with common opinion.

Bargle. Very well. But I, for one, have more trust in common opinions than I do in any philosophical reasoning whatever. In so far as you disagree with them, you must pay a great price in the plausibility of your theories.

Argle. Agreed. We have been measuring that price. I have shown that it is not so great as you thought; I am prepared to pay it. My theories can earn credence by their clarity and economy; and if they disagree a little with common opinion, then common opinion may be corrected even by a philosopher.

Bargle. The price is still too high.

Argle. We agree in principle; we're only haggling.

Bargle. We do. And the same is true of our other debates over ontic parsimony. Indeed, this argument has served us as an illustration—novel, simple, and self-contained—of the nature of our customary disputes.

Argle. And yet the illustration has interest in its own right. Your holes, had I been less successful, would have punctured my nominalistic materialism with the greatest of ease.

Bargle. Rehearsed and refreshed, let us return to—say—the question of classes.[5]

[5] There would be little truth to the guess that Argle is one of the authors and Bargle is the other. We thank Charles Chastain, who also is neither Argle nor Bargle, for many helpful comments.

· T W O ·

Anselm and Actuality

I. INTRODUCTION

Philosophy abounds in troublesome arguments—endlessly debated, perennially plausible, perennially suspect. The standards of validity for modal reasoning have long been unclear; they become clear only when we provide a semantic analysis of modal logic by reference to possible worlds and to possible things therein.[1] Thus insofar as we understand modal reasoning at all, we understand it as disguised reasoning about possible beings. But if these are intelligible enough to provide modal logic with foundations, they are intelligible enough to be talked about explicitly. Modal reasoning can be replaced by nonmodal, ordinary reasoning about possible things. Given an obscure modal argument, we can translate it into a nonmodal argument—or into several nonmodal arguments, if the given argument was ambiguous. Once we have a nonmodal argument, we have clear standards of validity; and once we have nonmodal translations of the premises, we can understand them well enough to judge whether they are credible. Foremost among our modal headaches is Anselm's ontological argument. How does it fare under the translation treatment I have prescribed? It turns out to have two principal nonmodal translations. One is valid; the other has credible premises; the difference between the two

I am grateful to Alvin Plantinga for his criticisms of an earlier version of this paper.

[1]See, for instance, Saul Kripke, "Semantical Considerations on Modal Logic," *Acta Philosophica Fennica* 16 (1963): 83–94.

is subtle. No wonder the argument has never been decisively refuted; no wonder it has never convinced the infidel.

II. FORMULATION OF THE ARGUMENT

The ontological argument notoriously comes in countless versions. We shall confine our attention to one of the arguments that can, with some plausibility, be extracted from Chapter II of the *Proslogion*—not the only one, but the one I take to be both simplest and soundest. The reader must judge for himself whether what I say can be adapted to his own favorite ontological argument.

The version we shall work on has the merit of bypassing some familiar difficulties that are not at the heart of the matter. It will have no chance to be invalid in some of the ways that ontological arguments have been said to be invalid. The proper name "God" will not appear, so we will not have to worry about the form or content of its definition. In fact, there will be no defining of anything. We will also not have to worry about the logic of definite descriptions. If I say "That which is red is not green" I might just mean "Whatever is red is not green," neither implying nor presupposing that at least or at most one thing is red. Similarly, we can construe Anselm's "that, than which nothing greater can be conceived" not as a definite description but rather as an idiom of universal quantification.

Our argument is as follows:

Premise 1. Whatever exists in the understanding can be conceived to exist in reality.

Premise 2. Whatever exists in the understanding would be greater if it existed in reality than if it did not.

Premise 3. Something exists in the understanding, than which nothing greater can be conceived.

Conclusion. Something exists in reality, than which nothing greater can be conceived.

III. THE FIRST PREMISE

It is our plan to reason explicitly about possible worlds and possible things therein. These possible beings will be included in our domain of discourse. The idioms of quantification, therefore, will be understood as ranging over all the beings we wish to talk about, whether existent or nonexistent.

In the context at hand, the appropriate sense of possibility is conceivability. Possible worlds are conceivable worlds. If some otherwise possible worlds are inconceivable—say, seventeen-dimensional worlds—we should not count those; whereas if some otherwise impossible worlds are conceivable—say, worlds in which there is a largest prime—we should count those. Given any statement about what may be conceived to be the case, we translate it into a statement about what is the case in some conceivable world.

Thus to say that something can be conceived to exist in reality is to say that in some conceivable world, it does exist. This makes sense only if existence is taken to be a relation between beings and worlds, so that we can say that something exists in one world but not in another.[2]

Premise 1 tells us that whatever exists in the understanding exists in some conceivable world or other. Thus the beings that may be said to exist in the understanding are among the beings we have already admitted into our domain of discourse. It is ill-advised to speak of them as existing in the understanding: they do not bear to the understanding the same relation which something existing in a world bears to that world! Let us simply call them *understandable* beings.

We are ready now to give a nonmodal translation of Premise 1, as follows:

1. $\forall x(Ux \supset \exists w(Ww \& xEw))$

(For any understandable being x, there is a world w such that x exists in w.)

Is the premise credible? I have no wish to contest it. Someone might say that a round square is an understandable being that does not exist in any conceivable world; and perhaps there is enough latitude in the notions of understandability and conceivability so that he might be within his rights. But the ontological arguer who construes those notions so that Premise 1 is a necessary truth is also within his rights, and that is what matters. It is not for me, but for the ontological arguer, to explain what existing in the understanding is supposed to be, and what is supposed to be the relation between the existence in one's understanding of a possible being and one's understanding of some or all descriptions that would apply to that being. I am willing to grant that he can give some adequate account.

He might wish to do so in such a way that the understandability of a given possible being is a contingent matter, so that a being might be *understandable in* one world but not in another. I may grant him this; but we shall only be concerned with actual understandability, understandability in the actual world. Hence the predicate "U" need not be relativized to worlds.[3]

IV. THE SECOND PREMISE

In some versions of the ontological argument, it seems that a hypothetical nonexistent God is supposed to be excelled in greatness by some *other* conceivable being:

---

[2] We will not need to settle the question whether anything—or any non-abstract thing—ever exists in more than one world, or in none, or partly in one and partly in another. For consideration of such questions, see my "Counterpart Theory and Quantified Modal Logic," in this volume.

[3] Similar remarks apply to "W". The ontological arguer might choose to explain conceivability in such a way that a world sometimes is *conceivable from* one world but not from another. However, we will be concerned only with actual conceivability of worlds; that is, conceivability from the actual world.

one that exists, but otherwise is just like the hypothetical nonexistent God. I am unable to see how this strategy could yield an argument close enough to soundness to be interesting. Moreover, it is not Anselm's strategy; he writes: "For suppose it exists in the understanding alone: then *it* can be conceived to exist in reality; which is greater." What excels a hypothetical nonexistent God is not some other being; it is that same being, conceived as existent.

To capture this idea, beings must have their greatnesses relative to worlds. Premise 2 says that any understandable being is greater in worlds in which it exists than in worlds in which it does not. We have the following nonmodal translation of Premise 2:

2. $\forall x \forall w \forall v (Ux \ \& \ Ww \ \& \ Wv \ \& \ xEw \ \& \sim xEv. \supset xwGxv)$

(For any understandable being x, and for any worlds w and v, if x exists in w but x does not exist in v, then the greatness of x in w exceeds the greatness of x in v.)

We need not regard the seeming hypostatization of greatnesses as more than a figure of speech, since we can take "the greatness of . . . in . . . exceeds the greatness of . . . in . . . " as an indivisible 4-place predicate.

I have no wish to dispute the second premise. In saying what makes for greatness, the ontological arguer is merely expounding his standards of greatness. Within wide limits, he is entitled to whatever standards of greatness he wants. All we can demand is that he stick to fixed standards throughout his argument, and throughout his subsequent account of the theological significance of the conclusion thereof.

V. THE THIRD PREMISE

The third premise says that there is some understandable being x whose greatness cannot be conceived to be exceeded by the greatness of anything. That is, the greatness of x is not exceeded by the greatness in any conceivable world w of any being y. We have seen that greatnesses, as thought of by the ontological arguer, belong to beings paired with worlds; according to the third premise, no such pair has a greatness exceeding the greatness of a certain understandable being x.

But if greatnesses belong to beings relative to worlds, what are we talking about when we say: the greatness of x? *Which* greatness of x? The greatness of x in which conceivable world? Different answers to the question yield different nonmodal translations of Premise 3.

We might construe Premise 3 as saying that what is unexceeded is the *actual* greatness of x, the greatness of x here in the actual world. If we speak of the greatness of something without mentioning a world, surely we ordinarily mean its greatness in the actual world; for we are ordinarily not talking about any worlds except the actual world. So it is plausible that even when other worlds *are* under discussion, we are speaking about the actual world unless we say otherwise. Thus, introducing a name "@" for the actual world, we obtain this first nonmodal translation of Premise 3:

3A. $\exists x(Ux \And \sim \exists w \exists y(Ww \And ywGx@))$

(There is an understandable being x, such that for no world w and being y does the greatness of y in w exceed the greatness of x in the actual world.)

Alternatively, we might construe Premise 3 as saying something weaker: that what is unexceeded is the *greatest* greatness of x, the greatness of x in any one of the worlds in which x is at its greatest. That is equivalent to saying merely that the greatness of x in some world v is unexceeded; for if the greatness of x in v is unexceeded, v is one of the worlds in which x is at its greatest. Thus we obtain a second nonmodal translation of Premise 3:

3B. $\exists x \exists v(Ux \And Wv \And \sim \exists w \exists y(Ww \And ywGxv))$

(There are an understandable being x and a world v, such that for no world w and being y does the greatness of y in w exceed the greatness of x in v.)

Or we might construe Premise 3 as saying something stronger: that what is unexceeded is *any* greatness of x, the greatness of x in any world whatever. Thus we obtain a third nonmodal translation of Premise 3:

3C. $\exists x(Ux \And \sim \exists v \exists w \exists y(Wv \And Ww \And ywGxv))$

(There is an understandable being x such that for no worlds v and w and being y does the greatness of y in w exceed the greatness of x in v.)

Under the auxiliary premise 4, which we shall take for granted henceforth,

4. $W@$

(The actual world is a world).

3C implies 3A, but not conversely, and 3A implies 3B, but not conversely.

Perhaps there is one more possibility: For any world w, the greatness in w of x is not exceeded by the greatness in w of anything. Thus we obtain a fourth translation:

3D. $\exists x(Ux \And \sim \exists w \exists y(Ww \And ywGxw))$

(There is an understandable being x such that for no world w and being y does the greatness of y in w exceed the greatness of x in w.)

3D is not a plausible translation, since it might be true even if the greatness of anything x in any world w is exceeded by the greatness of something else elsewhere.

Premise 3B, at least, is moderately credible. It says that there is a highest grade of greatness, and that this grade of greatness is occupied, in some world, by an understandable being. If, above some level, we were prepared to discriminate only finitely many grades of greatness (no matter how many), and if we were prepared to admit that any grade of greatness, however high, could be occupied by an understandable being, then we would thereby be committed to accepting 3B. I have no wish to dispute 3B.

We postpone consideration of the credibility of the stronger translations 3A and 3C of Premise 3. We will not need to consider whether 3D is credible.

VI. THE CONCLUSION

The conclusion says that there is some being x, existing in the actual world, whose greatness cannot be conceived to be exceeded by the greatness of anything. (We need not add that x is an understandable being, though that would follow if the rest did.) That is, the greatness of x is not exceeded by the greatness in any conceivable world w of any being y.

We ask again: *which* greatness of x? But this time the answer clearly should be: the *actual* greatness of x, the greatness of x here in the actual world. Other versions of the conclusion would either imply this version or be of no theological interest. The fool would not mind being convinced that there is an actual being who might conceivably have been—is, in some conceivable world—of unexcelled greatness. So our nonmodal translation of the conclusion resembles 3A, our first version of Premise 3:

C. $\exists x(xE@ \ \& \ \sim \exists w \exists y(Ww \ \& \ ywGx@))$

(There is a being x existing in the actual world such that for no world w and being y does the greatness of y in w exceed the greatness of x in the actual world.)

VII. VALIDITY OF THE ARGUMENT

We now have four precise, nonmodal translations of our original argument, one for each alternative translation of Premise 3. It is a routine matter to determine, by ordinary nonmodal logic, which are valid and which are not. It turns out that the arguments from 3A and 3C

$$\frac{1, 2, 3A, 4}{\therefore C} \qquad \frac{1, 2, 3C, 4}{\therefore C}$$

are valid, whereas the arguments from 3B and 3D

$$\frac{1, 2, 3B, 4}{\therefore C} \qquad \frac{1, 2, 3D, 4}{\therefore C}$$

are not valid. Hence, we shall not consider the arguments from 3B and 3D further, despite the moderate credibility of 3B. Moreover, since 3C implies 3A and the argument from 3A is already valid, we need not consider the argument from 3C separately. Rather, we shall regard the inference from 3C to 3A as a possible preliminary to the argument from 3A, and ask whether 3C has any credibility to pass on to 3A.

VIII. CREDIBILITY OF THE THIRD PREMISE

The success of our form of the ontological argument therefore turns out to depend on the credibility of 3A, our first nonmodal translation of the premise that something exists in the understanding, than which nothing greater can be conceived. Why might an ontological arguer accept 3A?

He might infer 3A from 3C, if 3C were credible. Why might he accept 3C?

He might infer 3C from premises he accepts concerning the existence and nature of God. But in that case he could not argue from 3C without circularity.

He might assume that for every description he understands, there is some understandable being answering to that description. But what of such well-understood descriptions as "largest prime" or "round square"? Possibly he can give some account of understandable beings such that one of them answers to any understood description; but if so, we can hardly continue to grant him Premise 1, according to which every understandable being can be conceived to exist. Premise 1 is indispensable to the argument from 3C, since without Premise 1, 3C might be true by virtue of a supremely great understandable being existing in no conceivable world.

He might obtain 3C by using the following *Principle of Saturation:* any sentence saying that there exists an understandable being of so-and-so description is true unless provably false. Such a principle would, of course, permit a much simpler ontological argument than ours: apply it to the description "Divine being existing in every world." But the Principle of Saturation can as easily be used to refute 3C as to defend it. Consider the sentence (*) saying that there is an understandable being which is greater than anything else in some world, but is exceeded in greatness in another world.

$$(*) \ \exists x \exists w \exists v (Ux \ \& \ Ww \ \& \ Wv \ \& \ \forall y(y \neq x \supset xwGyw) \ \& \ \exists yyvGxv)$$

If the Principle of Saturation supports 3C,[4] it should equally well support (*); otherwise it makes a discrimination unjustified by any visibly relevant difference between 3C and (*). But (*) is incompatible with 3C. So if the Principle of Saturation supports 3C, then it is a bad principle.

---

[4] I argue conditionally since we cannot say whether the Principle of Saturation supports 3C (and (*)) until we have formulated the Principle more precisely. In particular, we would have to settle whether the provability mentioned in the Principle is to include provability by means of the Principle itself.

I know of no other way to defend 3C. Therefore let us turn to the question whether 3A, unsupported by 3C, is credible in its own right.

The ontological arguer might accept 3A with or without also accepting G, a generalization over all worlds of which 3A is the instance pertaining to the actual world.

G. $\forall v(Wv \supset \exists x(Ux \ \& \ \sim \exists w \exists y(Ww \ \& \ ywGxv)))$

(For any world v, there is an understandable being x such that for no world w and being y does the greatness of y in w exceed the greatness of x in v.)

Why might he accept G? He might infer it from 3C; but we know of no noncircular reasons for him to believe 3C. Unless inferred from 3C, G does not seem credible. Let v be a bad world—say, one containing nothing but a small chunk of mud—and let w be the most splendid conceivable world. Then according to G there is some understandable being whose greatness in v is unexceeded by the greatness in w of anything—even the greatest of the inhabitants of w. What could this understandable being be? By 1 and 2 (which the ontological arguer accepts) it is something that exists in v. Is it part of the mud? Or is it an abstract entity that exists everywhere? If the latter, then there is no reason for it to be especially great at v, while if it is equally great everywhere then we are back to arguing from 3C. It seems that in order to believe G without inferring it from 3C, the ontological arguer would need to adopt standards of greatness so eccentric as to rob his conclusion of its expected theological import. If some mud in its mud-world is deemed to be as great as the greatest angel in his heavenly world, then it does not matter whether or not something exists in reality than which nothing greater—by *these* standards of greatness—can be conceived.

If the ontological arguer accepts 3A without also accepting G, then he is claiming that the actual world possesses a distinction which at least some other worlds lack: the actual world is one of those worlds at which something achieves a greatness unexceeded by the greatness of anything anywhere. For short: the actual world, unlike some other worlds, is a *place of greatest greatness*. Why is this credible? What is special about the actual world, compared to some others, that should lead us to think it a place of greatest greatness?

It will not do for the ontological arguer to cite various features of the actual world that impress him: its tall mountains, beautiful women, wise philosophers or what not. In the first place, the actual world is greatly excelled in all such respects by other worlds—it is possible for mountains to be taller than they actually are, and so on. In the second place, the ontological arguer is not supposed to be giving us empirical theology; we wish to know whether his premises are at all credible a priori.

It remains for the ontological arguer to hold that the actual world is special, and a fitting place of greatest greatness, precisely because it, alone out of the worlds, is actual. This reason seems prima facie to have some force: whatever actuality may be, it is something we deem tremendously important, and there *is* only one world that has it. We picture the actual world—indefensibly—as the one solid, vivid, energetic world among innumerable ghostly, faded, wispy, "merely" possible worlds. Therefore it may well seem plausible that the actual world, being special by its unique actuality, might also be special by being a place of greatest greatness. This does not pretend to be a proof of 3A, but we do not demand proof; we wish to know if the ontological arguer has any reason at all to accept 3A, even a reason that does no more than appeal to his sense of fitness.

IX. THE NATURE OF ACTUALITY

But this last reason to accept 3A is not only weak; it is mistaken. It is true that our world alone is actual; but that does not make our world special, radically different from all other worlds.

I suggest that "actual" and its cognates should be analyzed as *indexical* terms: terms whose reference varies, depending on relevant features of the context of utterance. The relevant feature of context, for the term "actual," is the world at which a given utterance occurs. According to the indexical analysis I propose, "actual" (in its primary sense) refers at any world w to the world w. "Actual" is analogous to "present," an indexical term whose reference varies depending on a different feature of context: "present" refers at any time t to the time t. "Actual" is analogous also to "here," "I," "you," "this," and "aforementioned"—indexical terms depending for their reference respectively on the place, the speaker, the intended audience, the speaker's acts of pointing, and the foregoing discourse.[5]

I do not mean to say that "actual" has different meanings in the languages used in different worlds, so that for any world w, "the actual world" is a proper name of w in the native language of w. That is false. (Just as it would be false to say that "today" changes its meaning every midnight). Rather, the *fixed* meaning we give to "actual" is such that, at any world w, "actual" refers in *our* language to w.

I use "refers" broadly to cover various semantic relations for indexical terms of various grammatical categories. To speak more precisely: at any world w, the name "the actual world" *denotes* or *names* w; the predicate "is actual" *designates* or *is true of* w and whatever exists in w; the operator "actually" *is true of* propositions true at w, and so on for cognate terms of other categories. Similarly, at any time t the name "the present time" denotes t, the predicate "is present" is true of t and whatever exists at t, the operator "presently" is true of propositions true at t, and so on.

---

[5] For a general account of indexicality, see Richard Montague, "Pragmatics," *Contemporary Philosophy,* ed. by Raymond Klibansky (Florence: La Nuova Italie Editrice, 1968.) A. N. Prior states the indexical analysis of actuality in "Modal Logic and the Logic of Applicability," *Theoria* 34 (1968): 191–92; but, sadly, he goes on to say "this seems a tall story, and . . . I doubt whether anyone seriously believes it."

A complication: we can distinguish primary and secondary senses of "actual" by asking what world "actual" refers to at a world w in a context in which some other world v is under consideration. In the primary sense, it still refers to w, as in "If Max ate less, he would be thinner than he actually is." In the secondary sense it shifts its reference to the world v under consideration, as in "If Max ate less, he would actually enjoy himself more." A similar distinction occurs among temporal indexicals: the unaccompanied present tense does, and the present tense accompanied by "now" does not, tend to shift its reference from the time of an utterance to another time under consideration.[6] "It will be the case in 2100 A.D. that there are men on Mars," said now, is probably true, whereas "It will be the case in 2100 A.D. that there are now men on Mars," said now, is probably false. The secondary, shifting sense of "actual" is responsible for our translation 3D. If we set out on the route that leads to 3A, we get "There is an understandable being x, such that for no world w and being y does the greatness of y in w exceed the actual greatness of x." Then if we take "actual" in the secondary sense, it shifts from referring to our own world to referring to the world w under consideration, thereby yielding 3D rather than 3A.

The strongest evidence for the indexical analysis of actuality is that it explains why skepticism about our own actuality is absurd. How do we know that we are not the unactualized possible inhabitants of some unactualized possible world? We can give no evidence: whatever feature of our world we may mention, it is shared by other worlds that are not actual. Some unactualized grass is no less green, some unactualized dollars buy no less (unactualized) bread, some unactualized philosophers are no less sure they are actual. Either we know in some utterly mysterious way that we are actual; or we do not know it at all.

But of course we do know it. The indexical analysis of actuality explains how we know it: in the same way I know that I am me, that *this* time is the present, or that I am here. All such sentences as "This is the actual world," "I am actual," "I actually exist," and the like are true on any possible occasion of utterance in any possible world. That is why skepticism about our own actuality is absurd.

"This is the actual world" is true whenever uttered in any possible world. That is not to say, of course, that all worlds are actual. "All worlds are actual" is *false* whenever uttered in any world. Everyone may truly call his own world actual, but no one, wherever located, may truly call all the worlds actual. It is the same with time. Sometimes it seems to the novice that indexical analysts of "present" are pretending that all times alike are present. But no: although "This time is present" is always true, "All times are present" is never true. If we take a timeless point of view and ignore our own location in time, the big difference between the present time and other times vanishes. That is not because we regard all times as equally present, but rather because if we ignore our own location in time we cannot use

---

[6] I owe this distinction to J. A. W. Kamp, "The Treatment of 'Now' As a 1-place Sentential Operator" (1967, unpublished). It is discussed also by A. N. Prior in "'Now,'" *Noûs* 2 (1968): 101–19.

temporally indexical terms like "present" at all. And similarly, I claim, if we take an a priori point of view and ignore our own location among the worlds, the big difference between the actual world and other worlds should vanish. That is not because we regard all worlds as equally actual[7] but rather because if we ignore our own location among the worlds we cannot use indexical terms like "actual."

If I am right, the ontological arguer who says that his world is special because his world alone is the actual world is as foolish as a man who boasts that he has the special fortune to be alive at a unique moment in history: the present. The actual world is not special in itself, but only in the special relation it bears to the ontological arguer. Other worlds bear the same relation to other ontological arguers. The ontological arguer has no reason to regard his own actual world as special except in its relation to him. Hence he has not even a weak reason to think that his world differs from some other worlds in being a place of greatest greatness—that is, not even a weak reason to accept 3A without also accepting its generalization G. We have already found that he has no reason to accept G without 3C and no good, non-circular reason to accept 3C. We should conclude, therefore, that the argument from 3A is a valid argument from a premise we have no non-circular reason to accept.

X. CONCLUSION

Of the alternative non-modal translations of our ontological argument, the best are the arguments from 3A and 3B. The premises of the argument from 3B enjoy some credibility, but the argument is invalid. The argument from 3A is valid, but 3A derives its credibility entirely from the illusion that because our world alone is actual, therefore our world is radically different from all other worlds—special in a way that makes it a fitting place of greatest greatness. But once we recognize the indexical nature of actuality, the illusion is broken and the credibility of 3A evaporates. It is true of *any* world, at that world but not elsewhere, that that world alone is actual. The world an ontological arguer calls actual is special only in that the ontological arguer resides there—and it is no great distinction for a world to harbor an ontological arguer. Think of an ontological arguer in some dismally mediocre world—there are such ontological arguers—arguing that his world alone is actual, hence special, hence a fitting place of greatest greatness, hence a world wherein something exists than which no greater can be conceived to exist. He is wrong to argue thus. So are we.

---

[7]Prior slips here in presenting the indexical analysis (as a tall story). He writes, "this word 'actual' must not be taken as signifying that the world in question is any more 'real' than those other worlds . . . " But "real" (even in scare-quotes) is presumably indexical in the same way as "actual." Hence we can no more say that all worlds are equally real than we can say that all worlds alike are actual.

Postscripts to

"Anselm and Actuality"

A. IMPOSSIBLE WORLDS

I retract my misguided stipulation that "If some otherwise impossible worlds are conceivable . . . we should count those [as worlds]." I thought to smooth over the difference between my own talk of possible worlds and Anselm's talk of what can be conceived, but I did so at an intolerable cost. Truth to tell, there are no impossible worlds, whatever feats of conceiving may be within our power.

Suppose there were. We would have to take great care in describing the impossible things that go on therein. We would have to distinguish very carefully between (1) the consistent truth about this extraordinary subject matter, and (2) false contradictions about it. For contradictions are not the truth about any subject matter whatsoever, no matter how exotic.[1] For instance, we would have to distinguish (1) the uncanny truth about a certain impossible world where pigs can fly and also they cannot from (2) the contradictory falsehood that, in that world, pigs can fly, although it is not so that, in that world, pigs can fly. —Nonsense! There is no such distinction to be drawn.

I am well aware that formal means are on offer for keeping track of the alleged distinction. It would suffice to imitate my own way of distinguishing between (1) the truth about the inconsistent content of an impossible story, and (2) contradictory falsehoods about that story. (See Postscript B to "Truth in Fiction," in this volume.) There are also the proposals of the relevantists.[2] But it's no use knowing how to keep track of a distinction that does not exist. If worlds were stories, or "set-ups," or suitably constructed models, or representations of some other sort, there could very well be impossible ones. They would purport to represent worlds, but could not really do so. We could very well distinguish between the truth about the content of an impossible representation and contradictory falsehoods about it. But worlds are not representations, as witness the case of this world. If anyone takes distinctions that make sense only for representations, and applies them to "worlds," charity dictates that really he is not speaking of worlds at all. He is not referring to those huge things, in one of which we live and move and have our being. Let us hope he didn't even intend to.

---

[1]This is uncontroversial, though it has been controverted. See, for instance, Graham Priest, "The Logic of Paradox," *Journal of Philosophical Logic* 8 (1979): 219–41.

[2]For instance, the *-function that governs "negation" in R. and V. Routley, "The Semantics of First Degree Entailment," *Noûs* 6 (1972): 335–59.

B. THE AMBIGUITY OF SHIFTINESS

I noted in passing that we can distinguish two senses of actual: a *primary* sense in which it refers to the world of utterance even in a context where another world is under consideration, and a *secondary* sense in which it shifts its reference in such a context. This ambiguity deserves more emphasis than I gave it, for without it my indexical analysis is indefensible. This has been shown by Peter van Inwagen[3] and Allen Hazen,[4] as follows. Consider these sentences.

(1)   The following is contingent: in the actual world, Caesar is murdered.

(2)   Let 'Alpha' name the actual world; Alpha might not have been actual.

(3)   Let 'Beta' name some nonactual world; Beta might have been actual.

(4)   There could have been objects other than those there actually are.

(5)   I could have been richer than I actually am.

Each of these sentences, I take it, is true on a natural reading. But if "actual" always has its primary, unshifty sense, how can (1)-(3) be true? If, on the other hand, it always has its secondary, shifty sense, how can (4)-(5) be true? Neither sense will serve for all cases. We need both.

C. SCEPTICISM REVIVIFIED?

According to my modal realism, there are countless unfortunates just like ourselves who rely on reasonable inductive methods and are sorely deceived. Not the best but the third best explanation of their total evidence is the true one; or all their newly examined emeralds turn out to be blue; or one dark day their sun fails to rise. To be sure, these victims of inductive error differ from us in that they are not actual. But I consider that no great difference. They are not our worldmates, but they do not differ from us in kind.

Among those who trust induction, those who are sorely deceived are just as numerous as those who are not. For it follows from plausible premises that both sets have the same cardinality as the set of worlds.

And yet we are confident that *we* are not among the deceived! Inductive disaster strikes ever so many victims no different from ourselves, and still we feel safe in continuing to trust induction. We have no reason at all for this faith in our own luck.

So it seems that the modal realist must be a sceptic about induction, else he is totally unreasonable in his optimism. —I disagree. As a modal realist, I have no more and no less reason than anyone else to give over my groundless faith in my inductive luck. I have the reason everyone has: it is possible, and possible in ever

[3]"Indexicality and Actuality," *Philosophical Review* 89 (1980): 403–26.

[4]"One of the Truths about Actuality," *Analysis* 39 (1979): 1–3.

so many ways, that induction will deceive me. That reason is metaphysically neutral. It becomes no better and no worse if reformulated in accordance with one or another ontology of modality.

Then why does it sound so much more disturbing when stated in the modal realist way? —Simply because it sounds fresh and new. We have never defeated the case for scepticism, we have only learned not to let it bother us. Let it reappear in new guise—any new guise—and our habit of ignoring it gives out.

No getting around it: there *is* a striking analogy between our inductive reason, on the one hand, and unreasonable optimism, on the other. For both consist in ignoring possibilities—perfectly good possibilities, which we cannot rule out—of disaster. It does not matter what the metaphysical nature of the ignored possibilities may be. The distressing analogy of reason to unreason remains. That analogy is no reason to start calling reason unreason, or vice versa. (Even if life is somehow very like a fountain, we had best go on calling the two by different names.) All the same it is disconcerting, especially if presented in a fresh way that gets past our defenses.[5]

D. THE ANTHROPIC PRINCIPLE

"Why is there something and not rather nothing?" —"If there were nothing, you wouldn't be here to ask the question." Ask a silly question, get a silly answer. But perhaps what makes the answer silly is just that it tells the questioner no more than he must have known already. What if an answer of the same sort were more informative?

"Why is the universe such as to make possible the evolution of intelligent life?"—"If it were not, you wouldn't be here to ask the question." A bit better, but still it gives no real news.

"Why does the recessional velocity of the universe after the big bang exactly equal the escape velocity?" —"If it did not, the universe would not be such as to make possible the evolution of intelligent life [here follows an elaborate demonstration], in which case you wouldn't be here to ask the question." This time, the answer deserves to be taken seriously. In recent cosmology, such questions sometimes do get such answers. They are called "anthropic."[6]

What is an anthropic answer? It might be meant as a veiled argument from design, or from natural teleology, or from subjective idealism. Let me assume that

---

[5] I am grateful to J. J. C. Smart, Robert M. Adams, and Peter Forrest, for forcefully putting to me the objection here considered. It is discussed at length by Forrest in "The Sceptical Implications of Realism about Possible Worlds," presented at the August 1981 conference of the Australasian Association of Philosophy. Forrest thinks, however, that to make the objection stick, we must find some sense in which the deceived vastly outnumber the undeceived.

[6] George Gale, "The Anthropic Principle." *Scientific American* 245, no. 6 (December 1981): 154–71; and John Leslie, "Anthropic Principle, World Ensemble, Design," *American Philosophical Quarterly* 9 (1982): 141–51.

it is none of these. Then it is not a straight answer to the "why"-question. The questioner sought information about the causal history of his explanandum.[7] He was not given any. (And not necessarily because there was none to give. In at least some of the cases in which anthropic answers are offered, he could truly have been told that his explanandum is so global a feature of the world that it leaves no room for causes distinct from itself, and hence it cannot have any causal history.) And yet he was told something that was responsive, in a way, to his request for explanatory information.

I think he was offered consolation for the lack of the explanatory information he sought. He was told: the thing is not so very mystifying after all, it was only to be expected. Therefore it is not so very bad if it must be left unexplained.

If actuality is a special distinction whereby one world is distinguished from all the rest, the anthropic consolation falls flat. For it seems that the capacity to support life also is a very special distinction, at least among worlds with roughly the same sort of physics as ours. It does not get rid of any mystery if we are told that both these rare distinctions happen to belong to the same world.

It is otherwise if actuality is not a rare distinction at all, but merely indexical. The anthropic answer serves its purpose well. For then the unexplained explanandum comes down, either immediately or by way of an elaborate demonstration, to this: the world we inhabit is one of the habitable worlds. However scarce the habitable worlds may be, it is no wonder that our world is one of them. We should turn out to live in a world that *isn't* habitable? Or, to return to the original question, in a world where there is nothing, and not rather something?[8]

E. TERMINOLOGICAL ACTUALISM

It is part of my view that many things—whole worlds and all their parts, including some people very like ourselves—are not actual. Hence my view is opposed to *actualism*: the thesis that everything there is (taking the quantifier as entirely unrestricted) is actual.

Actualism might be a metaphysical thesis to the effect that there are far fewer things than I believe in—only a large finite number of people, for instance, instead of an uncountable infinity of them spread over countless worlds.

But it might just be a terminological proposal, neutral with respect to ontology: whatever things there may or may not be, and however they may be related, all of them are to be called actual. "Actual" is to be used indiscriminately, as a blanket term applicable to everything there is (and again we take the quantifier as entirely unrestricted).

---

[7] See my "Causal Explanation" (to appear in the sequel to this volume).

[8] I am grateful to Peter van Inwagen, who called my attention to the connection between indexical actuality and certain anthropic answers. He comments on this connection in "Indexicality and Actuality," 403–4.

Terminological actualism will suit a philosopher who accepts common opinion as to what there is. It does not suit me. I would prefer to disagree with common opinion that everything is actual, so that I may instead agree with common opinion about the extent of actuality—about what sorts of things are actual, how many of them there are, how they are related to us. I cannot agree with common opinion on both points. I do not think there is any determinate convention of language that requires me to agree on the first point rather than the second. Why should there be? Why should our linguistic community have troubled to settle a point that has arisen so seldom?

But it scarcely matters. I have no objection of principle to absolutely indiscriminate blanket terms; I myself use "entity" that way. What does matter is that no one should foist metaphysical actualism on us by representing it as an innocent terminological stipulation.

If I had to, I too could say that everything is actual, only not all that is actual is part of this world. (Then I would advance an indexical analysis of thisworldliness.) But the game would begin over. Someone would be sure to say that by definition the world consists of everything there is, so there can be nothing that is not part of the world. . . . The moves go just as before.

· THREE ·

Counterpart Theory
and
Quantified Modal Logic

I. COUNTERPART THEORY

We can conduct formalized discourse about most topics perfectly well by means of our all-purpose extensional logic, provided with predicates and a domain of quantification suited to the subject matter at hand. That is what we do when our topic is numbers, or sets, or wholes and parts, or strings of symbols. That is not what we do when our topic is modality: what might be and what must be, essence and accident. Then we introduce modal operators to create a special-purpose, nonextensional logic. Why this departure from our custom? Is it a historical accident, or was it forced on us somehow by the very nature of the topic of modality?

It was not forced on us. We have an alternative. Instead of formalizing our modal discourse by means of modal operators, we could follow our usual practice. We could stick to our standard logic (quantification theory with identity and without ineliminable singular terms) and provide it with predicates and a domain of quantification suited to the topic of modality. That done, certain expressions are available which take the place of modal operators. The new predicates required, together with postulates on them, constitute the system I call *Counterpart Theory*.

I am indebted to David Kaplan, whose criticisms have resulted in many important improvements. A. N. Prior has informed me that my theory resembles a treatment of *de re* modality communicated to him by P. T. Geach in 1964.

The primitive predicates of counterpart theory are these four:

Wx (x is a possible world)
Ixy (x is in possible world y)
Ax (x is actual)
Cxy (x is a counterpart of y).

The domain of quantification is to contain every possible world and everything in every world. The primitives are to be understood according to their English readings and the following postulates:

P1: $\forall x \forall y (Ixy \supset Wy)$
        (Nothing is in anything except a world)
P2: $\forall x \forall y \forall z (Ixy \ \& \ Ixz \ . \supset y = z)$
        (Nothing is in two worlds)
P3: $\forall x \forall y (Cxy \supset \exists z Ixz)$
        (Whatever is a counterpart is in a world)
P4: $\forall x \forall y (Cxy \supset \exists z Iyz)$
        (Whatever has a counterpart is in a world)
P5: $\forall x \forall y \forall z (Ixy \ \& \ Izy \ \& \ Cxz \ . \supset x = z)$
        (Nothing is a counterpart of anything else in its world)
P6: $\forall x \forall y (Ixy \supset Cxx)$
        (Anything in a world is a counterpart of itself)
P7: $\exists x (Wx \ \& \ \forall y (Iyx \equiv Ay))$
        (Some world contains all and only actual things)
P8: $\exists x Ax$
        (Something is actual)

The world mentioned in P7 is unique, by P2 and P8. Let us abbreviate its description:

$$@ \ =_{df} \ \imath x \forall y (Iyx \equiv Ay) \text{ (the actual world)}$$

Unactualized possibles, things in worlds other than the actual world, have often been deemed "entia non grata,"[1] largely because it is not clear when they are or are not identical. But identity literally understood is no problem for us. Within any one world, things of every category are individuated just as they are in the actual world; things in different worlds are *never* identical, by P2. The counterpart relation is our substitute for identity between things in different worlds.[2] Where some would say that you are in several worlds, in which you have somewhat different properties and somewhat different things happen to you, I prefer to say that you are in the actual world and no other, but you have counterparts in several other

---

[1] W. V. Quine, *Word and Object* (Cambridge, Mass: MIT Press, 1960), p. 245.
[2] Yet with this substitute in use, it would not matter if some things *were* identical with their counterparts after all! P2 serves only to rule out avoidable problems of individuation.

worlds. Your counterparts resemble you closely in content and context in important respects. They resemble you more closely than do the other things in their worlds. But they are not really you. For each of them is in his own world, and only you are here in the actual world. Indeed we might say, speaking casually, that your counterparts are you in other worlds, that they and you are the same; but this sameness is no more a literal identity than the sameness between you today and you tomorrow. It would be better to say that your counterparts are men you *would have been,* had the world been otherwise.[3]

The counterpart relation is a relation of similarity. So it is problematic in the way all relations of similarity are: it is the resultant of similarities and dissimilarities in a multitude of respects, weighted by the importances of the various respects[4] and by the degrees of the similarities.[5]

Carnap,[6] Kanger,[7] Hintikka,[8] Kripke,[9] Montague,[10] and others have proposed interpretations of quantified modal logic on which one thing is allowed to be in several worlds. A reader of this persuasion might suspect that he and I differ only verbally: that what I call a thing in a world is just what he would call a ⟨thing, world⟩ pair, and that what he calls the same thing in several worlds is just what I would call a class of mutual counterparts. But beware. Our difference is not just verbal, for I enjoy a generality he cannot match. The counterpart relation will not, in general, be an equivalence relation. So it will not hold just between those of his ⟨thing, world⟩ pairs with the same first term, no matter how he may choose to identify things between worlds.

It would not have been plausible to postulate that the counterpart relation was transitive. Suppose x_1 in world w_1 resembles you closely in many respects, far more closely than anything else in w_1 does. And suppose x_2 in world w_2 resembles x_1 closely, far more closely than anything else in w_2 does. So x_2 is a counterpart of your counterpart x_1. Yet x_2 might not resemble you very closely, and something else in w_2 might resemble you more closely. If so, x_2 is not your counterpart.

It would not have been plausible to postulate that the counterpart relation was symmetric. Suppose x_3 in world w_3 is a sort of blend of you and your brother; x_3 resembles both of you closely, far more closely than anything else in w_3 resembles either one of you. So x_3 is your counterpart. But suppose also that the resemblance

[3]This way of describing counterparts is due to L. Sprague de Camp, "The Wheels of If," *Unknown Fantasy Fiction,* October, 1940.

[4]As discussed in Michael A. Slote, "The Theory of Important Criteria," *Journal of Philosophy* 63, no. 8 (Apr. 14, 1966): 211–24.

[5]The counterpart relation is very like the relation of intersubjective correspondence discussed in Rudolf Carnap, *Der Logische Aufbau der Welt* (Berlin-Schlachtensee: Weltkreis-Verlag, 1928), sec. 146.

[6]"Modalities and Quantification," *Journal of Symbolic Logic* 11, no. 2 (June 1946): 33–64.

[7]*Provability in Logic* (Stockholm: Almqvist and Wiksell, 1957).

[8]"Modality as Referential Multiplicity," *Ajatus* 20 (1957): 49–64.

[9]"A Completeness Theorem in Modal Logic," *Journal of Symbolic Logic* 24, no. 1 (March 1959): 1–14; "Semantical Considerations on Modal Logic," *Acta Philosophica Fennica* 16 (1963): 83–94.

[10]"Logical Necessity, Physical Necessity, Ethics, and Quantifiers," *Inquiry* 3 (1960): 259–69.

between x_3 and your brother is far closer than that between x_3 and you. If so, you are not a counterpart of x_3.

It would not have been plausible to postulate that nothing in any world had more than one counterpart in any other world. Suppose x_{4a} and x_{4b} in world w_4 are twins; both resemble you closely; both resemble you far more closely than anything else in w_4 does; both resemble you equally. If so, both are your counterparts.

It would not have been plausible to postulate that no two things in any world had a common counterpart in any other world. Suppose you resemble both the twins x_{4a} and x_{4b} far more closely than anything else in the actual world does. If so, you are a counterpart of both.

It would not have been plausible to postulate that, for any two worlds, anything in one was a counterpart of something in the other. Suppose there is something x_5 in world w_5—say, Batman—which does not much resemble anything actual. If so, x_5 is not a counterpart of anything in the actual world.

It would not have been plausible to postulate that, for any two worlds, anything in one had some counterpart in the other. Suppose whatever thing x_6 in world w_6 it is that resembles you more closely than anything else in w_6 is nevertheless quite unlike you; nothing in w_6 resembles you at all closely. If so, you have no counterpart in w_6.

II. TRANSLATION

Counterpart theory and quantified modal logic seem to have the same subject matter; seem to provide two rival ways of formalizing our modal discourse. In that case they should be intertranslatable; indeed they are. Hence I need not give directions for formalizing modal discourse directly by means of counterpart theory; I can assume the reader is accustomed to formalizing modal discourse by means of modal operators, so I need only give directions for translating sentences of quantified modal logic into sentences of counterpart theory.

Counterpart theory has at least three advantages over quantified modal logic as a vehicle for formalized discourse about modality. (1) Counterpart theory is a theory, not a special-purpose intensional logic. (2) Whereas the obscurity of quantified modal logic has proved intractable, that of counterpart theory is at least divided, if not conquered. We can trace it to its two independent sources. There is our uncertainty about analyticity, and, hence, about whether certain descriptions describe possible worlds; and there is our uncertainty about the relative importance of different respects of similarity and dissimilarity, and, hence, about which things are counterparts of which. (3) If the translation scheme I am about to propose is correct, every sentence of quantified modal logic has the same meaning as a sentence of counterpart theory, its translation; but not every sentence of counterpart theory is, or is equivalent to, the translation of any sentence of quantified modal logic. Therefore, starting with a fixed stock of predicates other than those of counterpart theory, we can say more by adding counterpart theory than we can by adding modal operators.

Now let us examine my proposed translation scheme.[11] We begin with some important special cases, leading up to a general definition.

First consider a closed (0-place) sentence with a single, initial modal operator: $\Box\phi$ or $\Diamond\phi$. It is given the familiar translation: $\forall\beta(W\beta \supset \phi^\beta)$ (ϕ holds in any possible world β) or $\exists\beta(W\beta \,\&\, \phi^\beta)$ (ϕ holds in some possible world β). To form the sentence ϕ^β (ϕ holds in world β) from the given sentence ϕ, we need only restrict the range of each quantifier in ϕ to the domain of things in the world denoted by β; that is, we replace $\forall\alpha$ by $\forall\alpha(I\alpha\beta \supset \cdots)$ and $\exists\alpha$ by $\exists\alpha(I\alpha\beta \,\&\, \cdots)$ throughout ϕ.

Next consider a 1-place open sentence with a single, initial modal operator: $\Box\phi\alpha$ or $\Diamond\phi\alpha$. It is given the translation $\forall\beta\forall\gamma(W\beta \,\&\, I\gamma\beta \,\&\, C\gamma\alpha \,.\supset\, \phi^\beta\gamma)$ (ϕ holds of every counterpart γ of α in any world β) or $\exists\beta\exists\gamma(W\beta \,\&\, I\gamma\beta \,\&\, C\gamma\alpha \,\&\, \phi^\beta\gamma)$ (ϕ holds of some counterpart γ of α in some world β). Likewise for an open sentence with any number of places.

If the modal operator is not initial, we translate the subsentence it governs. And if there are quantifiers that do not lie within the scope of any modal operator, we must restrict their range to the domain of things in the actual world; for that is their range in quantified modal logic, whereas an unrestricted quantifier in counterpart theory would range at least over all the worlds and everything in any of them. A sentence of quantified modal logic that contains *no* modal operator—a nonmodal sentence in a modal context—is therefore translated simply by restricting its quantifiers to things in the actual world.

Finally, consider a sentence in which there are modal operators within the scopes of other modal operators. Then we must work inward; to obtain ϕ^β from ϕ we must not only restrict quantifiers in ϕ but also translate any subsentences of ϕ with initial modal operators.

The general translation scheme can best be presented as a direct definition of the translation of a sentence ϕ of quantified modal logic:

> T1:   The translation of ϕ is $\phi^@$ (ϕ holds in the actual world); that is, in primitive notation, $\exists\beta(\forall\alpha(I\alpha\beta \equiv A\alpha) \,\&\, \phi^\beta)$

followed by a recursive definition of ϕ^β (ϕ holds in world β)

> T2a: ϕ^β is ϕ, if ϕ is atomic
> T2b: $(\sim \phi)^\beta$ is $\sim \phi^\beta$
> T2c: $(\phi \,\&\, \psi)^\beta$ is $\phi^\beta \,\&\, \psi^\beta$

---

[11]NOTATION: Sentences are mentioned by means of the Greek letters 'ϕ', 'ψ',. . .; variables by means of 'α', 'β', 'γ', 'δ',. . . If ϕ is any n-place sentence and α_1. . .α_n are any n different variables, then $\phi\alpha_1$. . .α_n is the sentence obtained by substituting α_1 uniformly for the alphabetically first free variable in ϕ, α_2 for the second, and so on. Variables introduced in translation are to be chosen in some systematic way that prevents confusion of bound variables. Symbolic expressions are used autonymously.

T2d: $(\phi \vee \psi)^\beta$ is $\phi^\beta \vee \psi^\beta$

T2e: $(\phi \supset \psi)^\beta$ is $\phi^\beta \supset \psi^\beta$

T2f: $(\phi \equiv \psi)^\beta$ is $\phi^\beta \equiv \psi^\beta$

T2g: $(\forall \alpha\, \phi)^\beta$ is $\forall \alpha\, (I\alpha\beta \supset \phi^\beta)$

T2h: $(\exists \alpha \phi)^\beta$ is $\exists \alpha (I\alpha\beta \,\&\, \phi^\beta)$

T2i: $(\Box\phi\alpha_1...\alpha_n)^\beta$ is $\forall \beta_1 \forall \gamma_1 \cdots \forall \gamma_n$

$\qquad\qquad (W\beta_1 \,\&\, I\gamma_1\beta_1 \,\&\, C\gamma_1\alpha_1 \,\&\cdots\&\, I\gamma_n\beta_1 \,\&\, C\gamma_n\alpha_n\, . \supset\, \phi^{\beta_1}\gamma_1\cdots\gamma_n)$

T2j: $(\Diamond\phi\alpha_1...\alpha_n)^\beta$ is $\exists \beta_1 \exists \gamma_1 \cdots \exists \gamma_n$

$\qquad\qquad (W\beta_1 \,\&\, I\gamma_1\beta_1 \,\&\, C\gamma_1\alpha_1 \,\&\cdots\&\, I\gamma_n\beta_1 \,\&\, C\gamma_n\alpha_n \,\&\, \phi^{\beta_1}\gamma_1\cdots\gamma_n)$

Using these two definitions, we find, for example, that

$\forall x Fx$

$\Diamond \exists x Fx$

$\Box Fx$

$\forall x(Fx \supset \Box Fx)$

$\Box\Diamond Fx$

are translated, respectively, as

$\forall x(Ix@ \supset Fx)$
(Everything actual is an *F*)

$\exists y(Wy \,\&\, \exists x(Ixy \,\&\, Fx))$
(Some possible world contains an *F*)

$\forall y_1 \forall x_1(Wy_1 \,\&\, Ix_1y_1 \,\&\, Cx_1x\, . \supset Fx_1)$
(Every counterpart of *x*, in any world, is an *F*)

$\forall x(Ix@ \supset . \; Fx \supset \forall y_1 \forall x_1(Wy_1 \,\&\, Ix_1y_1 \,\&\, Cx_1x\, . \supset Fx_1))$
(If anything is a counterpart of an actual *F*, then it is an *F*)

$\forall y_1 \forall x_1(Wy_1 \,\&\, Ix_1y_1 \,\&\, Cx_1x\, . \supset \exists y_2 \exists x_2(Wy_2 \,\&\, Ix_2y_2 \,\&\, Cx_2x_1 \,\&\, Fx_2))$
(Every counterpart of *x* has a counterpart which is an *F*)

The reverse translation, from sentences of counterpart theory to sentences of quantified modal logic, can be done by finite search whenever it can be done at all. For if a modal sentence ψ is the translation of a sentence ϕ of counterpart theory, then ψ must be shorter than ϕ and ψ must contain no predicates or variables not in ϕ. But not every sentence of counterpart theory is the translation of a modal sentence, or even an equivalent of the translation of a modal sentence. For instance, our postulates P1-P7 are not.

It may disturb us that the translation of $\forall x\Box\exists y(x = y)$ (everything actual necessarily exists) comes out true even if something actual lacks a counterpart in some world. To avoid this, we might be tempted to adopt the alternative translation scheme, brought to my attention by David Kaplan, in which T2i and T2j are replaced by

T2i': $(\Box\phi\alpha_1\cdots\alpha_n)^\beta$ is $\forall\beta_1(W\beta_1 \supset \exists\gamma_1\cdots\exists\gamma_n(I\gamma_1\beta_1\,\&\,C\gamma_1\alpha_1\,\&\,\cdots$

$\&\,I\gamma_n\beta_1\,\&\,C\gamma_n\alpha_n\,\&\,\phi^{\beta_1}\gamma_1\cdots\gamma_n))$

T2j': $(\Diamond\phi\alpha_1\cdots\alpha_n)^\beta$ is $\exists\beta_1(W\beta_1\,\&\,\forall\gamma_1\cdots\forall\gamma_n(I\gamma_1\beta_1\,\&\,C\gamma_1\alpha_1\,\&\,\cdots$

$\&\,I\gamma_n\beta_1\,\&\,C\gamma_n\alpha_n\,.\supset\,\phi^{\beta_1}\gamma_1\cdots\gamma_n))$

with heterogeneous rather than homogeneous quantifiers. Out of the frying pan, into the fire: with T2j', $\exists x\Diamond(x \neq x)$ (something actual is possibly non-self-identical) comes out true unless everything actual has a counterpart in every world! We might compromise by taking T2i' and T2j, but at the price of sacrificing the ordinary duality of necessity and possibility.[12] So I chose to take T2i and T2j.

III. ESSENTIALISM

Quine has often warned us that by quantifying past modal operators we commit ourselves to the view that "an object, of itself and by whatever name or none, must be seen as having some of its traits necessarily and others contingently, despite the fact that the latter traits follow just as analytically from some ways of specifying the object as the former traits do from other ways of specifying it."[13] This so-called "Aristotelian essentialism"—the doctrine of essences not relative to specifications—"should be every bit as congenial to [the champion of quantified modal logic] as quantified modal logic itself."[14]

Agreed. Essentialism is congenial. We do have a way of saying that an attribute is an essential attribute of an object—essential regardless of how the object happens to have been specified and regardless of whether the attribute follows analytically from any or all specifications of the object.

Consider the attribute expressed by a 1-place sentence ϕ and the object denoted by a singular term ζ.[15] To say that this attribute is an essential attribute of this object is to assert the translation of $\Box\phi\zeta$.

But we have not yet considered how to translate a modal sentence containing a singular term. For we know that any singular term ζ may be treated as a description $\imath\alpha(\psi\alpha)$ (although often only by letting ψ contain some artificial predicate made from a proper name); and we know that any description may be eliminated by Russell's contextual definition. Our translation scheme did not take account of singular terms because they need never occur in the primitive notation of quantified

---

[12] If we also postulate that the counterpart relation is an equivalence relation, we get an interpretation like that of Føllesdal in "Referential Opacity in Modal Logic" (unpublished Ph.D. dissertation, Harvard, 1961), sec. 20, and in "A Model-Theoretic Approach to Causal Logic," in *Det Kongeliger Norske Videnskabers Selskabs Forhandlinger* (1966): 3–13.

[13] "Reference and Modality," in *From a Logical Point of View*, 2d ed. (Cambridge, Mass.: Harvard, 1961), p. 155.

[14] "Reply to Professor Marcus," in *The Ways of Paradox* (New York: Random House, 1966), p. 182.

[15] NOTATION: Terms are mentioned by means of the Greek letters 'ζ', 'η',... The sentence $\phi\zeta$ is that obtained by substituting the term ζ uniformly into the 1-place sentence ϕ.

modal logic. We must always eliminate singular terms before translating; afterwards, if we like, we can restore them.

There is just one hitch: before eliminating a description, we must assign it a scope. Different choices of scope will, in general, lead to nonequivalent translations. This is so even if the eliminated description denotes precisely one thing in the actual world and in every possible world.[16]

Taking ζ as a description $\imath\alpha(\psi\alpha)$ and assigning it narrow scope, our sentence $\Box\phi\zeta$ is interpreted as

$$\Box\exists\alpha(\forall\delta(\psi\delta \equiv \delta = \alpha) \,\&\, \phi\alpha)$$

Its translation under this interpretation is

$$\forall\beta(W\beta \supset \exists\alpha(I\alpha\beta \,\&\, \forall\delta(I\delta\beta \supset . \, \psi^\beta\delta \equiv \delta = \alpha) \,\&\, \phi^\beta\alpha))$$

(Any possible world β contains a unique α such that $\psi^\beta\alpha$; and for any such α, $\phi^\beta\alpha$)

This is an interpretation *de dicto*: the modal operator attaches to the already closed sentence $\phi\zeta$. It is referentially opaque: the translation of an ostensible use of Leibniz's Law

$$\Box\phi\zeta$$
$$\underline{\eta = \zeta}$$
$$\therefore \Box\phi\eta$$

or of an ostensible existential generalization

$$\underline{\Box\phi\zeta}$$
$$\therefore \exists\alpha\Box\phi\alpha$$

is an invalid argument if the terms involved are taken as descriptions with narrow scope.

Taking ζ as a description with wide scope, $\Box\phi\zeta$ is interpreted as

$$\exists\alpha(\forall\delta(\psi\delta \equiv \delta = \alpha) \,\&\, \Box\phi\alpha)$$

and translated as

$$\exists\alpha(I\alpha@ \,\&\, \forall\delta(I\delta@ \supset . \, \psi^@\delta \equiv \delta = \alpha) \,\&\, \forall\beta\forall\gamma(W\beta \,\&\, I\gamma\beta \,\&\, C\gamma\alpha . \supset \phi^\beta\gamma))$$

(The actual world contains a unique α such that $\psi^@\alpha$; and for any counterpart γ thereof, in any world β, $\phi^\beta\gamma$)

This is an interpretation *de re*: the modal operator attaches to the open sentence ϕ to form a new open modal sentence $\Box\phi$, and the attribute expressed by $\Box\phi$ is then

---

[16] I follow Arthur Smullyan's treatment of scope ambiguity in modal sentences, given in "Modality and Description," *Journal of Symbolic Logic* 13, no. 1 (March 1948): 31–37, as qualified by Wilson's objection, in *The Concept of Language* (Toronto: University Press, 1959), p. 43, that some ostensible uses of Leibniz's law on modal sentences are invalid under *any* choice of scope in the conclusion.

predicated of the actual thing denoted by ζ. This interpretation is referentially transparent: the translation of an ostensible use of Leibniz's law or of an ostensible existential generalization is a valid argument if the terms involved are taken as descriptions with wide scope.

How are we to choose between the two interpretations of $\Box\phi\zeta$? Often we cannot, unless by fiat; there is a genuine ambiguity. But there are several conditions that tend to favor the wide-scope interpretation as the more natural: (1) whenever ζ is a description formed by turning a proper name into an artificial predicate; (2) whenever the description ζ has what Donnellan calls its referential use,[17] (3) whenever we are prepared to accept

ζ is something α such that necessarily $\phi\alpha$

as one possible English reading of $\Box\phi\zeta$. (The force of the third condition is due to the fact that $\exists\alpha(\zeta = \alpha \,\&\, \Box\phi\alpha)$ is unambiguously equivalent to $\Box\phi\zeta$ with ζ given wide scope.)[18]

The translations of $\Box\phi\zeta$ under its two interpretations are logically independent. Neither follows from the other just by itself. But with the aid of suitable auxiliary premises we can go in both directions. The inference from the narrow-scope translation to the wide-scope translation (exportation)[19] requires the further premise

$$\exists\alpha(I\alpha@ \,\&\, \forall\beta\forall\gamma(I\gamma\beta \,\&\, C\gamma\alpha . \supset \forall\delta(I\delta\beta \supset . \psi^\beta\delta \equiv \delta = \gamma)))$$

(There is something α in the actual world, any counterpart γ of which is the only thing δ in its world β such that $\psi^\beta\delta$)

which is a simplified equivalent of the translation of $\exists\alpha\Box(\zeta = \alpha)$ with ζ given narrow scope.[20] The inference from the wide-scope translation to the narrow-scope translation (importation) requires the same auxiliary premise, and another as well:

$$\exists\alpha(I\alpha@ \,\&\, \forall\delta(I\delta@ \supset . \psi^@\delta \equiv \delta = \alpha) \,\&\, \forall\beta(W\beta \supset \exists\gamma(I\gamma\beta \,\&\, C\gamma\alpha)))$$

(The unique α in the actual world such that $\psi^@\alpha$, has at least one counterpart γ in any world β)

This second auxiliary premise is not equivalent to the translation of any modal sentence.[21]

In general, of course, there will be more than two ways to assign scopes. Consider $\Box\Diamond(\eta = \zeta)$. Each description may be given narrow, medium, or wide scope; so there are nine nonequivalent translations.

It is the wide-scope, *de re*, transparent translation of $\Box\phi\zeta$ which says that the attribute expressed by ϕ is an essential attribute of the thing denoted by ζ. In short,

---

[17]"Reference and Definite Descriptions," *Philosophical Review* 75, no. 3 (July 1966): 281–304.

[18]Cf. Hintikka, *Knowledge and Belief* (Ithaca, N.Y.: Cornell Univ. Press, 1962), pp. 156–57.

[19]I follow Quine's use of this term in "Quantifiers and Propositional Attitudes," in *The Ways of Paradox*, p. 188.

[20]Cf. Hintikka, *op. cit.*, pp. 138–55.

[21]But under any variant translation in which T2i is replaced by T2i', it would be equivalent to the translation of $\Box\exists\alpha(\zeta = \alpha)$ (ζ necessarily exists) with ζ given wide scope.

an essential attribute of something is an attribute it shares with all its counterparts. All your counterparts are probably human; if so, you are essentially human. All your counterparts are even more probably corporeal; if so, you are essentially corporeal.

An attribute that something shares with all its counterparts is an essential attribute of that thing, part of its essence. The whole of its essence is the intersection of its essential attributes, the attribute it shares with all and only its counterparts. (*The* attribute, because there is no need to distinguish attributes that are coextensive not only in the actual world but also in every possible world.) There may or may not be an open sentence that expresses the attribute that is the essence of something; to assert that the attribute expressed by ϕ is the essence of the thing denoted by ζ is to assert

$$\exists \alpha(I\alpha@ \ \& \ \forall\delta(I\delta@ \supset. \ \psi^@\delta \equiv \delta = \alpha) \ \& \ \forall\beta\forall\gamma(I\gamma\beta \supset. \ C\gamma\alpha \equiv \phi^\beta\gamma))$$

(The actual world contains a unique α such that $\psi^@\alpha$; and for anything γ in any world β, γ is a counterpart of α if and only if $\phi^\beta\gamma$)

This sentence is not equivalent to the translation of any modal sentence.

Essence and counterpart are interdefinable. We have just defined the essence of something as the attribute it shares with all and only its counterparts; a counterpart of something is anything having the attribute which is its essence. (This is not to say that that attribute is the *counterpart's* essence, or even an essential attribute of the counterpart.)

Perhaps there are certain attributes that can only be essential attributes of things, never accidents. Perhaps every human must be essentially human; more likely, perhaps everything corporeal must be essentially corporeal. The attribute expressed by ϕ is of this sort, incapable of being an accident, just in case it is closed under the counterpart relation; that is, just in case

$$\forall\alpha\forall\beta\forall\gamma\forall\beta_1(I\alpha\beta \ \& \ I\gamma\beta_1 \ \& \ C\gamma\alpha \ \& \ \phi^\beta\alpha \ . \supset \ \phi^{\beta_1}\gamma)$$

(For any counterpart γ in any world β_1 of anything α in any world β, if $\phi^\beta\alpha$ then $\phi^{\beta_1}\gamma$)

This is a simplified equivalent of the translation of

$$\Box\forall\alpha(\phi\alpha \supset \Box\phi\alpha)$$

We might wonder whether these attributes incapable of being accidents are what we call "natural kinds." But notice first that we must disregard the necessarily universal attribute, expressed, for instance, by the open sentence $\alpha = \alpha$, since it is an essential attribute of everything. And notice second that arbitrary unions of attributes incapable of being accidents are themselves attributes incapable of being accidents; so to exclude gerrymanders we must confine ourselves to *minimal* attributes incapable of being accidents. All of these may indeed be natural kinds; but these cannot be the only natural kinds, since some unions and all intersections of natural kinds are themselves natural kinds.

IV. MODAL PRINCIPLES

Translation into counterpart theory can settle disputed questions in quantified modal logic. We can test a suggested modal principle by seeing whether its translation is a theorem of counterpart theory; or, if not, whether the extra postulates that would make it a theorem are plausible. We shall consider eight principles and find only one that should be accepted.

$\Box\phi \dashv\vdash \Box\Box\phi$ (Becker's principle)

The translation is not a theorem unless ϕ is a closed sentence, but would have been a theorem in general under the rejected postulate that the counterpart relation was transitive.

$\phi \dashv\vdash \Box\Diamond\phi$ (Brouwer's principle)

The translation is not a theorem unless ϕ is a closed sentence, but would have been a theorem in general under the rejected postulate that the counterpart relation was symmetric.

$\alpha_1 = \alpha_2 \dashv\vdash \Box\alpha_1 = \alpha_2$ (α_1 and α_2 not the same variable)

The translation is not a theorem, but would have been under the rejected postulate that nothing in any world had more than one counterpart in any other world.

$\alpha_1 \neq \alpha_2 \dashv\vdash \Box\alpha_1 \neq \alpha_2$ (α_1 and α_2 not the same variable)

The translation is not a theorem, but would have been under the rejected postulate that no two things in any world had a common counterpart in any other world.

$\forall\alpha\Box\phi\alpha \dashv\vdash \Box\forall\alpha\phi\alpha$ (Barcan's principle)

The translation is not a theorem, but would have been under the rejected postulate that, for any two worlds, anything in one was a counterpart of something in the other.

$\exists\alpha\Box\phi\alpha \dashv\vdash \Box\exists\alpha\phi\alpha$

The translation is not a theorem, but would have been under the rejected postulate that, for any two worlds, anything in one had some counterpart in the other.

$\Box\forall\alpha\phi\alpha \dashv\vdash \forall\alpha\Box\phi\alpha$ (Converse of Barcan's principle)

The translation is a theorem.

$\Box\exists\alpha\phi\alpha \dashv\vdash \exists\alpha\Box\phi\alpha$

The translation is not a theorem, nor would it have been under any extra postulates with even the slightest plausibility.

V. RELATIVE MODALITIES

Just as a sentence ϕ is necessary if it holds in all worlds, so ϕ is causally necessary if it holds in all worlds compatible with the laws of nature; obligatory for you if it holds in all worlds in which you act rightly; implicitly known, believed, hoped, asserted, or perceived by you if it holds in all worlds compatible with the content of your knowledge, beliefs, hopes, assertions, or perceptions. These, and many more, are *relative* modalities, expressible by quantifications over restricted ranges of worlds. We can write any dual pair of relative modalities as

$$\Box^i \delta_1 \cdots \delta_m$$
$$\Diamond^i \delta_1 \cdots \delta_m$$

where the index i indicates how the restriction of worlds is to be made and the m arguments $\delta_1, \ldots, \delta_m$, with $m \geq 0$, denote things to be considered in making the restriction (say, the person whose implicit knowledge we are talking about). To every dual pair of relative modalities there corresponds a characteristic relation

$$R^i x y z_1 \cdots z_m \quad \text{(world } x \text{ is } i\text{-related to world } y \text{ and } z_1, \ldots, z_m \text{ therein)}$$

governed by the postulate

P9: $\forall x \forall y \forall z_1 \cdots \forall z_m (R^i x y z_1 \cdots z_m \supset . Wx \ \& \ Wy \ \& \ Iz_1 y \ \& \cdots \& \ Iz_m y)$

The characteristic relation gives the appropriate restriction: we are to consider only worlds i-related to whatever world we are in (and certain things in it). Necessity and possibility themselves are that pair of relative modalities whose characteristic relation is just the 2-place universal relation between worlds.[22]

We can easily extend our translation scheme to handle sentences containing miscellaneous modal operators. We will treat them just as we do necessity and possibility, except that quantifiers over worlds will range over only those worlds which bear the appropriate characteristic relation to some world and perhaps some things in it. The translation of ϕ remains $\phi^\oplus$; we need only add two new clauses to the recursive definition of ϕ:

T2i*: $(\Box^i \delta_1 \cdots \delta_m \phi \alpha_1 \cdots \alpha_n)^\beta$ is $\forall \beta_1 \forall \gamma_1 \cdots \forall \gamma_n$
$(R^i \beta_1 \beta \delta_1 \cdots \delta_m \ \& \ I\gamma_1 \beta_1 \ \& \ C\gamma_1 \alpha_1 \ \& \cdots \& \ I\gamma_n \beta_1 \ \& \ C\gamma_n \alpha_n . \supset \phi^{\beta_1} \gamma_1 \cdots \gamma_n)$

T2j*: $(\Diamond^i \delta_1 \cdots \delta_m \phi \alpha_1 \cdots \alpha_n)^\beta$ is $\exists \beta_1 \exists \gamma_1 \cdots \exists \gamma_n$
$(R^i \beta_1 \beta \delta_1 \cdots \delta_m \ \& \ I\gamma_1 \beta_1 \ \& \ C\gamma_1 \alpha_1 \ \& \cdots \& \ I\gamma_n \beta_1 \ \& \ C\gamma_n \alpha_n \ \& \ \phi^{\beta_1} \gamma_1 \cdots \gamma_n)$

---

[22]Cf. Hintikka, "Quantifiers in Deontic Logic," *Societas Scientiarum Fennica, Commentationes Humanarum Litterarum* 23, no.4; Kanger, *op. cit.*; Kripke, *op. cit.*; Montague, *op. cit.*; Prior, "Possible Worlds," *Philosophical Quarterly* 12, no.46 (January 1962): 36–43; Hintikka, *Knowledge and Belief,* pp. 42–49; Føllesdal, "Quantification into Causal Contexts," in *Boston Studies in the Philosophy of Science* (New York: Humanities Press, 1965), pp. 263–74; Hintikka, "The Logic of Perception," in his *Models for Modalities* (Dordrecht: Reidel, 1969).

(since necessity and possibility are relative modalities, we no longer need T2i and T2j). For example, our translations of

$$\Box^i\phi$$
$$\Box^j\delta\psi\alpha$$
$$\Box\vdash^j\delta\phi$$

where ϕ is a 0-place sentence, ψ is a 1-place sentence, $\Box^i$ is a 0-place relative modality, and $\Box^j$ is a 1-place relative modality, are, respectively,

$$\forall\beta(R^i\beta@ \supset \phi^\beta)$$

(ϕ holds in any world i-related to the actual world)

$$\forall\beta\forall\gamma(R^j\beta_1@\delta \;\&\; I\gamma\beta \;\&\; C\gamma\alpha \;.\supset\; \psi^\beta\alpha)$$

(ψ holds of any counterpart γ of α in any world β j-related to the actual world and δ therein)

$$\forall\beta_1\forall\gamma(R^i\beta@ \;\&\; I\gamma\beta_1 \;\&\; C\gamma\delta \;.\supset\; \forall\beta_2(R^j\beta_2\beta_1\gamma \supset \phi^{\beta_2}))$$

(ϕ holds in any world β_2 such that, for some world β_1 that is i-related to the actual world and for some counterpart γ in β_1 of δ, β_2 is j-related to β_1 and γ)

The third example illustrates the fact that free variables occurring as arguments of relative modal operators may need to be handled by means of the counterpart relation.

Our previous discussion of singular terms as eliminable descriptions subject to ambiguity of scope carries over, with one change: in general, the auxiliary premise for exportation (and the first of two auxiliary premises for importation) must be the translation of $\Box^i\delta_1\cdots\delta_m(\zeta = \zeta)$ with one occurrence of ζ given wide scope and the other given narrow scope. The translation of $\exists\alpha\Box^i\delta_1\cdots\delta_m(\zeta = \alpha)$ will do only for those relative modalities, like necessity, for which $R^i@@\delta_1\cdots\delta_m$—and, hence, the translation of $\Box^i\delta_1\cdots\delta_m\phi \supset \phi$—are theorems under the appropriate postulates on the i-relation. More generally, the argument

$$\Box^i\delta_1\cdots\delta_m\phi\eta$$
$$\underline{\Box^i\delta_1\cdots\delta_m(\eta = \zeta)}$$
$$\therefore \Box^i\delta_1\cdots\delta_m\phi\zeta$$

where ϕ is a 1-place sentence, has a valid translation if ζ is given wide scope and η is given narrow scope throughout.

Principles corresponding to those discussed in section IV can be formulated for any relative modality (or, in the case of Becker's and Brouwer's principles, for any mixture of relative modalities). The acceptability of such principles will depend, in general, not just on the logical properties of the counterpart relation and the i-relations involved, but on the logical relations *between* the counterpart relation and the i-relations. For example, consider a relative necessity without arguments, so that its characteristic *i*-relation will be 2-place. (Such an *i*-relation is often called an *accessibility* relation between worlds). And consider Becker's principle for this relative necessity (but with '∃' still defined in terms of necessity itself): $\Box^i\phi \dashv 3 \Box^i\Box^i\phi$; that is, $\Box(\Box^i\phi \supset \Box^i\phi)$. It is often said that Becker's principle holds just in case accessibility is transitive, which is correct if ϕ is a closed sentence. But for open ϕ Becker's principle holds just in case

$$\forall x_1 \forall y_1 \forall x_2 \forall y_2 \forall x_3 \forall y_3 (Ix_1y_1 \ \& \ Ix_2y_2 \ \& \ Ix_3y_3 \ \& \ Cx_2x_1 \ \& \ Cx_3x_2$$
$$\& \ R^iy_2y_1 \ \& \ R^iy_3y_2 \ . \supset . \ Cx_3x_1 \ \& \ R^iy_3y_1)$$

even if neither accessibility nor the counterpart relation is transitive.

Postscripts to

"Counterpart Theory and Quantified Modal Logic"[1]

A. BEING IN A WORLD

I took as primitive the notion of an individual being *in* a possible world. I would now wish to distinguish the relation I had foremost in mind from two others.

A world is a large possible individual; it has smaller possible individuals as parts. A galaxy, a planet, a man, an electron—these things inhabit their world simply by being parts of it. Just as the electron is part of the man, and the man in turn is part of his planet which is part of its galaxy, so the galaxy in turn is part of its world. And so are its parts, and their parts, . . . , since the relation of part to whole is transitive. Any possible individual is part of a world, and in that sense it is *in* a world. (As a special case, a world is an improper part of itself.) Worlds do not overlap; unlike Siamese twins, they have no shared parts. Thus I stand by Postulate 2, construed as meaning that no possible individual is part of two worlds.

However, the possible individuals are not all the individuals. I wish to impose no restrictions on mereological summation of individuals, hence I must grant that there are individuals consisting of parts from several worlds. But such a cross-world sum is not a *possible* individual. There is no way for the whole of it to be actual.

[1]In these postscripts, I am much indebted to discussion with Allen Hazen, and to his "Counterpart-theoretic Semantics for Modal Logic," *Journal of Philosophy* 76 (1979): 319–38.

No matter which world is actual, at most a proper part of it actually exists. It is not in any world, in the sense just discussed, for it is not part of any world. But it is *partly in* each of many worlds, overlapping different worlds in virtue of different ones of its parts.

Finally, there are the non-individuals: that is, the sets. Provisionally,[2] my ontology consists of iterative set theory with individuals; the only unorthodox part is my view about what individuals there are. I take it that the part-whole relation applies to individuals, not sets. Then no set is in any world in the sense of being a part of it. Numbers, properties, propositions, events[3]—all these are sets, and not in any world. Numbers *et al.* are no more located in logical space than they are in ordinary time and space. Even a sequence of possible individuals all from the same world is not, strictly speaking, itself in that world.

When we evaluate the truth of a quantified sentence, we usually restrict the domain and quantify over less than all there is. If we evaluate a quantification at a world, we will normally omit many things not in that world, for instance the possible individuals that inhabit other worlds. But we will not omit the numbers, or some of the other sets. Let us say that an individual exists *from the standpoint of* a world iff it belongs to the least restricted domain that is normally—modal metaphysics being deemed abnormal—appropriate in evaluating the truth at that world of quantifications. I suppose that this domain will include all the indivduals in that world; none of the other individuals; and some, but not all, of the sets. There will be many sets that even exist from the standpoint of all worlds, for instance the numbers. Others may not; for instance the unit set of a possible individual might only exist from the standpoint of the world that the individual is in.

Thus we have three relations: being *in* a world, i.e. being part of a world; being *partly in* a world, i.e. having a part that is wholly in that world; and existing *from the standpoint of* a world. Postulate 2, the principle that nothing is in two worlds, applies only to the first of these.

The language of counterpart theory, and the modal language it replaces, had best be understood as quantifying only over possible individuals. Modifications are called for if we wish to quantify over more of what there is.

B. MODAL CONTINUANTS

I granted, none too enthusiastically, that there are individuals, not wholly in any world and hence incapable of being actualized in their entirety, that consist of parts from several worlds. Some of these cross-world individuals are unified by counterpart relations. For instance, there is the mereological sum of myself and all my

---

[2] I am not sure what to say about universals, as advocated in D. M. Armstrong, *Universals and Scientific Realism* (Cambridge University Press, 1978), except for this: they are not to be confused with the sets of individuals that I call properties. If there are universals, they differ in many ways from properties and they meet completely different theoretical needs.

[3] See my "Events" (in the sequel to this volume).

counterparts. Or (what is not the same) there is a cross-world individual which is a maximal counterpart-interrelated sum of possible individuals of whom I am one. In fact, there are many such.

More precisely, let us call X a *world-stage* of Y iff (1) X is a possible individual, entirely in one world, and is part of Y; and (2) X is not a proper part of any other individual of which the same is true. And let us call Y *counterpart-interrelated* iff any two world-stages of Y are counterparts. And let us call Y *maximal counterpart-interrelated*, or for short let us call it a *modal continuant*, iff (1) Y is counterpart-interrelated; and (2) Y is not a proper part of any other individual of which the same is true.

At this point it lies close to hand to suggest that ordinary things—stars, loco-motives, cats, ourselves—are modal continuants, just as they are temporal contin-uants having many temporal parts and not wholly located at any one time. Then we can have our counterpart theory and our identity across worlds as well, and everyone's intuitions will be satisfied.

I am not impressed. I have no objection to the theory of modal continuants. It is an equivalent reformulation of counterpart theory, so it is just as right as coun-terpart theory itself. It does not offend against Postulate 2, which merely prohibited individuals from being *wholly* in more than one world.

But I cannot see that the theory of modal continuants has any intuitive advan-tage. On the one hand, it makes a problem. Given the intransitivity of the coun-terpart relation, doubtless I—or rather, as we should now say, the actual world-stage of me—am part of ever so many different modal continuants. Which one is me? The puzzle is like that of Methuselah in "Survival and Identity" (in this vol-ume). Then let us borrow the solution. To be sure, I am (we are?) infinitely many different modal continuants. No worries: if we count by stage-sharing rather than identity, there is only one. —Will this really do? For temporal continuants, the pathological cases are fictional. It is only fitting and proper that such extraordinary goings on should force us to say something a bit counterintuitive. For modal con-tinuants, *every case is pathological*. Everything that can happen does. If we adopt the theory of modal continuants, we must count by stage-sharing not only when we want to treat the uncanny Methuselah as if he (they?) were an ordinary person, but also in the case of the ordinary people who are all, modally speaking, Methu-selahs.

And to what end? Presumably, to make Hubert Humphrey come out literally right when, after losing, he thinks: I myself might have won.[4] He is supposed to think: I am a modal continuant with a world-stage that wins. That is: the modal continuant of which one world-stage thinks this thought has a world-stage—a dif-ferent one—that wins. (It isn't "the" but let that pass.) For even if Humphrey is a modal continuant, it doesn't take the whole of him to do such things as winning or thinking the thought. The continuant does them by having a world-stage that

---

[4]See Saul Kripke, "Naming and Necessity," in Donald Davidson and Gilbert Harman, eds., *Semantics of Natural Language* (Dordrecht: Reidel, 1972), p. 344.

does them (in the senses appropriate respectively to continuants and to world-stages), just as a temporal continuant does this or that through its stages. But what good is that? If Humphrey yearns to think only of himself and nobody else, it is no use that he the thinker is part of the same mereological sum as some winner. That much is provided by the thisworldly sum of Humphrey and Nixon! No; what matters is that the modal continuant is counterpart-interrelated, so that the thinker of the thought has a winner for a counterpart. Then why not just say so, and leave the modal continuant out of it?

I think intuition is well enough satisfied if we take "myself" to modify "might have won." Humphrey thinks that he himself, and not someone else who resembles him, has the modal property expressed by "might have won." And that is true on anybody's theory. In counterpart theory, it is true because Humphrey himself, in virtue of his very own qualitative character, is such as to have some winners for counterparts.

If more is wanted, I do not think the theory of modal continuants can provide it.[5]

C. VAGUENESS AND VARIETY OF COUNTERPART RELATIONS

I am by no means offering a wholehearted defense of "Aristotelian essentialism." For the essences of things are settled only to the extent that the counterpart relation is, and the counterpart relation is not very settled at all. Like any relation of comparative overall similarity, it is subject to a great deal of indeterminacy (1) as to which respects of similarity and difference are to count at all, (2) as to the relative weights of the respects that do count, (3) as to the minimum standard of similarity that is required, and (4) as to the extent to which we eliminate candidates that are similar enough when they are beaten by competitors with stronger claims.

Further, as with vagueness generally, the vagueness of the counterpart relation—and hence of essence and *de re* modality generally—may be subject to pragmatic pressures, and differently resolved in different contexts.[6] The upshot is that it is hard to say anything false about essences. For any halfway reasonable statement will tend to create a context that (partially) resolves the vagueness of the counterpart relation in such a way as to make that statement true in that context. So almost anything goes. The true-hearted essentialist might well think me a false friend, a Quinean sceptic in essentialist's clothing.

---

[5] If it really must be Humphrey himself who does the winning, the very same Humphrey who thinks the modal thought, the best solution is to think not of genuine worlds but of world-stories—ersatz worlds—so that we think of Humphrey's actual losing and possible winning as two stories about him, one true and the other false. It is my impression that something like this, and not a theory of modal continuants, was Kripke's intention.

[6] See the Appendix to "General Semantics" and Example 5 of "Scorekeeping in a Language Game" (both in this volume) for discussions of vagueness and the effects of context on its resolution.

To take one extreme, a suitable context might deliver an antiessentialist counterpart relation—one on which anything is a counterpart of anything, and nothing has any essence worth mentioning. Or, as Hazen has suggested,[7] we might somehow partition things into kinds, and take a counterpart relation on which anything is a counterpart of anything of its kind. That would make the essence of a thing simply be its kind. Such unselective counterpart relations as these would violate my Postulate 5, since things would have counterparts in their own worlds besides themselves. But I needn't insist on Postulate 5 for any counterpart relation that might be appropriate in any context; it is enough to take it as a condition governing the more commonplace of them.

At the opposite extreme, a suitable context might deliver a hyperessentialist counterpart relation—one on which nothing has any counterpart except itself. Then by Postulate 2 nothing has otherworldly counterparts, and hence nothing has any of its attributes nonessentially. This counterpart relation, of course, is simply identity.

A common sort of counterpart relation, especially in the context of recent discussions of essentialism, is one that gives decisive weight to perfect match of origins. (I count this simply as one respect of similarity, *pace* Jaakko Hintikka who says that I ought to have considered match of origins *as well as* similarity.[8]) It is this sort of counterpart relation that we need to make sense of such possibilities as that of Hitler's leading a blameless life while someone else moves into his actual role and ends by living a wicked life just like the life that Hitler actually lived.[9]

Not only may the vagueness of the counterpart relation be very differently resolved in different contexts. Also we may need to play off one counterpart relation against another in a single context.[10] Or we may need to play off one relation of comparative similarity that governs the counterpart relation against another that governs explicit judgements of similarity. For as Fred Feldman has observed, one might truly say:

> I could have been more like what you in fact are like than like what in fact I am, and at the same time, you could have been more like what I in fact am like than what you in fact are.[11]

---

[7] *Op. cit.*, p. 332.

[8] See his *The Intentions of Intentionality and Other New Models for Modalities* (Dordrecht: Reidel, 1975), pp. 127–29 and 209.

[9] See my *Counterfactuals* (Oxford: Blackwell, 1973), p. 41. For the case of blameless Hitler, see Kripke, "Naming and Necessity," pp. 288–89.

[10] See Hintikka's discussion of "two kinds of cross-identification," in "On the Logic of Perception" in his *Models for Modalities* (Dordrecht: Reidel, 1969); my *Counterfactuals*, pp. 42–43; and "Counterparts of Persons and Their Bodies" (in this volume). The last shows how to use a harmless multiplicity of counterpart relations to replace an undesired multiplication of entities. Denis Robinson has applied the same method to many other cases, in a lecture at the Australasian Association of Philosophy Conference in Sydney in August 1980.

[11] "Counterparts," *Journal of Philosophy* 68 (1971): 406–9. A parallel problem about similarity and counterfactuals is discussed in "Counterfactual Dependence and Time's Arrow" (in the sequel to this volume).

D. PAIRS OF COUNTERPARTS AND COUNTERPARTS OF PAIRS

Consider the twin brothers Dee and Dum. Together they comprise a pair. In this easy case, we may take the pair simply as a mereological sum; then it is a possible individual, not a set, so counterpart theory applies to it without need for any modification.

In another world are two duplicate planets, far apart in time and space. On one planet there live a pair of twin brothers, Dee_1 and Dum_1; and together they comprise the pair Dee_1-cum-Dum_1. Likewise on the other planet there live Dee_2 and Dum_2, who comprise Dee_2-cum-Dum_2. Dee_1 and Dee_2 resemble Dee equally, and quite well, and better than anything else in their world does, and so they are both his counterparts. Likewise Dum_1 and Dum_2 are both counterparts of Dum.

Now we ask a doubly *de re* modal question about Dee and Dum: might they have been not twin brothers, but totally unrelated inhabitants of separated planets? Intuitively, it seems not. They are essentially related (or, at any rate, related if they both exist). But counterpart theory disagrees, and gives an answer that seems counterintuitive. For Dee and Dum satisfy the counterpart-theoretic translation of the formula

$\Diamond x$ and y are unrelated

as values respectively of its two variables. That is because there is a world in which there are unrelated counterparts of Dee and Dum respectively: namely, Dee_1 and Dum_2 in the world of the duplicate planets. (Or, for good measure, Dee_2 and Dum_1.)

But whether counterpart theory gives a counterintuitive answer depends on exactly how we put the question. Instead of a doubly *de re* question about Dee and Dum, we might better have asked a singly *de re* question about their pair, Dee-cum-Dum. Might *it* have been not a pair of twin brothers, but rather a pair of totally unrelated inhabitants of separate planets? Again it seems not. This time, counterpart theory agrees. For, under a reasonable counterpart relation, the pair Dee-cum-Dum does not satisfy the translation of the formula

$\Diamond \exists y \exists z(x$ is y-cum-z & y and z are unrelated$)$.

That is so because, for instance, the only counterparts of Dee-cum-Dum in the world of the duplicate planets are Dee_1-cum-Dum_1 and Dee_2-cum-Dum_2, and each of these is a related pair. We needn't worry about the unrelated pairs, Dee_1-cum-Dum_2 and Dee_2-cum-Dum_1. Nothing requires us to count these pairs as counterparts of Dee-cum-Dum, and the important difference between related pairs and unrelated ones gives us an excellent reason not to.

Two morals. First, we must learn the right way to apply counterpart theory. It seems that we do best to avoid doubly *de re* formulations if we want to respect intuition. And that seems plausible enough: doubly *de re* formulations may seem natural enough in the artificial language of quantified modal logic, but it is not so clear that they are part of our ordinary modal thought. Second, we should not accept any neat principle to the effect that a pair of counterparts is a counterpart of the pair, or any generalization thereof.[12]

E. DOES COUNTERPART THEORY CHANGE LOGIC?

If counterpart theory calls for the rejection of some popular modal principles, that needn't worry us. But if it forces us to reject principles of the logic of identity and quantification, that is more serious. Allen Hazen and Saul Kripke have said that it does.[13] I plead not guilty. I shall consider one case of the trouble they have in mind, but I think my defense carries over to other cases.

Consider schema (1) and sentence (2) below. (1) is a valid schema of the classical logic of identity and quantification. It says something very uncontroversial indeed, if by " = " we really mean identity: if we have one and the same thing, what's true of it is the same as what's true of it. (2), on the other hand, is an invalid sentence of quantified modal logic, since its counterpart-theoretic translation is not (and should not be) a theorem of counterpart theory.

(1) $\forall x \forall y (x = y \supset . \text{---} x \text{---} \equiv \text{---} y \text{---})$
(2) $\forall x \forall y (x = y \supset . \Diamond x \neq y \equiv \Diamond y \neq y)$

How can (2) fail? Would its denial mean that we have two different things that are contingently identical? Or perhaps one thing that is only contingently self-identical? No—the denial of (2) would mean no such nonsensical thing. To see what it would really mean, don't guess, but read the counterpart-theoretic translation. The translation of (2) turns out to say that nothing in the actual world has more than one counterpart in any other world. Then its denial says that something actual does have two counterparts in a single world. The case of Dee, Dee_1, and Dee_2 could serve as an illustration, if Dee is actual. Again, we are in trouble when a doubly *de re* formulation meets something with double counterparts.

So (1) is not to be challenged while its instance (2) may well be false! How is that? —I reply that (2) is not an instance of (1), so there is nothing at all wrong with accepting (1) and rejecting (2).

Compare another invalid sentence, (3). How can we accept (1) and reject (3)? — That's easy: to take (3) as an instance of (1) is to commit a fallacy of confusing bound variables.

(3) $\forall x \forall y (x = y \supset . \exists y y \neq x \equiv \exists y y \neq y)$

To make (3) an instance of (1), the final occurrence of "y" would have to be bound to the initial "$\forall y$". It isn't. It's bound to the nearby "$\exists y$".

---

[12]I have more or less followed Hazen, *op. cit.*, in stating and solving the problem. But with this minor technical difference: he builds the solution into a modified counterpart-theoretic semantics for multiply *de re* formulations, whereas I apply it in unmodified counterpart theory by steering clear of the multiply *de re*.

[13]Hazen, *ibid.* Kripke, "Naming and Necessity," footnote 13.

I say much the same about (2). To treat it as an instance of (1) is to confuse bound variables. The abbreviated notation of quantified modal logic conceals the true pattern of binding, but it is revealed when we examine the counterpart-theoretic translation. It is as follows.

(2) $\forall x \forall y (x = y \supset \Diamond \, x \neq y \equiv \Diamond \, y \neq y)$

The diamonds conceal quantifiers that bind the occurrences of "x" and "y" that follow. (Indeed, in the translation, the variables that follow would not be "x" and "y" at all, but different variables altogether.) The diamonds also conceal occurrences of "x" and "y" that are bound by the initial "$\forall x$" and "$\forall y$". This pattern of binding is not right for an instance of (1), any more than the pattern in (3) is.

So counterpart theory is no threat to standard logic. It is only a threat to simplistic methods of keeping track of variable-binding and instancehood when we are dealing with the perversely abbreviated language of quantified modal logic.

F. NONEXTENSIONALITY TOLERATED

Whatever else may fairly be said against the language of quantified modal logic, I withdraw my complaint against its nonextensionality. See "'Tensions" (in this volume), in which I argue that such violations of extensionality as it commits are of no deep significance. If we want to restore extensionality, we need only reanalyze the language in an otherwise pointless, but harmless, way.

G. ATTITUDINAL MODALITIES ABANDONED

In view of the arguments of "Attitudes *De Dicto* and *De Se*" (in this volume), I withdraw my statement that implicit knowledge, belief, etc. are relative modalities, expressible by quantification over restricted ranges of worlds. They are, however, something closely analogous to that: we need only put possible individuals in place of the worlds.

H. CONVENTIONALITY OF POSTULATE 2 DISOWNED

Footnote 2 has given some readers the impression that I regard Postulate 2 as a mere convention, and that we could just as truly say that some things are identical with their otherworldly counterparts after all. Not so. I was alluding to the possibility of a hybrid theory—a theory opposed to my own, a theory which I take to be false—according to which there are identities across worlds, but we use the counterpart relation anyway.

· F O U R ·

Counterparts of Persons
and
Their Bodies

Materialists like myself hold that persons and their bodies are identical. But there is a simple argument to show that this identity thesis is refuted by the mere possibility that a person might switch bodies. To defeat the argument it seems necessary to revise my counterpart theory by providing for a multiplicity of counterpart relations. This revision has an odd result. Modal predications may be *de re*, yet not referentially transparent.

The thesis I wish to defend here may be stated more precisely, as follows:

> (T) Necessarily, a person occupies a body at a time if and only if that person is identical with that body at that time.

Note that the thesis (T) is formulated not in terms of identity itself, a two-place relation, but in terms of a derivative three-place relation of identity at a time. I wish to regard enduring things such as persons and bodies as aggregates—sets, mereological sums, or something similar—of momentary stages. Enduring things X and Y are *identical at* a time t if and only if they both have stages at t—that is, *exist at t*—and their stages at t are identical. Therefore X and Y are identical *simpliciter* if and only if they are identical whenever either one exists. Note that (T) does not say that persons and bodies must be identical *simpliciter*. It does imply that *if* a certain person occupies a certain body whenever either the person or the

---

I am indebted to M. J. Cresswell, David Kaplan, and John Perry for illuminating discussion of these matters.

body exists, *then* the person and the body are identical. In such a case, all and only those stages which are stages of the person are stages of the body he occupies. But (T) also permits other cases: for instance, a body consisting of the stages of a certain person together with some final dead stages that are not stages of any person (and some initial prenatal stages that perhaps are not stages of any person); or a person consisting of stages of a certain body together with some initial or final ghostly stages that are not stages of any body; or even a body-switching person consisting partly of stages of one body and partly of stages of another body. A person consists of stages related pairwise by a certain relation we may call the relation of *personal unity*; a body consists of stages related pairwise by another relation we may call the relation of *bodily unity*.[1] Since for the most part persons occupy bodies and bodies are occupied by persons, it follows according to (T) that the two relations of unity are relations on almost the same set of stages. The exceptions are dead stages, perhaps prenatal stages, and perhaps ghostly stages. Moreover, if we leave out the dead or ghostly or perhaps prenatal stages, then at least for the most part the two relations of unity are coextensive. The exceptions would be body-switchers and perhaps split personalities. Nevertheless, the two relations of unity are different relations-in-intension; so they are coextensive only contingently if at all.

Now I shall present an argument against (T). I regard it as a simplified descendant of an argument put forth by Jerome Shaffer,[2] but I have changed it so much that he might not wish to acknowledge it as his own.

Body-switching is logically possible. Because I might have switched out of my present body yesterday, though in fact I did not, I and my actual present body are such that the former might not have occupied the latter today. Whether or not persons are identical with bodies they occupy, certainly persons are never identical with bodies they do not occupy. So we have:

(1)   I and my body are such that they might not have been identical today.

Suppose that, as is surely at least possible, I occupy the same body from the time when it and I began until the time when it and I will end. Then, by (T), it and I are identical whenever it or I exist. Hence my body and I, enduring things, are identical *simpliciter*. By this identity and Leibniz's law, (1) yields (2):

(2)   My body and my body are such that they might not have been identical today.

Since (2) is self-contradictory, (T) has apparently been refuted.

To rescue (T) without denying the possibility of body-switching and without denying that I might occupy the same body throughout the time that it or I exist,

---

[1]The so-called "problem of personal identity" is the problem of explicating the relation of personal unity between stages. This view is expounded more fully by John Perry in "Can the Self Divide?" *Journal of Philosophy* 69 (1972): 463–88.

[2]"Persons and Their Bodies," *Philosophical Review* 75, no. 1 (January 1966): 59–77.

I plan to show that the step from (1) to (2) by Leibniz's law is illegitimate—in other words, that (1) is not referentially transparent with respect to the term 'I'.

I have used the familiar "are such that" construction to indicate that (1) and (2) are to be taken as *de re* rather than *de dicto* modal predications. That is, we are to consider what happens in other possible worlds to the things denoted *here* in our actual world by the terms 'I' and 'my body,' not what happens in other worlds to the things denoted *there* by those terms. Suppose (1) were taken *de dicto*, as if it were this:

It might have been the case that I and my body were not identical today.

There is no problem explaining why this is not referentially transparent. Its truth conditions involve the denotations in other worlds of the terms 'I' and 'my body'; even if these denote the same thing here in our world, they denote different things in some other worlds, for instance in a world in which I switched bodies yesterday. Hence they are not interchangeable. But it would be wrong to take (1) as *de dicto*, for the argument leading up to (1) would then be incoherent and question-begging. As we understand (1) in the argument, it seems true even given (T) because of the fact that I might have switched bodies yesterday. But (1) taken *de dicto* is a straightforward denial of an instance of (T), and the possibility of body-switching is irrelevant to its truth or falsity. For (1) taken *de dicto* is true today if and only if there is some world such that the things denoted in that world today by 'I' and 'my body' are not identical today. But in any world, 'my body' today denotes whichever body is today occupied by the person who is today denoted by 'I', regardless of whether that person occupied that body yesterday. If (T) is true, then in any world the person today denoted there by 'I' and the body today denoted there by 'my body' are identical today; so (1) taken *de dicto* is false. (It should be understood that when I speak of the denotation in another world of 'I' and 'my body,' I am not concerned with any utterance of these terms by some inhabitant of the other world, but rather with the denotation of these terms in the other world on the occasion of their utterance by me here in our world.)

I have suggested elsewhere[3] that *de re* modal predications may best be understood by the method of counterparts. To say that something here in our actual world is such that it might have done so-and-so is not to say that there is a possible world in which that thing *itself* does so-and-so, but that there is a world in which a *counterpart* of that thing does so-and-so. To say that I am such that I might have been a Republican, but I am not such that I might have been a cockatrice, is to say that in some world I have a counterpart who is a Republican, but in no world do I have a counterpart who is a cockatrice. That is plausible enough, for the counterpart relation is a relation of similarity. X's counterparts in other worlds are all and only those things which resemble X closely enough in important respects, and

[3]"Counterpart Theory and Quantified Modal Logic," in this volume.

more closely than do the other things in their worlds. It is easier for a Republican than for a cockatrice to resemble me enough to be my counterpart.

The counterpart relation serves as a substitute for identity between things in different worlds. The principal advantage of the method of counterparts over the method of interworld identities is that if we adopted the latter in its most plausible form, we would say that things were identical with all and only those things which we would otherwise call their counterparts. But that could not be correct: first, because the counterpart relation is not transitive or symmetric, as identity is; and second, because the counterpart relation depends on the relative importances we attach to various different respects of similarity and dissimilarity, as identity does not.

To recapitulate: in each possible world there is a set of momentary stages and a set of enduring things composed of stages related pairwise by various relations of unity. An enduring thing and its stages exist only in one world, but may have counterparts in other worlds. We shall be concerned here only with counterparts of enduring things, though we can allow that stages also have their counterparts.

Applying the method of counterparts to the problem at hand, we immediately encounter a bothersome distraction. The translation of (2), which seemed self-contradictory, is this:

> There are a world W, a counterpart X in W of my body, and a counterpart Y in W of my body, such that X and Y are not identical today.

Unfortunately, this translation comes out true, but for an irrelevant reason. I, and also my body whether or not I am identical with it, might have been twins. My body therefore does have two different counterparts in certain worlds. Not only is the translation true; it seems to me to show that (2) itself is true. But the argument against (T) can easily be repaired. Replace (1) and (2) by:

> (1′)   I and my body are such that (without any duplication of either) they might not have been identical today.
>
> (2′)   My body and my body are such that (without any duplication of either) they might not have been identical today.

The argument works as well with (1′) and (2′) as it did with (1) and (2). Indeed, (1′) and (2′) correspond to (1) and (2) as we would have understood them if we had forgotten that I might have been twins.[4]

Applying counterpart theory to the repaired argument, we obtain these translations of (1′) and (2′):

> (1*)   There are a world W, a unique counterpart X in W of me, and a unique counterpart Y in W of my body, such that X and Y are not identical today.

---

[4] I do not know how or whether (1′) and (2′) can be expressed in the language of quantified modal logic. That does not bother me. I know how to express them in English and in counterpart theory.

(2*)   There are a world W, a unique counterpart X in W of my body, and a unique counterpart Y in W of my body, such that X and Y are not identical today.

The argument against (T) seems to go through, using (1*) and (2*): (1*) seems true because I might have switched bodies yesterday; (2*) is self-contradictory; yet (1*) implies (2*) by Leibniz's law, given (T) and the supposition that I occupy the same body whenever I or it exist.

In defense of (T), however, I claim that (1*) is *false,* despite the fact that I might have switched bodies yesterday. What is true because I might have switched bodies is not (1*) but rather (1**):

(1**)   There are a world W, a unique *personal counterpart* X in W of me, and a unique *bodily counterpart* Y in W of my body, such that X and Y are not identical today.

I now propose a revision of counterpart theory to the effect that, at least in the present context, (1**) rather than (1*) is the correct translation of (1′). What follows from (1**) by Leibniz's law, given (T) and the supposition that I occupy the same body whenever I exist, is not the self-contradiction (2*) but rather the truth:

There are a world W, a unique personal counterpart X in W of my body, and a unique bodily counterpart Y in W of my body, such that X and Y are not identical today.

Two other truths follow from (1**) in the same way:

There are a world W, a unique personal counterpart X in W of me, and a unique bodily counterpart Y in W of me, such that X and Y are not identical today.

There are a world W, a unique personal counterpart X in W of my body, and a unique bodily counterpart Y in W of me, such that X and Y are not identical today.

However, the translation of (2′) is none of these. If the translation of (1′) is (1**), the translation of (2′) should be (2**):

(2**)   There are a world W, a unique bodily counterpart X in W of my body, and a unique bodily counterpart Y in W of my body, such that X and Y are not identical today.

Though (2**) is not (2*), it is still a self-contradiction.

As we already noted, counterpart relations are a matter of over-all resemblance in a variety of respects. If we vary the relative importances of different respects of similarity and dissimilarity, we will get different counterpart relations. Two respects of similarity or dissimilarity among enduring things are, first, personhood and personal traits, and, second, bodyhood and bodily traits. If we assign great weight to the former, we get the *personal counterpart* relation. Only a person, or something very like a person, can resemble a person in respect of personhood and personal traits enough to be his personal counterpart. But if we assign great weight to the latter, we get the *bodily counterpart* relation. Only a body, or something very like a body, can resemble a body in respect to bodyhood and bodily traits enough to be its bodily counterpart.

If I am my body, then in many worlds there are things that are both personal and bodily counterparts of me and *ipso facto* of my body. These things, like me, are both persons and bodies. But in other worlds I (and my body) have neither personal counterparts nor bodily counterparts; or personal counterparts that are not bodily counterparts; or bodily counterparts that are not personal counterparts; or personal and bodily counterparts that are not identical. A world in which I switched out of my body—that is, my personal counterpart switched out of my bodily counterpart—yesterday is of this last sort. I and my body have there a personal counterpart that is a person but not a body and also a bodily counterpart that is a body but not a person. These are not identical today, and not identical *simpliciter*, though they were identical at times before yesterday since they shared their earlier stages. However, my personal counterpart is identical today with a different body. My bodily counterpart is identical today with a different person (if the body-switching was a trade) or with none.

We may draw an analogy between the relations of personal and bodily unity among stages of persons and bodies and the personal and bodily counterpart relations among enduring persons and bodies. If I ask of something that is both a stage of a body and a stage of a body-switching person "Was this ever in Borneo?" you should ask whether I mean this person or this body. If the former, I am asking whether the given stage is linked by personal unity to an earlier stage located in Borneo. If the latter, I am asking whether it is linked by bodily unity to an earlier stage located in Borneo. Similarly, if I ask of something that is both an enduring person and an enduring body "Might this have been an orangutan?" you should again ask whether I mean this person or this body. If the former, I am asking whether it has an orangutan for a personal counterpart; if the latter, whether it has an orangutan for a bodily counterpart.

But the analogy is imperfect. The two relations of unity are equivalence relations, at least for the most part and as a matter of contingent fact. Therefore it is easy and natural to form the concept of an enduring person or body, consisting of stages linked together pairwise by a relation of personal or bodily unity. It is tempting to do the same with the counterpart relations, forming the concept of a superperson or superbody consisting of persons or bodies in different worlds, linked together by a personal or bodily counterpart relation. But this cannot be done in any straightforward way because counterpart relations are not equivalence relations. Like all similarity relations on a sufficiently variegated domain, they fail to be transitive because chains of little differences add up to big differences.

Why should I think it plausible to employ multiple counterpart relations to translate (1′) as (1**) rather than (1*)? Precisely because by doing so I escape the refutation of (T), and I am convinced of (T). I am offered a trade: instead of a multiplicity of kinds of thing I can have a multiplicity of counterpart relations. A *reductio* refutes the whole combination of assumptions that led to contradiction; if all but one of those assumptions are highly plausible, whichever remains is the refuted one. And in addition, if I contemplate the propositions I express by means of (1') and (1**), it seems to me that they are the same.

I would like to present the translation of (1') by (1**) and (2') by (2**) as instances of a general scheme for translating English modal predications into sentences of counterpart theory with multiple counterpart relations. I do not know how to do this. Roughly, the idea is that the sense of a term somehow selects the counterpart relation that is to be used to find the counterparts of the thing denoted by that term. The terms 'I,' 'you,' 'that person,' 'the lady I saw you with last night,' 'George,' all select the personal counterpart relation. 'This thing' (pointing at myself), 'this body,' 'my body,' 'that which will be my corpse after I die,' all select the bodily counterpart relation. Similarly for indefinite terms (phrases of restricted quantification): 'everybody' selects the personal counterpart relation, whereas 'every body' selects the bodily counterpart relation. Even if everybody is his body, and conversely, "Everybody is such that he might have been a disembodied spirit" is true, whereas "Every body is such that it might have been a disembodied spirit" is false. The former means that each of those things which are both persons and bodies has a disembodied spirit as personal counterpart, whereas the latter means that each of those same things has a disembodied spirit as bodily counterpart.

In certain modal predications, the appropriate counterpart relation is selected not by the subject term but by a special clause. To say that something, regarded as a such-and-such, is such that it might have done so-and-so is to say that in some world it has a such-and-such-counterpart that does so-and-so. With these "regarded as" clauses in mind, I might say that I translate (1') as (1**) because I take it to be synonymous with (1''):

> (1'') I, regarded as a person, and my body, regarded as a body, are such that (without any duplication of either) they might not have been identical today.

Likewise I translated (2') as if it had contained two "regarded as a body" clauses.

If we are to have multiple counterpart relations, we may well wonder how many to have. One for every sortal? One for every natural kind? One for any common noun phrase whatever that can grammatically be inserted into 'regarded as a ————,' even the phrase 'yellow pig or prime number'? One for any kind of entity, even kinds that cannot be specified in our language?[5] I do not know. Nor do I know whether one of the counterpart relations, corresponding perhaps to the clause 'regarded as an entity,' can be identified with the single counterpart relation of my original counterpart theory.

---

[5] We could also put this question another way: given a three-place relation "———— is a ————al counterpart of ————," which kinds are appropriate middle arguments?

It is customary to distinguish real essences of things from their nominal essences under descriptions. Now, however, we have a third, intermediate, kind of essence. My real essence consists of the properties common to all my counterparts. (Here I use the original single counterpart relation.) My nominal essence under the description 'person' consists of the properties common to all possible persons. My intermediate essence under the description 'person' consists of the properties common to all my personal counterparts. I have no reason to think that any two of these sets of properties are the same. It may even be that none of the three is properly included in any other, if my personal counterparts include some entities (robots, say) which are almost persons but not quite. Counterpart relations are vague, being dependent on the relative weights assigned to respects of similarity or dissimilarity. Hence real essences are vague in a way nominal essences are not. Intermediate essences under descriptions share this vagueness, for the new multiple counterpart relations are no less vague than the original counterpart relation.

In my original counterpart theory, any *de re* modal predication is referentially transparent. Something has the same counterparts however we may choose to refer to it. Given a *de re* modal predication, we find the thing denoted by the subject term in the actual world; then we consider what befalls that thing—or rather, its counterparts—in other worlds. Only the denotation of the subject term matters. We can substitute another subject term with the same denotation but different sense, and the truth value of the modal predication will not change.

But in the present revision of counterpart theory, *de re* modal predications are not in general transparent. Not only the denotation of the subject term matters, but also the counterpart relation it selects. If we substitute another subject term with the same denotation but different sense, it may change the truth value of the modal predication by selecting a different counterpart relation. Then even though the denoted thing here in our world remains the same, we have a different way of following the fortunes of that thing in other worlds.

Nevertheless, these modal predications are still *de re*, not *de dicto*. We still find the denoted thing in our actual world and then find counterparts of that thing elsewhere. We do not at all consider the things denoted by the subject term in other worlds, as we would in the case of a *de dicto* modal predication.

Transparency of modal predications can fail whenever the sense of the subject term is used to do anything beyond determining the actual denotation of the subject term. One further thing it might do is determine the denotation of the subject term in other worlds; that is the *de dicto* case. Another, and altogether different, further thing it might do is select a counterpart relation. (These two are not the only alternatives.) It is the latter, I suggest, that happens in the argument we are considering. Therefore we can accept (1′) as a consequence of the possibility that I might have switched bodies, reject (2′) as self-contradictory, and yet accept (T) and its consequence that if I occupy the same body whenever I or it exist then I am my body.

· F I V E ·

Survival and Identity

What is it that matters in survival? Suppose I wonder whether I will survive the coming battle, brainwashing, brain transplant, journey by matter-transmitter, purported reincarnation or resurrection, fission into twins, fusion with someone else, or what not. What do I really care about? If it can happen that some features of ordinary, everyday survival are present but others are missing, then what would it take to make the difference between something practically as good as commonplace survival and something practically as bad as commonplace death?

I answer, along with many others: *what matters in survival is mental continuity and connectedness.* When I consider various cases in between commonplace survival and commonplace death, I find that what I mostly want in wanting survival is that my mental life should flow on. My present experiences, thoughts, beliefs, desires, and traits of character should have appropriate future successors. My total present mental state should be but one momentary stage in a continuing succession of mental states. These successive states should be interconnected in two ways. First, by bonds of similarity. Change should be gradual rather than sudden, and (at least in some respects) there should not be too much change overall. Second, by bonds of lawful causal dependence. Such change as there is should conform, for the most part, to lawful regularities concerning the succession of mental states—regularities, moreover, that are exemplified in everyday cases of survival. And this should be so not by accident (and also not, for instance, because some demon has set out to create a succession of mental states patterned to counterfeit our ordinary mental life) but rather because each succeeding mental state causally depends for its character on the states immediately before it.

I refrain from settling certain questions of detail. Perhaps my emphasis should be on *connectedness:* direct relations of similarity and causal dependence between my present mental state and each of its successors; or perhaps I should rather emphasize *continuity:* the existence of step-by-step paths from here to there, with extremely strong local connectedness from each step to the next. Perhaps a special place should be given to the special kind of continuity and connectedness that constitute memory;[1] or perhaps not. Perhaps the "mental" should be construed narrowly, perhaps broadly. Perhaps nonmental continuity and connectedness—in my appearance and voice, for instance—also should have at least some weight. It does not matter, for the present, just which version I would prefer of the thesis that what matters is mental continuity and connectedness. I am sure that I would endorse some version, and in this paper I want to deal with a seeming problem for any version.

The problem begins with a well-deserved complaint that all this about mental connectedness and continuity is too clever by half. I have forgotten to say what should have been said first of all. What matters in survival is survival. If I wonder whether I will survive, what I mostly care about is quite simple. When it's all over, will I myself—the very same person now thinking these thoughts and writing these words—still exist? Will any one of those who do exist afterward be me? In other words, *what matters in survival is identity*—identity between the I who exists now and the surviving I who will, I hope, still exist then.

One question, two answers! An interesting answer, plausible to me on reflection but far from obvious: that what matters is mental connectedness and continuity between my present mental state and other mental states that will succeed it in the future. And a compelling commonsense answer, an unhelpful platitude that cannot credibly be denied: what matters is identity between myself, existing now, and myself, still existing in the future.

If the two answers disagreed and we had to choose one, I suppose we would have to prefer the platitude of common sense to the interesting philosophical thesis. Else it would be difficult to believe one's own philosophy! The only hope for the first answer, then, is to show that we need not choose: the answers are compatible, and both are right. That is the claim I wish to defend. I say that it cannot happen that what matters in survival according to one answer is present while what matters in survival according to the other answer is lacking.

---

[1]Better, *quasi-memory:* that process which is memory when it occurs within one single person, but might not be properly so-called if it occurred in a succession of mental states that did not all belong to a single person.

I. PARFIT'S ARGUMENT

Derek Parfit has argued that the two answers cannot both be right, and we must therefore choose.[2] (He chooses the first). His argument is as follows:

(a) Identity is a relation with a certain formal character. It is one-one and it does not admit of degree.

(b) A relation of mental continuity and connectedness need not have that formal character. We can imagine problem cases in which any such relation is one-many or many-one, or in which it is present to a degree so slight that survival is questionable.

Therefore, since Parfit believes as I do that what matters in survival is some sort of mental continuity or connectedness,

(c) What matters in survival is not identity. At most, what matters is a relation that coincides with identity to the extent that the problem cases do not actually arise.

Parfit thinks that if the problem cases did arise, or if we wished to solve them hypothetically, questions of personal identity would have no compelling answers. They would have to be answered arbitrarily, and in view of the discrepancy stated in (a) and (b), there is no answer that could make personal identity coincide perfectly with the relation of mental continuity and connectedness that matters in survival.

Someone else could just as well run the argument in reverse. Of course what matters in survival is personal identity Therefore what matters cannot be mental continuity or connectedness, in view of the discrepancy stated in premises (a) and (b). It must be some better-behaved relation.

My task is to disarm both directions of the argument and show that the opposition between what matters and identity is false. We can agree with Parfit (and I think we should) that what matters in questions of personal identity is mental continuity or connectedness, and that this might be one-many or many-one, and admits of degree. At the same time we can consistently agree with common sense (and I think we should) that what matters in questions of personal identity—even in the problem cases—is identity.

I do not attack premises (a) and (b). We could, of course, say "identity" and just mean mental continuity and connectedness. Then we would deny that "identity" must have the formal character stated in (a). But this verbal maneuver would not meet the needs of those who think, as I do, that what matters in survival is literally *identity:* that relation that everything bears to itself and to no other thing. As for (b), the problem cases clearly are possible under Parfit's conception of the sort of mental continuity or connectedness that matters in survival: or under any

---

[2]Derek Parfit, "Personal Identity," *Philosophical Review* 80 (1971): 3–27.

conception I might wish to adopt. The questions about continuity and connectedness which I left open are not relevant, since no way of settling them will produce
a relation with the formal character of identity. So we do indeed have a discrepancy
of formal character between identity and any suitable relation of mental continuity
and connectedness.

But what does that show? Only that the two relations are different. And we
should have known that from the start, since they have different relata. He who
says that what matters in survival is a relation of mental continuity and connectedness is speaking of a relation among more or less momentary person-stages, or
time-slices of continuant persons, or persons-at-times. He who says that what matters in survival is identity, on the other hand, must be speaking of identity among
temporally extended continuant persons with stages at various times. What matters
is that one and the same continuant person should have stages both now and later.
Identity among stages has nothing to do with it, since stages are momentary. Even
if you survive, your present stage is not identical to any future stage.[3] You know
that your present stage will not survive the battle—that is not disconcerting—but
will *you* survive?

II. THE R-RELATION AND THE I-RELATION

Pretend that the open questions have been settled, so that we have some definite
relation of mental continuity and connectedness among person-stages in mind as
the relation that matters in survival. Call it the *R-relation,* for short. If you wonder
whether you will survive the coming battle or what-not, you are wondering whether
any of the stages that will exist afterward is R-related to you-now, the stage that
is doing the wondering. Similarly for other "questions of personal identity." If you
wonder whether this is your long-lost son, you mostly wonder whether the stage
before you now is R-related to certain past stages. If you also wonder whether he
is a reincarnation of Nero, you wonder whether this stage is R-related to other
stages farther in the past. If you wonder whether it is in your self-interest to save
for your old age, you wonder whether the stages of that tiresome old gaffer you
will become are R-related to you-now to a significantly greater degree than are all
the other person-stages at this time or other times. If you wonder as you step into
the duplicator whether you will leave by the left door, the right door, both, or
neither, you are again wondering which future stages, if any, are R-related to you-
now.

Or so say I. Common sense says something that sounds different: in wondering
whether you will survive the battle, you wonder whether you—a continuant person

---

[3]Unless time is circular, so that it is in its own future in the same way that places are to the west of
themselves. But that possibility also has nothing to do with survival.

consisting of your present stage along with many other stages—will continue beyond the battle. Will you be identical with anyone alive then? Likewise for other questions of personal identity.

Put this way, the two answers seem incomparable. It is pointless to compare the formal character of identity itself with the formal character of the relation R that matters in survival. Of course the R-relation among stages is not the same as identity either among stages or among continuants. But identity among continuant persons induces a relation among stages: the relation that holds between the several stages of a single continuant person. Call this the *I-relation*. It is the I-relation, not identity itself, that we must compare with the R-relation. In wondering whether you will survive the battle, we said, you wonder whether the continuant person that includes your present stage is identical with any of the continuant persons that continue beyond the battle. In other words: whether it is identical with any of the continuant persons that include stages after the battle. In other words: you wonder whether any of the stages that will exist afterward is I-related to—belongs to the same person as—your present stage. If questions of survival, or personal identity generally, are questions of identity among continuant persons, then they are also questions of I-relatedness among person-stages; and conversely. More precisely: *if common sense is right that what matters in survival is identity among continuant persons, then you have what matters in survival if and only if your present stage is I-related to future stages.* I shall not distinguish henceforth between the thesis that what matters in survival is identity and the thesis that what matters in survival is the I-relation. Either way, it is a compelling platitude of common sense.

If ever a stage is R-related to some future stage but I-related to none, or if ever a stage is I-related to some future stage but R-related to none, then the platitude that what matters is the I-relation will disagree with the interesting thesis that what matters is the R-relation. But no such thing can happen, I claim; so there can be no such disagreement. In fact, I claim that *any stage is I-related and R-related to exactly the same stages.* And I claim this not only for the cases that arise in real life, but for all possible problem cases as well. Let us individuate relations, as is usual, by necessary coextensiveness. Then I claim that *the I-relation is the R-relation.*

A continuant person is an aggregate[4] of person-stages, each one I-related to all the rest (and to itself). For short: a person is an I-*inter*related aggregate. Moreover, a person is not part of any larger I-interrelated aggregate; for if we left out any stages that were I-related to one another and to all the stages we included, then what we would have would not be a whole continuant person but only part of one. For short: a person is a maximal I-interrelated aggregate. And conversely, any maximal I-interrelated aggregate of person-stages is a continuant person. At least, I

---

[4]It does not matter what sort of "aggregate." I prefer a mereological sum, so that the stages are literally parts of the continuant. But a class of stages would do as well, or a sequence or ordering of stages, or a suitable function from moments or stretches of time to stages.

cannot think of any that clearly is not.[5] So far we have only a small circle, from personhood to I-interrelatedness and back again. That is unhelpful; but if the I-relation is the R-relation, we have something more interesting: a noncircular definition of personhood. I claim that *someting is a continuant person if and only if it is a maximal R-interrelated aggregate of person-stages*. That is: if and only if it is an aggregate of person-stages, each of which is R-related to all the rest (and to itself), and it is a proper part of no other such aggregate.

I cannot tolerate any discrepancy in formal character between the I-relation and the R-relation, for I have claimed that these relations are one and the same. Now although the admitted discrepancy between identity and the R-relation is harmless in itself, and although the I-relation is not identity, still it may seem that the I-relation inherits enough of the formal character of identity to lead to trouble. For suppose that S_1, S_2, . . .are person-stages; and suppose that C_1 is the continuant person of whom S_1 is a stage, C_2 is the continuant person of whom S_2 is a stage, and so on. Then any two of these stages S_i and S_j are I-related if and only if the corresponding continuant persons C_i and C_j are identical. The I-relations among the stages mirror the structure of the identity relations among the continuants.

I reply that the foregoing argument wrongly takes it for granted that every person-stage is a stage of one and only one continuant person. That is so ordinarily; and when that is so, the I-relation does inherit much of the formal character of identity. But ordinarily the R-relation also is well behaved. In the problem cases, however, it may happen that a single stage S is a stage of two or more different continuant persons. Worse, some or all of these may be persons to a diminished degree, so that it is questionable which of them should count as persons at all. If so, there would not be any such thing (in any straightforward way) as *the* person of whom S is a stage. So the supposition of the argument would not apply. It has not been shown that the I-relation inherits the formal character of identity in the problem cases. Rather it might be just as ill behaved as the R-relation. We shall examine the problem cases and see how that can happen.[6]

It would be wrong to read my definition of the I-relation as saying that person-stages S_1 and S_2 are I-related if and only if the continuant person of whom S_1 is a stage and the continuant person of whom S_2 is a stage are identical. The definite articles require the presupposition that I have just questioned. We should substitute the indefinite article: S_1 and S_2 are I-related if and only if a continuant person of whom S_1 is a stage and a continuant person of whom S_2 is a stage are identical.

---

[5]The least clear-cut cases are those in which the stages cannot be given any "personal time" ordering with respect to which they vary in the way that the stages of an ordinary person vary with respect to time. But it is so indeterminate what we want to say about such bizarre cases that they cannot serve as counter-examples to any of my claims.

[6]The argument also takes it for granted that every person-stage is a stage of at least one person. I do not object to that. If there is no way to unite a stage in a continuant with other stages, let it be a very short-lived continuant person all by itself.

More simply: if and only if there is some one continuant person of whom both S_1 and S_2 are stages.

One seeming discrepancy between the I-relation and the R-relation need not disturb us. The I-relation must be symmetrical, whereas the R-relation has a direction. If a stage S_2 is mentally connected to a previous stage S_1, S_1 is available in memory to S_2 and S_2 is under the intentional control of S_1 to some extent—not the other way around.[7] We can say that S_1 is R-related *forward* to S_2, whereas S_2 is R-related *backward* to S_1. The forward and backward R-relations are converses of one another. Both are (normally) antisymmetrical. But although we can distinguish the forward and backward R-relations, we can also merge them into a symmetrical relation. That is the R-relation I have in mind: S_1 and S_2 are R-related simpliciter if and only if S_1 is R-related either forward or backward to S_2.

While we are at it, let us also stipulate that every stage is R-related—forward, backward, and simpliciter—to itself. The R-relation, like the I-relation, is reflexive.

Parfit mentions two ways for a discrepancy to arise in the problem cases. First, the R-relation might be one-many or many-one. Second, the R-relation admits in principle of degree, and might be present to a degree that is markedly subnormal and yet not negligible. Both possibilities arise in connection with fission and fusion of continuant persons, and also in connection with immortality or longevity.

III. FISSION AND FUSION

Identity is one-one, in the sense that nothing is ever identical to two different things. Obviously neither the I-relation nor the R-relation is one-one in that sense. You-now are a stage of the same continuant as many other stages, and are R-related to them all. Many other stages are stages of the same continuant as you-now, and are R-related to you-now. But when Parfit says that the R-relation might be one-many or many-one, he does not just mean that. Rather, he means that one stage might be R-related to many stages that are not R-related to one another, and that many stages that are not R-related to one another might all be R-related to one single stage. (These possibilities do not differ once we specify that the R-relation is to be taken as symmetrical.) In short, the R-relation might fail to be transitive.

In a case of fission, for instance, we have a prefission stage that is R-related forward to two different, simultaneous postfission stages that are not R-related either forward or backward to each other. The forward R-relation is one-many, the backward R-relation is many-one, and the R-relation simpliciter is intransitive.

In a case of fusion we have two prefusion stages, not R-related either forward or backward to each other, that are R-related forward to a single postfusion stage. The forward R-relation is many-one, the backward R-relation is one-many, and the R-relation simpliciter is again intransitive.

[7] As before, it would be better to speak here of quasi-memory; and likewise of quasi-intentional control.

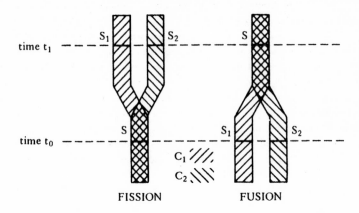

time t_1

time t_0

S_1 S_2 S

S S_1 S_2

C_1

C_2

FISSION   FUSION

Identity must be transitive, but the I-relation is not identity. The I-relation will fail to be transitive if and only if there is partial overlap among continuant persons. More precisely: if and only if two continuant persons C_1 and C_2 have at least one common stage, but each one also has stages that are not included in the other. If S is a stage of both, S_1 is a stage of C_1 but not C_2, and S_2 is a stage of C_2 but not C_1, then transitivity of the I-relation fails. Although S_1 is I-related to S, which in turn is I-related to S_2, yet S_1 is not I-related to S_2. In order to argue that the I-relation, unlike the R-relation, must be transitive, it is not enough to appeal to the uncontroversial transitivity of identity. The further premise is needed that partial overlap of continuant persons is impossible.

Figure 1 shows how to represent fission and fusion as cases of partial overlap. The continuant persons involved, C_1 and C_2, are the two maximal R-interrelated aggregates of stages marked by the two sorts of cross-hatching. In the case of fission, the prefission stages are shared by both continuants. In the case of fusion, the post-fusion stages are likewise shared. In each case, we have a shared stage S that is I-related to two stages S_1 and S_2 that are not I-related to each other. Also S is R-related to S_1 and S_2 (forward in the case of fission, backward in the case of fusion) but S_1 and S_2 are not R-related to each other. More generally, the I-relation and the R-relation coincide for all stages involved in the affair.

There is, however, a strong reason for denying that continuant persons can overlap in this way. From this denial it would indeed follow (as it does not follow from the transitivity of identity alone) that the I-relation cannot share the possible intransitivities of the R-relation.

The trouble with overlap is that it leads to overpopulation. To count the population at a given time, we can count the continuant persons who have stages at that time; or we can count the stages. If there is overlap, there will be more continuants than stages. (I disregard the possibility that one of the continuants is a time traveler with distinct simultaneous stages.) The count of stages is the count we accept; yet we think we are counting persons, and we think of persons as continuants rather than stages. How, then, can we tolerate overlap?

For instance, we say that in a case of fission *one* person becomes *two*. By describing fission as initial stage-sharing we provide for the two, but not for the one. There are two all along. It is all very well to say from an eternal or postfission standpoint that two persons (with a common initial segment) are involved, but we also demand to say that on the day before the fission only *one* person entered the duplication center; that his mother did not bear twins; that until he fissions he should only have one vote; and so on. Counting at a time, we insist on counting a person who will fission as one. We insist on a method of counting persons that agrees with the result of counting stages, though we do not think that counting persons just *is* counting (simultaneous) stages.

It is not so clear that we insist on counting a product of fusion as one (or a time traveler meeting himself as two). We are not sure what to say. But suppose we were fully devoted to the doctrine that the number of different persons in existence at a time is the number of different person-stages at that time. Even so, we would not be forced to deny that continuant persons could overlap. We would therefore not be driven to conclude that the I-relation cannot share the possible intransitivities of the R-relation.

The way out is to deny that we must invariably count two nonidentical continuants as two. We might count not by identity but by a weaker relation. Let us say that continuants C_1 and C_2 are *identical-at-time-t* if and only if they both exist at t and their stages at t are identical. (More precisely: C_1 and C_2 both have stages at t, and all and only stages of C_1 at t are stages of C_2 at t.) I shall speak of such relations of identity-at-a-time as relations of *tensed identity*. Tensed identity is not a kind of identity. It is not identity among stages, but rather a derivative relation among continuants which is induced by identity among stages. It is not identity among continuants, but rather a relation that is weaker than identity whenever different continuants have stages in common. If we count continuants by tensed identity rather than by identity, we will get the right answer—the answer that agrees with the answer we get by counting stages—even if there is overlap. How many persons entered the duplication center yesterday? We may reply: C_1 entered and C_2 entered, and no one else; although C_1 and C_2 are not identical today, and are not identical simpliciter, they were identical yesterday. So counting by identity-yesterday, there was only one. Counting by identity-today, there were two; but it is inappropriate to count by identity-today when we are talking solely about the events of yesterday. Counting by identity simpliciter there were two; but in talking about the events of yesterday it is as unnatural to count by identity as it is to count by identity-today. There is a way of counting on which there are two all along; but there is another way on which there are first one and then two. The latter has obvious practical advantages. It should be no surprise if it is the way we prefer.

It may seem far-fetched to claim that we ever count persons otherwise than by identity simpliciter. But we sometimes *do* count otherwise. If an infirm man wishes to know how many roads he must cross to reach his destination, I will count by identity-along-his-path rather than by identity. By crossing the Chester A. Arthur Parkway and Route 137 at the brief stretch where they have merged, he can cross both by crossing only one road. Yet these two roads are certainly not identical.

You may feel certain that you count persons by identity, not by tensed identity. But how can you be sure? Normal cases provide no evidence. When no stages are shared, both ways of counting agree. They differ only in the problem cases: fission, fusion, and another that we shall soon consider. The problem cases provide no very solid evidence either. They are problem cases just because we cannot consistently say quite all the things we feel inclined to. We must strike the best compromise among our conflicting initial opinions. Something must give way; and why not the opinion that of course we count by identity, if that is what can be sacrificed with least total damage?

A relation to count by does not have to be identity, as the example of the roads shows. But perhaps it should share the key properties of identity. It should at least be an *equivalence* relation: reflexive, symmetrical, and transitive. Relations of tensed identity are equivalence relations. Further, it should be an *indiscernibility* relation; not for all properties whatever, as identity is, but at least for some significant class of properties. That is, it ought to be that two related things have exactly the same properties in that class. Identity-at-time-t is an indiscernibility relation for a significant class of properties of continuant persons: those properties of a person which are logically determined by the properties of his stage at t. The class includes the properties of walking, being tall, being in a certain room, being thirsty, and believing in God at time t; but not the properties of being forty-three years old, gaining weight, being an ex-Communist, or remembering one's childhood at t. The class is sizable enough, at any rate, to make clear that a relation of tensed identity is more of an indiscernibility relation than is identity-along-a-path among roads.

If we are prepared to count a product of fusion as two, while still demanding to count a person who will fission as one, we can count at t by the relation of identity-at-all-times-up-to-t. This is the relation that holds between continuants C_1 and C_2 if and only if (1) they both exist at some time no later than t, (2) at any time no later than t, either both exist or neither does, and (3) at any time no later than t when both exist, they have exactly the same stages. Again, this is a relation among continuants that is weaker than identity to the extent that continuants share stages. Although derived from identity (among stages) it is of course not itself identity. It is even more of an indiscernibility relation than identity-at-t, since it confers indiscernibility with respect to such properties as being forty-three years old, gaining weight (in one sense), being an ex-Communist, and remembering one's childhood at t; though still not with respect to such properties as being, at t, the next winner of the State Lottery.

It may be disconcerting that we can have a single name for one person (counting by tensed identity) who is really two nonidentical persons because he will later fission. Isn't the name ambiguous? Yes; but so long as its two bearers are indiscernible in the respects we want to talk about, the ambiguity is harmless. If C_1 and C_2 are identical-at-all-times-up-to-now and share the name "Ned" it is idle to disambiguate such remarks as "Ned is tall," "Ned is waiting to be duplicated," "Ned is frightened," "Ned only decided yesterday to do it," and the like. These will be true on both disambiguations of "Ned," or false on both. Before the fission, only predictions need disambiguating. After the fission, on the other hand, the ambiguity of "Ned" will be much more bother. It can be expected that the ambiguous name "Ned" will then fall into disuse, except when we wish to speak of the shared life of C_1 and C_2 before the fission.

But what if we don't know whether Ned will fission? In that case, we don't know whether the one person Ned (counting by identity-now) is one person, or two, or many (counting by identity). Then we don't know whether "Ned" is ambiguous or not. But if the ambiguity is not a practical nuisance, we don't need to know. We can wait and see whether or not we have been living with a harmless ambiguity.

This completes my discussion of fission and fusion. To summarize: if the R-relation is the I-relation, and in particular if continuant persons are maximal R-interrelated aggregates of person-stages, then cases of fission and fusion must be treated as cases of stage-sharing between different, partially overlapping continuant persons. If so, the R-relation and the I-relation are alike intransitive, so there is no discrepancy on that score. If it is granted that we may count continuant persons by tensed identity, then this treatment does not conflict with our opinion that in fission one person becomes two; nor with our opinion (if it really is our opinion) that in fusion two persons become one.

IV. LONGEVITY

I turn now to a different problem case. Parfit has noted that mental connectedness will fade away eventually. If the R-relation is a matter of direct connectedness as well as continuity, then intransitivities of the R-relation will appear in the case of a person (if it is a person!) who lives too long.

Consider Methuselah. At the age of 100 he still remembers his childhood. But new memories crowd out the old. At the age of 150 he has hardly any memories that go back before his twentieth year. At the age of 200 he has hardly any memories that go back before his seventieth year; and so on. When he dies at the age of 969, he has hardly any memories that go beyond his 839th year. As he grows older he grows wiser; his callow opinions and character at age 90 have vanished almost without a trace by age 220, but his opinions and character at age 220 also have vanished almost without a trace by age 350. He soon learns that it is futile to set goals for himself too far ahead. At age 120, he is still somewhat interested in fulfilling the ambitions he held at age 40; but at age 170 he cares nothing for those ambitions, and it is beginning to take an effort of will to summon up an interest in fulfilling his aspirations at age 80. And so it goes.

We sometimes say: in later life I will be a different person. For us short-lived creatures, such remarks are an extravagance. A philosophical study of personal identity can ignore them. For Methuselah, however, the fading-out of personal identity looms large as a fact of life. It is incumbent on us to make it literally true that he will be a different person after one and one-half centuries or so.

I should imagine that this is so just in virtue of normal aging over 969 years. If you disagree, imagine that Methuselah lives much longer than a bare millennium (Parfit imagines the case of immortals who change mentally at the same rate as we do). Or imagine that his life is punctuated by frequent amnesias, brain-washings, psychoanalyses, conversions, and what not, each one of which is almost (but not quite) enough to turn him into a different person.

Suppose, for simplicity, that any two stages of Methuselah that are separated by no more than 137 years are R-related; and any two of his stages that are separated by more than 137 years are not R-related. (For the time being, we may pretend that R-relatedness is all-or-nothing, with a sharp cutoff.)

If the R-relation and the I-relation are the same, this means that two of Methuselah's stages belong to a single continuant person if and only if they are no more than 137 years apart. (Therefore the whole of Methuselah is not a single person.) That is the case, in particular, if continuant persons are maximal R-interrelated aggregates. For if so, then segments of Methuselah are R-interrelated if and only if they are no more than 137 years long; whence it follows that all and only the segments that are exactly 137 years long are maximal R-interrelated aggregates; so all and only the 137-year segments are continuant persons.

If so, we have intransitivity both of the R-relation and of the I-relation. Let S_1 be a stage of Methuselah at the age of 400; let S_2 be a stage of Methuselah at the age of 500; let S_3 be a stage of Methuselah at the age of 600. By hypothesis S_1 is R-related to S_2 and S_2 is R-related to S_3, but S_1 and S_3 are not R-related. Being separated by 200 years, they have no direct mental connections. Since S_1 and S_2 are linked by a 137-year segment (in fact, by infinitely many) they are I-related; likewise S_2 and S_3 are I-related. But S_1 and S_3 are not linked by any 137-year segment, so they are not I-related. The R-relation and the I-relation are alike intransitive.

The problem of overpopulation is infinitely worse in the case of Methuselah than in the cases of fission or fusion considered hitherto. Methuselah spends his 300th birthday alone in his room. How many persons are in that room? There are infinitely many different 137-year segments that include all of Methuselah's stages on his 300th birthday. One begins at the end of Methuselah's 163rd birthday and ends at the end of his 300th birthday; another begins at the beginning of his 300th and ends at the beginning of his 437th. Between these two are a continuum of other 137-year segments. No two of them are identical. Every one of them puts in an appearance (has a stage) in Methuselah's room on Methuselah's 300th birthday. Every one of them is a continuant person, given our supposition that Methuselah's stages are R-related if and only if they are not more than 137 years apart, and given that continuant persons are all and only maximal R-interrelated aggregates of person-stages. It begins to seem crowded in Methuselah's room!

Tensed identity to the rescue once more. True, there are continuum many non-identical continuant persons in the room. But, counting by the appropriate relation of tensed identity, there is only one. All the continuum many nonidentical continuant persons are identical-at-the-time-in-question, since they all share the single stage at that time. Granted that we may count by tensed identity, there is no over-crowding.

V. DEGREE

We turn now to the question of degree. Identity certainly cannot be a matter of degree. But the I-relation is not defined in terms of identity alone. It derives also from personhood: the property of being a continuant person. Thus personal identity may be a matter of degree because personhood is a matter of degree, even though identity is not. Suppose two person-stages S_1 and S_2 are stages of some one continuant that is a person to a low, but not negligible, degree. Suppose further that they are not stages of anything else that is a person to any higher degree. Then they are I-related to a low degree. So if personhood admits of degree, we have no discrepancy in formal character between the I-relation and the R-relation.

Parfit suggests, for instance, that if you fuse with someone very different, yielding a fusion product mentally halfway between you and your partner, then it is questionable whether you have survived. Not that there is a definite, unknown answer. Rather, what matters in survival—the R-relation—is present in reduced degree. There is less of it than in clear cases of survival, more than in clear cases of non-survival.[8] If we want the I-relation and the R-relation to coincide, we may take it that C_1 and C_2 (see Fig. 1 for cases of fusion) are persons to reduced degree because they are broken by abrupt mental discontinuities. If persons are maximal R-inter-related aggregates, as I claim, that is what we should expect; the R-relations across the fusion point are reduced in degree, hence the R-interrelatedness of C_1 and C_2 is reduced in degree, and hence the personhood of C_1 and C_2 is reduced in degree. C_1 and C_2 have less personhood than clear cases of persons, more personhood than continuant aggregates of stages that are clearly not persons. Then S and S_1, or S and S_2, are I-related to reduced degree just as they are R-related to reduced degree.

Personal identity to reduced degrees is found also in the case of Methuselah. We supposed before that stages no more than 137 years apart are R-related while states more than 137 years apart were not. But if the R-relation fades away at all—if it is a relation partly of connectedness as well as continuity—it would be more real-

---

[8]No similar problem arises in cases of fission. We imagine the immediate postfission stages to be pretty much alike, wherefore they can all be strongly R-related to the immediate prefission stages.

istic to suppose that it fades away gradually. We can suppose that stages within 100 years of each other are R-related to a high enough degree so that survival is not in doubt; and that stages 200 or more years apart are R-related to such a low degree that what matters in survival is clearly absent. There is no significant connectedness over long spans of time, only continuity. Then if we want the R-relation and the I-relation to coincide, we could say roughly this: 100-year segments of Methuselah are persons to a high degree, whereas 200-year segments are persons only to a low degree. Then two stages that are strongly R-related also are strongly I-related, whereas stages that are weakly R-related are also weakly I-related. Likewise for all the intermediate degrees of R-relatedness of stages, of personhood of segments of Methuselah, and hence of I-relatedness of stages.

It is a familiar idea that personhood might admit of degrees. Most of the usual examples, however, are not quite what I have in mind. They concern continuants that are said to be persons to a reduced degree because their stages are thought to be person-stages to a reduced degree. If anyone thinks that the wolf-child, the "dehumanized" proletarian, or the human vegetable is not fully a person, that is more because he regards the stages themselves as deficient than because the stages are not strongly enough R-interrelated. If anyone thinks that personhood is partly a matter of species membership, so that a creature of sorcery or a freak offspring of hippopotami could not be fully a person no matter how much he resembled the rest of us, that also would be a case in which the stages themselves are thought to be deficient. In this case the stages are thought to be deficient not in their intrinsic character but in their causal ancestry; there is, however, nothing wrong with their R-interrelatedness. A severe case of split personality, on the other hand, does consist of perfectly good person-stages that are not very well R-related. If he is said not to be fully a person, that *is* an example of the kind of reduced personhood that permits us to claim that the R-relation and the I-relation alike admit of degrees.

Let us ignore the complications introduced by deficient person-stages. Let us assume that all the stages under consideration are person-stages to more or less the highest possible degree. (More generally, we could perhaps say that the degree of I-relatedness of two stages depends not on the absolute degree of personhood of the continuant, if any, that links them; but rather on the relative degree of personhood of that continuant compared to the greatest degree of personhood that the degree of person-stage-hood of the stages could permit. If two wolf-child-stages are person-stages only to degree 0.8, but they are stages of a continuant that is a person to degree 0.8, we can say that the stages are thereby I-related to degree 1.)

If we say that a continuant person is an aggregate of R-interrelated person-stages, it is clear that personhood admits of degree to the extent that the R-relation does. We can say something like this: the degree of R-interrelatedness of an aggregate is the minimum degree of R-relatedness between any two stages in the aggregate. (Better: the greatest lower bound on the degrees of R-relatedness between any two stages.) But when we recall that a person should be a maximal such aggregate, confusion sets in. Suppose we have an aggregate that is R-interrelated to degree

0.9, and it is not included in any larger aggregate that is R-interrelated to degree 0.9 or greater. Suppose, however, that it *is* included in a much larger aggregate that is R-interrelated to degree 0.88. We know the degree to which it qualifies as an R-interrelated aggregate, but to what degree does it qualify as a maximal one? That is, to what degree does it qualify as a person, if persons are maximal R-interrelated aggregates? I am inclined to say: it passes the R-interrelatedness test for personhood to degree 0.9, but at the same time it flunks the maximality test to degree 0.88. Therefore it is a person only to degree 0.02!

This conclusion leads to trouble. Take the case of Methuselah. Assuming that R-relatedness fades out gradually, every segment that passes the R-interrelatedness test to a significant degree also flunks the maximality test to almost the same degree. (If the fadeout is continuous, delete "almost.") So *no* segment of Methuselah passes both tests for personhood to any significant degree. No two stages, no matter how close, are stages of some *one* continuant that is a person to high degree. Rather, nearby stages are strongly I-related by being common to many continuants, each one of which is strongly R-interrelated, is almost as strongly non-maximal, and therefore is a person only to a low degree.

We might sum the degrees of personhood of all the continuants that link two stages, taking the sum to be the degree of I-relatedness of the stages.

But there is a better way. Assume that R-relatedness can come in all degrees ranging from 0 to 1 on some scale. Then every number in the interval from 0 to 1 is a possible location for an arbitrary boundary between pairs of stages that are R-related and pairs that are not. Call every such number a *delineation* of this boundary. Every delineation yields a decision as to which stages are R-related. It thereby yields a decision as to which continuants are R-interrelated; a decision as to which continuants are included in larger R-interrelated aggregates; a decision as to which continuants are persons, given that persons are maximal R-interrelated aggregates; and thence a decision as to which stages are I-related. We can say that a certain continuant is a person, or that a certain pair of stages are I-related, *relative* to a given delineation. We can also say whether something is the case relative to a set of delineations, provided that all the delineations in the set agree on whether it is the case. Then we can take the degree to which it is the case as the size (more precisely: Lebesgue measure) of that set. Suppose, for instance, that two stages count as I-related when we set the cut-off for R-relatedness anywhere from 0 to 0.9, but not when we set the cut-off more stringently between 0.9 and 1. Then those two stages are I-related relative to delineations from 0 to 0.9, but not relative to delineations from 0.9 to 1. They are I-related to degree 0.9—the size of the delineation interval on which they are I-related. Yet there may not be any continuant linking those stages that is a person to degree more than 0. It may be that any continuant that links those stages is both R-interrelated and maximal only at a single delineation. At any more stringent delineation, it is no longer R-interrelated; while at any less stringent delineation it is still R-interrelated but not maximal.

The strategy followed here combines two ideas. (1) When something is a matter of degree, we can introduce a cutoff point. However, the choice of this cutoff point is more or less arbitrary. (2) When confronted with an arbitrary choice, the thing to do is not to make the choice. Rather, we should see what is common to all or most ways (or all or most reasonable ways) of making the choice, caring little what happens on any particular way of making it. The second idea is van Fraassen's method of supervaluations.[9]

On this proposal the I-relation admits of degree; and further, we get perfect agreement between degrees of I-relatedness and degrees of R-relatedness, regardless of the degrees of personhood of continuants. For at any one delineation, two stages are R-related if and only if they belong to some one maximal R-interrelated aggregate; hence if and only if they belong to some one continuant person; hence if and only if they are I-related. Any two stages are R-related and I-related relative to exactly the same set of delineations. Now if two stages are R-related to a degree x, it follows (given our choice of scale and measure) that they are R-related at all and only the delineations in a certain set of size x. Therefore they are I-related at all and only the delineations in a certain set of size x; which means that they are I-related to degree x. The degree of I-relatedness equals the degree of R-relatedness. In this way personal identity can be just as much a matter of degree as the mental continuity or connectedness that matters in survival.

VI. PERRY'S TREATMENT OF FISSION

It is instructive to contrast my way and John Perry's way[10] of overcoming the seeming discrepancies in character between personal identity and mental continuity or connectedness. Perry and I have the same goals, but our priorities differ. Perry does not need to resort to tensed identity to recue the common opinion that in fission there is only one person beforehand. However, Perry's way does not permit identification of the R-relation and the I-relation themselves, but only of certain time-dependent subrelations thereof. Further, he must introduce an unintuitive discrimination among the persons who exist at (have stages at) any given time. Some of them (all, except in the problem cases) are classified as *determinable* at that time. These are the ones who count. There may be others, not determinable at that time, who are left out of consideration for certain purposes.

Say that Stage S_1 is *R-related at time* t—for short, *R_t-related*—to stage S_2 if and only if stages S_1 and S_2 are R-related simpliciter, and also S_2 is located at time t. The R_t-relation, then, is the R-relation between stages at t and stages at other times (or at t).

---

[9]See Bas van Fraassen, "Singular Terms, Truth-Value Gaps, and Free Logic," *Journal of Philosophy* 63 (1966): 481–95. See also the discussion of vagueness in my "General Semantics," in this volume.
[10]John Perry, "Can the Self Divide?," *Journal of Philosophy* 69 (1972): 463–88

Say that stage S_1 is *I-related at time* t—for short, I_t-*related*—to stage S_2 if and only if both S_1 and S_2 are stages of some one continuant person who is determinable at time t, and S_2 is located at time t. The I_t-relation, then, is the I-relation between stages at t and stages at other times (or at t), if we leave out any continuant persons who are not determinable at t.

Perry proposes that something C is a continuant person determinable at t if and only if, for some person-stage S located at t, C is the aggregate comprising all and only the stages R_t-related to S. A continuant person, in general, is a continuant person determinable at some time. (No one is doomed to permanent indeterminability.) If something is a continuant person according to this proposal, Perry calls it a *lifetime*. If something is a continuant person according to my proposal—that is, if it is a maximal R-interrelated aggregate of person-stages—Perry calls it a *branch*. In normal cases, all and only lifetimes are branches.

In a case of fission, however, some lifetimes are not branches (see Fig. 1 for cases of fission). Branch C_1 is a lifetime determinable at t_1, since it comprises all and only the stages R_{t_1}-related to S_1. Likewise branch C_2 is a lifetime determinable at t_1. But C—the whole thing—though not a branch, is a lifetime determinable at t_0, since it comprises all and only the stages R_{t_0}-related to S. Note that C_1 and C_2 are not yet determinable at t_0, whereas C is no longer determinable at t_1.

On Perry's proposal, the R-relation is not the same as the I-relation in this case. Since C is a lifetime, and hence according to Perry a continuant person, S_1 and S_2 are I-related. However, they are not R-related.

What does follow from Perry's proposal is that, for any time t, the R_t-relation is the same as the I_t-relation. Perhaps that is good enough. Any particular question of survival, or of personal identity in general, arises at some definite time. If the question arises at time t, it is the R_t-relation and the I_t-relation that are relevant. We want them to give the same answer. The rest of the R-relation and the I-relation are not involved. In particular, it is harmless that S_1 and S_2 are I-related, since they are neither I_{t_0}-related nor I_{t_1}-related, nor indeed I_t-related for any time t whatever.

On Perry's proposal, any person-stage existing at any time must belong to exactly one continuant person who is determinable at that time. Persons can share stages, to be sure. More so on Perry's proposal than on mine, in fact: stage S in the fission case belongs to three lifetimes (C, C_1, and C_2) but only two branches (C_1 and C_2). Stage S_1 belongs to two lifetimes (C and C_1) but only one branch (C_1). But Perry's persons share stages only when all but one of the sharers is not determinable. Therefore we can count by identity, counting only the persons determinable at the time, and we will get the right answer. One determinable person (counting by identity) exists before the fission, but two exist afterward. There are three all along, counting by identity but including the nondeterminables; but at the fission one loses determinability and the other two gain it.

I grant that counting by tensed identity is somewhat counterintuitive; but isn't excluding the nondeterminable persons just as bad? They *are* (timelessly speaking) persons; they *do* exist at (have stages at) the time; they are *not* identical to persons we are counting. If we want to count the persons at the time, is it not gratuitous to exclude them? Perry can say: Yes, but we just do. Or: we do it for excellent practical reasons. I will say the same about counting by tensed identity without any exclusions. Both are counterintuitive; neither is unbearably so; either is better than not having any way to count that gives the correct answer; either is better than permitting the possibility of fission to create a discrepancy between personal identity and what matters in survival.

Perry considers only fission and fusion, but his proposal can apply also to the case of Methuselah. I do not know whether Perry would wish so to apply it. He might prefer to let mental continuity predominate over connectedness in the R-relation, so that the whole of Methuselah is both a branch and a lifetime, and thus an unproblematic person.

Suppose as before, however, that the R-relation fades out with an (arbitrary) cutoff at 137 years. For me, the 137-year segments (the branches) are the continuant persons; for Perry, the 274-year segments (the lifetimes) are the continuant persons. For instance, a segment that begins on Methuselah's 420th birthday and ends at the same time on his 694th comprises all and only the stages R_t-related to a certain stage S on his 557th, t being the time of that stage. The lifetimes are not branches and the branches are not lifetimes. (With a trivial exception: the initial and final 137-year segments are both branches and lifetimes. More generally: the initial and final lifetimes are shorter than the others, being cut off by birth or death.) Any stage at any time belongs to exactly one person determinable at that time, and to infinitely many nondeterminable persons. Counting by identity gives the right answer, provided the nondeterminable hordes are left out. The R_t-relation and the I_t-relation are the same for any time t, but the R-relation and the I-relation disagree for any two stages separated by more than 137 years but no more than 274.

Perry says nothing about degrees of personal identity. However, there is nothing to prevent him from taking over all I have said. If the R-relation admits of degree, then so does personhood, no matter whether continuant persons are branches or lifetimes. Then the I_t-relations also admit of degree, and there is no obstacle here to identifying them with the corresponding R_t-relations.

I have one serious misgiving about Perry's treatment of the problem. Perry has concentrated on making things come out as they should from the standpoint of any particular time, provided that persons not then determinable are not counted among the persons existing at that time. But what shall we do when we wish to generalize over persons existing at various times? Exclusion of the nondeterminables requires a definite point of reference, which is lacking. Overpopulation sets in again. Of course my cure for overpopulation—counting by tensed identity—also requires a definite point of reference. But let us count by identity, if we count from the standpoint of no definite time. How many persons were involved in an episode of fission long ago? I say: two. Perry says: three. Or else he says: none now determinable. Isn't two the correct answer?

Postscripts to

"Survival and Identity"

A. TWO MINDS WITH BUT A SINGLE THOUGHT

Derek Parfit rejects my attempt to square his views (which are mine as well) with common sense.[1] He objects that before I bring off the reconciliation, I must first misrepresent our commonsensical desire to survive. Consider a fission case as shown. I say there are two continuant persons all along, sharing their initial segments. One of them, C_1, dies soon after the fission. The other, C_2, lives on for many years. Let S be a shared stage at time t_0, before the fission but after it is known that fission will occur. The thought to be found in S is a desire for survival, of the most commonsensical and unphilosophical kind possible. Since S is a shared stage, this desire is a shared desire. Certainly C_2 has the survival he desired, and likewise has what we think matters: mental continuity and connectedness (the R-relation) between S and much later stages such as S_2. But how about C_1?

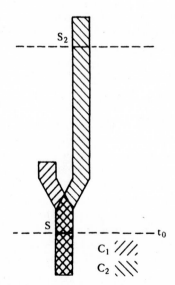

[1]"Lewis, Perry and What Matters," in Amélie Rorty, *The Identities of Persons* (Berkeley: University of California Press, 1976), pp. 91–96.

I wrote that "if common sense is right that what matters in survival is identity . . . , then you have what matters in survival if and only if your present stage is I-related to future stages" where stages are I-related iff they belong to some single continuant person (page 59). If that is right, then C_1 has what he commonsensically desired. For C_1's stage S at time t_0 is indeed I-related to stages far in the future such as S_2. These stages are I-related via the person C_2.—"But isn't this the *wrong* person?" says Parfit. C_1 himself survives only a short time. The one who lives longer is another person, one with whom C_1 once shared stages. If his desire is satisfied by this vicarious survival, it cannot really have been a commonsensical desire to survive.

If C_1 really had the commonsensical desire that he himself—the continuant person C_1—survive well into the future, then I grant that his desire is not satisfied. But I don't think he could have had exactly that desire. I said that the desire found in S was to be *of the most commonsensical and unphilosophical kind possible.* And there is a limit to how commonsensical one's desires can possibly be under the peculiar circumstance of stage-sharing.

The shared stage S does the thinking for both of the continuants to which it belongs. Any thought it has must be shared. It cannot desire one thing on behalf of C_1 and another thing on behalf of C_2. If it has an urgent, self-interested desire for survival on the part of C_1, that very thought must also be an urgent, self-interested (and not merely benevolent) desire for survival on the part of C_2. It is not possible that one thought should be both. So it is not possible for S to have such a desire on behalf of C_1. So it is not possible for C_1 at t_0 to have the straightforward commonsensical desire that he himself survive.

If C_1 and C_2 share the most commonsensical kind of desire to survive that is available to them under the circumstances, it must be a plural desire: let *us* survive. Now we must distinguish two different plural desires: existential and universal, weak and strong.

(weak)   Let at least one of us survive.
(strong)   Let all of us survive.

Because these desires are plural instead of singular, they are not perfectly commonsensical. Because they are put in terms of survival of continuants rather than relations of stages, they are more commonsensical than the "philosophical" desire for R-relatedness of one's present stage to future stages.

If C_1's (imperfectly) commonsensical desire for survival is predominantly the weak desire, then my reconciliation goes through. For C_1's weak desire is satisfied even though it is his stage-sharer rather than himself who survives. The weak desire is indeed equivalent to a desire for I-relatedness to future stages. Then if I am right that the I-relation is the R-relation, it is equivalent also to the desire for R-relatedness to future stages.

If C_1's desire is predominantly the strong desire, on the other hand, it is not satisfied. Then his desire for survival is not equivalent to the "philosophical" desire for R-relatedness to future stages, and my reconciliation fails. (However, the strong desire is equivalent to a more complicated desire concerning R-relatedness of stages.) But should we say that C_1 has the strong desire, and that since it is not satisfied, he does not have what commonsensically matters in survival? I think not. For if we say that of C_1, we must say it also of C_2. If one has the strong desire, both do. The strong desire is no more satisfied for C_2 than it is for C_1. But it seems clear that C_2, at least, *does* have what commonsensically matters in survival.

It is instructive to consider a system of survival insurance described by Justin Leiber, in *Beyond Rejection.*[2] (But let us imagine it without the risks and unpleasantness that Leiber supposes.) From time to time your mind is recorded; should a fatal accident befall you, the latest recording is played back into the blank brain of a fresh body. This system satisfies the weak desire for survival, but not the strong desire. Let S at t_0 be the stage that desires survival and therefore decides to have a recording made; the fission occurs at the time of recording; C_1 dies in an accident not long after; C_2 survives. The only extra peculiarities, compared with a simple case of fission, are that C_2 is interrupted in time and undergoes a body transplant. If this system would fairly well satisfy your desire for survival—or if your misgivings about it concern the body transplant rather than the fission—then your desire is predominantly the weak desire.

So far, I have supposed that C_1 and C_2 at t_0 already anticipate their fission. Now suppose not. Now, cannot they share the perfectly commonsensical singular desire: let *me* survive? After all, the desire to be found in the stage S in this case is no different from the desire that would be there if S were what it takes itself to be: a stage of a single person with no fission in his future. I agree that C_1 and C_2 have the singular desire. But it is not a desire that can be satisfied, for it rests on the false presupposition that they are a single person. The "me" in their shared thought (unless it refers to the thinking stage) has the status of an improper description. It cannot refer to C_1 in C_1's thought and to C_2 in C_2's thought, for these thoughts are one and the same. But their desire to survive *is* satisfied; at least C_2's is, and C_1's is no different. Therefore their desire for survival cannot consist only of their unsatisfiable singular desire. They must have the weak plural desire as well, despite the fact that they don't anticipate fission. And so must we. Doubtless we seldom have it as an occurrent desire. But many of our urgent desires are not occurrent, for instance your present desire not to suffer a certain torture too fiendish for you to imagine.

(At this point the reader of "Attitudes *De Dicto* and *De Se*" (in this volume) may wonder how well I have learned my own lesson. There I taught that desire is a relation of wanting-to-have—take this as indivisible—that the subject bears to a property. Why can't C_1 and C_2 bear the very same wanting-to-have relation to the very same property of surviving, so that they think the very same thought, and yet each thereby desire his own survival? But recall that the subject that wants-to-have

[2](New York: Ballantine, 1980).

properties was taken to be a stage, not a continuant. (See pages 143, 146.) Under this analysis, my point is that S's wanting-to-have the property

being such that the unique continuant of which it is a stage survives

is an unsatisfiable desire. That is so whether we think of it as a desire of S's or, more naturally, as a desire of C_1 and C_2. S had better want survival on behalf of C_1 and C_2 by wanting to have a different property:

being such that some continuant of which it is a stage survives.

This is the satisfied desire for survival that C_1 and C_2 share.)

B. IN DEFENSE OF STAGES[3]

Some would protest that they do not know what I mean by "more or less momentary person-stages, or time-slices of continuant persons, or persons-at-times". Others do know what I mean, but don't believe there are any such things.

The first objection is easy to answer, especially in the case where the stages are less momentary rather than more. Let me consider that case only; though I think that instantaneous stages also are unproblematic, I do not really need them. A person-stage is a physical object, just as a person is. (If persons had a ghostly part as well, so would person-stages.) It does many of the same things that a person does: it talks and walks and thinks, it has beliefs and desires, it has a size and shape and location. It even has a temporal duration. But only a brief one, for it does not last long. (We can pass over the question how long it can last before it is a segment rather than a stage, for that question raises no objection of principle.) It begins to exist abruptly, and it abruptly ceases to exist soon after. Hence a stage cannot do everything that a person can do, for it cannot do those things that a person does over a longish interval.

That is what I mean by a person-stage. Now to argue for my claim that they exist, and that they are related to persons as part to whole. I do not suppose the doubters will accept my premises, but it will be instructive to find out which they choose to deny.

First: it is possible that a person-stage might exist. Suppose it to appear out of thin air, then vanish again. Never mind whether it is a stage *of* any person (though in fact I think it is). My point is that it is the right sort of thing.

Second: it is possible that two person-stages might exist in succession, one right after the other but without overlap. Further, the qualities and location of the second at its appearance might exactly match those of the first at its disappearance. Here

[3]On this topic I am much indebted to discussions with Saul Kripke and with Denis Robinson. Kripke's views on related matters were presented in his lectures on "Identity through Time," given at Princeton in 1978 (and elsewhere); Robinson's in "Re-Identifying Matter," *Philosophical Review* (forthcoming).

I rely on a *patchwork principle* for possibility: if it is possible that X happen intrinsically in a spatiotemporal region, and if it is likewise possible that Y happen in a region, then also it is possible that both X and Y happen in two distinct but adjacent regions. There are no necessary incompatibilities between distinct existences. Anything can follow anything.

Third: extending the previous point, it is possible that there might be a world of stages that is exactly like our own world in its point-by-point distribution of intrinsic local qualities over space and time.

Fourth: further, such a world of stages might also be exactly like our own in its causal relations between local matters of particular fact. For nothing but the distribution of local qualities constrains the pattern of causal relations. (It would be simpler to say that the causal relations supervene on the distribution of local qualities, but I am not as confident of that as I am of the weaker premise.)

Fifth: then such a world of stages would be exactly like our own simpliciter. There are no features of our world except those that supervene on the distribution of local qualities and their causal relations.

Sixth: then our own world is a world of stages. In particular, person-stages exist.

Seventh: but persons exist too, and persons (in most cases) are not person-stages. They last too long. Yet persons and person-stages, like tables and table-legs, do not occupy spatiotemporal regions twice over. That can only be because they are not distinct. They are part-identical; in other words, the person-stages are parts of the persons.

Let me try to forestall two misunderstandings. (1) When I say that persons are maximal R-interrelated aggregates of person-stages, I do *not* claim to be reducing "constructs" to "more basic entities". (Since I do not intend a reduction to the basic, I am free to say without circularity that person-stages are R-interrelated aggregates of shorter person-stages.) Similarly, I think it is an informative necessary truth that trains are maximal aggregates of cars interrelated by the ancestral of the relation of being coupled together (count the locomotive as a special kind of car). But I do not think of this as a reduction to the basic. Whatever "more basic" is supposed to mean, I don't think it means "smaller." (2) By a part, I just mean a subdivision. I do not mean a well-demarcated subdivision that figures as a unit in causal explanation. Those who give "part" a rich meaning along these lines[4] should take me to mean less by it than they do.

---

[4] Such as D. H. Mellor, in his *Real Time* (Cambridge: Cambridge University Press, 1981), chapter 8.

How To Define
Theoretical Terms

Most philosophers of science agree that, when a newly proposed scientific theory introduces new terms, we usually cannot define the new terms using only the old terms we understood beforehand. On the contrary, I contend that there is a general method for defining the newly introduced theoretical terms.

Most philosophers of science also agree that, in order to reduce one scientific theory to another, we need to posit bridge laws: new laws, independent of the reducing theory, which serve to identify phenomena described in terms of the reduced theory with phenomena described in terms of the reducing theory. On the contrary, I deny that the bridge laws must be posited independently. They may follow from the reducing theory, via the definitions of the theoretical terms of the reduced theory. In such cases it would be wrong to think that theoretical reduction is done voluntarily, for the sake of parsimony, when the reduced and reducing theories are such as to permit it. Sometimes reduction is not only possible but unavoidable.

F. P. Ramsey proposed that theoretical terms might be eliminated in favor of existentially quantified bound variables. Rudolf Carnap, in his most recent discussions of theoretical terms, has used Ramsey's method to split any term-reducing theory into two parts: an analytic postulate to partially interpret the theoretical terms, and a synthetic postulate in which these terms do not occur. My proposal will be in the spirit of Ramsey's and Carnap's.

My proposal could be called an elimination of theoretical terms, if you insist: for to define them is to show how to do without them. But it is better called a vindication of theoretical terms; for to define them is to show that there is no good reason to want to do without them. They are no less fully interpreted and no less well understood than the old terms we had beforehand.

I am not planning to define theoretical terms within an observation language, whatever that is. Some statements report observations, and some do not; but I do not know of any special compartment of our language that is reserved for the reporting of observations. I do not understand what it is just to be a theoretical term, not of any theory in particular, as opposed to being an observational term (or a logical or mathematical term).[1] I believe I do understand what it is to be a *T-term:* that is, a theoretical term introduced by a given theory *T* at a given stage in the history of science. If so, then I also understand what it is to be an *O-term:* that is, any *other* term, one of our *original* terms, an *old* term we already understood before the new theory *T* with its new *T*-terms was proposed. An *O*-term can have any epistemic origin and priority you please. It can belong to any semantic or syntactic category you please. Any old term can be an *O*-term, provided we have somehow come to understand it. And by "understand" I mean "understand"—not "know how to analyze."

I am also not planning to "dispense with theoretical entities." Quite the opposite. The defining of theoretical terms serves the cause of scientific realism. A term correctly defined by means of other terms that admittedly have sense and denotation can scarcely be regarded as a mere bead on a formal abacus. If it purports to name something, then if the theory that introduced it is true it does name something. I suppose a theoretical entity is something we believe in only because its existence, occurrence, etc. is posited by some theory—especially some recent, esoteric, not-yet-well-established scientific theory. Theoretical entities might better be called (as they sometimes are called) *hypothetical* entities. Theoretical terms need not name theoretical entities: consider 'H_2O'. Theoretical entities need not be named by theoretical terms: consider "living creature too small to see." Theoretical entities need not be invisible, intangible, etc.: consider the dark companions of stars. Theoretical entities are not entities of a special category, but entities we know of (at present) in a special way.

I. THE POSTULATE OF *T*

Suppose the best scientific explanation we can devise for some body of data includes a new theory *T*, formulated by means of a postulate in which there occur some new terms $\tau_1 \ldots \tau_n$, terms we have never used before. We shall call these newly introduced terms the *theoretical terms of T*, or just *T-terms;* and we shall call all the

[1]My reasons are more or less those discussed by Hilary Putnam in "What Theories Are Not," *Logic, Methodology and Philosophy of Science* (Stanford: Stanford University Press, 1962), ed. by E. Nagel, P. Suppes, and A. Tarski.

other terms of our scientific vocabulary *O-terms*. We shall accordingly call any sentence of our language that is free of *T*-terms an *O-sentence*. Let us assume that the *O*-terms have conventionally established standard interpretations, well known to us. The *T*-terms, on the other hand, are unfamiliar. Our only clue to their meaning is the postulate of *T* that introduced them. We are accustomed to say that it implicitly defines them; but we would prefer explicit definitions.

We may stipulate that the postulate of *T* is a single sentence; if it was a set of sentences, take their conjunction. If it was a finite set, we can take their conjunction within ordinary logic. If it was a decidably infinite set, we must introduce devices for infinite conjunction—to do so would be bothersome, but not problematic.

We may stipulate that our *T*-terms are names, not predicates or functors. No generality is lost, since names can purport to name entities of any kind: individuals, species, states, properties, substances, magnitudes, classes, relations, or what not. Instead of a *T*-predicate 'F————', for instance, we can use '———— has *F*-hood'; '*F*-hood' is a *T*-name purporting to name a property, and '———— has ————' is an *O*-predicate. It is automatic to reformulate all *T*-terms as names, under the safe assumption that our *O*-vocabulary provides the needed copulas:

> ———— has the property ————
> ———— is in the state ———— at time ————
> ———— has ———— to degree ————

and the like. We will replace *T*-terms by bound variables; by making the *T*-terms grammatically uniform, we avoid the need to introduce variables of diverse types.

We must assume that all occurrences of *T*-terms in the postulate of *T* are purely referential, open to existential generalization and to substitution by Leibniz's law. We need not assume, however, that the language of *T* is an extensional language. Among the *O*-terms there may be nonextensional operators, for instance 'it is a law that————'; nonextensional connectives, for instance '———— because ————'; and so on.

We must assume, finally, that the postulate of *T* will be false in case any of the *T*-terms is denotationless. This is not a legitimate assumption for sentences in general: "There is no such substance as phlogiston" is true just because 'phlogiston' is denotationless. However, it does seem to be a legitimate assumption for the postulate of a term-introducing theory. The postulate of *T* will therefore imply, for each *T*-term τ_i, the sentence '$(\exists x)(x = \tau_i)$', which says that τ_i names something.

Such sentences sometimes count as logical truths. Many systems of logic avoid the difficulties of denotationless names by stipulating that an otherwise denotationless name is deemed artificially to name some arbitrarily chosen "null" individual. We must be able to take seriously the possibility of denotationless *T*-terms; it is worth the trouble to use a system of logic designed to tolerate them. Such a system has been given by Dana Scott;[2] its salient features are as follows.

---

[2]"Existence and Description in Formal Logic," in *Bertrand Russell: Philosopher of the Century* (London: Allen & Unwin, 1967), ed. by Ralph Schoenman.

(1) Improper descriptions and other denotationless terms are *really* denotationless: they name nothing in the domain of discourse. (The domain itself serves as a null individual for technical convenience; but it is not *in* the domain, and no term literally names it.)

(2) Atomic sentences containing denotationless terms are either true or false, depending on the predicate and other terms involved; we might, but need not, stipulate that they are always false.

(3) Identities containing denotationless terms on both sides are true; identities containing a denotationless term on one side only are false.

(4) Denotationless terms are interchangeable *salva veritate* in extensional contexts; necessarily denotationless names are interchangeable *salva veritate* even in intensional contexts.

II. THE RAMSEY AND CARNAP SENTENCES OF T

Let us write the postulate of our theory T in a way that exhibits the occurrences of T-terms therein: '$T[\tau_1 \ldots \tau_n]$'.

If we replace the T-terms uniformly by variables $x_1 \ldots x_n$ respectively (distinct variables that do not occur there already), we get a formula which we may call the *realization formula* of T: '$T[x_1 \ldots x_n]$'.

Any n-tuple of entities that satisfies this formula, under the fixed standard interpretations of its O-terms, may be said to *realize*, or to be a *realization* of, the theory T.

Therefore we recognize the postulate of T as the sentence that says that T is realized by the n-tuple of entities denoted, respectively, by the T-terms $\tau_1 \ldots \tau_n$. If so, then *a fortiori* T is realized. We can write another sentence, called the *Ramsey sentence* of T, which says only that T is realized: '$\exists x_1 \ldots x_n T[x_1 \ldots x_n]$'.

We can write a third sentence, called the *Carnap sentence* of T, which is neutral as to whether T is realized, but says that if T is realized, then the n-tuple of entities named respectively by $\tau_1 \ldots \tau_n$ is one realization of T. The Carnap sentence is the conditional of the Ramsey sentence and the postulate:

$$\exists x_1 \ldots x_n T[x_1 \ldots x_n] \supset T[\tau_1 \ldots \tau_n]$$

Our three sentences are related as follows: (1) The postulate is logically equivalent to the conjunction of the Ramsey sentence and the Carnap sentence. (2) The Ramsey sentence and the postulate logically imply exactly the same O-sentences. (3) The Carnap sentence logically implies no O-sentences except logical truths.

Therefore, insofar as the theory T serves as a device for systematizing O-sentences, the Ramsey sentence of T will do the job as well as the postulate itself. That was Ramsey's observation.[3] The Ramsey sentence can obviously do nothing to help

[3]"Theories," *The Foundations of Mathematics* (London: Routledge & Kegan Paul, 1931), ed. by R. B. Braithwaite.

interpret the T-terms, since they do not occur in it. The Carnap sentence, on the other hand, does nothing to help systematize O-sentences; but it does contain the T-terms, and it does seem to do as much toward interpreting them as the postulate itself does. And the Ramsey and Carnap sentences between them do exactly what the postulate does.

Accordingly, Carnap proposes[4] to take the Ramsey sentence as the synthetic postulate of T and the Carnap sentence as the analytic postulate of T. They divide the labor of the original postulate, which both systematized O-sentences and partially interpreted the T-terms. (Here and henceforth, when I speak of Carnap's proposal it should be understood that I mean Carnap's proposal *minus* Carnap's stipulation that the O-terms belong to an observation language.)

III. THE INTERPRETATION OF T-TERMS

Let us see whether we want to agree that the Carnap sentence does specify the appropriate interpretations of the T-terms, insofar as appropriate interpretations can be specified at all. Put aside, for the time being, Carnap's idea that the Ramsey and Carnap sentences in partnership should be a perfect substitute for the original postulate.

It is important to separate three cases. T may have precisely one realization, or no realization, or more than one realization.

In case T is uniquely realized, the Carnap sentence clearly gives exactly the right specification. It says that the T-terms name the entities in the n-tuple that is the unique realization of T. The first T-term, τ_1, names the first component of the unique realization of T; τ_2 names the second component; and so on.

In case T is not realized, the Carnap sentence says nothing about the denotation of the T-terms. But this modesty seems to be uncalled for. The T-terms were introduced on the assumption that T was realized, in order to name components of a realization of T. There is no realization of T. Therefore they should not name anything. 'Phlogiston' presumably is a theoretical term of an unrealized theory; we say without hesitation that there is no such thing as phlogiston. What else could we possibly say? Should we say that phlogiston is something or other, but (unless phlogiston theory turns out to be true after all) we have no hope of finding out what?

Let us say, then, that the theoretical terms of unrealized theories do not name anything. That will do very well, at least in the case of a theory like phlogiston

---

[4] *Philosophical Foundations of Physics* (New York: Basic Books, 1966), ed. by Martin Gardner, ch. 28; "Replies and Systematic Expositions," in *The Philosophy of Rudolf Carnap* (La Salle, Ill.: Open Court, 1963), ed. by P. A. Schilpp, section 24D; "On the Use of Hilbert's ϵ-Operator in Scientific Theories," in *Essays on the Foundations of Mathematics, Dedicated to A. A. Fraenkel on His Seventieth Anniversary* (Jerusalem: Magnes Press, 1961), ed. by Y. Bar-Hillel *et al.*; "Beobachtungssprache und theoretische Sprache," *Logica: Studia Paul Bernays dedicata* (Neuchâtel: Griffon, 1959).

theory which comes nowhere near being realized. It will not do so well in the case of unrealized theory with a (unique) *near*-realization: that is, an n-tuple that does not realize the original theory, but does realize some theory obtained from it by a slight weakening or a slight correction. We might want to say that the theoretical terms name the components of whichever n-tuple comes nearest to realizing the theory, if it comes near enough. We will ignore this complication, in part for the sake of simplicity and in part because we might hope to handle it as follows. Given a theory T, we might find a slightly weaker T', implied by but not implying T, such that an n-tuple is a realization of T' if and only if it is a near-realization of T. Then we could say that T', not T, is the real term-introducing theory; everything we have been saying about T really ought to be taken as applying to T' instead. T itself may be recovered as the conjunction of T' with further hypotheses containing the theoretical terms already introduced by T'.

There remains the case in which T is multiply realized. In this case, the Carnap sentence tells us that the T-terms name the components of some realization or other. But it does not tell us which; and there seems to be no nonarbitrary way to choose one of the realizations. So either the T-terms do not name anything, or they name the components of an arbitrarily chosen one of the realizations of T. Either of these alternatives concedes too much to the instrumentalist view of a theory as a mere formal abacus. Neither does justice to our naive impression that we understand the theoretical terms of a true theory, and without making any arbitrary choice among realizations. We should not accept Carnap's treatment in this case if we can help it. Can we?

We might say instead that the theoretical terms of multiply realized theories do not name anything. If multiple realization is a defect that theorists can reasonably hope to avoid, then we can afford to treat multiply realized theories as failures: call them false, and call their theoretical terms denotationless. But if multiple realization is inevitable, we cannot afford to disdain multiply realized theories. We can have denotations arbitrarily chosen, or no denotations at all.

A uniquely realized theory is, other things being equal, certainly more satisfactory than a multiply realized theory. We should insist on unique realization as a standard of correctness unless it is a standard too high to be met. Is there any reason to think that we must settle for multiply realized theories? I know of nothing in the way scientists propose theories which suggests that they do not hope for unique realization. And I know of no good reason why they should not hope for unique realization. Therefore I contend that we ought to say that the theoretical terms of multiply realized theories are denotationless.

Many philosophers do seem to think that unique realization is an extravagant hope, unlikely in scientific practice or even impossible in principle. Partly, this is professional skepticism; partly it is skepticism derived from confusions that I shall try to forestall.

In the first place, I am not claiming that scientific theories are formulated in such a way that they could not possibly be multiply realized. I am claiming only that it is reasonable to hope that a good theory will not in fact be multiply realized.

In the second place, I am not claiming that there is only one way in which a given theory *could* be realized; just that we can reasonably hope that there is only one way in which it *is* realized.

Finally, I should say again that we are talking only about realizations that make *T* true under a fixed interpretation of all of its *O*-vocabulary. And this *O*-vocabulary may be as miscellaneous as you please; in practice it is likely to be very miscellaneous indeed. An *O*-term is *any* term, of any character, which we already understood before the new theory *T* came along. It does not have to belong to an observation language. If anyone hopes to adapt my proposals to the task of interpreting theoretical terms using only an observation language—if there is any such thing—I would not be at all surprised if he ran into trouble with multiple realizations. But his project and his troubles are not mine.

John Winnie has announced a proof that scientific theories cannot be uniquely realized.[5] Though his proof is sound, it goes against nothing I want to say. Most of Winnie's multiple realizations of a given theory—all but one, perhaps—are not what I call realizations of the theory. I am concerned only with realizations under a fixed interpretation of the *O*-vocabulary; whereas Winnie permits variation in the interpretation of certain *O*-terms from one realization to another, provided that the variation is confined to theoretical entities. For instance, he would permit variation in the extension of the *O*-predicate '———— is bigger than ————' so long as the extension among observational entities remained fixed. Winnie's proof does not show that a theory is multiply realized in my sense unless the postulate of the theory is free of "mixed" *O*-terms: *O*-predicates whose extension includes theoretical entities, and the like. I would claim that mixed *O*-terms are omnipresent, and that there is no reason not to grant them a fixed interpretation even as applied to theoretical entities.

Perhaps another reason to think that theories cannot be uniquely realized comes from the idea that theoretical terms are somehow partially interpreted. It seems that the stronger a theory is, the better its theoretical terms are interpreted. If the postulate of the theory is a tautology, for instance, the theoretical terms are not interpreted at all. It is tempting to explain this by saying that the stronger theory has fewer realizations. Since no consistent theory interprets its terms so well that it could not have done better if it had been still stronger, it seems that unique realization—perfect interpretation—is a limit we can never reach. But this is a mistake. The stronger theory *may* have fewer actual realizations or it may not; but it *must* have less *risk* of multiple realization, and that is enought to explain why strength seems to make for better interpretation. On the other hand, the stronger theory must also have more risk of nonrealization.

Let us conclude, therefore, that the *T*-terms ought to name the components of the unique realization of *T* if there is one, and ought not to name anything oth-

[5]"The Implicit Definition of Theoretical Terms," *British Journal for the Philosophy of Science*, 18 (1967): 223–29.

erwise. We can record our conclusion by laying down three meaning postulates. The first

$$\exists y_1. . .y_n \forall x_1. . .x_n (T[x_1. . .x_n] \equiv .y_1 = x_1 \& . . .\& y_n = x_n) \supset T[\tau_1. . .\tau_n]$$

says that if T is uniquely realized, then it is realized by the entities named, respectively, by $\tau_1. . .\tau_n$. It is logically implied by the Carnap sentence of T. The second

$$\sim \exists x_1. . .x_n T[x_1. . .x_n] \supset .\sim \exists x(x = \tau_1) \& . . .\& \sim \exists x(x = \tau_n)$$

says that, if T is not realized, then $\tau_1. . .\tau_n$ do not name anything. It is logically independent of the Carnap sentence. The third

$$\exists x_1. . .x_n T[x_1. . .x_n] \& \sim \exists y_1. . .y_n \forall x_1. . .x_n$$
$$(T[x_1. . .x_n] \equiv .y_1 = x_1 \& . . .\& y_n = x_n).$$
$$\supset .\sim \exists x(x = \tau_1) \& . . .\& \sim \exists x(x = \tau_n)$$

says that, if T is mutiply realized, then, again, $\tau_1. . .\tau_n$ do not name anything. It disagrees with the Carnap sentence, inasmuch as the third postulate and the Carnap sentence together imply that T has at most one realization, but that conclusion ought not to follow from meaning postulates.

Now we have specified the denotations of the T-terms. What about their senses? We have specified their senses already. For we have specified their denotations in any possible world, not just here in our actual world. In any possible world, they are to name the components of whatever uniquely realizes T in that world, and they are to name nothing in that world unless T is uniquely realized there. We know what it is for an n-tuple of entities to realize T in an arbitrary possible world w: namely, the n-tuple satisfies the realization formula of T in the model determined jointly by the state of affairs in the possible world w and by the fixed interpretation of the O-vocabulary.

Here I rely on, but do not argue for, a doctrine of senses due originally to Carnap.[6] I am supposing that the sense of a name—at least, of a name that cannot be decomposed into constituents—is given in full by specifying what (if anything) it names in each possible world. If we like, we can say that a sense *is* a function from (some or all) possible worlds to named entities. The most important objection to this doctrine is that possible worlds and their unactualized inhabitants are occult; I have argued elsewhere[7] that they are no more occult than the infinite sets we have learned to live with, and just as useful in systematic philosophy.

Putnam, arguing against Carnap's notation of partial interpretation, has objected that "theories with false observational consequences have *no* interpretation (since they have no model that is 'standard' with respect to the observation terms). This certainly flies in the face of our usual notion of an interpretation, according to which

---

[6]*Meaning and Necessity*, 2nd ed. (Chicago: Chicago University Press, 1956), pp. 181–82.
[7]*Convention* (Cambridge, Mass.: Harvard University Press, 1969), p. 208.

such a theory is *wrong,* not *senseless.*"[8] The objection is mistaken. The theoretical terms of such a theory are not senseless, just *denotationless.* Their sense is given by their denotation in those possible worlds in which the theory *is* uniquely realized and, therefore, does *not* have false consequences. They have just as much sense as the denotationless term 'Santa Claus'.

A *logically determinate* name is one which names the same thing in every possible world. Its sense is a constant function. Numerals, for instance, seem to be logically determinate names of numbers. But 'the number of solar planets' is a logically indeterminate name of a number. Here in our actual world it happens to name the number 9. Elsewhere it may name other numbers, or nothing at all. *Anything* can have a logically indeterminate name—even a property. (This should have been obvious, but wasn't.) Take the name 'the physical property detected by means of the instrument with catalog number 12345 in so-and-so catalog' (filling in the name of a catalog). This happens, perhaps, to name the property of fluorescing in the ultraviolet. But if the catalog numbers had been different, it would have named some other property, or none.

We should notice that T-terms purporting to name properties will normally turn out to be logically indeterminate names of properties. Likewise for other T-terms; but let us stick to the special case. Suppose τ_1 is a T-term purporting to name a property. More precisely: T is formulated in such a way that the postulate of T cannot be true unless τ_1 names a property. It follows that if any n-tuple of entities uniquely realizes T in any possible world, the first component of that n-tuple is a property. But unless T is a very special theory, different n-tuples with different first components will uniquely realize T in different possible worlds. The sense of τ_1 will not be a constant function.

The logical indeterminacy of τ_1 makes for subtle equivocation in any context in which possible worlds other than our actual world are under discussion, either explicitly or implicitly. For instance, there will be trouble whenever τ_1 occurs in the scope of a modal operator, in the scope of a nomological operator, in the scope of an epistemic operator, or in a subjunctive conditional. We have to keep track of when τ_1 names the first component of the unique realization of T (if any) in our actual world, and when τ_1 instead names the first component of the unique realization of T (if any) in some other possible world under discussion.

For instance, someone might plausibly object that, on my account, it is impossible for T to have a unique realization but for the first component thereof not to be the property named by τ_1. But that does seem to be possible. Just consider the property named by τ_1. Fix your attention on that property, whatever it is. Now surely T could have a unique realization in which *that* property was not the first component! So what is impossible according to me is really possible. I reply that the objection commits a fallacy of equivocation. What I assert is this: for no possible world w is it the case that T has a unique realization in w but that the first component thereof is not the property named by τ_1 in the world w. What the objector properly denies is this: for no possible world w is it the case that T has a unique realization in w but that the first component thereof is not the property named by τ_1 in our actual world. Unfortunately, what I assert and what he properly denies can both be expressed by this ambiguous sentence: "It is impossible for T to have a unique realization but for the first component thereof not to be the property named by τ_1."

A similar difficulty arises over the name 'the property of having τ_1'. This name purports to name a property. We would suppose offhand that it names the same property as τ_1 itself. Indeed, we would suppose it has the same sense as τ_1. But at least on one reading it and τ_1 do not name the same property, neither in our actual world nor in any other possible world.

I take it that a property is identified when, and only when, we have specified exactly which things have it in every possible world. And I take it that a name of the form 'the property of doing so-and-so' names the property that belongs, in any world w, to exactly those things which, in the world w, do so-and-so. For instance, 'the property of having τ_1' names the property that belongs, in any world w, to exactly those things which, in the world w, have the property named by τ_1.

Now we can see the problem. Do we mean: (1) the property that belongs, in any world w, to exactly those things which, in the world w, have the property named by τ_1 *in our actual world?* That, of course, is just the same property which is named by τ_1 in our actual world. On this first reading, 'the property of having τ_1' and τ_1 do both name the same property.

Or do we rather mean: (2) the property that belongs, in any world w, to exactly those things which, in the world w, have the property named by τ_1 *in the world w?* On this second—and, I believe, better—reading, 'the property of having τ_1' is a logically determinate name of a certain property, which we may call the *diagonalized sense* of τ_1. The sense of τ_1 may be prepresented by a function $\|\tau_1\|$ which assigns to any world w a property $\|\tau_1\|_w$. A property in turn may be represented by a function P which assigns to any world w the set P_w of things which, in the world w, have the property. Then the diagonalized sense of τ_1 is the property whose representing function assigns to any world w the set of things $(\|\tau_1\|_w)_w$. It is not named by τ_1 in any world, unless T is a very peculiar theory. Neither is it the sense of τ_1; that is not a property at all, but rather a function from worlds to properties.

IV. THE DEFINITIONS OF T-TERMS

Given our conclusion that the T-terms $\tau_1 \ldots \tau_n$ denote the components of the unique realization of T if there is one, and should not denote anything otherwise, it is natural to define the T-terms by means of definite descriptions as follows.

$$\tau_1 = \imath y_1 \exists y_2 \ldots y_n \forall x_1 \ldots x_n \, (\mathsf{T}[x_1 \ldots x_n] \equiv . y_1 = x_1 \& \ldots \& y_n = x_n)$$

$$\ldots$$

$$\tau_n = \imath y_n \exists y_1 \ldots y_{n-1} \forall x_1 \ldots x_n (\mathsf{T}[x_1 \ldots x_n] \equiv . y_1 = x_1 \& \ldots \& y_n = x_n)$$

These are to be our *definition sentences* for the theory T. The first, for instance, says that τ_1 names that entity which, followed by some $n-1$ entities, comprises an n-tuple identical with all and only n-tuples that realize T. That is to say, τ_1 names the first component of the unique realization of T.

These definitions work properly, under the treatment of denotationless terms we have chosen. They are valid: true in any model in which the T-terms are interpreted as specified in the previous section, whether or not T is uniquely realized therein. They are jointly equivalent to the set of meaning postulates we put forth to replace the Carnap sentence of T. They do not imply any O-sentences except logical truths.

We can see now why it was worth the trouble to adopt Dana Scott's treatment of denotationless names rather than its more familiar alternatives.[9] Under Russell's theory of descriptions, the definition sentences are disguised existential quantifications, false unless T is uniquely realized. Under the truth-value-gap theory of Frege and Strawson, atomic contexts of denotationless names or descriptions have no truth value; so the definition sentences are neither true nor false unless T is uniquely realized. Either way, the definition sentences would not be valid identities, true whether or not T is uniquely realized. We would be forced to regard them as metalinguistic assertions of synonymy, or something of the sort. Under the chosen-individual theory of Frege and Carnap, improper descriptions name some arbitrarily chosen individual. So do the theoretical terms of unrealized or multiply realized theories, if the definition sentences are to be valid. But suppose T is multiply realized, and suppose the n-tuple consisting of the chosen individual taken n times over happens to be one of the realizations of T. In this case, by accident, the postulate of T turns out to be true, contrary to our decision that multiply realized theories should be false.

V. THE EXPANDED POSTULATE OF T

Given our definitions, we can eliminate T-terms in favor of the definite descriptions whereby we have defined them. Replacing each T-term by its definiens throughout the postulate of T, we obtain an O-sentence which we may call the *(definitionally) expanded postulate* of T. It says T is realized by the n-tuple consisting of the first, second, . . . , nth components of the unique realization of T. The expanded postulate is, of course, definitionally equivalent to the postulate. That is, the postulate together with the definition sentences is logically equivalent to the expanded postulate together with the definition sentences.

The expanded postulate says that T is uniquely realized. It is logically equivalent to a shorter O-sentence that says so in a more straightforward way; we may call this the *unique-realization sentence* of T:

---

[9]For a survey of the alternatives, see David Kaplan, "What Is Russell's Theory of Descriptions?" *Physics, Logic, and History* (New York: Plenum, 1969), ed. by Wolfgang Yourgrau.

$$\exists y_1 \ldots y_n \forall x_1 \ldots x_n (T[x_1 \ldots x_n] \equiv .y_1 = x_1 \& \ldots \& y_n = x_n)$$

Thus the postulate is definitionally equivalent to the unique-realization sentence. That is what we should expect, given our decision—*contra* Carnap—to interpret the T-terms in such a way that the postulate is true if and only if T is uniquely realized.

Still we may have misgivings. The expanded postulate is an O-sentence stronger than the Ramsey sentence of T, which said merely that T had *at least* one realization. Yet if the definition sentences are part of T, the expanded postulate is an O-theorem of T. So the definitions are giving us O-theorems that could not have been derived without them. That means that the definitions themselves, unlike the Carnap sentence, are not logically implied by the postulate.

Therefore, if I want to contend that the definition sentences of T are correct definitions, I must give up the idea that the theorems of T are all and only the logical consequences of the postulate of T. I am quite willing to give up that idea. I contend that the theorist who proposed T by asserting the postulate of T explicitly, labeling it as the postulate of a term-introducing theory, has also implicitly asserted the definition sentences of T. I contend that his audience *will* take him to have implicitly asserted the definition sentences of T. That is an empirical hypothesis about the conventional semantics of our language. To test it, we should find out what would happen if the audience came to think that T was multiply realized.

If they would thereupon call T a false theory, that confirms my account of the interpretation and definitions of the T-terms. If they would call T a true theory, that refutes my account and confirms Carnap's. What if they would be unable to decide which to say? Then my account and Carnap's are rival proposals for rational reconstruction within the range of free choice left open by our conventions. My proposal has the advantage that it permits theoretical terms to be fully interpreted and explicitly defined. Carnap's proposal has the advantage that it lets us live with multiply realized theories. But I see no reason why we need to be able to live with multiply realized theories.

The expanded postulate (and its logical equivalent, the unique-realization sentence) are not by any means the only interesting definitional equivalents of the postulate of T. For any T-term τ_i, consider the sentence that says τ_i names something: '$(\exists x)(x = \tau_i)$'. This sentence is definitionally equivalent to the postulate of T and to the expanded postulate of T (but logically equivalent to neither). That is what we should expect: T is uniquely realized if and only if there is something which is the ith component of the unique realization of T.

Therefore the postulate and expanded postulate of T are definitionally implied by any sentence which contains T-terms and which comes out false in case any of its T-terms are denotationless. There are many such sentences. Let τ_1, τ_2, and τ_3 be T-terms purporting to name, respectively, a property, a relation, and a function; and let ζ and η be O-terms purporting to name individuals. Let ν be an O-term naming a real number. Now consider such sentences as: 'ζ has the property τ_1', 'ζ bears the relation τ_2 to η', or 'the value of the function τ_3 for the argument ζ is

v'. Clearly each of these sentences should be false if its T-term is denotationless. Therefore each of them defnitionally implies the postulate and expanded postulate of T.

We would probably say, at first sight, that sentences such as these purport to state particular facts. Yet the theoretical postulates they imply—or some conjuncts thereof—will usually purport to state laws of nature, perhaps even laws of unrestricted universality. Therefore it is possible that a particular fact might be explained by a covering-law explanatory argument in which the explanans contains no explicit statement of any law! The required covering laws would be available by implication from certain particular-fact premises in the explanans. It seems that, if my account of theoretical terms is correct, the covering-law analysis of scientific explanation is in need of a slight reformulation. Take one of Hempel's definitions of deductive-nomological explanation:

> . . . deductive arguments whose conclusion is the explandum sentence . . . ; and whose premiss-set, the explanans, consists of general laws . . . , and of other statements . . . , which make assertions about particular facts.[10]

I contend we ought rather to say:

> . . . deductive arguments whose conclusion is the explanandum sentence; and whose premiss-set, the explanans, consists of statements which make assertions about particular facts and *perhaps* also of statements which assert general laws; and whose premiss-set implies statements which assert general laws.

I am confident that my objection goes against the letter, not the spirit, of Hempel's covering-law analysis.

VI. DERIVED BRIDGE LAWS FOR T

We can safely assume that there is a period, after the new theory T has been proposed, during which the T-terms retain the interpretations they received at the time of their introduction. At least for a while, our definition sentences for T remain valid. Suppose that, during this period, T is reduced by means of some other accepted scientific theory T^*. Let this be a reduction in which T survives intact; not, what is more common, a simultaneous partial reduction and partial falsification of T by T^*. We shall consider how this reduction might take place.

The reducing theory T^* need not be what we would naturally call a single theory; it may be a combination of several theories, perhaps belonging to different sciences. Parts of T^* may be miscellaneous unsystematized hypotheses which we

[10]*Philosophy of Natural Science* (Englewood Cliffs, N.J.: Prentice-Hall 1966), p. 51.

accept, and which are not properly called theories at all. Different parts of T^* may have been proposed or accepted at different times, either before or after T itself was proposed.

The most interesting case, however, is that in which T^* is well systematized, and at least part of T^* is newer than T. It is in that case that the reduction of T by means of T^* is likely to be an important advance toward the systematization of all empirical knowledge.

T^*, or parts of T^*, may introduce theoretical terms; if so, let us assume that these T^*-terms have been introduced by means of the same O-vocabulary which was used to introduce the theoretical terms of T. This is possible regardless of the order in which T and T^* were proposed. Any term that is either an O-term or a T^*-term may be called an O^*-term; so at the time T is reduced, the relevant part of our scientific vocabulary is divided into the T-vocabulary and the O^*-vocabulary.

Suppose the following O^*-sentence is a theorem of T^*; we may call it a *reduction premise* for T: '$T[\rho_1 \ldots \rho_n]$'. The terms $\rho_1 \ldots \rho_n$ are to be names belonging to the O^*-vocabulary. They may be elementary expressions and belong to the O^*-vocabulary in their own right, or they may be compound expressions—for instance, definite descriptions—whose ultimate constituents belong to the O^*-vocabulary. The reduction premise says that T is realized by an n-tuple of entities named, respectively, by the O^*-terms $\rho_1 \ldots \rho_n$. Notice that it cannot be true if any of those O^*-names are denotationless.

A reduction premise for T does not imply the postulate of T either logically or definitionally; nor conversely. But the postulate does follow logically from the reduction premise together with a set of *bridge laws* for T, as follows:

$$\rho_1 = \tau_1$$
$$\ldots$$
$$\rho_n = \tau_n$$

The bridge laws serve to identify phenomena described in terms of the reduced theory T with phenomena described in terms of the reducing theory T^* (including the O-vocabulary); and via these identifications, T can be derived from T^*.

But where do we get the bridge laws? The usual view[11] is that they are separate empirical hypotheses, independent of the reducing theory T^*. When T^* yields a reduction premise for T, we have the opportunity to choose between two rival bodies of theory. We may choose T^* augmented with bridge laws; if so, we can derive T, so we do not have to posit it. Or we may choose T^* without bridge laws, in which case we will have to posit T separately. Given this choice, we take whichever body of theory is better—more systematized, parsimonious, simple, credible, or what have you. We must decide whether the gain in systematization from reduc-

---

[11]Reviewed in the first two sections of John Kemeny and Paul Oppenheim, "On Reduction," *Philosophical Studies*, 7 (1956): 6–13. Since Kemeny and Oppenheim take the theoretical terms as predicates, their bridge laws are universally closed biconditionals rather than identities.

ing T is worth the loss of systematization from adding bridge laws. If it is, we choose to accept the bridge laws and perform the reduction.

The usual view assumes that it is impossible to derive the bridge laws from the unaugmented reducing theory T^*, since the bridge laws contain essential occurrences of the T-terms and these do not occur in T^*. But consider the *definitionally expanded bridge laws:* the sentences obtained from the bridge laws when we replace the T-terms by definite descriptions, according to our definition sentences for T.

$$\rho_1 = \imath y_1 \exists y_2 \ldots y_n \forall x_1 \ldots x_n (T[x_1 \ldots x_n] \equiv .y_1 = x_1 \& \ldots \& y_n = x_n)$$

$$\cdots$$

$$\rho_n = \imath y_n \exists y_1 \ldots y_{n-1} \forall x_1 \ldots x_n (T[x_1 \ldots x_n] \equiv .y_1 = x_1 \& \ldots \& y_n = x_n)$$

The definitionally expanded bridge laws are O^*-sentences. No incompatibility of vocabulary prevents them from being theorems of T^*. Yet they are definitional equivalents of the bridge laws; so if they are theorems of T^*, then T^* definitionally implies the bridge laws. There is no need for any empirical hypothesis other than theorems of T^*.

If T^* yields as theorems a reduction premise for T, and also a suitable set of definitionally expanded bridge laws for T, then T^*—without the aid of any other empirical hypothesis—reduces T. For T^* definitionally implies the postulate of T, as well as a set of bridge laws. Once T^* is accepted, there is no choice whether or not to reduce T. The reduction of T does not need to be justified by considerations of parsimony (or whatever) over and above the considerations of parsimony that led us to accept T^* in the first place.

It is useful to observe that the set of definitionally expanded bridge laws is logically implied by the following O^*-sentence, which we may call an *auxiliary reduction premise* for T:

$$\forall x_1 \ldots x_n (T[x_1 \ldots x_n] \equiv .\rho_1 = x_1 \& \ldots \& \rho_n = x_n)$$

It says that, unless one of the terms $\rho_1 \ldots \rho_n$ is denotationless, T is uniquely realized by an n-tuple of entities named, respectively, by $\rho_1 \ldots \rho_n$. Hence the reduction premise and the auxiliary reduction premise together say just this: T is uniquely realized by an n-tuple of entities named, respectively, by $\rho_1 \ldots \rho_n$. That is what T^* must imply in order to reduce T by means of derived bridge laws. In that case, indeed, we can by-pass the bridge laws. T^* definitionally implies T by an alternate route. Since T^* guarantees that T is uniquely realized, T^* logically implies the unique realization sentence of T, which is logically equivalent to the expanded postulate of T and definitionally equivalent to the postulate of T.

Let us briefly examine two examples of reduction by means of derived bridge laws.

(1) Let T be a theory explaining the operation of a machine by means of transition laws of the form: when the machine is in state τ_i, so-and-so input causes it to go into state τ_j and produce such-and-such output. The T-terms are $\tau_1 \ldots \tau_n$, purporting to name states of the machine. Later we obtain T^*: an account, pur-

porting to be complete, of the internal structure of the machine and the principles on which it works. Then, unless T^* falsifies T, we should be able to form state-names $\rho_1 \cdot \cdot \cdot \rho_n$ in the mechanical vocabulary of T^*, such that T^* implies that the states thus named are related to one another, and to the appropriate inputs and outputs, by the given transition laws. Thus T^* would yield a reduction premise for T. But also, since T^* purports to be a complete account of the working of the machine, we can reasonably expect T^* to leave no room for a second realization of T. T^* could imply that every n-tuple of states describable in its mechanical vocabulary, except for the n-tuple named by $\rho_1 \ldots \rho_n$, disobeys the given transition laws; and according to the completeness claimed by T^*, no states not so describable need be considered in explaining the input-output relations of the machine. (For instance, what we think we know about ordinary electromechanical machines seems to imply that the only states causally responsible for outputs are states describable in terms of positions and momenta of moving parts, currents, and voltages.) If so, T^* yields an auxiliary reduction premise for T; hence T^* together with the definitions of the state-names $\tau_1 \ldots \tau_n$ suffices to imply the bridge laws: '$\tau_i = \rho_i$'.

(2) Let T be a theory explaining the regulation of certain biological processes by positing hormones $\tau_1 \ldots \tau_n$: chemical substances of unspecified composition, secreted by specified cells under specified conditions and regulating the rates of specified chemical reactions in a specified way. The T-terms $\tau_1 \ldots \tau_n$, in this case, purport to name substances. Let T^* comprise our body of biochemical knowledge at some later time; T^* might imply that certain substances named by chemical formulas $\rho_1 \ldots \rho_n$ realized T, and that they alone did so. To exclude multiple realization of T, T^* would have to contain the information that, e.g., a certain gland secretes *nothing but* the substance with formula ρ_1; but we often do have such knowledge.

Not only is it possible for a theory to be reduced by means of derived bridge laws; we can even regard all possible reduction of theories as working in this way. Instead of saying that in some cases the bridge laws are posited independently of the reducing theory, we may rather say that in some cases the reducing theory must be strengthened ad hoc before it yields the bridge laws we want.

Suppose we want to reduce our theory T; and we accept a theory T^* which yields as a theorem some reduction premise for T, but does not yield the corresponding set of definitionally expanded bridge laws. Let T^{**} be the theory obtained from T^* by providing these definitionally expanded bridge laws. T^* does not reduce T by means of derived bridge laws, but only by means of bridge laws posited independently of T^*. T^{**}, a theory obtained by suitable strengthening of T^*, does reduce T by means of derived bridge laws. How shall we describe what happens when we add bridge laws to T^* in order to reduce T? If we say that T^* is the reducing theory, we must say that T^* reduces T by means of independently posited bridge laws. But we could just as well say that T^{**} was the reducing theory, and that we strengthened T^* to T^{**} in order that T^{**} might reduce T by means of derived bridge laws. Of course, it does not matter very much which we say. Either way, the bridge laws have been posited ad hoc in return for the reduction of T; for T^{**} is definitionally equivalent to T^* plus the bridge laws.

Still, I think it best to say that the strengthening of the reducing theory is a precondition, not a part, of the reduction. For that will remind us that strengthening is not necessarily needed. A body of theory already accepted before we thought of using it to reduce T may already be strong enough, without any more strengthening ad hoc, to reduce T by means of derived bridge laws. I do not know whether most cases of theoretical reduction are of this sort; but we should at least leave the possibility open, as the usual account of reduction does not.

VII. LATER REVISIONS OF T

So far, we have discussed the interpretation of T-terms at the time of their introduction, the time when their parent theory T is first proposed. It remains to ask what happens later when T is amended and extended. This matters especially in connection with reduction, since theories do not often survive reduction intact. More often the original theory is falsified while a corrected version is reduced. If T is thus partially reduced and partially falsified, or revised for any other reason, do the T-terms retain their meanings?

We might say that the T-terms should always be defined using the currently accepted version of T. As T is corrected, modified, extended, or perhaps even when we accept miscellaneous hypotheses that contain T-terms but do not belong integrally to any version of T, the T-terms gradually change their meaning. In particular, they change their meanings in the revisions preparatory to partial reduction of T.[12] But these are very peculiar changes of meaning—so peculiar that this position seems to change the meaning of 'change the meaning of'. They occur continually, unnoticed, without impeding communication. We might try saying that a *small* enough change of meaning is not really a change of meaning, but that would imply that enough nonchanges in meaning could add up to a change in meaning. The position has other problems. How are we to define the theoretical terms of defunct or never-accepted theories? Should we use the best-known version, or what? What if different scientists accept slightly different versions of T, disagreeing, say, on the exact value of some physical constant? We ought not to say they give the T-terms different meanings. What do the T-terms mean if we have suspended judgment between two slightly different versions of T?

We might therefore prefer to say that the T-terms keep the meanings they received at their first introduction. They should still be defined using the original version of T even after it has been superseded by revised versions.

---

[12]As suggested by Paul Feyerabend, "Explanation, Reduction, and Empiricism," *Minnesota Studies in the Philosophy of Science* 3 (Minneapolis: University of Minnesota Press, 1962), ed. by H. Feigl and G. Maxwell.

This position will work only if we permit the T-terms to name components of the nearest near-realization of T, even if it is not a realization of T itself. For after T has been corrected, no matter how slightly, we will believe that the original version of T is unrealized. We will want the T-terms to name components of the unique realization (if any) of the corrected version of T. They can do so without change of meaning if a realization of the corrected version is also a near-realization of the original version.

According to this position, we may be unable to discover the meanings of theoretical terms at a given time just by looking into the minds of the most competent language-users at that time. We will need to look at the past episodes of theory-proposing in which those terms were first introduced into their language. The working physicist is the expert on electrons; but the historian of physics knows more than he about the meaning of 'electron', and hence about which things could truly have been called electrons if the facts had been different. If we were ignorant of history, we could all be ignorant or mistaken about the meanings of words in common use among us. This situation is surprising, but it has precedent: a parallel doctrine about proper names has recently been defended.[13] To know what 'Moses' means among us it is not enough to look into our minds; you must look at the man who stands at the beginning of the causal chain leading to our use the word 'Moses'.

I do not wish to decide between these alternatives. Either seems defensible at some cost. I hope the truth lies in between, but I do not know what an intermediate position would look like.

---

[13]See David Kaplan, "Quantifying In," *Synthese*, 19 (1968): 178–214.

PART TWO

Philosophy of Mind

An Argument
for the
Identity Theory

I. INTRODUCTION

The (Psychophysical) Identity Theory is the hypothesis that—not necessarily but as a matter of fact—every experience[1] is identical with some physical state.[2] Specifically, with some neurochemical state. I contend that we who accept the materialistic working hypothesis that physical phenomena have none but purely physical explanations must accept the identity theory. This is to say more than do most friends of the theory, who say only that we are free to accept it, and should for the sake of some sort of economy or elegance. I do not need to make a case for the

---

[1] Experiences herein are to be taken in general as universals, not as abstract particulars. I am concerned, for instance, with pain, an experience that befalls many people at many times; or with pain of some definite sort, an experience which at least *might* be common to different people at different times. Both are universals, capable of repeated instantiation. The latter is a narrower universal than the former, as crimson of some definite shade is narrower than red, but still a universal. I am not concerned with the particular pain of a given person at a given time, an abstract entity which cannot itself recur but can only be similar—at best, exactly similar—to other particular pains of other people or at other times. We might identify such abstract particulars with pairs of a universal and a single concrete particular instance thereof; or we might leave them as unanalyzed, elementary beings, as in Donald C. Williams, "On the Elements of Being," *Review of Metaphysics* 7 (1953): 3–18 and 171–92. [All but the first sentence of this note was added in October 1969.]

[2] States also are to be taken in general as universals. I shall not distinguish between processes, events, phenomena, and states in a strict sense.

identity theory on grounds of economy,[3] since I believe it can and should rest on a stronger foundation.

My argument is this: The definitive characteristic of any (sort of) experience as such is its causal role, its syndrome of most typical causes and effects. But we materialists believe that these causal roles which belong by analytic necessity to experiences belong in fact to certain physical states. Since those physical states possess the definitive characteristics of experience, they must be the experiences.

My argument parallels an argument which we will find uncontroversial. Consider cylindrical combination locks for bicycle chains. The definitive characteristic of their state of being unlocked is the causal role of that state, the syndrome of its most typical causes and effects: namely, that setting the combination typically causes the lock to be unlocked and that being unlocked typically causes the lock to open when gently pulled. That is all we need know in order to ascribe to the lock the state of being or of not being unlocked. But we may learn that, as a matter of fact, the lock contains a row of slotted discs; setting the combination typically causes the slots to be aligned; and alignment of the slots typically causes the lock to open when gently pulled. So alignment of slots occupies precisely the causal role that we ascribed to being unlocked by analytic necessity, as the definitive characteristic of being unlocked (for these locks). Therefore alignment of slots is identical with being unlocked (for these locks). They are one and the same state.

II. THE NATURE OF THE IDENTITY THEORY

We must understand that the identity theory asserts that certain physical states are experiences, introspectible processes or activities, not that they are the supposed intentional objects that experiences are experiences *of*. If these objects of experience really exist separate from experiences of them, or even as abstract parts thereof, they may well also be something physical. Perhaps they are also neural, or perhaps they are abstract constituents of veridically perceived surroundings, or perhaps they are something else, or nothing at all; but that is another story. So I am not claiming that an experience of seeing red, say, is itself somehow a red neural state.

Shaffer has argued that the identity theory is impossible because (abstract particular) experiences are, by analytic necessity, unlocated, whereas the (abstract particular) neural events that they supposedly are have a location in part of the subject's nervous system.[4] But I see no reason to believe that the principle that experiences are unlocated enjoys any analytic, or other, necessity. Rather it is a metaphysical prejudice which has no claim to be respected. Or if there is, after all,

---

[3] I am therefore invulnerable to Brandt's objection that the identity theory is not clearly more economical than a certain kind of dualism. "Doubts about the Identity Theory," in *Dimensions of Mind,* Sidney Hook, ed. (New York: NYU Press, 1960), pp. 57–67.

[4] "Could Mental States Be Brain Processes?" *Journal of Philosophy* 58, no. 26 (Dec. 21, 1961): 813–22.

a way in which it is analytic that experiences are unlocated, that way is irrelevant: perhaps in our presystematic thought we regard only concreta as located in a primary sense, and abstracta as located in a merely derivative sense by their inherence in located concreta. But this possible source of analytic unlocatedness for experiences does not meet the needs of Shaffer's argument. For neural events are abstracta too. Whatever unlocatedness accrues to experiences not because they are mental but because they are abstract must accrue as much to neural events. So it does not discriminate between the two.

The identity theory says that experience-ascriptions have the same reference as certain neural-state-ascriptions: both alike refer to the neural states which are experiences. It does not say that these ascriptions have the same sense. They do not; experience-ascriptions refer to a state by specifying the causal role that belongs to it accidentally, in virtue of causal laws, whereas neural-state-ascriptions refer to a state by describing it in detail. Therefore the identity theory does not imply that whatever is true of experiences as such is likewise true of neural states as such, nor conversely. For a truth about things of any kind *as such* is about things of that kind not by themselves, but together with the sense of expressions by which they are referred to as things of that kind.[5] So it is pointless to exhibit various discrepancies between what is true of experiences as such and what is true of neural states as such. We can explain those discrepancies without denying psychophysical identity and without admitting that it is somehow identity of a defective sort.

We must not identify an experience itself with the attribute that is predicated of somebody by saying that he is having that experience.[6] The former *is* whatever state it is that occupies a certain definitive causal role; the latter is the attribute of *being in* whatever state it is that occupies that causal role. By this distinction we

---

[5] Here I have of course merely applied to states Frege's doctrine of sense and reference. See "On Sense and Reference," in *Translations from the Philosophical Writings of Gottlob Frege*, ed. by Peter Geach and Max Black. (New York: Oxford University Press, 1960), pp. 56–78.

[6] Here I mean to deny all identities of the form ⌜α is identical with the attribute of having α⌝ where α is an experience-name definable as naming the occupant of a specified causal role. I deny, for instance, that pain is identical with the attribute of having pain. On my theory, 'pain' is a *contingent* name—that is, a name with different denotations in different possible worlds—since in any world, 'pain' names whatever state happens in that world to occupy the causal role definitive of pain. If state X occupies that role in world V while another state Y (incompatible with X) occupies that role in world W, then 'pain' names X in V and Y in W. I take 'the attribute of having pain', on the other hand, as a *non-contingent* name of that state or attribute Z that belongs, in any world, to whatever things have pain in that world—that is, to whatever things have in that world the state named in that world by 'pain'. (I take states to be attributes of a special kind: attributes of things at times.) Thus Z belongs in V to whatever things have X in V, and in W to whatever things have Y in W; hence Z is identical neither with X nor with Y.

Richard Montague, in "On the Nature of Certain Philosophical Entities," *Monist* 53 (1969): 172–73, objects that I seem to be denying a logical truth having as its instances all identities of the form ⌜α is identical with the attribute of having α⌝ where α is a *non-contingent* name of a state which is (either contingently or necessarily) an experience. I would agree that such identities are logically true; but those are not the identities I mean to deny, since I claim that our ordinary experience-names—'pain' and the like—are *contingent* names of states. [This note was added in October 1969.]

can answer the objection that, since experience-ascriptions and neural-state-descriptions are admittedly never synonymous and since attributes are identical just in case they are predicated by synonymous expressions, therefore experiences and neural states cannot be identical attributes. The objection does establish a nonidentity, but not between experiences and neural states. (It is unfair to blame the identity theory for needing the protection of so suspiciously subtle a distinction, for a parallel distinction is needed elsewhere. Blue is, for instance, the color of my socks, but blue is not the attribute predicated of things by saying they are the color of my socks, since ' . . . is blue' and ' . . . is the color of my socks' are not synonymous.)

III. THE FIRST PREMISE: EXPERIENCES DEFINED BY CAUSAL ROLES

The first of my two premises for establishing the identity theory is the principle that the definitive characteristic of any experience as such is its causal role. The definitive causal role of an experience is expressible by a finite[7] set of conditions that specify its typical causes and its typical effects under various circumstances. By analytic necessity these conditions are true of the experience and jointly distinctive of it.

My first premise is an elaboration and generalization of Smart's theory that avowals of experience are, in effect, of the form 'What is going on in me is like what is going on in me when . . .' followed by specification of typical stimuli for, or responses to, the experiences.[8] I wish to add explicitly that . . . may be an elaborate logical compound of clauses if necessary; that . . . must specify typical causes or effects of the experience, not mere accompaniments; that these typical causes and effects may include other experiences; and that the formula does not apply only to first-person reports of experience.

This is not a materialist principle, nor does it ascribe materialism to whoever speaks of experiences. Rather it is an account of the parlance common to all who believe that experiences are something or other real and that experiences are efficacious outside their own realm. It is neutral between theories—or a lack of any theory—about what sort of real and efficacious things experiences are: neural states or the like, pulsations of ectoplasm or the like, or just experiences and nothing else. It is not neutral, however, between all current theories of mind and body. Epiphenomenalist and parallelist dualism are ruled out as contradictory because they

---

[7] It would do no harm to allow the set of conditions to be infinite, so long as it is recursive. But I doubt the need for this relaxation.

[8] *Philosophy and Scientific Realism* (New York: Humanities Press, 1963), ch. 5. Smart's concession that his formula does not really translate avowals is unnecessary. It results from a bad example: 'I have a pain' is not translatable as 'What is going on in me is like what goes on when a pin is stuck into me', because the concept of pain might be introduced without mention of pins. Indeed; but the objection is no good against the translation 'What is going on in me is like what goes on when (i.e. when and because) my skin is damaged'.

deny the efficacy of experience. Behaviorism as a thoroughgoing dispositional analysis of all mental states, including experiences,[9] is likewise ruled out as denying the reality and a fortiori the efficacy of experiences. For a pure disposition is a fictitious entity. The expressions that ostensibly denote dispositions are best construed as syncategorematic parts of statements of the lawlike regularities in which (as we say) the dispositions are manifest.

Yet the principle that experiences are defined by their causal roles is itself behaviorist in origin, in that it inherits the behaviorist discovery that the (ostensibly) causal connections between an experience and its typical occasions and manifestations somehow contain a component of analytic necessity. But my principle improves on the original behavioristic embodiment of that discovery in several ways:

First, it allows experiences to be something real and so to be the effects of their occasions and the causes of their manifestations, as common opinion supposes them to be.

Second, it allows us to include other experiences among the typical causes and effects by which an experience is defined. It is crucial that we should be able to do so in order that we may do justice, in defining experiences by their causal roles, to the introspective accessibility which is such an important feature of any experience. For the introspective accessibility of an experience is its propensity reliably to cause other (future or simultaneous) experiences directed intentionally upon it, wherein we are aware of it. The requisite freedom to interdefine experiences is not available in general under behaviorism; interdefinition of experiences is permissible only if it can in principle be eliminated, which is so only if it happens to be possible to arrange experiences in a hierarchy of definitional priority. We, on the other hand, may allow interdefinition with no such constraint. We may expect to get mutually interdefined families of experiences, but they will do us no harm. There will be no reason to identify anything with one experience in such a family without regard to the others—but why should there be? Whatever occupies the definitive causal role of an experience in such a family does so by virtue of its own membership in a causal isomorph of the family of experiences, that is, in a system of states having the same pattern of causal connections with one another and the same causal connections with states outside the family, viz., stimuli and behavior. The isomorphism guarantees that if the family is identified *throughout* with its isomorph then the experiences in the family will have their definitive causal roles. So, ipso facto, the isomorphism requires us to accept the identity of all the experiences of the family with their counterparts in the causal isomorph of the family.[10]

[9] Any theory of mind and body is compatible with a dispositional analysis of mental states other than experiences or with so-called "methodological behaviorism."

[10] Putnam discusses an analogous case for machines: a family of ("logical" or "functional") states defined by their causal roles and mutually interdefined, and a causally isomorphic system of ("structural") states otherwise defined. He does not equate the correlated logical and structural states. "Minds and Machines," in *Dimensions of Mind*, pp. 148–79.

Third, we are not obliged to define an experience by the causes and effects of exactly all and only its occurrences. We can be content rather merely to identify the experience as that state which is *typically* caused in thus-and-such ways and *typically* causes thus-and-such effects, saying nothing about its causes and effects in a (small) residue of exceptional cases. A definition by causes and effects in typical cases suffices to determine what the experience is, and the fact that the experience has some characteristics or other besides its definitive causal role confers a sense upon ascriptions of it in some exceptional cases for which its definitive typical causes and effects are absent (and likewise upon denials of it in some cases for which they are present). Behaviorism does not acknowledge the fact that the experience is something apart from its definitive occasions and manifestations, and so must require that the experience be defined by a strictly necessary and sufficient condition in terms of them. Otherwise the behaviorist has merely a partial explication of the experience by criteria, which can never give more than a presumption that the expreience is present or absent, no matter how much we know about the subject's behavior and any lawlike regularities that may govern it. Relaxation of the requirement for a strictly necessary and sufficient condition is welcome. As anybody who has tried to implement behaviorism knows, it is usually easy to find conditions which are *almost* necessary and sufficient for an experience. All the work—and all the complexity which renders it incredible that the conditions found should be known implicitly by every speaker—comes in trying to cover a few exceptional cases. In fact, it is just impossible to cover some atypical cases of experiences behavioristically: the case of a perfect actor pretending to have an experience he does not really have; and the case of a total paralytic who cannot manifest any experience he does have (both cases under the stipulation that the pretense or paralysis will last for the rest of the subject's life no matter what happens, in virtue of regularities just as lawlike as those by which the behaviorist seeks to define experiences).

It is possible, and probably good analytic strategy, to reconstrue any supposed pure dispositional state rather as a state defined by its causal role. The advantages in general are those we have seen in this case: the state becomes recognized as real and efficacious; unrestricted mutual interdefinition of the state and others of its sort becomes permissible; and it becomes intelligible that the state may sometimes occur despite prevention of its definitive manifestations.[11]

I do not offer to prove my principle that the definitive characteristics of experiences as such are their causal roles. It would be verified by exhibition of many suitable analytic statements saying that various experiences typically have thus-and-such causes and effects. Many of these statements have been collected by behaviorists; I inherit these although I explain their status somewhat differently. Behaviorism is widely accepted. I am content to rest my case on the argument that my

---

[11]Quine advocates this treatment of such dispositional states as are worth saving in *Word and Object* (Cambridge, Mass.: MIT Press, and New York: Wiley, 1960), pp. 222–25. "They are conceived as built-in, enduring structural traits."

principle can accommodate what is true in behaviorism and can escape attendant difficulties.

IV. THE SECOND PREMISE: EXPLANATORY ADEQUACY OF PHYSICS

My second premise is the plausible hypothesis that there is some unified body of scientific theories, of the sort we now accept, which together provide a true and exhaustive account of all physical phenomena (i.e. all phenomena describable in physical terms). They are unified in that they are cumulative: the theory governing any physical phenomenon is explained by theories governing phenomena out of which that phenomenon is composed and by the way it is composed out of them. The same is true of the latter phenomena, and so on down to fundamental particles or fields governed by a few simple laws, more or less as conceived of in present-day theoretical physics. I rely on Oppenheim and Putnam for a detailed exposition of the hypothesis that we may hope to find such a unified physicalistic body of scientific theory and for a presentation of evidence that the hypothesis is credible.[12]

A confidence in the explanatory adequacy of physics is a vital part, but not the whole, of any full-blooded materialism. It is the empirical foundation on which materialism builds its superstructure of ontological and cosmological doctrines, among them the identity theory. It is also a traditional and definitive working hypothesis of natural science—what scientists say nowadays to the contrary is defeatism or philosophy. I argue that whoever shares this confidence must accept the identity theory.

My second premise does not rule out the existence of nonphysical phenomena; it is not an ontological thesis in its own right. It only denies that we need ever explain physical phenomena by nonphysical ones. Physical phenomena are physically explicable, or they are utterly inexplicable insofar as they depend upon chance in a physically explicable way, or they are methodologically acceptable primitives. All manner of nonphysical phenomena may coexist with them, even to the extent of sharing the same space-time, provided only that the nonphysical phenomena are entirely inefficacious with respect to the physical phenomena. These coexistent nonphysical phenomena may be quite unrelated to physical phenomena; they may be causally independent but for some reason perfectly correlated with some physical phenomena (as experiences are, according to parallelism); they may be epiphenomena, caused by some physical phenomena but not themselves causing any (as experiences are, according to epiphenomenalism). If they are epiphenomena they may even be correlated with some physical phenomena, perfectly and by virtue of a causal law.

[12]"Unity of Science as a Working Hypothesis," in *Minnesota Studies in the Philosophy of Science 2* (Minneapolis: Univ. of Minnesota Press, 1958), Herbert Feigl, Michael Scriven, and Grover Maxwell, eds., pp. 3–36.

V. CONCLUSION OF THE ARGUMENT

But none of these permissible nonphysical phenomena can be experiences. For they must be entirely inefficacious with respect to all physical phenomena. But all the behavioral manifestations of experiences are (or involve) physical phenomena and so cannot be effects of anything that is inefficacious with respect to physical phenomena. These behavioral manifestations are among the typical effects definitive of any experience, according to the first premise. So nothing can be an experience that is inefficacious with respect to physical phenomena. So nothing can be an experience that is a nonphysical phenomenon of the sort permissible under the second premise. From the two premises it follows that experiences are some physical phenomena or other.

And there is little doubt which physical phenomena they must be. We are far from establishing positively that neural states occupy the definitive causal roles of experiences, but we have no notion of any other physical phenomena that could possibly occupy them, consistent with what we do know. So if nonphysical phenomena are ruled out by our confidence in physical explanation, only neural states are left. If it could be shown that neural states do not occupy the proper causal roles, we would be hard put to save materialism itself.

A version of epiphenomenalism might seem to evade my argument: let experiences be nonphysical epiphenomena, precisely correlated according to a causal law with some simultaneous physical states which are themselves physically (if at all) explicable. The correlation law (it is claimed) renders the experiences and their physical correlates causally equivalent. So the nonphysical experiences have their definitive physical effects after all—although they are not needed to explain those effects, so there is no violation of my second premise (since the nonphysical experiences redundantly redetermine the effects of their physical correlates). I answer thus: at best, this position yields nonphysical experiences alongside the physical experiences, duplicating them, which is not what its advocates intend. Moreover, it is false that such a physical state and its epiphenomenal correlate are causally equivalent. The position exploits a flaw in the standard regularity theory of cause. We know on other grounds that the theory must be corrected to discriminate between genuine causes and the spurious causes which are their epiphenomenal correlates. (The "power on" light does not cause the motor to go, even if it is a lawfully perfect correlate of the electric current that really causes the motor to go.) Given a satisfactory correction, the nonphysical correlate will be evicted from its spurious causal role and thereby lose its status as the experience. So this epiphenomenalism is not a counterexample.

The dualism of the common man holds that experiences are nonphysical phenomena which are the causes of a familiar syndrome of physical as well as nonphysical effects. This dualism is a worthy opponent, daring to face empirical refutation, and in due time it will be rendered incredible by the continuing advance of physicalistic explanation. I have been concerned to prevent dualism from finding a safe fall-back position in the doctrine that experiences are nonphysical and physically inefficacious. It is true that such phenomena can never be refuted by any amount of scientific theory and evidence. The trouble with them is rather that they cannot be what we call experiences. They can only be the nonphysical epiphenomena or correlates of physical states which are experiences. If they are not the experiences themselves, they cannot rescue dualism when it is hard-pressed. And if they cannot do that, nobody has any motive for believing in them. Such things may be—but they are of no consequence.

· E I G H T ·

Radical Interpretation

Imagine that we have undertaken the task of coming to know Karl as a person. We would like to know what he believes, what he desires, what he means, and anything else about him that can be explained in terms of these things. We seek a two-fold interpretation: of Karl's language, and of Karl himself. And we want to know his beliefs and desires in two different ways. We want to know their content as Karl could express it in his own language, and also as we could express it in our language. (For instance, we want to know whether 'owsnay isyay itewhay' is a sentence that Karl could use to express something or other that he believes; and also whether Karl believes that, as we would put it, snow is white. Of course, Karl's language just might turn out to be the same as ours—that is part of what we want to find out—but the two questions are independent even so.)

Imagine also that we must start from scratch. At the outset we know nothing about Karl's beliefs, desires, and meanings. Whatever we may know about persons in general, our knowledge of Karl in particular is limited to our knowledge of him as a physical system. But at least we have plenty of that knowledge—in fact, we have all that we could possibly use. Now, how can we get from that knowledge to the knowledge we want?

I can diagram the problem of radical interpretation as follows. **Given P, the facts about Karl as a physical system, solve for the rest.**

P, our ultimate data base, gives us the whole truth about Karl as a physical system. It tells us how Karl moves, what forces he exerts on his surroundings, what light or sound or chemical substances he absorbs or emits. It tells us the same

```
┌─────────────────────────────────────┐
│                                      │
│      P   Karl as a physical          │
│          system                      │
│                                      │
└─────────────────────────────────────┘

┌───────────────────────────┐   ┌───────────────────────────┐
│                           │   │                           │
│  Ao   Karl's attitudes:   │   │  Ak   Karl's attitudes:   │
│       beliefs and desires,│   │       beliefs and desires,│
│       as expressed in     │   │       as expressed in     │
│       *our* language      │   │       *Karl's* language   │
│                           │   │                           │
└───────────────────────────┘   └───────────────────────────┘

        ┌───────────────────────────────┐
        │                               │
        │   M   Karl's meanings:        │
        │       truth conditions of     │
        │       his full sentences      │
        │  ............................ │
        │                               │
        │       (and denotations, etc.  │
        │       of constituents of      │
        │       sentences)              │
        │                               │
        └───────────────────────────────┘
```

things about all of Karl's material parts, great or small, permanent or temporary. It tells us all the masses and charges of the particles that compose him, and all the magnitudes and directions of the fields and potentials and radiation that pervade him. It tells us not only his present physical state but also his physical history; and not only the actual particular physical facts but also the nomic or counterfactual or causal dependences among them. It tells us higher order facts, if need be: as that there exist some or other states of Karl, of unspecified character, that realize such-and-such patterns of causal relations to one another and to such-and-such specified physical states. And in case the material parts of Karl interact with any psionic fields, astral bodies, entelechies, or what-not, then **P** must tell us the physics and the physical states of those things as well.

Both **Ao** and **Ak** are to be specifications of Karl's propositional attitudes—in particular, of Karl's system of beliefs and desires. (I limit my attention to these attitudes in the hope that all others will prove to be analyzable as patterns of belief and desire, actual or potential; but if not, then whatever attitudes resist such analysis also should be included in **Ao** and **Ak**.) To specify the propositional content of Karl's beliefs and desires, we may specify how to express the believed or desired proposition, in some language, by a sentence in a context. **Ao** specifies Karl's beliefs and desires as expressed in *our* language; **Ak** specifies them as expressed in *Karl's* language; until we find out what the sentences of Karl's language mean, the two sorts of information are different. We take Karl's beliefs and desires to admit of degree, with the zero and unit of desire fixed arbitrarily. Also we allow them to vary with time. Thus **Ao** and **Ak** will consist of ascriptions of the form:

$Karl \begin{Bmatrix} believes \\ desires \end{Bmatrix}$, *to degree d, at time t, the proposition expressed, in context c, by the*

sentence '———' of $\begin{Bmatrix} our \\ Karl's \end{Bmatrix}$ *language.* Take this, if you wish, as a single relation

between Karl, a degree (*i.e.* a number), a time, a context, and a sentence of our language or Karl's. I would prefer to take the seeming reference to a proposition at face value: Karl is related (to a degree, at a time) to a proposition, and that proposition in turn is related (in a context) to a sentence. For if our interest is in the philosophy of mind and of language, then the pursuit of ontological parsimony seems to me an unnecessary distraction. Propositions may be dispensable or they may not, but at least they seem harmless. True, Quine has rightly warned us against the question-begging myth of the museum;[1] but the myth begs questions not because it countenances propositions or other abstract entities, but rather because it uncritically takes for granted that our mental and semantic relations to these entities are determinate and need no explanation.

M, the third component of our desired interpretation of Karl, is to be a specification, in our language, of the meanings of expressions of Karl's language. Primarily, **M** specifies the truth conditions of full sentences of Karl's language (perhaps relative to contexts of utterance). I leave it open, here, just what a 'truth condition' is; in particular, whether it should specify only the actual truth value of the sentence, or whether it should also specify what the truth value would be in various counterfactual situations not too remote from actuality, or whether it should specify the truth value at all possible worlds whatever. Secondarily, **M** specifies a way of parsing the sentences of Karl's language, the denotation or sense or comprehension or what-not of the constituents from which sentences may be compounded, and the way that the denotation (or whatever) of a compound depends on that of its constituents. In short, it specifies the syntactic and semantic rules of a grammar capable of generating Karl's sentences plus the truth conditions thereof.

It should be obvious by now that my problem of radical interpretation is not any real-life task of finding out about Karl's beliefs, desires, and meanings. I am not really asking how *we* could determine these facts. Rather: how do *the facts* determine these facts? By what constraints, and to what extent, does the totality of physical facts about Karl determine what he believes, desires, and means? To speak of a mighty knower, who uses his knowledge of these constraints to advance from omniscience about the physical facts **P** to omniscience about the other facts determined thereby, is a way of dramatizing our problem—safe enough, so long as we can take it or leave it alone. The real-life knower has all the problems of our fic-

---

[1] W. V. Quine, *Ontological Relativity and Other Essays* (New York: Columbia University Press, 1969), pp. 27–29.

titious knower, and more besides: he does not have all of **P** to draw on, and he may be limited in endurance, intelligence, or memory. (On the other hand, he does not aspire to omniscience about **Ao, Ak**, and **M**.) But these further obstacles to his investigation are irrelevant to our real topic.

If I ask *how* **P** determines all the rest, my question requires the presupposition that **P** *does* determine all the rest. Or, at least, that **P** determines all the rest to the extent that anything does—that where determination by **P** leaves off, there indeterminacy begins. In other words, I am presupposing that there cannot possibly be two Karls exactly alike with respect to **P** but differing somehow with respect to **Ao, Ak**, or **M**. (It does not matter that there might be two equally correct ways to resolve some mental or semantic indeterminacy, so long as *both* ways are available for *both* Karls. The two Karls still do not differ.) This basic presupposition of our enterprise is a sort of minimal materialism. 'Minimal', first, because we have allowed **P** to include the physics of astral bodies or what-not if need be; and second, because even if all the mental and semantic facts about Karl are determined by the physical facts, it does not follow that they can be stated in the langauge of physics. (I think they can be, if the language of physics is taken fairly broadly, but that is another story.)

What are the constraints by which the problem of radical interpretation is to be solved? Roughly speaking, they are the fundamental principles of our general theory of persons. They tell as how beliefs and desires and meanings are normally related to one another, to behavioral output, and to sensory input.

The general theory of persons serves as a schema for particular theories of particular persons. A particular theory of Karl, for instance, may be constructed by ascribing particular beliefs, desires, and meanings to him. That is: by filling in **Ao, Ak**, and **M**. But not just any filling-in will do. The relations of **Ao, Ak**, and **M** to one another and to **P** must conform—for the most part, more or less—to the principles of the general theory. Else the particular theory of Karl is inconsistent. In this way, the general theory provides the constraining power to make radical interpretation possible.

Our general theory of persons, like a term-introducing scientific theory, has a mixed character. On the one hand, it implicitly defines its key theoretical concepts: in particular, the concepts of belief, desire, and meaning. On the other, it uses these concepts to make an empirical claim about human beings—a claim so well confirmed that we take it quite for granted. If we disentangle the definitional content and the empirical content, we have something roughly like this. Definitional content: something may count as a person's system of beliefs, desires, and meanings if and only if it is a system that more or less conforms to the principles of the theory. Empirical content: for any human being (with certain exceptions) there will exist a system of beliefs, desires, and meanings correctly so-called—that is, one that conforms to the principles. That is: almost whatever **P** may be, within the limits of human possibility, the problem of radical interpretation should have a solution.

The concepts of belief, desire, and meaning are common property. The theory that implicitly defines them had better be common property too. It must amount to nothing more than a mass of platitudes of common sense, though these may be reorganized in perspicuous and unfamiliar ways. Esoteric scientific findings that go beyond common sense must be kept out, on pain of changing the subject.

I have said, rather loosely, that the fundamental principles of our common-sense theory of persons implicitly define such concepts as belief, desire, and meaning. Actually, I would like to claim something stronger: that the implicit definitions can be made explicit,[2] and that the explicit definitions so obtained would be analytic. If so, then our constraining principles would themselves have a status akin to analyticity: Karl might have no beliefs, desires, or meanings at all, but it is analytic that if he does have them then they more or less conform to the constraining principles by which the concepts of belief, desire, and meaning are defined. But it would not be appropriate to press this claim here. For the question of whether analyticity is a legitimate notion is part of the broader question of the extent to which semantic facts are determinate, and that question is part of the very problem of radical interpretation that we are right now considering. I do not think I need to claim analyticity; it is enough that the constraining principles should be very firmly built into our common system of belief.

The principles that I would like to put forward as constraints on radical interpretation are the following six. They are not independent, and some may be entirely redundant given the others. On the other hand, I may well have overlooked important ones that should have been listed.

The *Principle of Charity* constrains Ao, or the relation between Ao and P: Karl should be represented as believing what he ought to believe, and desiring what he ought to desire. And what is that? In our opinion, he ought to believe what *we* believe, or perhaps what we would have believed in his place; and he ought to desire what we desire, or perhaps what we would have desired in his place. (But that's only our opinion! Yes. Better we should go by an opinion we *don't* hold?) A crude version of the Principle of Charity might just require that, so far as other constraints allow it, the beliefs and desires ascribed to Karl by Ao should be the same as our own beliefs and desires. "We will try for a theory that finds him consistent, a believer of truths, and a lover of the good (all by our own lights, it goes without saying)" as Davidson puts it.[3] But it would be more charitable to make allowances for the likelihood that Karl's circumstances—his life history of evidence and training, recounted in physical terms in our data base P—may have led him understandably into error. We should at least forbear from ascribing to Karl those of our beliefs and desires which, according to P and our notions of

---

[2] In the way I suggest in "An Argument for the Identity Theory," and "How To Define Theoretical Terms," both in this volume; and in my "Psychophysical and Theoretical Identifications," *Australasian Journal of Philosophy* 50 (1972): 249–58.

[3] Donald Davidson, 'Mental Events,' in *Essays on Actions and Events* (Clarendon Press: Oxford, 1980), pp. 207–25.

reason, he has been given no reason to share. We should even ascribe to him those errors which we think we would have made, or should have made, if our evidence and training had been like his. Perhaps an improved Principle of Charity would require Karl's beliefs and ours to be related as follows: there must exist some common inductive method $\mathcal{M}$ which would lead to approximately our present systems of belief if given our life histories of evidence, and which would likewise lead to approximately the present system of beliefs ascribed to Karl by **Ao** if given Karl's life history of evidence according to **P**. As for desires: there must exist some common underlying system of basic intrinsic values $\mathcal{U}$ which would yield approximately our systems of desires if given our systems of beliefs, and which would likewise yield approximately the system of desires ascribed to Karl by **Ao** if given the system of beliefs ascribed to Karl by **Ao**. Diagrammatically: there must exist $\mathcal{M}$ and $\mathcal{U}$ such that:

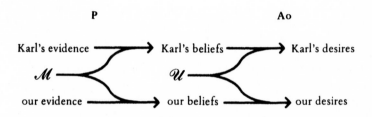

approximately. That 'approximately' is important: our common-sense theory of persons tells us that Karl's beliefs and desires may differ from ours not just because of Karl's different evidence, but also because of the effects of Karl's different training on his underlying inductive method and basic intrinsic values. He may or may not have learned to beware of hasty generalization, or to like raw eel. If our common-sense theory (without benefit of esoteric scientific knowledge) told us just what these effects of training were, we could build them into a still better version of the Principal of Charity. But if not, we must idealize them away, and then not apply the idealized Principle too stringently.

The *Rationalization Principle* constrains the relation between **Ao** and **P**: Karl should be represented as a rational agent; the beliefs and desires ascribed to him by **Ao** should be such as to provide good reasons for his behavior, as given in physical terms by **P**. Thus if it is in **P** that Karl's arm goes up at a certain time, **Ao** should ascribe beliefs and desires according to which it is a good thing for his arm to go up then. I would hope to spell this out in decision-theoretic terms, as follows. Take a suitable set of mutually exclusive and jointly exhaustive propositions about Karl's behavior at any given time; of these alternatives, the one that comes true according to **P** should be the one (or: one of the ones) with maximum expected utility according to the total system of beliefs and desires ascribed to Karl at that time by **Ao**. A precondition: those ascribed beliefs and desires should be coherent enough to permit the comparison of expected utilities of alternative ways of behaving.[4]

Would such use of the machinery of decision theory go against my requirement that the constraining principles should come from our common-sense theory of persons, not from esoteric science? I think not. Decision theory (at least, if we omit the frills) is not esoteric science, however unfamiliar it may seem to an outsider. Rather, it is a systematic exposition of the consequences of certain well-chosen platitudes about belief, desire, preference, and choice. It is the very core of our common-sense theory of persons, dissected out and elegantly systematized. The same goes for my previous mention of underlying inductive methods and systems of basic intrinsic values: to the extent that unfamiliar theories are involved, they are not scientific theories but philosophical systematizations of parts of the common-sense theory of persons. The machinery derived from such systematizations is common property, whether or not the accompanying jargon is.

There is an ambiguity in the term 'behavior'. Note that I am using it to refer to raw behavior—body movements and the like—given by **P** alone; not to refer to behavior specified partly in terms of the agent's intentions. The latter is given jointly by **P** and **Ao**. That Karl's fingers move on certain trajectories and exert certain forces is what I call 'behavior'; that he signs a check is not. If anyone prefers, however, we could restate the Rationalization Principle in terms of the second sense of 'behavior': the beliefs and desires ascribed to Karl by **Ao** should be such as to provide good reasons—preferably, decision-theoretic explanations—for his nonraw behavior as given jointly by **P** and **Ao**.[5]

The Principle of Truthfulness constrains the relation between **Ao** and **M**: Some of the beliefs and desires ascribed to Karl by **Ao**—in particular, some of those that pertain to speech behavior or responses to it on the part of Karl and his usual partners in conversation—should constitute Karl's part of the pattern of attitudes that I have elsewhere[6] called a convention of truthfulness in Karl's language, under the truth conditions assigned by **M** to sentences thereof. For instance, if **M** assigns to 'Ionlay!' the truth condition that a lion is present, then some of the beliefs and desires ascribed to Karl by **Ao** should be as follows: (1) a desire not to utter 'Ionlay!' unless a lion is present; (2) a belief that his partners have a like desire; (3) a belief that a lion is present, at times when he hears 'Ionlay!' uttered; (4) a belief that his partners respond in the same way to utterances of 'Ionlay!'; (5) a belief that his partners expect him to have the beliefs and desires (1)—(4), or at least that

---

[4]See, for instance, the exposition of decision theory in Richard Jeffrey, *The Logic of Decision* (New York: McGraw-Hill, 1965); or the less formal account of rationalization of behavior in Donald Davidson, "Actions, Reasons, and Causes," in *Essays on Actions and Events* (Clarendon Press: Oxford, 1980), pp. 3–21.

[5]This second version would fit better the account of rationalization in Donald Davidson, "Actions, Reasons, and Causes."

[6]David Lewis, *Convention: A Philosophical Study* (Cambridge, Mass.: Harvard University Press, 1969) and "Languages and Language"in this volume.

they have no contrary expectations about him; (6) a belief that they expect him also to have the belief (5), or at least that they have no contrary expectations; and so on.[7]

The Principle of Generativity constrains **M**: **M** should assign truth conditions to the sentences of Karl's language in a way that is at least finitely specifiable, and preferably also reasonably uniform and simple. Perhaps we may add that it should do so by means of syntactic and semantic rules that fit some standardized format: the format of a Tarski-style truth theory, as proposed by Davidson;[8] or a categorically based transformational grammar with intensional semantic functions, as I have proposed;[9] or the sort of semantically based grammar proposed by some transformational grammarians, with some sort of specification of truth conditions for the base structures.

The Manifestation Principle constrains the relation between **P** and **Ak**, and to a slight extent also **Ao**: Karl's beliefs, as expressed in his own language, should normally be manifest in his dispositions to speech behavior. The sentences (in context) that he could be made to utter should normally be among those that express propositions that he believes to a high degree. So unless **Ao** ascribes to Karl some special reason for deception or secrecy, it should be possible to read off the beliefs in **Ak** from the dispositions-to-utter given in **P**. (I do not see quite how to state a companion Manifestation Principle for the desires in **Ak**, but I rather think that there should be one.)

The Triangle Principle constrains the three-way relation between **Ao**, **M**, and **Ak**: Karl's beliefs and desires should be the same whether expressed in his language or in ours. Suppose that **M** assigns a certain truth condition to a sentence s (in context c) in Karl's language, and suppose that a sentence s' (in context c') of our language has the same truth condition. Then if **M** is correct (and assigns truth conditions of a sufficiently rich sort), we ought to be entitled to regard s (in c) and s' (in c') as expressing the same propositions in their respective languages. If so, the status of s (in c) in **Ak** should be the same as that of s' (in c'), in **Ao**: if **Ak** ascribes to Karl a certain degree of belief in the proposition expressed by s (in c), then **Ao** should ascribe to him the same degree of belief in the proposition expressed by s' (in c'), and likewise for Karl's degrees of desire.

How might we use these six constraining principles to solve the problem of radical interpretation? (I still mean the unreal problem of advancing from omniscience about **P** alone to omniscience also about **Ao**, **Ak**, and **M**.) I should like to contrast three rather different methods.

Method 1 is meant to borrow as much as possible from discussions of radical

---

[7]Rather similar constraints on the relations between Karl's attitudes and his meanings could be taken from the discussions of meaning in H. P. Grice, "Meaning," *Philosophical Review* 66 (1957): 377–88; Stephen Schiffer, *Meaning* (Oxford: Oxford University Press, 1972); or Erik Stenius, "Mood and Language-Game," *Synthese* 17 (1967): 254–74.

[8]In Donald Davidson, "Truth and Meaning," *Synthese* 17 (1967): 304–33, and elsewhere.

[9]In "General Semantics" in this volume.

interpretation by Davidson.[10] Davidson's problem of radical interpretation is not the same as mine, but can be treated as a sub-problem of mine. Given Karl's beliefs as expressed in his own language (part of **Ak**), Davidson asks how to solve both for Karl's beliefs as expressed in our language (part of **Ao**) and for the truth conditions of full sentences of Karl's language (part of **M**). As a by-product we may also get parsings of Karl's sentences and some sort of meanings for their constituents (the rest of **M**), since these are needed to play an auxiliary role in generating the truth conditions of the full sentences. Davidson's suggested method of attacking this sub-problem (which he regards as only a sketch of the main features of a fully adequate method) is to fill in the beliefs in **Ao** and the truth conditions (and auxiliary machinery) in **M** simultaneously, subject to three constraints: the Triangle Principle, and the Principles of Charity and Generativity. We must strike a balance as best we can between the demands of Charity on **Ao** and the demands of Generativity on **M**; it is not to be expected that we can satisfy both constraints perfectly.

To incorporate Davidson's method of solving the sub-problem into a method for solving my problem of radical interpretation, we must first use the Manifestation Principle to fill in the beliefs in **Ak**. But for that we need some input from **Ao**: so we must proceed by successive approximations. Method 1 goes as follows.

First step: fill in **Ao**, tentatively, by means of the Principle of Charity. We may or may not draw on **P** at this point; it depends on which version of the Principle of Charity we use.

Second step: using the tentative filling-in of **Ao** to exclude the cases in which Karl seems to have reason for deception or secrecy, and using Karl's dispositions to speech behavior as given in **P**, fill in the beliefs in **Ak** by means of the Manifestation Principle. This brings us up to the beginning of Davidson's sub-problem.

Third step: simultaneously revise the beliefs in **Ao** and fill in **M**, in such a way that the Triangle Principle is satisfied and a satisfactory balance is struck between the demands of the Principle of Charity on the beliefs in **Ao** and the demands of the Principle of Generativity on **M**.

Fourth step: using Karl's behavior of all sorts, as given in **P**, and using the revised beliefs in **Ao**, revise the desires in **Ao** by means of the Rationalization Principle. Then fill in the desires in **Ak** by means of the Triangle Principle. This gives a complete, but tentative, solution.

Fifth step: see whether the subsequent revision of **Ao** would have made any difference to the outcome of the second step. If so, start over at the second step using the revised **Ao**; if not, a stable solution has been reached. If the outcome at the second step is not too sensitive to the details of **Ao**, and if the revision of **Ao** at the third and fourth steps is not too great, then we may hope for a stable solution after not too many rounds of iteration.

---

[10]In Donald Davidson, "Mental Events," in *Essays on Actions and Events*, pp. 207–25; *idem*, the Locke Lectures, given at Oxford University, 1970; *idem*, "Conceptual Relativism," two lectures given at the University of London, 1971.

I doubt the adequacy of Method 1; mostly because it wastes the constraining power of the Principle of Truthfulness, but also because it fails to constrain the ascribed beliefs in Ao, as well as the desires, by means of the Rationalization Principle. Too much emphasis goes to language as a vehicle for manifestation of belief and belief as manifest in langauge; not enough either to language as a social practice or to belief as manifest in non-linguistic behavior. It may well be that my full problem of radical interpretation (for Karl, or in general) does have a fairly determinate solution by virtue of the constraints that are left out of Method 1, and yet that Davidson's sub-problem—the problem that has to be solved as the third step of Method 1—is severely indeterminate if taken by itself.

Method 2, the method I am inclined to favor, is almost opposite to Method 1 in its plan of attack. The idea is to start by securing Ao, go on to M, and fill in Ak only at the end. If we proceed in that order, Davidson's sub-problem never arises. Two other sub-problems arise instead: the problem of determining Karl's attitudes (as expressed in our language) on the basis of certain of the physical facts about him, and then the problem of determining his meanings on the basis of certain of these attitudes. I hope that these are sub-problems that can safely be taken by themselves, without loss of determinacy. Method 2 goes as follows.

First step: using P both as a source of information on Karl's behavior and as a source of information on his life history of evidence, fill in Ao completely by means of the Rationalization Principle and the Principle of Charity. No special attention is given to Karl's language at this step; his speech behavior is merely included along with all the rest of his behavior to be rationalized.

Second step: using Ao to give information about those of Karl's attitudes that pertain to speech behavior, fill in M in such a way that, first, the relation of these attitudes to the truth conditions of the full sentences conforms to the Principle of Truthfulness; and second, the demands of the Principle of Generativity on the truth conditions and auxiliary apparatus of M are satisfied as well as they can be.

Third step: given Ao and M, fill in Ak by means of the Triangle Principle. (The Manifestation Principle should then be satisfied automatically; it is redundant, given the Principle of Truthfulness, the Rationalization Principle as applied to speech behavior, and the Triangle Principle.) This completes the solution.

Method 3, finally, is the obvious holistic non-method: try to fill in Ao, Ak, and M all at once, satisfying all six of our constraining principles or balancing them off as best we can. That is the method we would have to fall back on if we decided that no sub-problem could be separated out without loss of some determinacy, and hence gave up hope of solving the full problem step by step. That would be no great defeat. Our fictitious mighty knower will not mind trying all possible complete solutions to find out which are the ones that fit the constraints! After all, we are not really interested in a practical method of finding out anything; we are interested in the determination of the mental and semantic facts by the physical facts via the constraining principles. Plans of attack and the determinacy of various sub-problems are side issues.

The things that matter are: (1) what the problem of radical interpretation **is**; (2) the set of constraints by which it is solved, and the source of their constraining power; (3) the presupposition that the physical facts determine the mental and semantic facts, somehow, to the extent that anything does; and (4) the extent of the determinacy.

As regards the extent of determinacy, all that I have said so far is meant to be neutral between optimism and pessimism. I have only tried to say what a solution to the problem of radical interpretation is—namely, a filling-in of **Ao**, **Ak**, and **M**—and what constraints it must satisfy to be correct. That leaves it open whether there is one correct solution or many; and, if many, how different two correct solutions can be.

Indeterminacy might come in more or less virulent forms. It is worth distinguishing, for the worst sort is also the least credible—by my lights, always far less credible than the hypothesis that we have misconceived the whole problem!

It seems hopeless to deny, in the face of such examples as have been offered by Quine,[11] that the truth conditions of full sentences in **M** do not suffice to determine the rest of **M**: the parsings and the meanings of the constituents of sentences. At least, that is so unless there is something more than our Principle of Generativity to constrain this auxiliary syntactic and semantic apparatus.

It also seems hard to deny that a more general indeterminacy can arise because no solution fits all the constraints perfectly, and many different ways to strike a balance give many different compromise solutions. The 'unsharp analyticity' of some so-called definitions in physics, or the confused desires of a compulsive thief, might exemplify this indeterminacy of compromise.

Grant these two sorts of indeterminacy, and set them aside. Could indeterminacy of beliefs, desires, and truth conditions also arise because two different solutions both fit all the constraints perfectly? Here is the place to hold the line. This sort of indeterminacy has not been shown by convincing examples, and neither could it be shown—to me—by proof. *Credo:* if ever you prove to me that all the constraints we have yet found could permit two perfect solutions, differing otherwise than in the auxiliary apparatus of **M**, then you will have proved that we have not yet found all the constraints.

---

[11]In *Ontological Relativity and Other Essays* (New York: Columbia University Press, 1969).

Postscripts to

"Radical Interpretation"

A. KARL AND OTHERS OF HIS KIND

I stated my problem in an unduly individualistic way: given the facts *about Karl* as a physical system, solve for the facts *about him* as a person—*his* beliefs, desires, and meanings. If Karl were a unique being, this would be the right question to ask. If not—if he is, for instance, human—it is not. In "Mad Pain and Martian Plain" (in this volume), I argued that a "madman" might be in pain not because his state occupied the causal role of pain in him but rather because that state occupies that role, for the most part, in members of the kind to which he belongs. The same possibility should be recognized for attitudes as well. Karl might believe himself a fool, and might desire fame, even though the best interpretation of Karl considered in isolation might not assign those attitudes to him. For the best interpretation of Karl's kind generally might be one that interprets two states respectively as belief that one is a fool and as desire for fame, and Karl might be in those two states.

Compare a less controversial case. We have a certain kind of mass-produced calculator: the Texas Instruments 58C, let us say. A certain hardware state S of the 58C is the state of having the number 6099241494 stored in register 17. The state S is to be thus interpreted because of its causal role in the functional organization of the 58C. Now suppose that one 58C comes out defective. It still *is* a 58C, and the defect is not such as to prevent it from ever being in state S; but the defect does mean that the role of S in this calculator differs from the normal role of S in the 58C. Considering the defective calculator in isolation, there is no reason to interpret S as the state of having 6099241494 in register 17. But that is how we interpret S for the 58C generally, so that is what S is for any 58C—even the defective one. We would say, and rightly so, that when the defective 58C is in state S, then it does have 6099241494 in register 17.

An interpretation just of Karl at the present moment need only specify his attitudes and his meanings. But an interpretation of Karl's kind generally—or even of Karl himself as he is at various times, or as he might have been under various different circumstances—must be something more complicated. It must be a scheme of interpretation specifying the attitudes and meanings as a function of the momentary total physical state. On the basis of such states, the scheme assigns interpretations to individuals at times. (Indeed it might—and should, I think—do this simply by identifying certain attitudes with certain (partial) physical states.)

The best scheme is the one that does the best job overall of conforming to the constraining principles, taking one individual and time with another. (The individuals in question being not only Karl and others of his kind as they actually are, but also some of their might-have-been counterparts.) The best interpretation for Karl is the one assigned to him by the scheme of interpretation that does best overall, even if it does not do so well in his exceptional case. And the best scheme is *ipso facto* correct: to believe that one is a fool, or to desire fame, is to be such that the best scheme for your kind assigns these attitudes to you.

(What if there is no unique best scheme? Suppose there are several that beat the rest, these are tied or incomparable, and they yield conflicting assignments of attitudes and meanings. Then to the extent that there is conflict, Karl's attitudes and meanings are indeterminate. And what if it is not clear which of all the broader and narrower kinds Karl belongs to should be taken as "his kind" in determining the best scheme of interpretation for his kind?[1] As I noted in "Mad Pain and Martian Pain," we cannot rely on our criteria of selection to settle hard cases unequivocally. If they do not, and if different choices favor schemes that assign conflicting attitudes and meanings to Karl, we have here a further source of indeterminacy. Given indeterminacy, there are two natural senses in which we may nevertheless speak of Karl's attitudes and meanings. (1) We may take only what is agreed upon between the conflicting eligible schemes. Or, more daringly, (2) we may take him to have all the attitudes and meanings assigned by all the conflicting eligible schemes. The problem resembles that of truth in inconsistent fiction, discussed in Postscript B to "Truth in Fiction" (in this volume), and the alternative proposed solutions to the problems are parallel.

Any broadly functionalist theory of mind is under intuitive pressure from two directions. On the one hand, it seems wrong to make it invariable or necessary that the mental states occupy their definitive causal roles. Couldn't there be occasional exceptions, comparable to the case of the defective calculator? On the other hand, the mental states of Karl seem intrinsic to him. Why should whether he now feels pain—or believes himself to be a fool, or desires fame—depend on what causes what in the case of someone else? I do not see any acceptable way to respect both intuitions in their full strength. Individualistic functionalism respects the second at the expense of the first. I have tried to strike a more credible compromise, one that grants some of the force of each. The first intuition is respected to this extent: indeed it is possible that there be exceptional cases in which a mental state fails entirely to occupy its definitive role. However, such cases must be exceptional, such failures cannot be too common. The second intuition is respected to this extent:

---

[1] It might indeed turn out that humans have such vast differences in hardware from one to the next (unlike 58C calculators) that the salient kind does after all contain only Karl and some of his counterparts. If so, the correction I have been advocating will turn out to make little difference. Still, I do not think we should adopt an individualistic approach to interpretation on principle, even if we should be prepared to have it forced on us by the facts of individual difference.

one's mental states are intrinsic states that one is in. However, what makes one's states be the mental states they are—what makes them occupy the role they do—is not entirely intrinsic. To a limited extent it concerns others of one's kind. But that extent *is* limited since, necessarily, most cases are not exceptional.

B. THE SYSTEMS OF ATTITUDES

In view of my arguments in "Attitudes *De Dicto* and *De Se*" (in this volume), of course I must withdraw my statement that Ao and Ak are to be specifications of Karl's *propositional* attitudes. His egocentric, irreducibly *de se* attitudes should not be left out, although these are not (in my sense of the word) propositional. But even these might be expressed, in context, by sentences of our language, or of Karl's:[2] we must use first-person sentences, and we must regard these as expressing properties rather than propositions. Thus Karl may believe (to a certain degree, at a certain time) that he is a fool; this belief is expressed in our language by "I am a fool", but only if this is regarded as expressing the property of being a fool rather than the proposition that Karl is a fool. (What if Karl thinks that he himself is a fool and Karl isn't, from which he concludes that he must not be Karl?) There is of course a good sense in which a first-person sentence does express a proposition, but this sort of expression is beside the point for our present purposes.

The ascriptions of belief that comprise Ao will not much resemble the belief sentences of ordinary language. (Likewise *mutatis mutandis* for the ascriptions of desire.) For our object is to specify belief in a narrowly psychological sense: the belief that governs behavior, the belief that is "in the head", determined by brain states and their causal roles. But our ordinary belief sentences often are not narrowly psychological. Take the case of puzzling Pierre.[3] He believes that the city he has heard of under the name of *Londres* is pretty—this much is narrow psychology and belongs in Ao. The city he has heard of under that name is London—that is not a psychological matter at all. Thanks to this mixed situation, only partly psychological, an ordinary belief sentence is true: Pierre believes that London is pretty. This is *not* an ascription that belongs in Ao. If Pierre had been just the same psychologically, but otherwise situated, the city he had heard of as *Londres* might have been Bristol. Then he would have believed that Bristol, not London, was pretty. But the beliefs assigned to him in our interpretation should have been just the same.

---

[2]Here I am simplifying matters by assuming what may well be false: that the languages have resources adequate to describe the complex shapes, tunes, etc. that may figure in Karl's attitudes.

[3]Discussed in Saul Kripke, "A Puzzle about Belief," in Avishai Margalit, ed., *Meaning and Use* (Dordrecht: Reidel, 1979); and in my "What Puzzling Pierre Does Not Believe," *Australasian Journal of Philosophy* 59 (1981): 283–89.

· NINE ·

Mad Pain
and
Martian Pain

I

There might be a strange man who sometimes feels pain, just as we do, but whose pain differs greatly from ours in its causes and effects. Our pain is typically caused by cuts, burns, pressure, and the like; his is caused by moderate exercise on an empty stomach. Our pain is generally distracting; his turns his mind to mathematics, facilitating concentration on that but distracting him from anything else. Intense pain has no tendency whatever to cause him to groan or writhe, but does cause him to cross his legs and snap his fingers. He is not in the least motivated to prevent pain or to get rid of it. In short, he feels pain but his pain does not at all occupy the typical causal role of pain. He would doubtless seem to us to be some sort of madman, and that is what I shall call him, though of course the sort of madness I have imagined may bear little resemblance to the real thing.

I said there might be such a madman. I don't know how to prove that something is possible, but my opinion that this is a possible case seems pretty firm. If I want a credible theory of mind, I need a theory that does not deny the possibility of mad pain. I needn't mind conceding that perhaps the madman is not in pain in *quite* the same sense that the rest of us are, but there had better be some straightforward sense in which he and we are both in pain.

This paper was presented at a conference on mind-body identity held at Rice University in April 1978. I am grateful to many friends, and especially to Patricia Kitcher, for valuable discussions of the topic.

Also, there might be a Martian who sometimes feels pain, just as we do, but whose pain differs greatly from ours in its physical realization. His hydraulic mind contains nothing like our neurons. Rather, there are varying amounts of fluid in many inflatable cavities, and the inflation of any one of these cavities opens some valves and closes others. His mental plumbing pervades most of his body—in fact, all but the heat exchanger inside his head. When you pinch his skin you cause no firing of C-fibers—he has none—but, rather, you cause the inflation of many smallish cavities in his feet. When these cavities are inflated, he is in pain. And the effects of his pain are fitting: his thought and activity are disrupted, he groans and writhes, he is strongly motivated to stop you from pinching him and to see to it that you never do again. In short, he feels pain but lacks the bodily states that either are pain or else accompany it in us.

There might be such a Martian; this opinion too seems pretty firm. A credible theory of mind had better not deny the possibility of Martian pain. I needn't mind conceding that perhaps the Martian is not in pain in *quite* the same sense that we Earthlings are, but there had better be some straightforward sense in which he and we are both in pain.

II

A credible theory of mind needs to make a place both for mad pain and for Martian pain. Prima facie, it seems hard for a materialist theory to pass this two-fold test. As philosophers, we would like to characterize pain a priori. (We might settle for less, but let's start by asking for all we want.) As materialists, we want to characterize pain as a physical phenomenon. We can speak of the place of pain in the causal network from stimuli to inner states to behavior. And we can speak of the physical processes that go on when there is pain and that take their place in that causal network. We seem to have no other resources but these. But the lesson of mad pain is that pain is associated only contingently with its causal role, while the lesson of Martian pain is that pain is connected only contingently with its physical realization. How can we characterize pain a priori in terms of causal role and physical realization, and yet respect both kinds of contingency?

A simple identity theory straightforwardly solves the problem of mad pain. It goes just as straightforwardly wrong about Martian pain. A simple behaviorism or functionalism goes the other way: right about the Martian, wrong about the madman. The theories that fail our twofold test so decisively are altogether too simple. (Perhaps they are too simple ever to have had adherents.) It seems that a theory that can pass our test will have to be a mixed theory. It will have to be able to tell us that the madman and the Martian are both in pain, but for different reasons: the madman because he is in the right physical state, the Martian because he is in a state rightly situated in the causal network.

Certainly we can cook up a mixed theory. Here's an easy recipe: First, find a theory to take care of the common man and the madman, disregarding the Martian—presumably an identity theory. Second, find a theory to take care of the common man and the Martian, disregarding the madman—presumably some sort of behaviorism or functionalism. Then disjoin the two: say that to be in pain is to be in pain either according to the first theory or according to the second. Alternatively, claim ambiguity: say that to be in pain in one sense is to be in pain according to the first theory, to be in pain in another sense is to be in pain according to the second theory.

This strategy seems desperate. One wonders why we should have a disjunctive or ambiguous concept of pain, if common men who suffer pain are always in pain according to both disjuncts or both disambiguations. It detracts from the credibility of a theory that it posits a useless complexity in our concept of pain—useless in application to the common man, at least, and therefore useless almost always.

I don't object to the strategy of claiming ambiguity. As you'll see, I shall defend a version of it. But it's not plausible to cook up an ambiguity ad hoc to account for the compossibility of mad pain and Martian pain. It would be better to find a widespread sort of ambiguity, a sort we would believe in no matter what we thought about pain, and show that it will solve our problem. That is my plan.

III

A dozen years or so ago, D. M. Armstrong and I (independently) proposed a materialist theory of mind that joins claims of type-type psychophysical identity with a behaviorist or functionalist way of characterizing mental states such as pain.[1] I believe our theory passes the twofold test. Positing no ambiguity without independent reason, it provides natural senses in which both madman and Martian are in pain. It wriggles through between Scylla and Charybdis.

Our view is that the concept of pain, or indeed of any other experience or mental state, is the concept of a state that occupies a certain causal role, a state with certain typical causes and effects. It is the concept of a state apt for being caused by certain stimuli and apt for causing certain behavior. Or, better, of a state apt for being caused in certain ways by stimuli plus other mental states and apt for combining with certain other mental states to jointly cause certain behavior. It is the concept of a member of a system of states that together more or less realize the pattern of causal generalizations set forth in commonsense psychology. (That system may be

---

[1] D. M. Armstrong, *A Materialist Theory of the Mind* (London: Routledge, 1968); "The Nature of Mind," in C. V. Borst, ed., *The Mind/Brain Identity Theory* (London: Macmillan, 1970), pp. 67–97; "The Causal Theory of the Mind," *Neue Heft für Philosophie*, no. 11 (Vendenhoek & Ruprecht, 1977), pp. 82–95. David Lewis, "An Argument for the Identity Theory," in this volume; review of *Art, Mind, and Religion, Journal of Philosophy* 66 (1969): 22–27, particularly pp. 23–25; "Psychophysical and Theoretical Identifications," *Australasian Journal of Philosophy* 50 (1972): 249–58; "Radical Interpretation," in this volume.

characterized as a whole and its members characterized afterward by reference to their place in it.)

If the concept of pain is the concept of a state that occupies a certain causal role, then whatever state does occupy that role is pain. If the state of having neurons hooked up in a certain way and firing in a certain pattern is the state properly apt for causing and being caused, as we materialists think, then that neural state is pain. But the concept of pain is not the concept of that neural state. ("The concept of . . ." is an intensional functor.) The concept of pain, unlike the concept of that neural state which in fact is pain, would have applied to some different state if the relevant causal relations had been different. Pain might have not been pain. The occupant of the role might have not occupied it. Some other state might have occupied it instead. Something that is not pain might have been pain.

This is not to say, of course, that it might have been that pain was not pain and nonpain was pain; that is, that it might have been that the occupant of the role did not occupy it and some nonoccupant did. Compare: "The winner might have lost" (true) versus "It might have been that the winner lost" (false). No wording is entirely unambiguous, but I trust my meaning is clear.

In short, the concept of pain as Armstrong and I understand it is a *nonrigid* concept. Likewise the word "pain" is a nonrigid designator. It is a contingent matter what state the concept and the word apply to. It depends on what causes what. The same goes for the rest of our concepts and ordinary names of mental states.

Some need hear no more. The notion that mental concepts and names are nonrigid, wherefore what *is* pain might not have been, seems to them just self-evidently false.[2] I cannot tell why they think so. Bracketing my own theoretical commitments, I think I would have no opinion one way or the other. It's not that I don't care about shaping theory to respect naive opinion as well as can be, but in this case I have no naive opinion to respect. If I am not speaking to your condition, so be it.

If pain is identical to a certain neural state, the identity is contingent. Whether it holds is one of the things that varies from one possible world to another. But take care. I do not say that here we have two states, pain and some neural state, that are contingently identical, identical at this world but different at another. Since I'm serious about the identity, we have not two states but one. This one state, this neural state which is pain, is not contingently identical to itself. It does not differ from itself at any world. Nothing does.[3] What's true is, rather, that the concept and name of pain contingently apply to some neural state at this world, but do not

---

[2] For instance, see Saul A. Kripke, "Naming and Necessity," in Gilbert Harman and Donald Davidson, eds., *Semantics of Natural Language* (Dordrecht: Reidel, 1972), pp. 253–355, 763–69, particularly pp. 335–36. Note that the sort of identity theory that Kripke opposes by argument, rather than by appeal to self-evidence, is not the sort that Armstrong and I propose.

[3] The closest we can come is to have something at one world with twin counterparts at another. See my "Counterpart Theory and Quantified Modal Logic," in this volume. That possibility is irrelevant to the present case.

apply to it at another. Similarly, it is a contingent truth that Bruce is our cat, but it's wrong to say that Bruce and our cat are contingently identical. Our cat Bruce is necessarily self-identical. What is contingent is that the nonrigid concept of being our cat applies to Bruce rather than to some other cat, or none.

IV

Nonrigidity might begin at home. All actualities are possibilities, so the variety of possibilities includes the variety of actualities. Though some possibilities are thoroughly otherworldly, others may be found on planets within range of our telescopes. One such planet is Mars.

If a nonrigid concept or name applies to different states in different possible cases, it should be no surprise if it also applies to different states in different actual cases. Nonrigidity is to logical space as other relativities are to ordinary space. If the word "pain" designates one state at our actual world and another at a possible world where our counterparts have a different internal structure, then also it may designate one state on Earth and another on Mars. Or, better, since Martians may come here and we may go to Mars, it may designate one state for Earthlings and another for Martians.

We may say that some state *occupies a causal role for a population*. We may say this whether the population is situated entirely at our actual world, or partly at our actual world and partly at other worlds, or entirely at other worlds. If the concept of pain is the concept of a state that occupies that role, then we may say that a state *is pain for a population*. Then we may say that a certain pattern of firing of neurons is pain for the population of actual Earthlings and some but not all of our otherworldly counterparts, whereas the inflation of certain cavities in the feet is pain for the population of actual Martians and some of their otherworldly counterparts. Human pain is the state that occupies the role of pain for humans. Martian pain is the state that occupies the same role for Martians.

A state occupies a causal role for a population, and the concept of occupant of that role applies to it, if and only if, with few exceptions, whenever a member of that population is in that state, his being in that state has the sort of causes and effects given by the role.

The thing to say about Martian pain is that the Martian is in pain because he is in a state that occupies the causal role of pain for Martians, whereas we are in pain because we are in a state that occupies the role of pain for us.

V

Now, what of the madman? He is in pain, but he is not in a state that occupies the causal role of pain for him. He is in a state that occupies that role for most of

us, but he is an exception. The causal role of a pattern of firing of neurons depends on one's circuit diagram, and he is hooked up wrong.

His state does not occupy the role of pain for a population comprising himself and his fellow madmen. But it does occupy that role for a more salient population—mankind at large. He is a man, albeit an exceptional one, and a member of that larger population.

We have allowed for exceptions. I spoke of the definitive syndrome of *typical* causes and effects. Armstrong spoke of a state *apt for* having certain causes and effects; that does not mean that it has them invariably. Again, I spoke of a system of states that *comes near* to realizing commonsense psychology. A state may therefore occupy a role for mankind even if it does not at all occupy that role for some mad minority of mankind.

The thing to say about mad pain is that the madman is in pain because he is in the state that occupies the causal role of pain for the population comprising all mankind. He is an exceptional member of that population. The state that occupies the role for the population does not occupy it for him.

VI

We may say that X is in pain simpliciter if and only if X is in the state that occupies the causal role of pain for the *appropriate* population. But what is the appropriate population? Perhaps (1) it should be *us*; after all, it's our concept and our word. On the other hand, if it's X we're talking about, perhaps (2) it should be a population that X himself belongs to, and (3) it should preferably be one in which X is not exceptional. Either way, (4) an appropriate population should be a natural kind—a species, perhaps.

If X is you or I—human and unexceptional—all four considerations pull together. The appropriate population consists of mankind as it actually is, extending into other worlds only to an extent that does not make the actual majority exceptional.

Since the four criteria agree in the case of the common man, which is the case we usually have in mind, there is no reason why we should have made up our minds about their relative importance in cases of conflict. It should be no surpr[ise] if ambiguity and uncertainty arise in such cases. Still, some cases do seem reasonably clear.

If X is our Martian, we are inclined to say that he is in pain when the cav[ities] in his feet are inflated; and so says the theory, provided that criterion (1) is weighed by the other three, so that the appropriate population is taken to [be the] species of Martians to which X belongs.

If X is our madman, we are inclined to say that he is in pain when he i[s in the] state that occupies the role of pain for the rest of us; and so says the the[ory pro]vided that criterion (3) is outweighed by the other three, so that the ap[propriate] population is taken to be mankind.

We might also consider the case of a mad Martian, related to other Martians as the madman is to the rest of us. If X is a mad Martian, I would be inclined to say that he in pain when the cavities in his feet are inflated; and so says our theory provided that criteria (2) and (4) together outweigh either (1) or (3) by itself.

Other cases are less clear-cut. Since the balance is less definitely in favor of one population or another, we may perceive the relativity to population by feeling genuinely undecided. Suppose the state that plays the role of pain for us plays instead the role of thirst for a certain small subpopulation of mankind, and vice versa. When one of them has the state that is pain for us and thirst for him, there may be genuine and irresolvable indecision about whether to call him pained or thirsty—that is, whether to think of him as a madman or as a Martian. Criterion (1) suggests calling his state pain and regarding him as an exception; criteria (2) and (3) suggest shifting to a subpopulation and calling his state thirst. Criterion (4) could go either way, since mankind and the exceptional subpopulation may both be natural kinds. (Perhaps it is relevant to ask whether membership in the subpopulation is hereditary.)

The interchange of pain and thirst parallels the traditional problem of inverted spectra. I have suggested that there is no determinate fact of the matter about whether the victim of interchange undergoes pain or thirst. I think this conclusion accords well with the fact that there seems to be no persuasive solution one way or the other to the old problem of inverted spectra. I would say that there is a good sense in which the alleged victim of inverted spectra sees red when he looks at grass: he is in a state that occupies the role of seeing red for mankind in general. And there is an equally good sense in which he sees green: he is in a state that occupies the role of seeing green for him, and for a small subpopulation of which he is an unexceptional member and which has some claim to be regarded as a natural kind. You are right to say either, though not in the same breath. Need more be said?

To sum up. Armstrong and I claim to give a schema that, if filled in, would characterize pain and other states a priori. If the causal facts are right, then also we characterize pain as a physical phenomenon. By allowing for exceptional members of a population, we associate pain only contingently with its causal role. Therefore we do not deny the possibility of mad pain, provided there is not too much of it. By allowing for variation from one population to another (actual or merely possible) we associate pain only contingently with its physical realization. Therefore we do not deny the possibility of Martian pain. If different ways of filling in the relativity to population may be said to yield different senses of the word "pain," then we plead ambiguity. The madman is in pain in one sense, or relative to one population. The Martian is in pain in another sense, or relative to another population. (So is the mad Martian.)

But we do not posit ambiguity ad hoc. The requisite flexibility is explained simply by supposing that we have not bothered to make up our minds about semantic niceties that would make no difference to any commonplace case. The

ambiguity that arises in cases of inverted spectra and the like is simply one instance of a commonplace kind of ambiguity—a kind that may arise whenever we have tacit relativity and criteria of selection that sometimes fail to choose a definite relatum. It is the same kind of ambiguity that arises if someone speaks of relevant studies without making clear whether he means relevance to current affairs, to spiritual well-being, to understanding, or what.

VII

We have a place for commonplace pain, mad pain, Martian pain, and even mad Martian pain. But one case remains problematic. What about pain in a being who is mad, alien, and unique? Have we made a place for that? It seems not. Since he is mad, we may suppose that his alleged state of pain does not occupy the proper causal role for him. Since he is alien, we may also suppose that it does not occupy the proper role for us. And since he is unique, it does not occupy the proper role for others of his species. What is left?

(One thing that might be left is the population consisting of him and his unactualized counterparts at other worlds. If he went mad as a result of some improbable accident, perhaps we can say that he is in pain because he is in the state that occupies the role for most of his alternative possible selves; the state that would have occupied the role for him if he had developed in a more probable way. To make the problem as hard as possible, I must suppose that this solution is unavailable. He did *not* narrowly escape being so constituted that his present state would have occupied the role of pain.)

I think we cannot and need not solve this problem. Our only recourse is to deny that the case is possible. To stipulate that the being in this example is in pain was illegitimate. That seems credible enough. Admittedly, I might have thought off-hand that the case was possible. No wonder; it merely combines elements of other cases that are possible. But I am willing to change my mind. Unlike my opinions about the possibility of mad pain and Martian pain, my naive opinions about this case are not firm enough to carry much weight.

VIII

Finally, I would like to try to preempt an objection. I can hear it said that I have been strangely silent about the very center of my topic. *What is it like* to be the madman, the Martian, the mad Martian, the victim of interchange of pain and thirst, or the being who is mad, alien, and unique? What is the *phenomenal character* of his state? If it *feels* to him like pain, then it *is* pain, whatever its causal role or physical nature. If not, it isn't. It's that simple!

Yes. It would indeed be a mistake to consider whether a state is pain while ignoring what it is like to have it. Fortunately, I have not made that mistake. Indeed, it is an impossible mistake to make. It is like the impossible mistake of considering whether a number is composite while ignoring the question of what factors it has.

Pain is a feeling.[4] Surely that is uncontroversial. To have pain and to feel pain are one and the same. For a state to be pain and for it to feel painful are likewise one and the same. A theory of what it is for a state to be pain is inescapably a theory of what it is like to be in that state, of how that state feels, of the phenomenal character of that state. Far from ignoring questions of how states feel in the odd cases we have been considering, I have been discussing nothing else! Only if you believe on independent grounds that considerations of causal role and physical realization have no bearing on whether a state is pain should you say that they have no bearing on how that state feels.

Postscript to

"Mad Pain
and
Martian Pain"

KNOWING WHAT IT'S LIKE

The most formidable challenge to any sort of materialism and functionalism comes from the friend of phenomenal qualia. He says we leave out the phenomenal aspect of mental life: we forget that pain is a feeling, that there is something it is like to hold one's hand in a flame, that we are aware of something when we suffer pain, that we can recognize that something when it comes again. . . . So far, our proper reply is the one sketched in Section VIII: we deny none of that! We say to the friend of qualia that, beneath his tendentious jargon, he is just talking about pain and various aspects of its functional role. We have already said what we take pain to be; and we do not doubt that part of its causal role is to give rise to judgments that one is in pain, and part is to enable one to recognize pain (the same realizer of the same role) when it comes again.

---

[4]Occurrent pain, that is. Maybe a disposition that sometimes but not always causes occurrent pain might also be called "pain."

So far, so good. But if he persists, the friend of qualia can succeed in escaping our unwelcome agreement; and when he does, we must reverse our strategy. Suppose he makes his case as follows.[1]

> You have not tasted Vegemite (a celebrated yeast-based condiment). So you do not know what it is like to taste Vegemite. And you never will, unless you taste Vegemite. (Or unless the same experience, or counterfeit traces of it, are somehow produced in you by artificial means.) No amount of the information whereof materialists and functionalists speak will help you at all. But if you taste Vegemite, *then* you will know what it is like. So you will have gained a sort of information that the materialists and functionalists overlook entirely. Call this *phenomenal information*. By *qualia* I mean the special subject matter of this phenomenal information.

Now we must turn eliminative. We dare not grant that there is a sort of information we overlook; or, in other words, that there are possibilities exactly alike in the respects we know of, yet different in some other way. That would be defeat. Neither can we credibly claim that lessons in physics, physiology, . . . could teach the inexperienced what it is like to taste Vegemite. Our proper answer, I think, is that knowing what it's like is not the possession of information at all. It isn't the elimination of any hitherto open possibilities. Rather, knowing what it's like is the possession of abilities: abilities to recognize, abilities to imagine, abilities to predict one's behavior by means of imaginative experiments. (Someone who knows what it's like to taste Vegemite can easily and reliably predict whether he would eat a second helping of Vegemite ice cream.) Lessons cannot impart these abilities—who would have thought that they could? There is a state of knowing what it's like, sure enough. And Vegemite has a special power to produce that state. But phenomenal information and its special subject matter do not exist.[2]

Imagine a smart data bank. It can be told things, it can store the information it is given, it can reason with it, it can answer questions on the basis of its stored information. Now imagine a pattern-recognizing device that works as follows. When exposed to a pattern it makes a sort of template, which it then applied to patterns presented to it in future. Now imagine one device with both faculties,

[1]This is the "knowledge argument" of Frank Jackson, "Epiphenomenal Qualia," *Philosophical Quarterly* 32 (1982): 127–36. It appears also, in less purified form, in Thomas Nagel, "What Is It Like To Be a Bat?" *Philosophical Review* 83 (1974): 435–50, and in Paul Meehl, "The Compleat Autocerebroscopist," in Paul Feyerabend and Grover Maxwell, eds., *Mind, Matter, and Method: Essays in Philosophy and Science in Honor of Herbert Feigl* (Minneapolis: University of Minnesota Press, 1966).
[2]This defense against the knowledge argument is presented in detail in Laurence Nemirow, *Functionalism and the Subjective Quality of Experience* (Ph.D. dissertation, Stanford University, 1979), chapter 2; and more briefly in his review of Thomas Nagel's *Mortal Questions*, *Philosophical Review* 89 (1980): 473–77.

rather like a clock radio. There is no reason to think that any such device must have a third faculty: a faculty of making templates for patterns it has never been exposed to, using its stored information about these patterns. If it has a full description about a pattern but no template for it, it lacks an ability but it doesn't lack information. (Rather, it lacks information in usable form.) When it is shown the pattern it makes a template and gains abilities, but it gains no information. We might be rather like that.

· T E N ·

Attitudes *De Dicto*
and *De Se*

I

If I hear the patter of little feet around the house, I expect Bruce. What I expect is a cat, a particular cat. If I heard such a patter in another house, I might expect a cat but no particular cat. What I expect then seems to be a Meinongian incomplete cat. I expect winter, expect stormy weather, expect to shovel snow, expect fatigue—a season, a phenomenon, an activity, a state. I expect that someday mankind will inhabit at least five planets. This time what I expect is a state of affairs.

If we let surface grammar be our guide, the objects of expectation seem quite a miscellany. The same goes for belief, since expectation is one kind of belief. The same goes for desire: I could want Bruce, want a cat but no particular cat, want winter, want stormy weather, want to shovel snow, want fatigue, or want that someday mankind will inhabit at least five planets. The same goes for other attitudes to the extent that they consist partly of beliefs or desires or lacks thereof.

But the seeming diversity of objects might be an illusion. Perhaps the objects of attitudes are uniform in category, and it is our ways of speaking elliptically about these uniform objects that are diverse. That indeed is our consensus. We mostly think that the attitudes uniformly have propositions as their objects. That is why we speak habitually of "propositional attitudes."

When I hear a patter and expect Bruce, for instance, there may or may not be some legitimate sense in which Bruce the cat is an object of my attitude. But, be that as it may, according to received opinion my expectation has a propositional object. It is directed upon a proposition to the effect that Bruce is about to turn up. If instead I expect a cat but no particular cat, then the object of my expectation is a different proposition to the effect that some cat or other is about to turn up. Likewise for our other examples.

The case of expecting a cat shows one advantage of our policy of uniformly assigning propositional objects. If we do not need a Meinongian incomplete cat as object of this attitude, then we dodge the problem of saying what manner of strange cat that might be. That problem (and others like it) may be worth dodging, even if not beyond hope of solution.

There is a second advantage. When we assign a propositional object rather than, say, a Meinongian incomplete cat, we characterize the attitude more fully. If I want a cat, most likely what I want is that I enjoy the company of some cat. But my want might involve some other relationship; for instance, I might want that I be the legal owner of some cat. Saying just that I want a cat leaves it unclear which of these wants I have. Assigning a propositional object makes it clear.

(There is a genuinely unspecific want, namely wanting that I either own or enjoy the company of some cat. But to say that I want a cat is not to ascribe this unspecific want; it is to ascribe an underspecified want which may be this one, but more likely isn't.)

The third advantage is most important. Our attitudes fit into a causal network. In combination, they cause much of our behavior; they are caused in part by the stimuli we receive from our surroundings and in part by one another. In attempting to systematize what we know about the causal roles of attitudes, we find it necessary to refer to the logical relations among the objects of the attitudes. Those relations will be hard to describe if the assigned objects are miscellaneous. Uniform propositional objects, on the other hand, facilitate systematic common-sense psychology.

I fully support the policy of assigning objects of uniform category. But I think we have not chosen the right category. Rather than standardizing on *propositions,* I think we should standardize on *properties.* I want to make a case for two theses. (1) When propositional objects will do, property objects also will do. (2) Sometimes property objects will do and propositional objects won't.

II

The general agreement that the objects of the attitudes are propositions is to some extent phony. Not everyone means the same thing by the word "proposition." I mean a set of possible worlds, a region of logical space. Others mean something more like a sentence, something with indexicality and syntactic structure but taken in abstraction from any particular language. Such a thing might be regarded as a sentential meaning.[1] My target in this paper is the view, until recently my own,

[1] As in my "General Semantics," in this volume.

that the objects of attitudes are propositions in the sense of sets of worlds. I need not quarrel with the view that they are propositions in some other sense.

You may think it goes without saying that the objects of attitudes are not sets of worlds because, for instance, believing that $2 + 2 = 4$ is not the same as believing that $123 + 456 = 579$ though both equations hold at exactly the same worlds—namely, all. I know perfectly well that there is such a thing as ignorance of noncontingent matters. I do not know what is the proper treatment of such ignorance; several very different strategies have been proposed. They depart to different degrees, and in different directions, from the assignment of sets of possible worlds as propositional objects. My hunch is that this problem cuts across the issues I want to discuss, so I shall ignore it. If you wish, you may take it that I hope to cast some indirect light on our own attitudes by talking about the attitudes of imaginary hyper-rational creatures.

The word "property" also is used in many senses. I mean a set: the set of exactly those possible beings, actual or not, that have the property in question. That means that I shall confine myself to properties that things have or lack *simpliciter*. For instance I shall not speak of a property that a road has in some counties but not in others, or of a property that a person has at some times of his life but not at others; instead I shall speak of properties that segments of the road or the person simply have or lack. Apart from that, I am using the word "property" broadly. I do not limit myself to natural properties, as opposed to gruesome gerrymanders. Nor do I limit myself to intrinsic properties like size or shape; I include also properties that things have in virtue of their relations to other things. Thus I include the property of being taller than any Swede ever was or ever will be; the property of inhabiting a country where the 7'¼" gauge once flourished; and even the property of inhabiting a possible world where someday mankind will inhabit at least five planets.

More generally: to any set of worlds whatever, there corresponds the property of inhabiting some world in that set. In other words, to any proposition there corresponds the property of inhabiting some world where that proposition holds. These properties that correspond to propositions may not be intrinsic properties, but they count as properties in the broader sense I have in mind.

Note that if a property corresponds to any proposition, it corresponds to exactly one. Else the property of inhabiting some world where X holds would be the property of inhabiting some world where Y holds, for two propositions X and Y. Since X and Y are two, there is a world where one holds but not both; then an inhabitant of that world both has and lacks the property, which is impossible. (I take it that the world in question is inhabited, on the grounds that every world is a part (an improper part), and hence an inhabitant, of itself.)

Now I am ready to defend my first thesis: when propositional objects of attitudes will do, property objects also will do. Since I construe properties broadly, this thesis is not very bold. We have a one-one correspondence between all propositions and some properties. Whenever it would be right to assign a proposition as the object of an attitude, I shall simply assign the corresponding property. Since the correspondence is one-one, no information is lost and no surplus information is added. The attitude is equally well characterized either way. And since it is easy to go back and forth, there can be no significant difference in convenience.

The exercise would be pointless if we stopped here. It gets its point from my second thesis: sometimes property objects will do and propositional objects won't. Remember that our correspondence runs from *all* propositions to only *some* properties: if a property belongs to some but not all inhabitants of some world, it corresponds to no proposition and cannot replace a propositional object. But once we switch from propositional objects to the corresponding properties, then the way is open for expansion. We can include other properties also as objects for attitudes, without losing the categorial uniformity of objects. It remains to be shown that such an expansion serves any purpose.

III

First I hope to persuade you that there is an arbitrary restriction built into the view that the objects of attitudes are sets of worlds. Consider the subjects of attitudes. These are spread out. Some are here, some are in New Zealand. But not only are they spread out through space; also they are spread out through time. Some live now, others live in the 14th century. Admittedly, when we quantify over them we often omit all but our contemporaries. But that is a restriction we can drop at will, as when we say that few of the great philosophers are now alive.

But not only are the subjects of attitudes spread out through time and space; also they are spread out through logical space. Some live here at our actual world, others live at other possible worlds. Admittedly, when we quantify over them we often omit all but our worldmates. But that again is a restriction we can drop at will.[2]

I shall assume that each subject of attitudes inhabits only one world. He may have counterparts to stand in for him at other worlds, related to him by bonds of similarity, but he himself is not there.[3] I need not quarrel, here, with those who say that Adam is a vast aggregate, partly in each of many worlds. But this vast

---

[2] I can. Some say they can't. They say their understanding is limited to what can be expressed by modalities and world-restricted quantifiers. I have no help to offer these unfortunates, since it is known that the expressive power of a language that quantifies across worlds outruns that of the sort of language they understand. See, for instance, Allen Hazen, "Expressive Completeness in Modal Language," *Journal of Philosophical Logic* 5 (1976): 25–46. His examples of theses inexpressible by modalities and world-restricted quantifiers alone are notable for their seeming intelligibility.

[3] See my "Counterpart Theory and Quantified Modal Logic" and "Counterparts of Persons and Their Bodies," both in this volume; and section 1.9 of *Counterfactuals* (Oxford: Blackwell, 1973).

Adam—if we may call him that—consists of many causally isolated parts each with attitudes of its own. The vast Adam is surely not a single subject of attitudes.

So, putting aside our occasional indulgences in tacitly restricted quantification, we have an enormous population spread out through space, through time, and through the worlds. That sets the stage. Now, what happens when one member of this scattered population has a propositional attitude, rightly so called? Take belief. What happens when he believes a proposition, say the proposition that cyanoacrylate glue dissolves in acetone?

Answer: he locates himself in a region of logical space. There are worlds where cyanoacrylate dissolves in acetone and worlds where it doesn't. He has a belief about himself: namely, that he inhabits one of the worlds where it does. Thereby he ascribes to himself the property of inhabiting one of the worlds included in the set which is the proposition that cyanoacrylate dissolves in acetone. This property that he self-ascribes is exactly the property that corresponds to the proposition that cyanoacrylate dissolves in acetone.

So it is in general. To believe a proposition is to self-ascribe the corresponding property. The property that corresponds to a proposition is a locational property: it is the property that belongs to all and only the inhabitants of a certain region of logical space.

We could just as well think of it a little differently. A proposition divides the populace. Some are privileged to inhabit worlds where cyanoacrylate dissolves in acetone, others are not. (I seem to be one of the unlucky ones.) Someone who believes a proposition, and thereby locates himself in logical space, also places himself within the divided population. He has a partial opinion as to who he is: he is one of *this* class, not one of *that* class. To believe a proposition is to identify oneself as a member of a subpopulation comprising the inhabitants of the region of logical space where the proposition holds. Note that the boundaries of such a subpopulation follow the borders between world and world. Either all the inhabitants of a world belong, or none do. To place oneself in such a subpopulation is to self-ascribe the property that distinguishes it from the rest of the population. And that, of course, is the property that corresponds to the believed proposition. It comes to the same in the end.

If you are willing to view our topic from the modal realist perspective just set forth, you will see why there is something arbitrary about taking the objects of belief always as sets of worlds. We are scattered not only through logical space, but also through ordinary time and space. We can have beliefs whereby we locate ourselves in logical space. Why not also beliefs whereby we locate ourselves in ordinary time and space? We can self-ascribe properties of the sort that correspond to propositions. Why not also properties of the sort that don't correspond to propositions? We can identify ourselves as members of subpopulations whose boundaries follow the borders of the worlds. Why not also as members of subpopulations whose boundaries don't follow the borders of the worlds?

IV

Why not? No reason! We can and we do have beliefs whereby we locate ourselves in ordinary time and space; whereby we self-ascribe properties that don't correspond to propositions; and whereby we identify ourselves as members of subpopulations whose boundaries don't follow the borders of the worlds. These beliefs are attitudes whose objects might better be taken as self-ascribed properties than as believed-true propositions.[4] They show that sometimes property objects will do and propositional objects won't.

Let us begin with an example of John Perry's: the case of Lingens lost in the library.[5]

> An amnesiac, Rudolf Lingens, is lost in the Stanford library. He reads a number of things in the library, including a biography of himself, and a detailed account of the library in which he is lost. . . . He still won't know who he is, and where he is, no matter how much knowledge he piles up, until that moment when he is ready to say, "*This* place is aisle five, floor six, of Main Library, Stanford. *I* am Rudolf Lingens."

It seems that the Stanford library has plenty of books, but no helpful little maps with a dot marked "location of this map." Book learning will help Lingens locate himself in logical space. The more he reads, the more he finds out about the world he lives in, so the fewer worlds are left where he may perhaps be living. The more he reads, the more propositions he believes, and the more he is in a position to self-ascribe properties of inhabiting such-and-such a kind of world. But none of this, by itself, can guarantee that he knows where in the world he is. He needs to locate himself not only in logical space but also in ordinary space. He needs to self-ascribe the property of being in aisle five, floor six, of Main Library, Stanford; and this is not one of the properties that corresponds to a proposition. He needs to identify himself as a member of a subpopulation whose boundaries don't follow the borders of the worlds—a subpopulation whose sole member at Lingen's own world is Lingens himself.

Book learning will help, no doubt, but only because Lingens has more than book learning. He is in a position to self-ascribe the property of being in a certain perceptual situation. This is a property that does not correspond to any proposition, since there are worlds where some have it and others do not. Book learning may eventually convince Lingens that he inhabits a world where exactly one person is in that perceptual situation, and where that one is Rudolf Lingens, who is in aisle five, floor six, of Main Library, Stanford. Then his problem is solved. But not

---

[4]Brian Loar, "The Semantics of Singular Terms," *Philosophical Studies* 30 (1976): 353–77, suggests analyzing certain exceptional beliefs as self-ascription of properties (or "propositional functions"). My suggestion is that Loar's analysis works not only in exceptional cases but in general, thus giving us a uniform treatment.

[5]From John Perry, "Frege on Demonstratives," *Philosophical Review* 86 (1977): 474–97.

because he has managed to conjure nonpropositional belief out of propositional belief. He relied on his perceptual belief, and that was already nonpropositional. Nonpropositional plus propositional belief can give more nonpropositional belief. That is how Lingens can find out who and where in the world he is.

We can imagine a more difficult predicament. Consider the case of the two gods. They inhabit a certain possible world, and they know exactly which world it is. Therefore they know every proposition that is true at their world. Insofar as knowledge is a propositional attitude, they are omniscient. Still I can imagine them to suffer ignorance: neither one knows which of the two he is. They are not exactly alike. One lives on top of the tallest mountain and throws down manna; the other lives on top of the coldest mountain and throws down thunderbolts. Neither one knows whether he lives on the tallest mountain or on the coldest mountain; nor whether he throws manna or thunderbolts.

Surely their predicament is possible. (The trouble might perhaps be that they have an equally perfect view of every part of their world, and hence cannot identify the perspectives from which they view it.) But if it is possible to lack knowledge and not lack any propositional knowledge, then the lacked knowledge must not be propositional. If the gods came to know which was which, they would know more than they do. But they wouldn't know more propositions. There are no more to know. Rather, they would self-ascribe more of the properties they possess. One of them, for instance, would correctly self-ascribe the property of living on the tallest mountain. He has this property and his worldmate doesn't, so self-ascribing this property is not a matter of knowing which is his world.

I think these examples suffice to establish my second thesis: sometimes property objects will do and propositional objects won't. Some belief and some knowledge cannot be understood as propositional, but can be understood as self-ascription of properties.

When there is a propositional object, we are accustomed to speak of an attitude *de dicto*. Self-ascription of properties might suitably be called belief or knowledge *de se*. My thesis is that the *de se* subsumes the *de dicto*. but not vice versa. A general account of belief or knowledge must therefore be an account of belief or knowledge *de se*.

I am greatly indebted to Perry *(op. cit.)* and he in turn acknowledges a debt to several papers by Hector-Neri Castañeda.[6] Castañeda argues that the "he" (or "he himself") that appears for instance in "The editor of *Soul* knows that he is a millionaire" is ineliminable. As I would put it, this typical attribution of knowledge *de se* is not equivalent to any attribution of knowledge *de dicto*. To support this claim, we need only find a case in which the editor knows well enough which of

[6]The first is "'He': A Study in the Logic of Self-Consciousness," *Ratio* 8 (1966): 130–57. The best introduction is "On the Logic of Attributions of Self-Knowledge to Others," *Journal of Philosophy* 65 (1968): 439–56. Similar arguments are found also in Peter Geach "On Beliefs about Oneself," *Analysis* 18 (1957): 23–24; and in Arthur N. Prior, "On Spurious Egocentricity," *Philosophy* 42 (1967): 326–35.

the worlds is his without knowing whether he is among the millionaires of his world: suppose, for instance, that the god on the tallest mountain is the editor of *Soul,* and is a millionaire, but that the god on the coldest mountain is not a millionaire. Castañeda concerns himself with the logic of knowledge *de se;* Perry and I are concerned instead with the problem of finding appropriate objects for such knowledge.

Perry distinguishes believing Fregean thoughts from what he calls "self-locating belief." The former is belief *de dicto,* near enough. (Perry is not committed to any analysis of Fregean thoughts in terms of worlds; and he might wish to endow them with something like syntactic structure, and thereby to distinguish between equivalent thoughts.) The latter is what I call belief irreducibly *de se,* exemplified by that which Lingens can't get from books. I reject Perry's terminology: I say that *all* belief is "self-locating belief." Belief *de dicto* is self-locating belief with respect to logical space; belief irreducibly *de se* is self-locating belief at least partly with respect to ordinary time and space, or with respect to the population. I propose that any kind of self-locating belief should be understood as self-ascription of properties. Perry has a different proposal, which we shall consider later.

V

Some people, called Haecceitists,[7] may find even the case of the two gods unconvincing. They might analyze that case as follows.

The gods inhabit a world *W;* there is another world *V,* which is qualitatively just like *W* but which differs in that the gods have traded places. The god on the tallest mountain in *W* and the god on the coldest mountain in *V,* though not qualitative counterparts, are united by a primitive bond that somehow makes them one. (Likewise for the god on the coldest mountain in *W* and the god on the tallest mountain in *V.*) If the god on the tallest mountain in *W* does not know whether he is on the tallest or the coldest mountain, he must not really know *quite* which world is his. He may know everything qualitative that there is to know about his world, but not know whether his world is *W* or *V.* If he knew that, he would know every proposition that holds at his world. But it seems there is one he doesn't know: the proposition he would express if he said, in English, "I am on the tallest mountain." If his pronoun "I" applies both to him and to his brother in Haecceity on the coldest mountain in *V,* then indeed this proposition holds at *W* but not at

---

[7]For discussions of Haecceitism, see David Kaplan, "How To Russell a Frege-Church," *Journal of Philosophy* 72 (1975): 716–29; and Robert M. Adams, "Primitive Thisness and Primitive Identity," *Journal of Philosophy* 76 (1979): 5–26. I do not mean to suggest, however, that Kaplan or Adams would endorse the whole of the Haecceitist analysis here considered.

V. If he knew this proposition, would he not know that he is on the tallest mountain?

I would be well content to discover what I ought to believe about the objects of the attitudes, and leave the Haecceitists to sort out their affairs for themselves. But I can't resist the urge to meddle. Should you be a Haecceitist, I advise you to spit out the analysis I've put into your mouth. Haecceitism or no, there is a kind of ignorance that cannot be remedied by any amount of self-location in logical space.

Let's grant, briefly, that the world *W* of the gods has its qualitative duplicate *V* in which the gods have traded places. Let the god on the tallest mountain know that his world is *W*, not *V*. Let him be omniscient about *all* propositions, not only qualitative ones. How does that help? Never mind *V*, where he knows he doesn't live. There are still two different mountains in *W* where he might, for all he knows, be living.

What about the proposition he would express if he said "I am on the tallest mountain"? Doesn't he know it? Of course he does—he knows all the propositions that hold at *W*, and this is one of them. Doesn't he therefore know that he is on the tallest mountain?

No. That doesn't follow. Since he is the god on the tallest mountain, his sentence expresses a certain proposition, one true at *W* but not *V*, one that he knows to be true. Had he been the god on the coldest mountain—as he might be, for all he knows—his sentence would have expressed a different proposition, one true at *V* but not *W*, one that he knows to be false. If he doesn't know which he is, he doesn't know which proposition his sentence expresses and he doesn't know whether his sentence expresses a truth. He knows the proposition that he would in fact express by "I am on the tallest mountain," but that doesn't mean that he knows whether he is on the tallest mountain.

VI

Perry (*op. cit.*) considers the case of the mad Heimson, who falsely believes himself to be David Hume. The case poses two problems for those who think of belief as a propositional attitude. Both problems vanish when we rather think of Heimson's mad belief as the mistaken self-ascription of a property he does not possess.

The first problem is that Heimson *couldn't* be Hume. If he believes the proposition that holds at just those worlds where he is Hume, then he believes the empty proposition that holds at no worlds. In the first place, there is no world where Heimson and Hume are literally identical. Suppose there were; then from the standpoint of that world, their difference at this world would be a difference between Hume and Hume, which is absurd. At most they could be vicariously identical, by having a common counterpart at some world. (Or if, as some think, Hume and Heimson are aggregates spread over many worlds, there could be some world such that the Hume-part and the Heimson-part that inhabit that world are identical. But if these aggregates are unified by a counterpart relation, this is simply a redescription of the vicarious identify just considered.) But in the second place, there is not even any world where Heimson and Hume are vicariously identical. For let me stipulate that they have precious little in common. Their origins don't match at all, neither do their noteworthy attributes and deeds. That stops them from having a common counterpart, under any reasonable counterpart relation, but does not at all hinder mad Heimson from believing that he is Hume.

The proposition that Heimson is Hume, even if charitably reconstrued as a matter of vicarious identity, is the empty proposition, hence unfit to be believed. (Admittedly, we who are not hyper-rational do seemingly believe the empty proposition in some of its guises, as when we get our sums wrong; but Heimson's mistake seems nothing like that.) Yet Heimson does believe that he is Hume. How can that be? I reply that the property of being Hume is a perfectly possible property. Hume actually had it. Heimson couldn't possibly have this property (not even vicariously); but that doesn't stop him from self-ascribing it, and that is what he does. The empty proposition doesn't enter into it.

The second problem arises when we ask why Heimson is wrong. He believes he is Hume. Hume believed that too. Hume was right. If Hume believed he was Hume by believing a proposition, that proposition was true. Heimson believes just what Hume did. But Hume and Heimson are worldmates. Any proposition true for Hume is likewise true for Heimson. So Heimson, like Hume, believes he is Hume by believing a true proposition. So he's right. But he's not right. He's wrong, because he believes he's Hume and he isn't.

There are two ways out. (1) Heimson does not, after all, believe what Hume did. Or (2) Heimson does believe what Hume did, but Heimson believes falsely what Hume believed truly.

Doubtless it is true in *some* sense that Heimson does not believe what Hume did. But there had better also be a central and important sense in which Heimson and Hume believe alike. For one thing, the predicate "believes he is Hume" applies alike to both: Heimson believes he is Hume and Hume believes he is Hume. Do not say that I equivocate, and that what is true is only that Heimson believes that he (Heimson) is Hume and Hume believes that he (Hume) is Hume. Everyone believes that Hume is Hume, but not everyone believes that he—he himself—is Hume. There is a genuine, univocal predicate, which appears for instance in "Not everyone believes that he is Hume," and that is the predicate that applies alike to Heimson and Hume.

What is more important, Heimson may have got his head into perfect match with Hume's in every way that is at all relevant to what he believes. If nevertheless Heimson and Hume do not believe alike, then *beliefs ain't in the head!* They depend partly on something else, so that if your head is in a certain state and you're Hume you believe one thing, but if your head is in that same state and you're Heimson you believe something else. Not good. The main purpose of assigning objects of attitudes is, I take it, to characterize states of the head; to specify their causal roles with respect to behavior, stimuli, and one another. If the assignment of objects depends partly on something besides the state of the head, it will not serve this purpose. The states it characterizes will not be the occupants of the causal roles.

(The New Theory of Reference teaches that meanings ain't in the head. That may be right—it depends on which of the many sorts of semantic values that new theorists of reference must distinguish best deserve the name "meanings." If it is right, it applies *inter alia* to the sentences whereby we express our beliefs to others and to ourselves. But the proper moral is not that beliefs ain't in the head. The proper moral is that beliefs are ill-characterized by the meanings of the sentences that express them. Hilary may express one of his beliefs by the sentence "Elms are threatened by disease," although the meaning of this sentence, in some sense of "meaning," depends on more than is in his head. But if so, then it seems that what Hilary believes and what his sentence means cannot be quite the same.)

Mean what you will by "object of an attitude." But if you mean something that is not determined by the state of the head, and that cannot do the job of characterizing states of the head by their causal roles, then I think you had better introduce something else that can do that job. I would prefer to reserve the term "object of an attitude" for that something else.

If we can agree that beliefs are in the head, so that Heimson and Hume may indeed believe alike, then the first way out is shut. We must take the second. Heimson's belief and Hume's have the same object, but Heimson is wrong and Hume is right. Then the object of their shared belief is not a proposition. Else it would be a proposition that either does or doesn't hold at their common world, making them either both right or both wrong. The solution is that the object is not a proposition at all. It is a property: the property of being Hume. Hume self-ascribes this property; he has it; he is right. Heimson, believing just what Hume does, self-ascribes the very same property; he lacks it; he is wrong.

VII

So far, I have regarded the subjects of attitudes as ordinary people, or the like. And people are continuants, extended through time. But some cases of belief *de se* can be better understood if we take the believer not as a continuant but as a more-or-less momentary time-slice thereof. Earlier I assumed that each subject of attitudes inhabits only one world, even if, as some think, persons are extended across the worlds. Now I make a parallel assumption with respect to extension through time.

Consider the insomniac. Tonight, as most nights, he lies awake for hours. While he lies awake, his state of mind changes little. He does not keep track of the time. So all through the night he wonders what time it is.

To wonder is to lack knowledge, but what relevant knowledge does he lack?

Not propositional knowledge; he knows, well enough, what sort of world is his. And not self-ascription of properties to his continuant self; he knows, well enough, what locus through space and time he occupies and what his various segments are like. He knows, for instance, that he spends the night of 13–14 February 1978 lying awake and wondering what time it is.

To understand how he wonders, we must recognize that it is time-slices of him that do the wondering. A slice of the insomniac may locate the whole of the insomniac well enough in logical space and space and time. Yet that slice may fail to locate itself in space, in time, and in the population of slices of the well-located continuant insomniac. The slice at 3:49 A.M. may self-ascribe the property of being one slice of an insomniac who lies awake all night on such-and-such date at such-and-such place at such-and-such a kind of world, and yet may fail to self-ascribe the property of being at 3:49 A.M. That is how this slice may be ignorant, and wonder what time it is, without failing in any relevant way to locate the continuant to which it belongs. It is the slice, not the continuant, that fails to self-ascribe a property.

VIII

Some say, condescendingly, that scientific knowledge of our world is all very well in its place; but it ignores something of the utmost importance. They say there is a kind of personal, subjective knowledge that we have or we seek, and it is altogether different from the impersonal, objective knowledge that science and scholarship can provide.

Alas, I must agree with these taunts, in letter if not in spirit. Lingens has studied the encyclopedias long and hard. He knows full well that he needs a kind of knowledge they do not contain. Science and scholarship, being addressed to all the world, provide knowledge of the world; and that is knowledge *de dicto,* which is not the whole of knowledge *de se.*

But *distinguo!* I admit that knowledge *de dicto* is incomplete; but not that it is in any way misleading or distorted by its incompleteness. A map that is incomplete because the railways are left off is faulty indeed. By a misleading omission, it gives a distorted representation of the countryside. But if a map is made suitable for portable use by leaving off the "location of this map" dot, its incompleteness is not at all misleading. It cannot be said to misrepresent or distort the countryside at all, though indeed there is something that cannot be found out from it. A signpost that tells you where you are is none the worse for not being a clock that tells you when you are. An encyclopedia that tells you where in logical space you are is none the worse for being neither signpost nor clock. Knowledge *de dicto* is not the whole of knowledge *de se.* But there is no contradiction, or conflict, or unbridgeable gap, or even tension, between knowledge *de dicto* and the rest. They fit together as nicely as you please.

IX

My title concerns attitudes in general. Yet so far I've concentrated on belief and knowledge (without heeding the difference between them). Now I shall argue that my two theses hold for desire as well. When propositional objects of desire can be assigned, property objects also will do; but sometimes property objects will do and propositional objects won't. Desire *de se* subsumes desire *de dicto*, but not vice versa.

If my theses hold for belief and knowledge and desire, then also they hold for any attitude which amounts to lack of belief or knowledge or desire. Further, they hold for any attitude that is at least in part a combination of suitably related beliefs or unbeliefs, bits of knowledge or of ignorance, desires or indifferences. Now we have a broad class indeed, and I think the generality of my title is well justified. I'm not sure anything is left out—perhaps some ill-understood attitudes of imagining, conceiving, contemplating, or entertaining a thought.

Typical cases of desire *de se* are wanting to be healthy, wealthy, and wise; wanting to visit Swindon; wanting not to read admissions folders. Each of these desires can be understood as a relation of the subject to some property he desires to possess.

Propositional objects of desire may be traded in for the corresponding properties. Wishing that cyanoacrylate dissolved in acetone is wishing to have the property of inhabiting a world where it does. More often, however, we desire properties that do not correspond to propositions. All those listed in the previous paragraph, for instance, belong to some but not all inhabitants of our world.

But that does not yet establish that desire *de se* outruns desire *de dicto*. Is it so, perhaps, that anyone who desires a property X thereby desires a proposition Y; and hence also desires the property of inhabiting a world where Y holds, which need not be the same as the original property X? To refute this conjecture, we may return to the case of the two gods. Imagine that besides knowing exactly which world is theirs, they see all of that world and behold, it is very good. So they want to inhabit exactly that world, and no other. So far as wanting *de dicto* goes, they are as choosy as can be. But they are not quite as choosy as can be, for neither god cares much which of the two he is. The want they lack cannot be a propositional want, since they are not indifferent to any proposition. For every proposition that holds at their world, they want it to hold; for every other proposition, they want it not to hold. But when it comes to living on the tallest mountain and throwing down manna, they can take it or leave it. If instead one of them did want to be the god on the tallest mountain, then he would want more than he does. But he would not want another proposition.

Or take lost Lingens. Doubtless he wants to find his way out. We might say that he likes those worlds where he finds his way out and dislikes those where he doesn't. (He or one of his counterparts, as the case may be.) But that is too simple. There are worlds where some are lost in libraries and find their way out and others are lost in libraries and don't. And there are some of these worlds where Lingens is unable to locate himself either among the winners or among the losers. That is, some worlds have winners with all the properties that Lingens self-ascribes and also have losers with all those properties. What does Lingens think of these worlds? Does he want to inhabit them? Yes and no—he wants to inhabit such a world as one of its winners, but not as one of its losers. He does not like or dislike that world as such. Rather, he likes the lot of some of its inhabitants who might for all he knows be he, and he dislikes the lot of others. He wants a property that some but not all of them have. His liking for certain locations in certain worlds is not simply a liking for certain worlds. His want *de se* is not equivalent to any want *de dicto*.

I suppose I might want to be a poached egg. (An ordinary poached egg—not an eggy creature that walks and talks.) Would I then want to inhabit one of the worlds where I am a poached egg? That's not it. I take it there are no such worlds. No poached egg is a counterpart of mine! If the object of my want is a proposition, it is the empty proposition. How could I want the empty proposition, in such a guise that I recognize it for what it is? But if the object is a property, it is nonempty. It is a property that plenty of poached eggs actually have.

As I write this, I know that next Wednesday evening I will be done with graduate admissions for the year. Afterwards I'll go home and sit down by the fire, and I'll think "Thank goodness that's over!"[8] I will be content. There is something—namely, for that to be over—that I want now and will still want then, and I will then take it that I have what I want. What is this thing—a proposition? No. My contented time-slice will not be especially pleased about inhabiting a world where the chore of graduate admissions goes on at certain times and not at others. What's good about that? After all, there are plenty of other time-slices of me whose tastes are no different, and who also know that they inhabit such a world, but who are most discontented because the chore is not yet over. The contented time-slice will not be especially fortunate in its location in logical space, but rather will take delight in its location in time. What it will want, and what it will take itself to have, is the property of being located after the end of graduate admissions.

I note an analogy.[9] The saintly crusader, who would like to live in a world without avoidable misery, is something like the snob who would like to live in a better part of town. Each wants a locational property. The crusader wants to be in a nice part of logical space, whereas the snob wants to be in a nice part of ordinary space. I trust the analogy redounds more to the credit of the snob than to the discredit of the crusader.

---

[8]See Arthur N. Prior's paper of that name, *Philosophy* 34 (1959): 12–17. Prior uses the example of saying "Thank goodness that's over" to argue that not all we say can be expressed with a timeless copula and dates. It doesn't mean: "Thank goodness that's over before 11 p.m., 22 February 1978." I am echoing Prior, but in the material mode.

[9]At this point I am indebted to Robert M. Adams, "Theories of Actuality," *Noûs* 8 (1974): 211–31 and especially pp. 215–16; and to discussion with Adams.

X

Quine once defended something very close to my present account of desire *de se*.[10] He considers a cat, chased by a dog, who wants to get on to a roof. He considers attitudes *de dicto*.

> What the cat wants, then, is the state of affairs that is the class of all possible worlds in which he is on that roof. What he fears is the class of all possible worlds in which the dog has him.

Then he finds trouble. After discussing the familiar problem of identity across worlds for Catiline and for the Great Pyramid, he returns to the cat.

> In a possible world with many similar cats and dogs and roofs, which cat is to be he? One of these possible worlds will have a cat like him on a roof like his, and another cat like him in the dog's jaws; does it belong to both the desired state of affairs and the feared one?

He therefore suggests that we take *centered possible worlds*—in effect, pairs of a world and a designated space-time point therein—and regard the wanted or feared state of affairs as a class of centered worlds. A centered world is *centered on* a cat therein if and only if the designated point is in the midst of the cat—more precisely, is the center of gravity of the cat's pineal gland. The cat wants a class of centered worlds that are centered on a cat safely on a roof. He fears a class of centered worlds that are centered instead on a cat in the jaws of a dog. No centered world belongs to both classes. A problematic world with many similar cats is a world that belongs to the wanted class under some centerings and to the feared class under other centerings.

(Quine does not in the end adopt the theory just stated. He prefers a divided theory, on which the objects of some "primitive" attitudes are classes of stimulation patterns, whereas the objects of less primitive attitudes are linguistic. I protest that the advantages of uniform objects are not to be lightly forsaken.)

A class of centered worlds corresponds to a property. Most directly it corresponds to a property of space-time points, but also it corresponds to a property of cats. Let X be a class of centered worlds; there corresponds to it the property of being a cat on which some member of X is centered. Let Y be a property; there corresponds to it the class of exactly those centered worlds that are centered on a cat having the property Y. (Here I assume that one centered world cannot be centered on two different cats, cats who occupy the same place at the same time. To avoid that assumption, as perhaps we should, we might redefine centered worlds as pairs of a world and a designated inhabitant thereof.) By centering the worlds, Quine has in effect replaced propositions by properties as objects of the attitudes.

[10]"Propositional Objects," in W. V. Quine, *Ontological Relativity and Other Essays* (New York: Columbia University Press, 1969).

I am not sure how far Quine's reasons are the same as mine. Insofar as he was dealing with the problem of a world with many similar cats, our reasons are the same. But insofar as he was trying to avoid all need for a counterpart relation, as is suggested by his discussion of Catiline and the Great Pyramid, our reasons are not the same. If I thought it could be done, I would be glad to rescue the doctrine of propositional objects by means of a counterpart relation. I would regard all that depended on the counterpart relation as infected with vagueness, but would not worry unduly about that.

I haven't yet mentioned one big difference between Quine's treatment and mine. By "possible worlds" I simply mean certain big concrete particulars, of which this world of ours is one. Quine rather means certain abstract entities—certain classes of classes of quadruples of real numbers, as it happens. I trust that he distinguishes the concrete world we're part of from that one of his abstract ersatz worlds that represents it. Call that one the "actualized ersatz world" to distinguish it from the world itself. Up to a point it makes little difference whether you believe as I do in a multitude of concrete worlds of which ours is one, or whether instead you believe as Quine does[11] in a multitude of abstract ersatz worlds, of which one is special in that it represents the one and only concrete world. Most analyses involving possible worlds go through equally well either way. (Further, as has been rightly emphasized by Stalnaker *(op. cit.)*, a view of other worlds as abstract accords better than mine with the tendency of ordinary usage to speak of possibilities as "ways things might have been." That phrase certainly does suggest that possibilities are abstract.) All the same, I think that Quine's view, or any similarly moderate version of modal realism, comes to grief in the end. The actualized ersatz world is special, since it alone represents the one concrete world. And it is special not just from its own standpoint, but from the standpoint of any world. So it is noncontingently special, since contingency is variation from world to world. But it is part of the theory that the actualized ersatz world is the special one. So it seems to turn out to be a noncontingent matter which of the ersatz worlds is actualized. That is wrong, and needs explaining away.

XI

I think that common-sense psychology implicitly defines the attitudes—they are whatever states occupy the causal roles it sets forth[12]—and I think common-sense

---

[11]And many others. Abstract ersatz worlds are ably defended, for instance, in Adams, "Theories of Actuality," and in Robert Stalnaker, "Possible Worlds," *Noûs* 10 (1976): 65–75. Adams, Stalnaker, and Quine differ about the exact nature of the ersatz worlds, but all regard them as abstract entities of some sort.

[12]See my "An Argument for the Identity Theory," in this volume; "Psychophysical and Theoretical Identifications," *Australasian Journal of Philosophy* 50 (1972): 249–58; and "Radical Interpretation," in this volume.

psychology, systematized, should look a lot like Bayesian decision theory. Then it is interesting to ask what happens to decision theory if we take all attitudes as *de se*. Answer: very little. We replace the space of worlds by the space of centered worlds, or by the space of all inhabitants of worlds. All else is just as before. Whatever the points of the space of possibilities may be, we have probability distributions over the space and assignments of utility values to the points. For any rational agent at any time there is a pair of a probability distribution and a utility assignment. The probabilities change under the impact of his perception; the probabilities and utilities jointly goven his action. His degrees of belief at a time are got by taking the total probability of regions of the space; his degrees of desirability are got by integrating the point-by-point utilities, weighted by probability, over regions of the space. But since the space of possibilities is no longer the space of worlds, its regions to which degrees of belief and desirability attach are no longer propositions. Instead they are properties.

Robert Stalnaker has argued that propositions, taken as sets of worlds, are just the right objects of attitudes to assign if we want the assignment to be part of a theory of rational action.[13] But he was not considering the question of propositional versus property objects. In fact, the very considerations he gives turn out to call for a version of decision theory based on attitudes *de se*. He describes the rational agent as one who

> sees various alternative possible futures with the one to become actual depending in part on his choice of action. The function of desire is simply to divide these alternative courses of events into the ones to be sought and the ones to be avoided, or . . . to provide an ordering or measure of the alternative possibilities with respect to their desirability. The function of belief is simply to determine which are the relevant alternative possible situations, or . . . to rank them with respect to their probability on various conditions of becoming actual.

He goes on to argue that objects for attitudes ought to be identified if and only if they are functionally equivalent, and are functionally equivalent if and only if they disagree on none of the agent's alternative possible situations.

If the agent's alternative possible situations are always alternative worlds, as Stalnaker assumes, this is indeed an argument for propositional objects. But I claim that sometimes the agent has alternative possibilities in a single world. Consider Lingens when he knows almost enough to get out. He has narrowed the possibilities down to two. Perhaps he is in aisle five, floor six, of Main Library, Stanford, in which case the way out is to go downstairs. Or perhaps he is on one of the lower floors in the stacks of Widener, in which case the thing to do is to go up. The books tell him that there are amnesiacs lost in both places, and he has figured out that he is one of the two. His deliberation concerns eight alternative possibilities.

[13]"Propositions," in Alfred MacKay and Daniel Merrill, eds., *Issues in the Philosophy of Language* (New Haven: Yale University Press, 1976).

| | He is the Stanford amnesiac | | He is the Widener amnesiac | |
	Stanford amnesiac goes down	Stanford amnesiac goes up	Stanford amnesiac goes down	Stanford amnesiac goes up
Widener amnesiac goes down	Case 1 Good	Case 2 Bad	Case 3 Bad	Case 4 Bad
Widener amnesiac goes up	Case 5 Good	Case 6 Bad	Case 7 Good	Case 8 Good

He must choose whether to go down, and thereby actualize one of cases 1, 3, 4, or 5, or whether to go up and actualize one of 2, 6, 7, or 8. The eight cases are spread over only four sorts of worlds. The good case 1 and the bad case 3, for instance, do not belong to different worlds. They are separated by about 3000 miles within a single world. If the objects of Lingen's attitudes are to play their proper role in a systematic account of his deliberation, they must discriminate between these two cases. Propositions won't, properties will.

XII

I hope I've convinced you that propositions won't quite do as uniform objects for the attitudes, and that properties will do at least somewhat better. But I haven't tried to show that *only* properties will do. I presume there are workable alternatives to my theory, as to most philosophical theories.

Some philosophers would favor sentential objects, drawn either from natural language or from some hypothetical language of thought. Others would favor sentence meanings, entities enough like sentences to have syntactic structure and indexicality. If you are of one of these persuasions, my advice to you is by no means new: do not limit yourself to complete, closed, nonindexical sentences or meanings. Be prepared to use predicates, open sentences, indexical sentences, or meanings thereof—something that can be taken to express properties rather than propositions.

Another proposal, given by Perry (*op. cit.*), is roughly as follows. (I shall disregard any difference there may be between properties and Perry's "incomplete Fregean senses" and I shall not use Perry's terminology.) Take belief; the cases of knowledge, desire, and the rest would be parallel. In Perry's scheme, a belief has *two* objects.

The first object is a pair of an individual and a property. To have the belief is to ascribe the property to the individual, and if the individual has the property then the belief is true. (More generally we should take pairs of an *n*-tuple of individuals and an *n*-ary relation. The case of an individual-property pair is the case *n* = 1, near enough; and ordinary propositional belief could be taken as the case *n* = 0. But let's keep to individual-property pairs for the sake of simplicity.)

Insofar as belief is characterized by the first object, Perry claims that beliefs ain't in the head. Hume and Heimson are alike in the head. But the first object of Hume's belief that he himself is Hume is the pair of Hume and the property of being Hume, whereas the first object of Heimson's like belief is the pair of Heimson and the property of being Hume. Perry asks how can it be, if Hume and Heimson are alike, that Hume is right and Heimson is crazy? He takes the first way out: despite the likeness of their heads, they don't believe the same thing. The first object of Hume's belief is true, that of Heimson's belief is false.

Perry fully appreciates that attributions of beliefs enter into a systematic common-sense psychology, and that for this purpose beliefs had better be in the head. Hence the second object. The second object is a function that takes the subject as argument and delivers as value the first object, the pair of an individual and a property ascribed to it. Characterized by second object, beliefs *are* in the head. Hume and Heimson have the same second object of belief: a function that assigns to Hume the pair of Hume and the property of being Hume, and that assigns to Heimson the pair of Heimson and the property of being Hume. So Perry recognizes, as he should, a sense in which Hume and Heimson believe alike.

Perry's second object has a job to do, sure enough, but what about the first? It has two jobs. It determines whether one's belief is true, as we saw. In addition, it serves to explain agreement in belief. Suppose Heimson manages to convince his psychiatrist that he is right, so that the psychiatrist also ascribes to Heimson the property of being Hume. Then Heimson and his psychiatrist share a common belief. Not in the sense in which Heimson and Hume do—the psychiatrist doesn't believe that he himself is Hume—but in another, equally legitimate sense. They agree in that they share as a first object of belief the pair of Heimson and the property of being Hume.

That is Perry's proposal. I am sure it works as well as mine, but it is more complicated. I doubt that the extra complexity buys anything.

Perry's proposal must work at least as well as mine, because mine can be subsumed under his. Whenever I say that someone self-ascribes a property *X*, let Perry say that the first object of his belief is the pair of himself and the property *X*. Let Perry say also that the second object is the function that assigns to any subject *Y* the pair of *Y* and *X*.

The apparent advantage of Perry's scheme is that it provides, in the most straightforward way possible, for other-ascription as well as self-ascription of properties. Ascription of properties to individuals, in general, is called belief *de re*. Perry's scheme is made for belief *de re,* and belief *de se* falls under that as a special case. By providing for ascription of properties in general, Perry gives an account of agreement in the ascription of properties. Heimson and his gullible psychiatrist agree in that they both ascribe to Heimson the property of being Hume.

Certainly we need to be able to make sense of belief *de re* in general—of other-ascription as well as self-ascription of properties. But do we need a scheme as elaborate as Perry's? I think not.

On the account I shall suggest, the subject's self-ascriptions are the whole of his system of beliefs. Other-ascriptions of properties are not some further beliefs along-side the self-ascriptions. Beliefs are in the head; but I agree with Perry that beliefs *de re*, in general, are not. Beliefs *de re* are not really beliefs. They are states of affairs that obtain in virtue of the relations of the subject's beliefs to the *res* in question. If I am right, Perry's scheme for representing beliefs actually represents beliefs and more besides. As a scheme for representing beliefs, it is redundant. Given just a few of the first objects—those that represent the subject's self-ascriptions—and given the requisite facts not about beliefs, we have all the first and second objects of belief. And the same goes *mutatis mutandis* for other attitudes, though I shall continue to discuss only the case of belief.

XIII

Unaware that the Lord High Auditor and the Paymaster-General are the same man, Go-To ascribes rectitude to this man under the description "Lord High Auditor" but not under the description "Paymaster-General." This familiar notion of ascription of properties to individuals under descriptions is not yet belief *de re*, but it is a step in that direction.

We needn't take the so-called descriptions as verbal, thereby limiting ourselves to what can be expressed in some particular language. I might ascribe espionage to a stranger under a description given by a visual image of his face. We might take descriptions as properties, not as particular expression of properties in thought and language. As a preliminary definition, we might say that a subject ascribes property X to individual Y under description Z if and only if (1) Y uniquely has the property Z, and (2) the subject believes the proposition that there is something which uniquely has property Z and also has property X. (By "uniquely" I mean "uniquely in its world.") But this is not general enough, because it requires the subject's belief to be propositional. We want to be able to raise the question whether one of our two gods ascribes to his mountain, under the description "mountain I live on top of," the property of being the tallest mountain. The answer should be that he does if and only if he self-ascribes the property of living on top of the tallest mountain, and that is a matter of his nonpropositional belief *de se*. So let us take relations of the subject to the described individual, such as the relation expressed by "mountain I live on top of," also as descriptions under which properties may be ascribed. (There is a sense in which "mountain I live on top of" expresses a property relative to any given subject; but also there is a sense in which what it expresses is not relative to subject, and it expresses a relation. The latter sense is more convenient for present purposes.) If we take relations as descriptions, we need not consider separately the case in which the description is a property: we can trade in such a property for a peculiar sort of relation, a relation which a subject bears to an individual if and only if the individual has the given property.

Here is a final definition. A subject ascribes property X to individual Y under description Z if and only if (1) the subject bears the relation Z uniquely to Y, and (2) the subject self-ascribes the property of bearing relation Z uniquely to something which has property X.

Now for belief *de re*. Up to a point it is obvious what to say. To ascribe property X to individual Y *simpliciter*—to believe *de re* of Y that Y has X—is to ascribe X to Y under some suitable description of Y. It remains to ask what makes a description "suitable."

Certainly not just any description is suitable. Ascribing espionage to someone under the description "shortest spy" is notoriously not an example of belief *de re*.[14] Neither is any ascription I might make under the description "shortest of my ancestors," to take an example in which the description must be regarded as a relation. An ascription under the description "the murderer" may or may not be an example of belief *de re*, depending on how close the subject is to solving the crime in question.

It will not be possible to say precisely which relations are suitable, since it is often quite vague whether some case should or should not count as an example of belief *de re*. The vagueness is partly resolved in context, but differently in different contexts. Still, I can at least say something about what tends to make a relation be a suitable description.

If our topic were modality *de re*, the suitable descriptions would be those that capture the essence of the thing described. It is necessary *de re* of individual Y that Y has property X if and only if, for some property Z, (1) Z is the essence of Y, and (2) the proposition that whatever has Z also has X is the necessary proposition. (This and a definition of belief *de re* are not quite parallel in form; rightly not, I think.) I have elsewhere[15] suggested that the essence of Y is that property which belongs to Y and all its counterparts, and to nothing else. If so, essence is infected with the vagueness of the counterpart relation. The balancing of respects of similarity and difference—for instance, the question whether perfect match of origins should have decisive weight—goes differently in different contexts, and is never

---

[14] See David Kaplan, "Quantifying In," *Synthese* 19 (1968): 178–214. My account of belief *de re* is broadly similar to Kaplan's. The most important difference is that Kaplan takes the subject's causal *rapport* with the described individual under the description as an extra condition; whereas I take it as part of the content of a suitable description, at least in most cases. (I am indebted at this point to David Lumsden.)

[15] "Counterpart Theory and Quantified Modal Logic," in this volume. Others would define the essence differently, or not at all.

fully determinate. That is as it should be. In veiw of our difficulty in applying it, the concept of essence had better not turn out to be a precise concept.

The trouble with essences, as "suitable descriptions" in the analysis of belief *de re*, is not that the concept of essence is imprecise. The trouble is that essences are hard to come by. Hume's essence is an extremely rich property, rich enough to apply to Hume alone out of all the inhabitants of this world and rich enough to distinguish Hume's counterparts from all of his not-quite-counterparts at other worlds. Certainly I don't know Hume's essence. I doubt that anyone does, even the scholars who know most about Hume. I doubt that Hume did himself. Yet I think I have beliefs *de re* about Hume, and I'm certain that many of his contemporaries did. If I could never have a *de re* belief about Y without knowing that there is something which uniquely has Z, where Z is Y's essence under some reasonable counterpart relation, I would have scarcely any beliefs *de re*. (Beliefs *de re* about numbers might be the most likely survivors.) And that is just what would follow if the only "suitable descriptions" were those rich enough to capture essences.

The psychiatrist ascribes to Heimson the property of being Hume. He would be unlikely to do so under a description that captures Heimson's essence. Heimson's essence is quite unlike Hume's, so it would be quite difficult to believe that there is something that uniquely has Heimson's essence and that also has the property of being Hume. For this reason also, it seems wrong that the only "suitable descriptions" are those that capture essences.

(A complication arises. It is plausible that ordinary proper names express essences, so that the description "Hume" applies exactly to Hume and his counterparts under some reasonable counterpart relation. If I ascribe a property to Hume *by name*, having a belief I might express by saying "Hume was noble," do I thereby ascribe nobility to Hume under a description that captures his essence? No. As I have noted already in sections V and VI, the sentential expression of belief is not a straightforward matter.[16] I may say "Hume was noble," not knowing quite which proposition it expresses because I don't know Hume's essence. And I may thereby express a belief, indeed a belief in virtue of which I believe *de re* of Hume that he was noble. And still I do not believe that something noble uniquely has Z, where Z is Hume's unknown essence.)

Leaving essences in abeyance, we will do well to look elsewhere for "suitable descriptions." It will help to have a collection of examples, uncontroversial or so I hope, of relationships in which belief *de re* is possible. I can have beliefs *de re* (1) about my acquaintances, present or absent; (2) about contemporary public figures prominent in the news; (3) about the famous dead who feature prominently in history; (4) about authors whose works I have read; (5) about strangers now face

---

[16]That is why it seems to me unfortunate that the study of the objects of belief has become entangled with the semantic analysis of attributions of belief. I hope that in this paper I have managed to keep the topics separate.

to face with me; (6) about strangers I am somehow tracing, such as the driver of the car ahead of me, or the spy I am about to catch because he has left so many legible traces; and (7) about myself.

What have these cases in common? To put a name to it: a *relation of acquaintance*.[17] To make it a little more precise: in each case, I and the one of whom I have beliefs *de re* are so related that there is an extensive causal dependence of my states upon his; and this causal dependence is of a sort apt for the reliable transmission of information.

It is too much to require that information actually be reliably transmitted. In every case, a lot might go wrong and I might be very badly misinformed, and yet I could have beliefs *de re*—many of them wrong, perhaps—about the one to whom I bear a relation of acquaintance.

It is not enough just to require an extensive causal dependence. My life may be remarkably entangled with that of some stranger. I may have caught his germs time and again. His driving may have caused traffic jams that made me late to many important appointments. He may have caused many people to go to places where they happened to meet me. And so on. In short, maybe my life would have been very different but for his doings. None of this, by itself, makes it possible for me to have beliefs *de re* about this stranger.

Here is my proposal. A subject ascribes property X to individual Y if and only if the subject ascribes X to Y under some description Z such that either (1) Z captures the essence of Y, or (2) Z is a relation of acquantance that the subject bears to Y.

(If I have a belief that I might express by saying "Hume was noble," I probably ascribe nobility to Hume under the description "the one I have heard of under the name of 'Hume'." That description is a relation of acquantance that I bear to Hume. This is the real reason why I believe *de re* of Hume that he was noble. The fact that "Hume" expresses Hume's unknown essence is irrelevant.)

Seldom do we know essences; seldom do we believe *de re* by ascribing properties to individuals under descriptions that capture their essences. If I did manage to know someone's essence, probably it would be by dint of much investigation. But in that case I would bear a relation of acquaintance to the one I had investigated. Then I don't need his essence to have beliefs *de re* about him. I can ascribe properties to him under the description "target of such-and-such investigations of mine." So it is unclear that anything is gained by providing for essence-capturing descriptions as well as relations of acquaintance. If we have the former, we will have the latter. (But again, beliefs *de re* about numbers may be an exception—how can you be acquainted with a number?)

This has not been a very thorough study of belief *de re*. But I hope it is enough

[17]Compare Charles Chastain's discussion of "knowledge of" in section 12 of "Reference and Context," in *Language, Mind, and Knowledge (Minnesota Studies in the Philosophy of Science 7)*, ed. by Keith Gunderson, (Minneapolis: Univ. of Minnesota Press, 1975).

to make my point: other-ascriptions of properties are not further beliefs alongside the self-ascriptions, but rather are state of affairs that obtain partly in virtue of the subject's self-ascriptions and partly in virtue of facts not about his attitudes.

XIV

Self-ascription of properties is ascription of properties to oneself under the relation of identity. Certainly identity is a relation of acquaintance par excellence. So belief *de se* falls under belief *de re*.

But there are other relations of acquaintance, besides identity, that a subject may bear to himself. So belief *de re* about oneself turns out to cover more than self-ascription of properties. To take an example due to David Kaplan,[18] watching is a relation of acquaintance. I watch myself in reflecting glass, unaware that I am watching myself. I ascribe to myself, under the description "the one I am watching," the property of wearing pants that are on fire. I therefore believe *de re* of the one I am watching—that is, myself—that his pants are on fire. But I do not self-ascribe the property of wearing pants that are on fire. Very soon I will, but not yet. So self-ascription isn't quite the same thing as ascription, *de re,* to oneself.[19]

Postscripts to

"Attitudes *De Dicto* and *De Se*"

A. *DE RE* AND *DE SE*

It should have been said more clearly: the analysis of belief *de re* that I propose in Section XIII is *not* a reduction of *de re* to *de dicto*. Rather, it is a reduction of *de re* generally to *de se*. We are normally left with an irreducibly *de se* belief in the analysans: the subject self-ascribes the property of bearing the relation Z uniquely to something which has property X. As it might be: I self-ascribe staring at something furry (and at nothing else); I am in fact staring only at Bruce, staring is a

---

[18] *Demonstratives* (unpublished manuscript).

[19] I am grateful to many people for conversations about this material; especially Paul Benacerraf, Max Cresswell, and David Lumsden.

suitable relation of acquaintance, and that is how I believe *de re* of Bruce that he is furry.

If I am right, there can be no reduction of *de re* to *de dicto*. For such a reduction would apply, *inter alia*, to the special case in which the subject ascribes a property to himself under the relation of identity—that is, to the special case of belief *de se*. But I have argued that *de se* is not in general reducible to *de dicto*.

Since belief *de se* is a special case of belief *de re*, a question arises.[1] I said that belief *de se* was (narrowly) psychological, whereas belief *de re* is only partly psychological: "Beliefs *de re* are not really beliefs. They are states of affairs that obtain in virtue of the relations of the subject's beliefs to the *res* in question." Then is belief *de se* wholly psychological, or is it not?—It is. In this exceptional case, the nonpsychological part drops out. The nonpsychological part of *de re* belief generally is that the subject bears a suitable relation uniquely to the *res*. But when the *res* is himself and the relation is identity, this nonpsychological part reduces to the mere necessary truth that he is identical to himself and to nothing else.

B. GRIEF FOR MODERATE MODAL REALISM?[2]

I suggested in Section X that the moderate modal realist has a problem about actuality. On his view, there is one of the abstract ersatz worlds, and one only, that is special because it is the one that represents the concrete world. This one, he says, is actualized. Now, consider W, another of the abstract ersatz worlds. It is not special, not the one that represents the concrete world, not actualized. But it could have been. Surely it is a contingent matter which of the ersatz worlds is actualized, and in particular it is possible that W be actualized. What is possible is what is true at some world. Which world?—Presumably W itself. So the moderate realist must be able to say: it is true at W that W is actualized, for at W, W is the ersatz world that alone represents the concrete world.

I asked: what does this mean? There is only one concrete world, according to the moderate realist. *Ex hypothesi,* W does not represent it. Then how can it be that, at W, W does represent it?

The problem is part of a more general one. What does it mean when we say that something that is not true *simpliciter* is nevertheless true at a world? For me, truth at a world is a simple matter. It is just truth, with world-dependent linguistic elements evaluated at the world in question. For instance—and this alone will take us a lot of the way—quantifiers must (usually) be restricted to inhabitants of the proper world.[3] Thus it is true at a certain world that some pigs fly iff some inhab-

---

[1]It was brought to my attention by Mark Johnston.

[2]In this postscript, I am much indebted to correspondence with John G. Bennett.

[3]See the translation scheme proposed in "Counterpart Theory and Quantified Modal Logic" (in this volume), in particular clauses T2g–T2h, page 31.

itants of that world are pigs that fly. It is not true *simpliciter* that some pigs fly, since no pigs that fly inhabit this world.

If that is what truth at a world means, I do not see how it can be true at one ersatz world and false at another that W represents the concrete world. It just does or it just doesn't. The concrete world is not part of any ersatz world. Still less are there supposed to be different concrete worlds to inhabit different ersatz worlds. That was my objection.

But, as should have been clear all along, the moderate modal realist cannot and does not think of truth at a world in the same way that I do. If he did, how could he even agree that it is true at a certain world that pigs fly? Pigs that fly are parts of some worlds, or so I think, but they are not parts of any ersatz worlds. (Maybe, representations of them are parts of some ersatz worlds.) So my objection should be in part withdrawn and in part generalized. I should ask: what does the moderate realist mean when he says that *anything* is true at an ersatz world?

That was not meant as an unanswerable question. There are many answers the moderate realist might offer. I think that all of them, except for some that don't even get the facts of modality right, succeed only by giving up on some of the analytic goals that modal realism was meant to serve. We are left with theories that may help to systematize our opinions about modality, counterfactuals, truth in a representation, . . . but that no longer offer instructive analyses.

It will suffice to consider one of all the answers that might be given: the modal answer. The moderate realist might say that it is true at ersatz world W that ϕ iff, necessarily, if W represented the concrete world, then it would be that ϕ. (Despite the subjunctive verbs, this is to be taken simply as a strict implication—the necessitation of a truth-functional conditional.) Taking ϕ as "W represents the concrete world," this answer handles my original objection with the greatest of ease. But if it is given, then it becomes uninstructive to analyze necessity as truth at all (ersatz) worlds!

C. *POSSIBILIA* POWER?

According to what I have said, our beliefs and desires consist in relations to properties. These properties are sets of possible individuals. In any realistic case, most of these *possibilia* are unactualized. But we act as we do because we believe and desire as we do. Then do our relations with unactualized *possibilia* enter into the causal histories of actual events? That would never do!

No; what's true is rather this. Certain of our states, presumably brain states, jointly cause our acts. Because of the ways they cause and get caused, we classify them as certain beliefs and desires. We classify beliefs and desires by associating them with "objects of attitudes"—namely, with sets consisting in part of unactualized individuals. They bear interpretations, according to such principles as are discussed in "Radical Interpretation" (in this volume). But they stand in relations to unactualized *possibilia* because they bear interpretations, and they bear interpretations because of their causal powers—not vice versa.

You might as well worry that numbers have causal powers, since the water boils because it reaches the centigrade temperature of 100. The answer is the same. The state of the water is indexed by the number in virtue of its causal powers—not vice versa.

PART THREE

Philosophy of Language

· E L E V E N ·

Languages and Language

I. THESIS

What is a language? Something which assigns meanings to certain strings of types of sounds or of marks. It could therefore be a function, a set of ordered pairs of strings and meanings. The entities in the domain of the function are certain finite sequences of types of vocal sounds, or of types of inscribable marks; if σ is in the domain of a language $\mathcal{L}$, let us call σ a *sentence* of $\mathcal{L}$. The entities in the range of the function are meanings: if σ is a sentence of $\mathcal{L}$, let us call $\mathcal{L}(\sigma)$ the *meaning* of σ in $\mathcal{L}$. What could a meaning of a sentence be? Something which, when combined with factual information about the world—or factual information about *any* possible world—yields a truth-value. It could therefore be a function from worlds to truth-values—or more simply, a set of worlds. We can say that a sentence σ is *true in* a language $\mathcal{L}$ *at* a world w if and only if w belongs to the set of worlds $\mathcal{L}(\sigma)$. We can say that σ is *true in* $\mathcal{L}$ (without mentioning a world) if and only if our actual world belongs to $\mathcal{L}(\sigma)$. We can say that σ is *analytic in* $\mathcal{L}$ if and only if every possible world belongs to $\mathcal{L}(\sigma)$. And so on, in the obvious way.

This paper was originally prepared in 1968 and was revised in 1972. The 1968 draft appears in Italian translation as "Lingue e lingua," *Versus* 4 (1973): 2–21.

II. ANTITHESIS

What is a language? A social phenomenon which is part of the natural history of human beings; a sphere of human action, wherein people utter strings of vocal sounds, or inscribe strings of marks, and wherein people respond by thought or action to the sounds or marks which they observe to have been so produced.

This verbal activity is, for the most part, rational. He who produces certain sounds or marks does so for a reason. He knows that someone else, upon hearing his sounds or seeing his marks, is apt to form a certain belief or act in a certain way. He wants, for some reason, to bring about that belief or action. Thus his beliefs and desires give him a reason to produce the sounds or marks, and he does. He who responds to the sounds or marks in a certain way also does so for a reason. He knows how the production of sounds or marks depends upon the producer's state of mind. When he observes the sounds or marks, he is therefore in a position to infer something about the producer's state of mind. He can probably also infer something about the conditions which caused that state of mind. He may merely come to believe these conclusions, or he may act upon them in accordance with his other beliefs and his desires.

Not only do both have reasons for thinking and acting as they do; they know something about each other, so each is in a position to replicate the other's reasons. Each one's replication of the other's reasons forms part of his own reason for thinking and acting as he does; and each is in a position to replicate the other's replication of his own reasons. Therefore the Gricean mechanism[1] operates: X intends to bring about a response on the part of Y by getting Y to recognize that X intends to bring about that response; Y does recognize X's intention, and is thereby given some sort of reason to respond just as X intended him to.

Within any suitable population, various regularities can be found in this rational verbal activity. There are regularities whereby the production of sounds or marks depends upon various aspects of the state of mind of the producer. There are regularities whereby various aspects of responses to sounds or marks depend upon the sounds or marks to which one is responding. Some of these regularities are accidental. Others can be explained, and different ones can be explained in very different ways.

Some of them can be explained as conventions of the population in which they prevail. Conventions are regularities in action, or in action and belief, which are arbitrary but perpetuate themselves because they serve some sort of common interest. Past conformity breeds future conformity because it gives one a reason to go on conforming; but there is some alternative regularity which could have served instead, and would have perpetuated itself in the same way if only it had got started.

More precisely: a regularity R, in action or in action and belief, is a *convention*

---

[1] H. P. Grice, "Meaning," *Philosophical Review* 66 (1957): 377–88.

in a population P if and only if, within P, the following six conditions hold. (Or at least they almost hold. A few exceptions to the "everyone"s can be tolerated.)

(1) Everyone conforms to R.

(2) Everyone believes that the others conform to R.

(3) This belief that the others conform to R gives everyone a good and decisive reason to conform to R himself. His reason may be that, in particular, those of the others he is now dealing with conform to R; or his reason may be that there is general or widespread conformity, or that there has been, or that there will be. His reason may be a practical reason, if conforming to R is a matter of acting in a certain way; or it may be an epistemic reason, if conforming to R is a matter of believing in a certain way. First case: according to his beliefs, some desired end may be reached by means of some sort of action in conformity to R, provided that the others (all or some of them) also conform to R; therefore he wants to conform to R if they do. Second case: his beliefs, together with the premise that others conform to R, deductively imply or inductively support some conclusions; and in believing this conclusion, he would thereby conform to R. Thus reasons for conforming to a convention by believing something—like reasons for belief in general—are believed premises tending to confirm the truth of the belief in question. Note that I am *not* speaking here of practical reasons for acting so as to somehow produce in oneself a certain desired belief.

(4) There is a general preference for general conformity to R rather than slightly-less-than-general conformity—in particular, rather than conformity by all but any one. (This is not to deny that some state of *widespread* nonconformity to R might be even more preferred.) Thus everyone who believes that at least almost everyone conforms to R will want the others, as well as himself, to conform. This condition serves to distinguish cases of convention, in which there is a predominant coincidence of interest, from cases of deadlocked conflict. In the latter cases, it may be that each is doing the best he can by conforming to R, given that the others do so; but each wishes the others did not conform to R, since he could then gain at their expense.

(5) R is not the only possible regularity meeting the last two conditions. There is at least one alternative R' such that the belief that the others conformed to R' would give everyone a good and decisive practical or epistemic reason to conform to R' likewise; such that there is a general preference for general conformity to R' rather than slightly-less-than-general conformity to R'; and such that there is normally no way of conforming to R and R' both. Thus the alternative R' could have perpetuated itself as a convention instead of R; this condition provides for the characteristic arbitrariness of conventions.

(6) Finally, the various facts listed in conditions (1) to (5) are matters of *common* (or *mutual*) *knowledge:* they are known to everyone, it is known to everyone that they are known to everyone, and so on. The knowledge mentioned here may be merely potential: knowledge that would be available if one bothered to think hard enough. Everyone must potentially know that (1) to (5) hold; potentially know

that the others potentially know it; and so on. This condition ensures stability. If anyone tries to replicate another's reasoning, perhaps including the other's replication of his own reasoning, . . . , the result will reinforce rather than subvert his expectation of conformity to R. Perhaps a negative version of (6) would do the job: no one disbelieves that (1) to (5) hold, no one believes that others disbelieve this, and so on.

This definition can be tried out on all manner of regularities which we would be inclined to call conventions. It is a convention to drive on the right. It is a convention to mark poisons with skull and crossbones. It is a convention to dress as we do. It is a convention to train beasts to turn right on "gee" and left on "haw." It is a convention to give goods and services in return for certain pieces of paper or metal. And so on.

The common interests which sustain conventions are as varied as the conventions themselves. Our convention to drive on the right is sustained by our interest in not colliding. Our convention for marking poisons is sustained by our interest in making it easy for everyone to recognize poisons. Our conventions of dress might be sustained by a common aesthetic preference for somewhat uniform dress, or by the low cost of mass-produced clothes, or by a fear on everyone's part that peculiar dress might be thought to manifest a peculiar character, or by a desire on everyone's part not to be too conspicuous, or—most likely—by a mixture of these and many other interests.

It is a platitude—something only a philosopher would dream of denying—that there are conventions of language, although we do not find it easy to say what those conventions are. If we look for the fundamental difference in verbal behavior between members of two linguistic communities, we can be sure of finding something which is arbitrary but perpetuates itself because of a common interest in coordination. In the case of conventions of language, that common interest derives from our common interest in taking advantage of, and in preserving, our ability to control others' beliefs and actions to some extent by means of sounds and marks. That interest in turn derives from many miscellaneous desires we have; to list them, list the ways you would be worse off in Babel.

III. SYNTHESIS

What have languages to do with language? What is the connection between what I have called *languages*, functions from strings of sounds or of marks to sets of possible worlds, semantic systems discussed in complete abstraction from human affairs, and what I have called *language*, a form of rational, convention-governed human social activity? We know what to *call* this connection we are after: we can say that a given language £ is *used by*, or is a (or the) language *of*, a given population P. We know also that this connection holds by virtue of the conventions of language prevailing in *P*. Under suitably different conventions, a different language would be used by *P*. There is some sort of convention whereby *P* uses £—but what is it? It is worthless to call it a convention to use £, even if it can correctly be so described, for we want to know what it is to use £.

My proposal[2] is that the convention whereby a population *P* uses a language £ is a convention of *truthfulness* and *trust* in £. To be truthful in £ is to act in a certain way: to try never to utter any sentences of £ that are not true in £. Thus it is to avoid uttering any sentence of £ unless one believes it to be true in £. To be trusting in £ is to form beliefs in a certain way: to impute truthfulness in £ to others, and thus to tend to respond to another's utterance of any sentence of £ by coming to believe that the uttered sentence is true in £.

Suppose that a certain language £ is used by a certain population *P*. Let this be a perfect case of normal language use. Imagine what would go on; and review the definition of a convention to verify that there does prevail in *P* a convention of truthfulness and trust in £.

(1) There prevails in *P* at least a regularity of truthfulness and trust in £. The members of *P* frequently speak (or write) sentences of £ to one another. When they do, ordinarily the speaker (or writer) utters one of the sentences he believes to be true in £; and the hearer (or reader) responds by coming to share that belief of the speaker's (unless he already had it), and adjusting his other beliefs accordingly.

(2) The members of *P* believe that this regularity of truthfulness and trust in £ prevails among them. Each believes this because of his experience of others' past truthfulness and trust in £.

(3) The expectation of conformity ordinarily gives everyone a good reason why he himself should conform. If he is a speaker, he expects his hearer to be trusting in £; wherefore he has reason to expect that by uttering certain sentences that are true in £ according to his beliefs—by being truthful in £ in a certain way—he can impart certain beliefs that he takes to be correct. Commonly, a speaker has some reason or other for wanting to impart some or other correct beliefs. Therefore his beliefs and desires constitute a practical reason for acting in the way he does: for uttering some sentence truthfully in £.

As for the hearer: he expects the speaker to be truthful in £, wherefore he has good reason to infer that the speaker's sentence is true in £ according to the speaker's beliefs. Commonly, a hearer also has some or other reason to believe that the speaker's beliefs are correct (by and large, and perhaps with exceptions for certain topics); so it is reasonable for him to infer that the sentence he has heard is probably true in £. Thus his beliefs about the speaker give him an epistemic reason to respond trustingly in £.

We have coordination between truthful speaker and trusting hearer. Each con-

[2]This propsal is adapted from the theory given in Erik Stenius, "Mood and Language-Game," *Synthese* 17 (1967): 254–74.

forms as he does to the prevailing regularity of truthfulness and trust in £ because he expects complementary conformity on the part of the other.

But there is also a more diffuse and indirect sort of coordination. In coordinating with his present partner, a speaker or hearer also is coordinating with all those whose past truthfulness and trust in £ have contributed to his partner's present expectations. This indirect coordination is a four-way affair: between present speakers and past speakers, present speakers and past hearers, present hearers and past speakers, and present hearers and past hearers. And whereas the direct coordination between a speaker and his hearer is a coordination of truthfulness with trust for a single sentence of £, the indirect coordination with one's partner's previous partners (and with *their* previous partners, etc.) may involve various sentences of £. It may happen that a hearer, say, has never before encountered the sentence now addressed to him; but he forms the appropriate belief on hearing it—one such that he has responded trustingly in £—because his past experience with truthfulness in £ has involved many sentences grammatically related to this one.

(4) There is in *P* a general preference for general conformity to the regularity of truthfulness and trust in £. Given that most conform, the members of *P* want all to conform. They desire truthfulness and trust in £ from each other, as well as from themselves. This general preference is sustained by a common interest in communication. Everyone wants occasionally to impart correct beliefs and bring about appropriate actions in others by means of sounds and marks. Everyone wants to preserve his ability to do so at will. Everyone wants to be able to learn about the parts of the world that he cannot observe for himself by observing instead the sounds and marks of his fellows who have been there.

(5) The regularity of truthfulness and trust in £ has alternatives. Let £' be any language that does not overlap £ in such a way that is is possible to be truthful and trusting simultaneously in £ and in £', and that is rich and convenient enough to meet the needs of *P* for communication. Then the regularity of truthfulness and trust in £' is an alternative to the prevailing regularity of truthfulness and trust in £. For the alternative regularity, as for the actual one, general conformity by the others would give one a reason to conform; and general conformity would be generally preferred over slightly-less-than-general conformity.

(6) Finally, all these facts are common knowledge in *P*. Everyone knows them, everyone knows that everyone knows them, and so on. Or at any rate none believes that another doubts them, none believes that another believes that another doubts them, and so on.

In any case in which a language £ clearly is used by a population *P*, then, it seems that there prevails in *P* a convention of truthfulness and trust in £, sustained by an interest in communication. The converse is supported by an unsuccessful search for counterexamples: I have not been able to think of any case in which there is such a convention and yet the language £ is clearly not used in the population *P*. Therefore I adopt this definition, claiming that it agrees with ordinary usage in the cases in which ordinary usage is fully determinate:

a language £ is *used by* a population *P* if and only if there prevails in *P* a convention of truthfulness and trust in £, sustained by an interest in communication.

Such conventions, I claim, provide the desired connection between languages and language-using populations.

Once we understand how languages are connected to populations, whether by conventions of truthfulness and trust for the sake of communication or in some other way, we can proceed to redefine relative to a population all those semantic concepts that we previously defined relative to a language. A string of sounds or of marks is a *sentence of P* if and only if it is a sentence of some language £ which is used in *P*. It has a certain *meaning in P* if and only if it has that meaning in some language £ which is used in *P*. It is *true in P at* a world *w* if and only is it is true at *w* in some language £ which is used in *P*. It is *true in P* if and only if it is true in some language £ which is used in *P*.

The account just given of conventions in general, and of conventions of language in particular, differs in one important respect from the account given in my book *Convention*.[3]

Formerly, the crucial clause in the definition of convention was stated in terms of a conditional preference for conformity: each prefers to conform if the others do, and it would be the same for the alternatives to the actual convention. (In some versions of the definition, this condition was subsumed under a broader require-ment of general preference for general conformity.) The point of this was to explain why the belief that others conform would give everyone a reason for conforming likewise, and so to explain the rational self-perpetuation of conventions. But a rea-son involving preference in this way must be a practical reason for acting, not an epistemic reason for believing. Therefore I said that conventions were regularities in action alone. It made no sense to speak of believing something in conformity to convention. (Except in the peculiar case that others' conformity to the convention gives one a practical reason to conform by acting to somehow produce a belief in oneself; but I knew that this case was irrelvant to ordinary language use.) Thus I was cut off from what I now take to be the primary sort of conventional coordi-nation in language use: that between the action of the truthful speaker and the responsive believing of his trusting hearer. I resorted to two different substitutes.

Sometimes it is common knowledge how the hearer will want to act if he forms various beliefs, and we can think of the speaker not only as trying to impart beliefs but also as trying thereby to get the hearer to act in a way that speaker and hearer alike deem appropriate under the circumstances that the speaker believes to obtain. Then we have speaker-hearer coordination of action. Both conform to a convention of truthfulness for the speaker plus appropriate responsive action by the hearer.

[3]Cambridge, Mass.: Harvard University Press, 1969. A similar account was given in the original version of this paper, written in 1968.

The hearer's trustful believing need not be part of the content of the convention, though it must be mentioned to explain why the hearer acts in conformity. In this way we reach the account of "signaling" in *Convention,* chapter IV.

But signaling was all-too-obviously a special case. There may be no appropriate responsive action for the hearer to perform when the speaker imparts a belief to him. Or the speaker and hearer may disagree about how the hearer ought to act under the supposed circumstances. Or the speaker may not know how the hearer will decide to act; or the hearer may not know that he knows; and so on. The proper hearer's response to consider is *believing,* but that is not ordinarily an action. So in considering language use in general, in *Convention,* chapter V, I was forced to give up on speaker-hearer coordination. I took instead the diffuse coordination between the present speaker and the past speakers who trained the present hearer. Accordingly, I proposed that the convention whereby a population P used a language $\mathcal{L}$ was simply a convention of truthfulness in $\mathcal{L}$. Speakers conform; hearers do not, until they become speakers in their turn, if they ever do.

I think now that I went wrong when I went beyond the special case of signaling. I should have kept my original emphasis on speaker-hearer coordination, broadening the definition of convention to fit. It was Jonathan Bennett[4] who showed me how that could be done: by restating the crucial defining clause not in terms of preference for conformity but rather in terms of reasons for conformity—practical *or epistemic* reasons. The original conditional preference requirement gives way now to clause (3): the belief that others conform gives everyone a reason to conform likewise, and it would be the same for the alternatives to the actual convention. Once this change is made, there is no longer any obstacle to including the hearer's trust as part of the content of a convention.

(The old conditional preference requirement is retained, however, in consequence of the less important clause (4). Clause (3) as applied to practical reasons, but not as applied to epistemic reasons, may be subsumed under (4).)

Bennett pointed out one advantage of the change: suppose there is only one speaker of an idiolect, but several hearers who can understand him. Shouldn't he and his hearers comprise a population that uses his idiolect? More generally, what is the difference between (a) someone who does not utter sentences of a language because he does not belong to any population that uses it, and (b) someone who does not utter sentences of the language although he does belong to such a population because at present—or always, perhaps—he has nothing to say? Both are alike, so far as action in conformity to a convention of truthfulness goes. Both are vacuously truthful. In *Convention* I made it a condition of truthfulness in $\mathcal{L}$ that one sometimes does utter sentences of $\mathcal{L}$, though not that one speaks up on any particular occasion. But that is unsatisfactory: what degree of truthful talkativeness

---

[4]Personal communication, 1971. Bennett himself uses the broadened concept of convention differently, wishing to exhibit conventional meaning as a special case of Gricean meaning. See his "The Meaning-Nominalist Strategy," *Foundations of Language* 10 (1973): 141–68.

does it take to keep up one's active membership in a language-using population? What if someone just never thought of anything worth saying?

(There is a less important difference between my former account and the present one. Then and now, I wanted to insist that cases of convention are cases of predominant coincidence of interest. I formerly provided for this by a defining clause that seems now unduly restrictive; in any instance of the situation to which the convention applies, everyone has approximately the same preferences regarding all possible combinations of actions. Why *all?* It may be enough that they agree in preferences to the extent specified in my present clause (4). Thus I have left out the further agreement-in-preference clause.)

IV. OBJECTIONS AND REPLIES

Objection: Many things which meet the definition of a language given in the thesis—many functions from strings of sounds or of marks to sets of possible worlds—are not really possible languages. They could not possibly be adopted by any human population. There may be too few sentences, or too few meanings, to make as many discriminations as language-users need to communicate. The meanings may not be anything language-users would wish to communicate about. The sentences may be very long, impossible to pronounce, or otherwise clumsy. The language may be humanly unlearnable because it has no grammar, or a grammar of the wrong kind.

Reply: Granted. The so-called languages of the thesis are merely an easily specified superset of the languages we are really interested in. A language in a narrower and more natural sense is any one of these entities that could possibly—possibly in some appropriately strict sense—be used by a human population.

Objection: The so-called languages discussed in the thesis are excessively simplified. There is no provision for indexical sentences, dependent on features of the context of their utterance: for instance, tensed sentences, sentences with personal pronouns or demonstratives, or anaphoric sentences. There is no provision for ambiguous sentences. There is no provision for non-indicative sentences: imperatives, questions, promises and threats, permissions, and so on.

Reply: Granted. I have this excuse: the phenomenon of language would be not too different if these complications did not exist, so we cannot go too far wrong by ignoring them. Nevertheless, let us sketch what could be done to provide for indexicality, ambiguity, or non-indicatives. In order not to pile complication on complication we shall take only one at a time.

We may define an *indexical language* $\mathcal{L}$ as a function that assigns sets of possible worlds not to its sentences themselves, but rather to sentences paired with possible occasions of their utterance. We can say that σ is true in $\mathcal{L}$ at a world w on a possible occasion o of the utterance of σ if and only if w belongs to $\mathcal{L}(\sigma, o)$. We can say that σ is true in $\mathcal{L}$ on o (without mentioning a world) if and only if the world in which o is located—our actual world if o is an actual occasion of utterance of σ, or some other world if not—belongs to $\mathfrak{L}(\sigma, o)$. We can say that a speaker is truthful in $\mathfrak{L}$ if he tries not to utter any sentence σ of $\mathfrak{L}$ unless σ would be true in $\mathfrak{L}$ on the occasion of his utterance of σ. We can say that a hearer is trusting in $\mathfrak{L}$ if he believes an uttered sentence of $\mathfrak{L}$ to be true in $\mathfrak{L}$ on its occasion of utterance.

We may define an *ambiguous language* $\mathfrak{L}$ as a function that assigns to its sentences not single meanings, but finite sets of alternative meanings. (We might or might not want to stipulate that these sets are non-empty.) We can say that a sentence σ is true in $\mathfrak{L}$ at w under some meaning if and only if w belongs to some member of $\mathfrak{L}(\sigma)$. We can say that σ is true in $\mathfrak{L}$ under some meaning if and only if our actual world belongs to some member of $\mathfrak{L}(\sigma)$. We can say that someone is (minimally) truthful in $\mathfrak{L}$ if he tries not to utter any sentence σ of $\mathfrak{L}$ unless σ is true in $\mathfrak{L}$ under some meaning. He is trusting if he believes an uttered sentence of $\mathfrak{L}$ to be true in $\mathfrak{L}$ under some meaning.

We may define a *polymodal language* $\mathfrak{L}$ as a function which assigns to its sentences meanings containing two components: a set of worlds, as before; and something we can call a *mood:* indicative, imperative, etc. (It makes no difference what things these are—they might, for instance, be taken as code numbers.) We can say that a sentence σ is indicative, imperative, etc., in $\mathfrak{L}$ according as the mood-component of the meaning $\mathfrak{L}(\sigma)$ is indicative, imperative, etc. We can say that a sentence σ is true in $\mathfrak{L}$, regardless of its mood in $\mathfrak{L}$, if and only if our actual world belongs to the set-of-worlds-component of the meaning $\mathfrak{L}(\sigma)$. We can say that someone is truthful in $\mathfrak{L}$ with respect to indicatives if he tries not to utter any indicative sentence of $\mathfrak{L}$ which is not true in $\mathfrak{L}$; truthful in $\mathfrak{L}$ with respect to imperatives if he tries to act in such a way as to make true in $\mathfrak{L}$ any imperative sentence of $\mathfrak{L}$ that is addressed to him by someone in a relation of authority to him; and so on for other moods. He is trusting in $\mathfrak{L}$ with respect to indicatives if he believes uttered indicative sentences of $\mathfrak{L}$ to be true in $\mathfrak{L}$; trusting in $\mathfrak{L}$ with respect to imperatives if he expects his utterance of an imperative sentence of $\mathfrak{L}$ to result in the addressee's acting in such a way as to make that sentence true in $\mathfrak{L}$, provided he is in a relation of authority to the addressee; and so on. We can say simply that he is truthful and trusting in $\mathfrak{L}$ if he is so with respect to all moods that occur in $\mathfrak{L}$. It is by virtue of the various ways in which the various moods enter into the definition of truthfulness and of trust that they deserve the familiar names we have given them. (I am deliberating stretching the ordinary usage of "true," "truthfulness," and "trust" in extending them to non-indicatives. For instance, truthfulness with respect to imperatives is roughly what we might call *obedience* in $\mathfrak{L}$.)

Any natural language is simultaneously indexical, ambiguous, and polymodal; I leave the combination of complications as an exercise. Henceforth, for the most part, I shall lapse into ignoring indexicality, ambiguity, and non-indicatives.

Objection: We cannot always discover the meaning of a sentence in a population just by looking into the minds of the members of the population, no matter what we look for there. We may also need some information about the causal origin of what we find in their minds. So, in particular, we cannot always discover the meaning of a sentence in a population just by looking at the conventions prevailing therein. Consider an example: What is the meaning of the sentence "Mik Karthee was wise" in the language of our 137th-century descendants, if all we can find in any of their minds is the inadequate dictionary entry: "Mik Karthee: controversial American politician of the early atomic age"? It depends, we might think, partly on which man stands at the beginning of the long causal chain ending in that inadequate dictionary entry.

Reply: If this doctrine is correct, I can treat it as a subtle sort of indexicality. The set of worlds in which a sentence σ is true in a language $\pounds$ may depend on features of possible occasions of utterance of σ. One feature of a possible occasion of utterance—admittedly a more recondite feature than the time, place, or speaker—is the causal history of a dictionary entry in a speaker's mind.

As with other kinds of indexicality, we face a problem of nomenclature. Let a *meaning*$_1$ be that which an indexical language $\pounds$ assigns to a sentence σ on a possible occasion o of its utterance: $\pounds(\sigma, o)$, a set of worlds on our account. Let a *meaning*$_2$ be that fixed function whereby the meaning$_1$ in $\pounds$ of a sentence σ varies with its occasions of utterance. Which one is a meaning? That is unclear—and it is no clearer which one is a sense, intension, interpretation, truth-condition, or proposition.

The objection says that we sometimes cannot find the meaning$_1$ of σ on o in P by looking into the minds of members of P. Granted. But what prevents it is that the minds do not contain enough information about o: in particular, not enough information about its causal history. We have been given no reason to doubt that we can find the meaning$_2$ of σ in P by looking into minds; and that is all we need do to identify the indexical language used by P.

An exactly similar situation arises with more familiar kinds of indexicality. We may be unable to discover the time of an utterance of a tensed sentence by looking into minds, so we may know the meaning$_2$ of the sentence uttered in the speaker's indexical language without knowing its meaning$_1$ on the occasion in question.

Objection: It makes no sense to say that a mere string of sounds or of marks can bear a meaning or a truth-value. The proper bearers of meanings and truth-values are particular speech acts.

Reply: I do not say that a string of types of sounds or of marks, by itself, can bear a meaning or truth-value. I say it bears a meaning and truth-value relative to a language, or relative to a population. A particular speech act by itself, on the other hand, can bear a meaning and truth-value, since in most cases it uniquely determines the language that was in use on the occasion of its performance. So can a particular uttered string of vocal sounds, or a particular inscribed string of marks, since in most cases that uniquely determines the particular speech act in which it was produced, which in turn uniquely determines the language.

Objection: It is circular to give an account of meanings in terms of possible worlds. The notion of a possible world must itself be explained in semantic terms.

Possible worlds are models of the analytic sentences of some language, or they are the diagrams or theories of such models.[5]

Reply: I do not agree that the notion of a possible world ought to be explained in semantic terms, or that possible worlds ought to be eliminated from our ontology and replaced by their linguistic representatives—models or whatever.

For one thing, the replacement does not work properly. Two worlds indistinguishable in the representing language will receive one and the same representative.

But more important, the replacement is gratuitous. The notion of a possible world *is* familiar in its own right, philosophically fruitful, and tolerably clear. Possible worlds are deemed mysterious and objectionable because they raise questions we may never know how to answer: are any possible worlds five-dimensional? We seem to think that we do not understand possible worlds at all unless we are capable of omniscience about them—but why should we think that? Sets also raise unanswerable questions, yet most of us do not repudiate sets.

But if you insist on repudiating possible worlds, much of my theory can be adapted to meet your needs. We must suppose that you have already defined truth and analyticity in some base language—that is the price you pay for repudiating possible worlds—and you want to define them in general, for the language of an arbitrary population *P*. Pick your favorite base language with any convenient special properties you like: Latin, Esperanto, Begriffsschrift, Semantic Markerese, or what have you. Let's say you pick Latin. Then you may redefine a language as any function from certain strings of sound or of marks to sentences of Latin. A sentence σ of a language £ (in your sense) is true, analytic, etc., if and only if £(σ) is true, analytic, etc., in Latin.

You cannot believe in languages in my sense, since they involve possible worlds. But I can believe in languages in your sense. And I can map your languages onto mine by means of a fixed function from sentences of Latin to sets of worlds. This function is just the language Latin, in my sense. My language £ is the composition of two functions: your language £, and my language Latin. Thus I can accept your approach as part of mine.

Objection: Why all this needless and outmoded hypostasis of meanings? Our ordinary talk about meaning does not commit us to believing in any such entities as meanings, any more than our ordinary talk about actions for the sake of ends commits us to believing in any such entities as sakes.

Reply: Perhaps there are some who hypostatize meanings compulsively, imagining that they could not possibly make sense of our ordinary talk about meaning

---

[5]Possible worlds are taken as models in S. Kripke, "A Completeness Theorem in Modal Logic," *Journal of Symbolic Logic* 24 (1959): 1–15; in Carnap's recent work on semantics and inductive logic, discussed briefly in secs. 9, 10, and 25 of "Replies and Systematic Expositions," *The Philosophy of Rudolf Carnap*, ed. by P. Schilpp, (La Salle, Ill.: Open Court,, 1963) and elsewhere. Worlds are taken as state-descriptions—diagrams of models—in Carnap's earlier work: for instance, sec. 18 of *Introduction to Semantics* (Cambridge, Mass.: Harvard Univ. Press, 1942). Worlds are taken as complete, consistent novels—theories of models—in R. Jeffrey, *The Logic of Decision* (New York: McGraw-Hill, 1965), sec. 12.8.

if they did not. Not I. I hypostatize meanings because I find it convenient to do so, and I have no good reason not to. There is no point in being a part-time nominalist. I am persuaded on independent grounds that I ought to believe in possible worlds and possible beings therein, and that I ought to believe in sets of things I believe in. Once I have these, I have all the entities I could ever want.

Objection: A language consists not only of sentences with their meanings, but also of constituents of sentences—things sentences are made of—with their meanings. And if any language is to be learnable without being finite, it must somehow be determined by finitely many of its constituents and finitely many operations on constituents.

Reply: We may define a class of objects called *grammars*. A grammar Γ is a triple comprising (1) a large finite *lexicon* of *elementary constituents* paired with meanings; (2) a finite set of *combining operations* which build larger constituents by combining smaller constituents, and derive a meaning for the new constituent out of the meanings of the old ones; and (3) a *representing operation* which effectively maps certain constituents onto strings of sounds or of marks. A grammar Γ generates a function which assigns meanings to certain constituents, called *constituents in Γ*. It generates another function which assigns meanings to certain strings of sounds or of marks. Part of this latter function is what we have hitherto called a language. A grammar uniquely determines the language it generates. But a language does not uniquely determine the grammar that generates it, not even when we disregard superficial differences between grammars.

I have spoken of meanings for constituents in a grammer, but what sort of things are these? Referential semantics tried to answer that question. It was a near miss, failing because contingent facts got mixed up with the meanings. The cure, discovered by Carnap,[6] is to do referential semantics not just in our actual world but in every possible world. A meaning for a name can be a function from worlds to possible individuals; for a common noun, a function from worlds to sets; for a sentence, a function from worlds to truth-values (or more simply, the set of worlds where that function takes the value truth). Other derived categories may be defined by their characteristic modes of combination. For instance, an adjective combines with a common noun to make a compound common noun; so its meaning may be a function from common-noun meanings to common-noun meanings, such that the meaning of an adjective-plus-common-noun compound is the value of this function when given as argument the meaning of the common noun being modified. Likewise a verb phrase takes a name to make a sentence; so its meaning may be a function that takes the meaning of the name as argument to give the meaning of the sentence as value. An adverb (of one sort) takes a verb phrase to make a verb phrase, so its meaning may be a function from verb-phrase meanings to verb-phrase

---

[6]"Replies and Systematic Expositions," sec. 9.v. A better-known presentation of essentially the same idea is in S. Kripke, "Semantical Considerations on Modal Logic," *Acta Philosophica Fennica* 16 (1963): 83–94.

meanings. And so on, as far as need be, to more and more complicated derived categories.[7]

If you repudiate possible worlds, an alternative course is open to you: let the meanings for constituents in a grammar be phrases of Latin, or whatever your favorite base language may be.

A grammar, for us, is a semantically interpreted grammar—just as a language is a semantically interpreted language. We shall not be concerned with what are called grammars or languages in a purely syntactic sense. My definition of a grammar is meant to be general enough to encompass transformational or phrase-structure grammars for natural language[8] (when provided with semantic interpretations) as well as systems of formation and valuation rules for formalized languages. Like my previous definition of a language, my definition of a grammar is too general: it gives a large superset of the interesting grammars.

A grammar, like a language, is a set-theoretical entity which can be discussed in complete abstraction from human affairs. Since a grammar generates a unique language, all the semantic concepts we earlier defined relative to a language £—sentencehood, truth, analyticity, etc.—could just as well have been defined relative to a grammar Γ. We can also handle other semantic concepts pertaining to constituents, or to the constituent structure of sentences.

We can define the meaning in Γ, denotation in Γ, etc., of a subsentential constituent in Γ. We can define the meaning in Γ, denotation in Γ, etc., of a *phrase:* a string of sounds or of marks representing a subsentential constituent in Γ via the representing operation of Γ. We can define something we may call the *fine structure of meaning* in Γ of a sentence or phrase: the manner in which the meaning of the sentence or phrase is derived from the meanings of its constituents and the way it is built out of them. Thus we can take account of the sense in which, for instance, different analytic sentences are said to differ in meaning.

Now the objection can be restated: what ought to be called a language is what I have hitherto called a grammar, not what I have hitherto called a language. Different grammar, different language—at least if we ignore superficial differences between grammars. Verbal disagreement aside, the place I gave to my so-called languages ought to have been given instead to my so-called grammars. Why not begin by saying what it is for a grammar Γ to be used by a population P? Then we could go on to define sentencehood, truth, analyticity, etc., in P as sentencehood, truth, analyticity, etc., in whatever grammar is used by P. This approach would have the advantage that we could handle the semantics of constituents in a

---

[7] See my "General Semantics," in this volume.

[8] For a description of the sort of grammars I have in mind (minus the semantic interpretation) see N. Chomsky, *Aspects of the Theory of Syntax* (Cambridge, Mass.: M.I.T. Press, 1965), and G. Harman, "Generative Grammars without Transformation Rules," *Language* 37 (1963): 597–616. My "constituents" correspond to semantically interpreted deep phrase-markers, or sub-trees thereof, in a transformational grammar. My "representing operation" may work in several steps and thus subsumes both the transformational and the phonological components of a transformational grammar.

population in an exactly similar way. We could say that a constituent or phrase has a certain meaning, denotation, etc., in *P* if it has that meaning, denotation, etc., in whatever grammar is used by *P*. We could say that a sentence or phrase has a certain fine structure of meaning in *P* if it has it in whatever grammar is used by *P*.

Unfortunately, I know of no promising way to make objective sense of the assertion that a grammar Γ is used by a population *P* whereas another grammar Γ', which generates the same language as Γ, is not. I have tried to say how there are facts about *P* which objectively select the languages used by *P*. I am not sure there are facts about *P* which objectively select privileged grammars for those languages. It is easy enough to define truthfulness and trust in a grammar, but that will not help: a convention of truthfulness and trust in Γ will also be a convention of truthfulness and trust in Γ' whenever Γ and Γ' generate the same language.

I do not propose to discard the notion of the meaning in *P* of a constituent or phrase, or the fine structure of meaning in *P* of a sentence. To propose that would be absurd. But I hold that these notions depend on our methods of evaluating grammars, and therefore are no clearer and no more objective than our notion of a *best* grammar for a given language. For I would say that a grammar Γ is used by *P* if and only if Γ is a best grammar for a language £ that is used by *P* in virtue of a convention in *P* of truthfulness and trust in £; and I would define the meaning in *P* of a constituent or phrase, and the fine structure of meaning in *P* of a sentence, accordingly.

The notions of a language used by *P*, of a meaning of a sentence in *P*, and so on, are independent of our evaluation of grammars. Therefore I take these as primary. The point is not to refrain from ever saying anything that depends on the evaluation of grammars. The point is to do so only when we must, and that is why I have concentrated on languages rather than grammars.

We may meet little practical difficulty with the semantics of constituents in populations, even if its foundations are as infirm as I fear. It may often happen that all the grammars anyone might call best for a given language will agree on the meaning of a given constituent. Yet there is trouble to be found: Quine's examples of indeterminacy of reference[9] seem to be disagreements in constituent semantics between alternative good grammars for one language. We should regard with suspicion any method that purports to settle objectively whether, in some tribe, "gavagai" is true of temporally continuant rabbits or time-slices thereof. You can give their language a good grammar of either kind—and that's that.

It is useful to divide the claimed indeterminacy of constituent semantics into three separate indeterminacies. We begin with undoubted objective fact: the dependence of the subject's behavioral output on his input of sensory stimulation (both as it actually is and as it might have been) together with all the physical laws and

---

[9]W. V. Quine, "Ontological Relativity," *Journal of Philosophy* 65 (1968): 185–212; *Word and Object*, pp. 68–79.

anatomical facts that explain it. (a) This information either determines or under-determines the subject's system of propositional attitudes: in particular, his beliefs and desires. (b) These propositional attitudes either determine or underdetermine the truth conditions of full sentences—what I have here called his language. (c) The truth conditions of full sentences either determine or underdetermine the meanings of sub-sentential constituents—what I have here called his grammar.

My present discussion has been directed at the middle step, from beliefs and desires to truth conditions for full sentences. I have said that the former determine the latter—provided (what need not be the case) that the beliefs and desires of the subject and his fellows are such as to comprise a fully determinate convention of truthfulness and trust in some definite language. I have said nothing here about the determinacy of the first step; and I am inclined to share in Quine's doubts about the determinacy of the third step.

Objection: Suppose that whenever anyone is party to a convention of truthfulness and trust in any language $\mathcal{L}$, his competence to be party to that convention—to conform, to expect conformity, etc.—is due to his possession of some sort of uncon-scious internal representation of a grammar for $\mathcal{L}$. That is a likely hypothesis, since it best explains what we know about linguistic competence. In particular, it explains why experience with some sentences leads spontaneously to expectations involving others. But on that hypothesis, we might as well bypass the conventions of language and say that $\mathcal{L}$ is used by P if and only if everyone in P possesses an internal representation of a grammar for $\mathcal{L}$.

Reply: In the first place, the hypothesis of internally represented grammars is not an explanation—best or otherwise—of anything. Perhaps it is *part* of some theory that best explains what we know about linguistic competence; we can't judge until we hear something about what the rest of the theory is like.

Nonetheless, I am ready enough to believe in internally represented grammars. But I am much less certain that there are internally represented grammars than I am that languages are used by populations; and I think it makes sense to say that languages might be used by populations even if there were no internally represented grammars. I can tentatively agree that $\mathcal{L}$ is used by P if and only if everyone in P possesses an internal representation of a grammar for $\mathcal{L}$, if that is offered as a sci-entific hypothesis. But I cannot accept it as any sort of analysis of "$\mathcal{L}$ is used by P", since the analysandum clearly could be true although the analysans was false.

Objection: The notion of a convention of truthfulness and trust in $\mathcal{L}$ is a needless complication. Why not say, straightforwardly, that $\mathcal{L}$ is used by P if and only if there prevails in P a convention to bestow upon each sentence of $\mathcal{L}$ the meaning that $\mathcal{L}$ assigns to it? Or, indeed, that a grammar Γ of $\mathcal{L}$ is used by P if and only if there prevails in P a convention to bestow upon each constituent in Γ the mean-ing that Γ assigns to it?

Reply: A convention, as I have defined it, is a regularity in action, or in action and belief. If that feature of the definition were given up, I do not see how to salvage any part of my theory of conventions. It is essential that a convention is a regularity such that conformity by others gives one a reason to conform; and such a reason must either be a practical reason for acting or an epistemic reason for believing. What other kind of reason is there?

Yet there is no such thing as an action of bestowing a meaning (except for an irrelevant sort of action that is performed not by language-users but by creators of language) so we cannot suppose that language-using populations have conventions to perform such actions. Neither does bestowal of meaning consist in forming some belief. Granted, bestowal of meaning is conventional in the sense that it depends on convention: the meanings would have been different if the conventions of truthfulness and trust had been different. But bestowal of meaning is not an action done in conformity to a convention, since it is not an action, and it is not a belief-formation in conformity to a convention, since it is not a belief-formation.

Objection: The beliefs and desires that constitute a convention are inaccessible mental entities, just as much as hypothetical internal representations of grammars are. It would be best if we could say in purely behavioristic terms what it is for a language £ to be used by a population *P*. We might be able to do this by referring to the way in which members of *P* would answer counterfactual questionnaires; or by referring to the way in which they would or would not assent to sentences under deceptive sensory stimulation; or by referring to the way in which they would intuitively group sentences into similarity-classes; or in some other way.

Reply: Suppose we succeeded in giving a behavioristic operational definition of the relation "£ is used by *P*." This would not help us to understand what it is for £ to be used by *P*; for we would have to understand that already, and also know a good deal of common-sense psychology, in order to check that the operational definition was a definition of what it is supposed to be a definition of. If we did not know what it meant for £ to be used by *P*, we would not know what sort of behavior on the part of members of *P* would indicate that £ was used by *P*.

Objection: The conventions of language are nothing more nor less than our famously obscure old friends, the rules of language, renamed.

Reply: A convention of truthfulness and trust in £ might well be called a rule, though it lacks many features that have sometimes been thought to belong to the essence of rules. It is not promulgated by any authority. It is not enforced by means of sanctions except to the extent that, because one has some sort of reason to conform, something bad may happen if one does not. It is nowhere codified and therefore is not "laid down in the course of teaching the language" or "appealed to in the course of criticizing a person's linguistic performance."[10] Yet it is more than a mere regularity holding "as a rule"; it is a regularity accompanied and sustained by a special kind of system of beliefs and desires.

A convention of truthfulness and trust in £ might have as consequences other regularities which were conventions of language in their own right: specializations of the convention to certain special situations. (For instance, a convention of truth-

---

[10] P. Ziff, *Semantic Analysis*, pp. 34–35.

fulness in £ on weekdays.) Such derivative conventions of language might also be called rules; some of them might stand a better chance of being codified than the overall convention which subsumes them.

However, there are other so-called rules of language which are not conventions of language and are not in the least like conventions of language: for instance, "rules" of syntax and semantics. They are not even regularities and cannot be formulated as imperatives. They might better be described not as rules, but as clauses in the definitions of entities which are to be mentioned in rules: clauses in the definition of a language £, of the act of being truthful in £, of the act of stating that the moon is blue, etc.

Thus the conventions of language might properly be called rules, but it is more informative and less confusing to call them conventions.

Objection: Language is not conventional. We have found that human capacities for language acquisition are highly specific and dictate the form of any language that humans can learn and use.

Reply: It may be that there is less conventionality than we used to think: fewer features of language which depend on convention, more which are determined by our innate capacities and therefore are common to all languages which are genuine alternatives to our actual language. But there are still conventions of language; and there are still convention-dependent features of language, differing from one alternative possible convention of language to another. That is established by the diversity of actual languages. There are conventions of language so long as the regularity of truthfulness in a given language has even a single alternative.

Objection: Unless a language-user is also a set-theorist, he cannot expect his fellows to conform to a regularity of truthfulness and trust in a certain language £. For to conform to this regularity is to bear a relation to a certain esoteric entity: a set of ordered pairs of sequences of sound-types or of mark-types and sets of possible worlds (or something more complicated still, if £ is a natural language with indexicality, ambiguity, and non-indicatives). The common man has no concept of any such entity. Hence he can have no expectations regarding such an entity.

Reply: The common man need not have any concept of £ in order to expect his fellows to be truthful and trusting in £. He need only have suitable particular expectations about how they might act, and how they might form beliefs, in various situations. He can tell whether any actual or hypothetical particular action or belief-formation on their part is compatible with his expectations. He expects them to conform to a regularity of truthfulness and trust in £ if any particular activity or belief-formation that would fit his expectations would fall under what *we*—but not *he*—could describe as conformity to that regularity.

It may well be that his elaborate, infinite system of potential particular expectations can only be explained on the hypothesis that he has some unconscious mental entity somehow analogous to a general concept of £—say, an internally represented grammar. But it does not matter whether this is so or not. We are concerned only to say what system of expectations a normal member of a language-using population must have. We need not engage in psychological speculation about how those expectations are generated.

Objection: If there are conventions of language, those who are party to them should know what they are. Yet no one can fully describe the conventions of language to which he is supposedly a party.

Reply: He may nevertheless know what they are. It is enough to be able to recognize conformity and non-conformity to his convention, and to be able to try to conform to it. We know ever so many things we cannot put into words.

Objection: Use of language is almost never a rational activity. We produce and respond to utterances by habit, not as the result of any sort of reasoning or deliberation.

Reply: An action may be rational, and may be explained by the agent's beliefs and desires, even though that action was done by habit, and the agent gave no thought to the beliefs or desires which were his reason for acting. A habit may be under the agent's rational control in this sense: if that habit ever ceased to serve the agent's desires according to his beliefs, it would at once be overridden and corrected by conscious reasoning. Action done by a habit of this sort is both habitual and rational. Likewise for habits of believing. Our normal use of language is rational, since it is under rational control.

Perhaps use of language by young children is not a rational activity. Perhaps it results from habits which would not be overridden if they ceased to serve the agent's desires according to his beliefs. If that is so, I would deny that these children have yet become party to conventions of language, and I would deny that they have yet become normal members of a language-using population. Perhaps language is first acquired and afterward becomes conventional. That would not conflict with anything I have said. I am not concerned with the way in which language is acquired, only with the condition of a normal member of a language-using population when he is done acquiring language.

Objection: Language could not have originated by convention. There could not have been an agreement to begin being truthful and trusting in a certain chosen language, unless some previous language had already been available for use in making the agreement.

Reply: The first language could not have originated by an agreement, for the reason given. But that is not to say that language cannot be conventional. A convention is so-called because of the way it persists, not because of the way it originated. A convention need not originate by convention—that is, by agreement—though many conventions do originate by agreement, and others could originate by agreement even if they actually do not. In saying that language is convention-governed, I say nothing whatever about the origins of language.

Objection: A man isolated all his life from others might begin—through genius or a miracle—to use language, say to keep a diary. (This would be an accidentally private language, not the necessarily private language Wittgenstein is said to have proved to be impossible.) In this case, at least, there would be no convention involved.

Reply: Taking the definition literally, there would be no convention. But there would be something very similar. The isolated man conforms to a certain regularity at many different times. He knows at each of these times that he has conformed to that regularity in the past, and he has an interest in uniformity over time, so he continues to conform to that regularity instead of to any of various alternative regularities that would have done about as well if he had started out using them. He knows at all times that this is so, knows that he knows at all times that this is so, and so on. We might think of the situation as one in which a convention prevails in the population of different time-slices of the same man.

Objection: It is circular to define the meaning in *P* of sentences in terms of the beliefs held by members of *P*. For presumably the members of *P* think in their language. For instance, they hold beliefs by accepting suitable sentences of their language. If we do not already know the meaning in *P* of a sentence, we do not know what belief a member of *P* would hold by accepting that sentence.

Reply: It may be true that men think in language, and that to hold a belief is to accept a sentence of one's language. But it does not follow that belief should be analyzed as acceptance of sentences. It should not be. Even if men do in fact think in language, they might not. It is at least possible that men—like beasts—might hold beliefs otherwise than by accepting sentences. (I shall not say here how I think belief should be analyzed.) No circle arises from the contingent truth that a member of *P* holds beliefs by accepting sentences, so long as we can specify his beliefs without mentioning the sentences he accepts. We can do this for men, as we can for beasts.

Objection: Suppose a language £ is used by a population of inveterate liars, who are untruthful in £ more often than not. There would not be even a regularity—still less a convention, which implies a regularity—of truthfulness and trust in £.

Reply: I deny that £ is used by the population of liars. I have undertaken to follow ordinary usage only where it is determinate; and, once it is appreciated just how extraordinary the situation would have to be, I do not believe that ordinary usage is determinate in this case. There are many similarities to clear cases in which a language is used by a population, and it is understandable that we should feel some inclination to classify this case along with them. But there are many important differences as well.

Although I deny that the population of liars *collectively* uses £, I am willing to say that each liar *individually* may use £, provided that he falsely believes that he is a member—albeit an exceptional, untruthful member—of a population wherein there prevails a convention of truthfulness and trust in £. He is in a position like that of a madman who thinks he belongs to a population which uses £, and behaves accordingly, and so can be said to use £, although in reality all the other members of this £-using population are figments of his imagination.

Objection: Suppose the members of a population are untruthful in their language £ more often than not, not because they lie, but because they go in heavily for irony, metaphor, hyperbole, and such. It is hard to deny that the language £ is used by such a population.

Reply: I claim that these people are truthful in their language £, though they are not *literally truthful* in £. To be literally truthful in £ is to be truthful in another language related to £, a language we can call literal-£. The relation between £ and literal-£ is as follows: a good way to describe £ is to start by specifying literal-£ arnd then to describe £ as obtained by certain systematic departures from literal-£. This two-stage specification of £ by way of literal-£ may turn out to be much simpler than any direct specification of £.

Objection: Suppose they are often untruthful in £ because they are not communicating at all. They are joking, or telling tall tales, or telling white lies as a matter of social ritual. In these situations, there is neither truthfulness nor trust in £. Indeed, it is common knowledge that there is not.

Reply: Perhaps I can say the same sort of thing about this non-serious language use as I did about non-literal language use. That is: their seeming untruthfulness in non-serious situations is untruthfulness not in the language £ that they actually use, but only in a simplified approximation to £. We may specify £ by first specifying the approximation language, then listing the signs and features of context by which non-serious language use can be recognized, then specifying that when these signs or features are present, what would count as untruths in the approximation language do not count as such in £ itself. Perhaps they are automatically true in £, regardless of the facts; perhaps they cease to count as indicative.

Example: what would otherwise be an untruth may not be one if said by a child with crossed fingers. Unfortunately, the signs and features of context by which we recognize non-serious language use are seldom as simple, standardized, and conventional as that. While they must find a place somewhere in a full account of the phenomenon of language, it may be inexpedient to burden the specification of £ with them.

Perhaps it may be enough to note that these situations of non-serious language use must be at least somewhat exceptional if we are to have anything like a clear case of use of £; and to recall that the definition of a convention was loose enough to tolerate some exceptions. We could take the non-serious cases simply as violations—explicable and harmless ones—of the conventions of language.

There is a third alternative, requiring a modification in my theory. We may say that a *serious communication situation* exists with respect to a sentence σ of £ whenever it is true, and common knowledge between a speaker and a hearer, that (a) the speaker does, and the hearer does not, know whether σ is true in £; (b) the hearer wants to know; (c) the speaker wants the hearer to know; and (d) neither the speaker nor the hearer has other (comparably strong) desires as to whether or not the speaker utters σ. (Note that when there is a serious communication situation with respect to σ, there is one also with respect to synonyms or contradictories in £ of σ, and probably also with respect to other logical relatives in £ of σ.) Then we may say that the convention whereby P uses £ is a convention of truthfulness and trust in £ in serious communication situations. That is: when a serious communication situation exists with respect to σ, then the speaker tries not to utter σ unless it is true in £, and the hearer responds, if σ is uttered, by coming to believe that σ is true in £. If that much is a convention in P, it does not matter what goes on in other situations: they use £.

The definition here given of a serious communication resembles that of a signaling problem in *Convention*, chapter IV, the difference being that the hearer may respond by belief-formation only, rather than by what speaker and hearer alike take to be appropriate action. If this modification were adopted, it would bring my general account of language even closer to my account in *Convention* of the special case of signaling.

Objection: Truthfulness and trust cannot be a convention. What could be the alternative to uniform truthfulness—uniform *un*truthfulness, perhaps? But it seems that if such untruthfulness were not intended to deceive, and did not deceive, then it too would be truthfulness.

Reply: The convention is not the regularity of truthfulness and trust *simpliciter*. It is the regularity of truthfulness and trust in some particular language £. Its alternatives are possible regularities of truthfulness and trust in other languages. A regularity of uniform untruthfulness and non-trust in a language £ can be redescribed as a regularity of truthfulness and trust in a different language anti-£ complementary to £. Anti-£ has exactly the same sentences as £, but with opposite truth conditions. Hence the true sentences of anti-£ are all and only the untrue sentences of £.

There is a different regularity that we may call a regularity of truthfulness and trust *simpliciter*. That is the regularity of being truthful and trusting in whichever language is used by one's fellows. This regularity neither is a convention nor depends on convention. If any language whatever is used by a population P, then a regularity (perhaps with exceptions) of truthfulness and trust *simpliciter* prevails in P.

Objection: Even truthfulness and trust in £ cannot be a convention. One conforms to a convention, on my account, because doing so answers to some sort of interest. But a decent man is truthful in £ if his fellows are, whether or not it is in his interest. For he recognizes that he is under a moral obligation to be truthful in £; an obligation to reciprocate the benefits he has derived from others' truthfulness in £, or something of that sort. Truthfulness in £ may bind the decent man against his own interest. It is more like a social contract than a convention.

Reply: The objection plays on a narrow sense of "interest" in which only selfish interests count. We commonly adopt a wider sense. We count also altruistic interests and interests springing from one's recognition of obligations. It is this wider sense that should be understood in the definition of convention. In this wider sense, it is nonsense to think of an obligation as outweighing one's interests. Rather, the obligation provides one interest which may outweigh the other interests.

A convention of truthfulness and trust in £ is sustained by a mixture of selfish interests, altruistic interests, and interests derived from obligation. Usually all are present in strength; perhaps any one would be enough to sustain the convention. But occasionally truthfulness in £ answers only to interests derived from obligation and goes against one's selfish or even altruistic interests. In such a case, only a decent man will have an interest in remaining truthful in £. But I dare say such cases are not as common as moralists might imagine. A convention of truthfulness and trust among scoundrels might well be sustained—with occasional lapses—by selfish interests alone.

A convention persists because everyone has reason to conform if others do. If the convention is a regularity in action, this is to say that it persists because everyone prefers general conformity rather than almost-general conformity with himself as the exception. A (demythologized) social contract may also be described as a regularity sustained by a general preference for general conformity, but the second term of the preference is different. Everyone prefers general conformity over a certain state of general non-conformity called the state of nature. This general preference sets up an obligation to reciprocate the benefits derived from others' conformity, and that obligation creates an interest in conforming which sustains the social contract. The objection suggests that, among decent men, truthfulness in £ is a social contract. I agree; but there is no reason why it cannot be a social contract and a convention as well, and I think it is.

Objection: Communication cannot be explained by conventions of truthfulness alone. If I utter a sentence σ of our language £, you—expecting me to be truthful in £—will conclude that I take σ to be true in £. If you think I am well informed, you will also conclude that probably σ is true in £. But you will draw other conclusions as well, based on your legitimate assumption that it is for some good reason that I chose to utter σ rather than remain silent, and rather than utter any of the other sentences of £ that I also take to be true in £. I can communicate all sorts of misinformation by exploiting your beliefs about my conversational purposes, without ever being untruthful in £. Communication depends on principles of helpfulness and relevance as well as truthfulness.

Reply: All this does not conflict with anything I have said. We do conform to conversational regularities of helpfulness and relevance. But these regularities are not independent conventions of language; they result from our convention of truthfulness and trust in £ together with certain general facts—not dependent on any convention—about our conversational purposes and our beliefs about one another. Since they are by-products of a convention of truthfulness and trust, it is unnecessary to mention them separately in specifying the conditions under which a language is used by a population.

Objection: Let £ be the language used in P, and let $£^-$ be some fairly rich fragment of £. That is, the sentences of $£^-$ are many but not all of the sentences of £ (in an appropriate special sense if £ is infinite); and any sentence of both has the same meaning in both. Then $£^-$ also turns out to be a language used by P; for by my definition there prevails in P a convention of truthfulness and trust in $£^-$, sustained by an interest in communication. Not one but many—perhaps infinitely many—languages are used by P.

Reply: That is so, but it is no problem. Why not say that any rich fragment of a language used by P is itself a used language?

Indeed, we will need to say such things when P is linguistically inhomogeneous. Suppose, for instance, that P divides into two classes: the learned and the vulgar. Among the learned there prevails a convention of truthfulness and trust in a language $\pounds$; among P as a whole there does not, but there does prevail a convention of truthfulness and trust in a rich fragment $\pounds^-$ of $\pounds$. We wish to say that the learned have a common language with the vulgar, but that is so only if $\pounds^-$, as well as $\pounds$, counts as a language used by the learned.

Another case: the learned use $\pounds_1$, the vulgar use $\pounds_2$, neither is included in the other, but there is extensive overlap. Here $\pounds_1$ and $\pounds_2$ are to be the most inclusive languages used by the respective classes. Again we wish to say that the learned and the vulgar have a common language: in particular, the largest fragment common to $\pounds_1$ and $\pounds_2$. That can be so only if this largest common fragment counts as a language used by the vulgar, by the learned, and by the whole population.

I agree that we often do not count the fragments; we can speak of *the* language of P, meaning by this not the one and only thing that is a language used by P, but rather the most inclusive language used by P. Or we could mean something else: the union of all the languages used by substantial sub-populations of P, provided that some quite large fragment of this union is used by (more or less) all of P. Note that the union as a whole need not be used at all, in my primary sense, either by P or by any sub-population of P. Thus in my example of the last paragraph, the language of P might be taken either as the largest common fragment of $\pounds_1$ and $\pounds_2$ or as the union of $\pounds_1$ and $\pounds_2$.

Further complications arise. Suppose that half of the population of a certain town uses English, and also uses basic Welsh; while the other half uses Welsh, and also uses basic English. The most inclusive language used by the entire population is the union of basic Welsh and basic English. The union of lagnuages used by substantial sub-populations is the union of English and Welsh, and the proviso is satisfied that some quite large fragment of this union is used by the whole population. Yet we would be reluctant to say that either of these unions is the language of the population of the town. We might say that Welsh and English are the two languages of the town, or that basic English and basic Welsh are. It is odd to call either of the two language-unions a language; though once they *are* called that, it is no further oddity to say that one or other of them is the language of the town. There are two considerations. First: English, or Welsh, or basic English, or basic Welsh, can be given a satisfactory unified grammar; whereas the language-unions cannot. Second: English, or Welsh, or basic Welsh, or basic English, is (in either of the senses I have explained) the language of a large population outside the town; whereas the language-unions are not. I am not sure which of the two considerations should be emphasized in saying when a language is the language of a population.

Objection: Let £ be the language of *P*; that is, the language that ought to count as the most inclusive language used by *P*. (Assume that *P* is linguistically homogeneous.) Let £⁺ be obtained by adding garbage to £; some extra sentences, very long and difficult to pronounce, and hence never uttered in *P*, with arbitrarily chosen meanings in £⁺. Then it seems that £⁺ is a language used by *P*, which is absurd.

A sentence never uttered at all is *a fortiori* never uttered untruthfully. So truthfulness-as-usual in £ plus truthfulness-by-silence on the garbage sentences constitutes a kind of truthfulness in £⁺; and the expectation thereof constitutes trust in £⁺. Therefore we have a prevailing regularity of truthfulness and trust in £⁺. This regularity qualifies as a convention in *P* sustained by an interest in communication.

Reply: Truthfulness-by-silence is truthfulness, and expectation thereof is expectation of truthfulness; but expectation of truthfulness-by-silence is not yet trust. Expectation of (successful) truthfulness—expectation that a given sentence will not be uttered falsely—is a necessary but not sufficient condition for trust. There is no regularity of trust in £⁺, so far as the garbage sentences are concerned. Hence there is no convention of truthfulness and trust in £⁺, and £⁺ is not used by *P*.

For trust, one must be able to take an utterance of a sentence as evidence that the sentence is true. That is so only if one's degree of belief that the sentence will be uttered falsely is low, not only absolutely, but as a fraction of one's degree of belief—perhaps already very low—that the sentence will be uttered at all. Further, this must be so not merely because one believes in advance that the sentence is probably true: one's degree of belief that the sentence will be uttered falsely must be substantially lower than the product of one's degree of belief that the sentence will be uttered times one's prior degree of belief that it is false. A garbage sentence of £⁺ will not meet this last requirement, not even if one believes to high degrees both that it is true in £⁺ and that it never will be uttered.

This objection was originally made, by Stephen Schiffer, against my former view that conventions of language are conventions of truthfulness. I am inclined to think that it succeeds as a counter-example to that view. I agree that £⁺ is not used by *P*, in any reasonable sense, but I have not seen any way to avoid conceding that £⁺ is a possible language—it might *really* be used—and that there does prevail in *P* a convention of truthfulness in £⁺, sustained by an interest in communication. Here we have another advantage of the present account over my original one.

Objection: A sentence either is or isn't analytic in a given language, and a language either is or isn't conventionally adopted by a given population. Hence there is no way for the analytic-synthetic distinction to be unsharp. But not only can it be unsharp; it usually is, at least in cases of interest to philosophers. A sharp analytic-synthetic distinction is available only relative to particular rational reconstructions of ordinary language.

Reply: One might try to explain unsharp analyticity by a theory of degrees of convention. Conventions do admit of degree in a great many ways: by the strengths of the beliefs and desires involved, and by the fraction of exceptions to the many almost-universal quantifications in the definition of convention. But this will not help much. It is easy to imagine unsharp analyticity even in a population whose conventions of language are conventions to the highest degree in every way.

One might try to explain unsharp analyticity by recalling that we may not know whether some worlds are really possible. If a sentence is true in our language in all worlds except some worlds of doubtful possibility, then that sentence will be of doubtful analyticity. But this will not help much either. Unsharp analyticity usually seems to arise because we cannot decide whether a sentence would be true in some bizarre but clearly possible world.

A better explanation would be that our convention of language is not exactly a convention of truthfulness and trust in a single language, as I have said so far. Rather it is a convention of truthfulness and trust in whichever we please of some cluster of similar languages: languages with more or less the same sentences, and more or less the same truth-values for the sentences in worlds close to our actual world, but with increasing divergence in truth-values as we go to increasingly remote, bizarre worlds. The convention confines us to the cluster, but leaves us with indeterminacies whenever the languages of the cluster disagree. We are free to settle these indeterminacies however we like. Thus an ordinary, open-textured, imprecise language is a sort of blur of precise languages—a region, not a point, in the space of languages. Analyticity is sharp in each language of our cluster. But when different languages of our cluster disagree on the analyticity of a sentence, then that sentence is unsharply analytic among us.

Rational reconstructions have been said to be irrelevant to philosophical problems arising in ordinary, unreconstructed language. My hypothesis of conventions of truthfulness and trust in language-clusters provides a defense against this accusation. Reconstruction is not—or not always—departure from ordinary language. Rather it is selection from ordinary language: isolation of one precise language, or of a sub-cluster, out of the language-cluster wherein we have a convention of truthfulness and trust.

Objection: The thesis and the antithesis pertain to different subjects. The thesis, in which languages are regarded as semantic systems, belongs to the philosophy of artificial languages. The antithesis, in which language is regarded as part of human natural history, belongs to the philosophy of natural language.

Reply: Not so. *Both* accounts—just like almost any account of almost anything—can most easily be applied to simple, artificial, imaginary examples. Language-games are just as artificial as formalized calculi.

According to the theory I have presented, philosophy of language is a single subject. The thesis and antithesis have been the property of rival schools; but in fact they are complementary essential ingredients in any adequate account either of languages or of language.

· T W E L V E ·

General Semantics

I. INTRODUCTION

On the hypothesis that all natural or artificial languages of interest to us can be given transformational grammars of a certain not-very-special sort, it becomes possible to give very simple general answers to the questions:

(1) What sort of thing is a meaning?
(2) What is the form of the semantic rules whereby meanings of compounds are built from the meanings of their constituent parts?

It is not my plan to make any strong empirical claim about language. To the contrary: I want to propose a convenient format for semantics general enough to work for a great variety of logically possible languages. This paper therefore belongs not to empirical linguistic theory but to the philosophy thereof.

My proposals regarding the nature of meanings will not comform to the expectations of those linguists who conceive of semantic interpretation as the assignment to sentences and their constituents of compounds of 'semantic markers' or the like.[1]

This paper is derived from a talk given at the Third La Jolla Conference on Linguistic Theory, March 1969. I am much indebted to Charles Chastain, Frank Heny, David Kaplan, George Lakoff, Richard Montague, and Barbara Partee for many valuable criticisms and suggestions.

[1]Jerrold Katz and Paul Postal, *An Integrated Theory of Linguistic Descriptions* (Cambridge, Mass.: MIT Press, 1964), for instance.

Semantic markers are *symbols:* items in the vocabulary of an artificial language we may call *Semantic Markerese.* Semantic interpretation by means of them amounts merely to a translation algorithm from the object language to the auxiliary language Markerese. But we can know the Markerese translation of an English sentence without knowing the first thing about the meaning of the English sentence: namely, the conditions under which it would be true. Semantics with no treatment of truth conditions is not semantics. Translation into Markerese is at best a substitute for real semantics, relying either on our tacit competence (at some future date) as speakers of Markerese or on our ability to do real semantics at least for the one language Markerese. Translation into Latin might serve as well, except insofar as the designers of Markerese may choose to build into it useful features—freedom from ambiguity, grammar based on symbolic logic—that might make it easier to do real semantics for Markerese than for Latin.[2]

The Markerese method is attractive in part just because it deals with nothing but symbols: finite combinations of entities of a familiar sort out of a finite set of elements by finitely many applications of finitely many rules. There is no risk of alarming the ontologically parsimonious. But it is just this pleasing finitude that prevents Markerese semantics from dealing with the relations between symbols and the world of non-symbols—that is, with genuinely semantic relations. Accordingly, we should be prepared to find that in a more adequate method, meanings may turn out to be complicated, infinite entities built up out of elements belonging to various ontological categories.

My proposals will also not conform to the expectations of those who, in analyzing meaning, turn immediately to the psychology and sociology of language users: to intentions, sense-experience, and mental ideas, or to social rules, conventions, and regularities. I distinguish two topics: first, the description of possible languages or grammars as abstract semantic systems whereby symbols are associated with aspects of the world; and second, the description of the psychological and sociological facts whereby a particular one of these abstract semantic systems is the one used by a person or population. Only confusion comes of mixing these two topics. This paper deals almost entirely with the first.[3]

My proposals are in the tradition of *referential,* or *model-theoretic,* semantics descended from Frege, Tarski, Carnap (in his later works), and recent work of Kripke and others on semantic foundations of intensional logic.[4] The project of

---

[2]For similar criticisms, see Bruce Vermazen, review of Jerrold Katz and Paul Postal, *An Integrated Theory of Linguistic Descriptions,* and of Katz, *Philosophy of Language,* in *Synthese* 17 (1967): 350–65.

[3]I discuss the second elsewhere: David Lewis, "Languages and Language," in this volume; *Convention: A Philosophical Study* (Cambridge, Mass.: Harvard Univ. Press, 1969), chapter 5.

[4]See Gottlob Frege, "Über Sinn und Bedeutung," *Zeitschrift für Philosophie und philosophische Kritik* 100 (1892): 25–50, translated as "On Sense and Reference," in P. T. Geach and M. Black, *Translations from the Philosophical Writings of Gottlob Frege* (Oxford: Blackwell, 1960); Alfred Tarski, "Der Wahrheitsbegriff in den formalisierten Sprachen," *Studia Philosophica* 1 (1936): 261–405, translated as "The Concept of Truth in Formalized Languages," in Tarski, *Logic, Semantics, Metamathematics*

transplanting referential semantics from artificial to natural languages has recently been undertaken, in various ways, by several philosophers and linguists.[5] I have no quarrel with these efforts; indeed, I have here adapted features from several of them. I hope, however, that the system set forth in this paper offers a simpler way to do essentially the same thing. But simplicity is a matter of taste, and simplicity at one place trades off against simplicity elsewhere. It is in these trade-offs that my approach differs most from the others.

II. CATEGORIALLY BASED GRAMMARS

A *categorial grammar* in the sense of Ajdukiewicz[6] is a context-free phrase structure grammar of the following sort.

First, we have a small number of *basic categories*. One of these is the category *sentence* (S). Others might be, for instance, the categories *name* (N) and *common noun* (C). Perhaps we can get by with these three and no more; indeed, Ajdukiewicz went so far as to do without the category *common noun*. Or perhaps we might do better to use different basic categories; we will consider dispensing with the category *name* in favor of an alternative basic category *verb phrase* (VP), or perhaps *noun phrase* (NP).

Second, we have infinitely many *derived categories*. Whenever $c, c_1, \ldots, c_n$ ($n \geq 1$) are any categories, either basic or derived, we have a derived category which we will write $(c/c_1 \ldots c_n)$. (However, we usually omit the outermost parentheses.)

(Oxford: Oxford Univ. Press, 1956); Rudolf Carnap, *Meaning and Necessity* (Chicago: Univ. of Chicago Press, 1947) and "Replies and Systematic Expositions," in P. Schilpp, ed., *The Philosophy of Rudolf Carnap* (La Salle, Ill.: Open Court, 1963), sec. 9; Saul Kripke, "Semantical Considerations on Modal Logic," *Acta Philosophica Fennica* 16 (1963): 83–94; David Kaplan, *Foundations of Intensional Logic* (Ph.D. dissertation, U.C.L.A., 1964); Richard Montague, "Logical Necessity, Physical Necessity, Ethics, and Quantifiers," *Inquiry* 3 (1960): 259–69; Richard Montague, "Pragmatics," in *Contemporary Philosophy—La philosophie contemporaine,* ed. by R. Klibansky, (Florence: La Nuova Italia Editrice, 1968); Richard Montague, "Pragmatics and Intensional Logic," *Synthese* 22 (1970): 68–94; Dana Scott, "Advice on Modal Logic," in *Philosophical Problems in Logic: Recent Developments,* ed. by Karel Lambert, (Dordrecht: Reidel, 1970), pp. 143–73.

[5] Donald Davidson, "Truth and Meaning," *Synthese* 17 (1967): 304–23; Terence Parsons, *A Semantics for English* (duplicated, 1968); Richard Montague, "Intensional Logic and Some of Its Connections with Ordinary Language," talk delivered to the Southern California Logic Colloquim, April 1969, and to the Association of Symbolic Logic meeting at Cleveland, Ohio, May 1969; Richard Montague, "English as a Formal Language I" in *Linguaggi nella società e nella technica* (Milan: Edizoni di Communità, 1970); Richard Montague, "Universal Grammar," *Theoria* 36 (1970); Edward Keenan, *A Logical Base for a Transformational Grammar of English* (Ph.D. dissertation, University of Pennsylvania, 1969).

[6] Kazimierz Ajdukiewicz, "Die syntaktische Konnexität," *Studia Philosophica* 1 (1935): 1–27; translated as "Syntactic Connexion," in S. McCall, *Polish Logic,* (Oxford: Clarendon Press, 1967), pp. 207–31; part one translated as "On Syntactical Coherence," *Review of Metaphysics* 20 (1967): 635–47. Yehoshua Bar-Hillel, *Language and Information* (Reading, Mass.: Addison-Wesley, 1964), part two.

Third, we have context-free phrase-structure rules of the form

$$c \rightarrow (c/c_1 \ldots c_n) + c_1 + \cdots + c_n$$

corresponding to each derived category. That is to say: for any categories c, $c_1, \ldots, c_n$, the result of concatenating any expression of category $(c/c_1 \ldots c_n)$, then any expression of category c_1, then. . . , and finally any expression of category c_n is an expression of category c. Accordingly, we will say that a $(c/c_1 \ldots c_n)$ *takes* a c_1 and . . . and a c_n and *makes* a c. The phrase-structure rules are implicit in the system of derived categories.

Finally, we have a lexicon wherein finitely many expressions—words or word-like morphemes—are assigned to categories. The categories of these lexical expressions may be either basic or derived; unless some lexical expressions belong to derived categories, no non-lexical compound expressions can be generated. Notice that although there are infinitely many derived categories and infinitely many phase-structure rules, nevertheless with any given lexicon all but finitely many categories and rules will be unemployed. This is true even though many lexica will generate infintely many compound expressions.

To specify a categorial grammar, we need only specify its lexicon. The rest is common to all categorial grammars. Consider this lexicon:

⟨a	(S/(S/N))/C⟩	⟨pig	C⟩
⟨believes	(S/N)/S⟩	⟨piggishly	(S/N)/(S/N)⟩
⟨every	(S/(S/N))/C⟩	⟨Porky	N⟩
⟨grunts	S/N⟩	⟨something	S/(S/N)⟩
⟨is	(S/N)/N⟩	⟨the	(S/(S/N))/C⟩
⟨loves	(S/N)/N⟩	⟨which	(C/C)/(S/N)⟩
⟨Petunia	N⟩	⟨yellow	C/C⟩

It gives us a categorial grammar which is simply a notational variant of this rather commonplace context-free grammar:

S →	NP + VP VP + Npr	Npr →	Porky Petunia
VP →	Adv + VP Vt + Npr Vs + S	NP →	something
		Nco →	pig
		VP →	grunts
NP →	Art + Nco	Vt →	loves is
Nco →	Adj + Nco		
Adj →	Rel + VP	Vs →	believes
		Art →	a every the
		Adj →	yellow
		Adv →	piggishly
		Rel →	which

There are three peculiarities about the grammar. First, proper nouns are distinguished from noun phrases. Proper nouns or noun phrases may be subjects (though with different word order) but only proper nouns may be objects. Second, there is nothing to prevent inappropriate iteration of modifiers. Third, the word order is sometimes odd. We will see later how these peculiarities may be overcome.

The employed rules in this example are the eight phrase-structure rules corresponding to the eight employed derived categories.

In this example, I have used only derived categories of the form (c/c_1) that take a single argument. I shall adopt this restriction for the most part in practice, but not in principle.

It is apparent that categorial grammars of this sort are not reasonable grammars for natural language. For that matter, they are not reasonable grammars for most artificial languages either—the exception being symbolic logic in Polish notation. Hence, despite their elegance, categorial grammars have largely been ignored since the early 1950's. Since then, however, we have become interested in the plan of using a simple phrase-structure grammar as a base for a transformational grammar. The time therefore seems ripe to explore *categorially based transformational grammars,* obtained by taking an Ajdukiewicz categorial grammar as base and adding a transformational component. So far as I know, this proposal has been made only once before,[7] but it seems an obvious one.

It is obvious that by adding a transformational component to the categorial grammar of our example, we could rectify the word order and filter out inappropriate iterations of modifiers. Less obviously, we could provide for noun phrase objects by means of a transformational component together with a few additional lexical items—items that need never appear in the final generated sentences.

If reasonable categorially based transformational grammars can be given for all languages of interest to us, and if this can be done under the constraint that meanings are to be determined entirely by base structure, so that the transformational component is irrelevant to semantics, then it becomes extremely easy to give general answer to the questions: What is a meaning? What is the form of a semantic projection rule? Let us see how this can be done.

III. INTENSIONS FOR BASIC CATEGORIES

In order to say what a meaning *is,* we may first ask what a meaning *does,* and then find something that does that.

A meaning for a sentence is something that derermines the conditions under which the sentence is true or false. It determines the truth-value of the sentence in various possible states of affairs, at various times, at various places, for various

[7]John Lyons, "Towards a 'Notional' Theory of the Parts of Speech," *Journal of Linguistics* 2 (1966): 209–236.

speakers, and so on. (I mean this to apply even to non-declarative sentences, but postpone consideration of them.) Similarly, a meaning for a name is something that determines what thing, if any, the name names in various possible states of affairs, at various times, and so on. Among 'things' we include things that do not actually exist, but *might* exist in states of affairs different from the actual state of affairs. Similarly, a meaning for a common noun is something that determines which (possible or actual) things, if any, that common noun applies to in various possible states of affairs, at various times, and so on.

We call the truth-value of a sentence the *extension* of that sentence; we call the thing named by a name the *extension* of that name; we call the set of things to which a common noun applies the *extension* of that common noun. The extension of something in one of these three categories depends on its meaning and, in general, on other things as well: on facts about the world, on the time of utterance, on the place of utterance, on the speaker, on the surrounding discourse, etc. It is the meaning which determines how the extension depends upon the combination of other relevant factors. What sort of things determine how something depends on something else? *Functions,* of course; functions in the most general set-theoretic sense, in which the domain of arguments and the range of values may consist of entities of any sort whatever, and in which it is not required that the function be specifiable by any simple rule. We have now found something to do at least part of what a meaning for a sentence, name, or common noun does: a function which yields as output an appropriate extension when given as input a package of the various factors on which the extension may depend. We will call such an input package of relevant factors an *index;* and we will call any function from indices to appropriate extensions for a sentence, name, or common noun an *intension.*

Thus an *appropriate intension for* a sentence is any function from indices to truth-values; an *appropriate intension for* a name is any function from indices to things; an *appropriate intension for* a common noun is any function from indices to sets. The plan to construe intensions as extension-determining functions originated with Carnap.[8] Accordingly, let us call such functions *Carnapian intensions.* But whereas Carnap's extension-determining functions take as their arguments models or state-descriptions representing possible worlds, I will adopt the suggestion[9] of letting the arguments be packages of miscellaneous factors relevant to determining extensions.

We may take indices as *n*-tuples (finite sequences) of the various items other than meaning that may enter into determining extensions. We call these various items *coordinates* of the index, and we shall assume that the coordinates are given some arbitrary fixed order.

---

[8] Rudolf Carnap, *Meaning and Necessity* (Chicago: Univ. of Chicago Press, 1947), sec. 40; and Rudolf Carnap, "Replies and Systematic Expositions," in P. Schilpp, ed., *The Philosophy of Rudolf Carnap,* (La Salle, Ill.: Open Court, 1963).

[9] Richard Montague, "Pragmatics," in *Contemporary Philosophy—La philosophie contemporaine;* Dana Scott, "Advice on Modal Logic."

First, we must have a *possible-world coordinate.* Contingent sentences depend for their truth value on facts about the world, and so are true at some possible worlds and false at others. A possible world corresponds to a possible totality of facts, determinate in all respects. Common nouns also have different extensions at different possible worlds; and so do some names, at least if we adopt the position[10] that things are related to their counterparts in other worlds by ties of strong similarity rather than identity.

Second, we must have several *contextual coordinates* corresponding to familiar sorts of dependence on features of context. (The world coordinate itself might be regarded as a feature of context, since different possible utterances of a sentence are located in different possible worlds.) We must have a *time coordinate,* in view of tensed sentences and such sentences as 'Today is Tuesday'; a *place coordinate,* in view of such sentences as 'Here there are tigers'; a *speaker coordinate* in view of such sentences as 'I am Porky'; an *audience coordinate* in view of such sentences as 'You are Porky'; an *indicated-objects coordinate* in view of such sentences as 'That pig is Porky' or 'Those men are Communists'; and a *previous discourse coordinate* in view of such sentences as 'The aforementioned pig is Porky'.

Third, it is convenient to have an *assignment coordinate:* an infinite sequence of things, regarded as giving the values of any variables that may occur free in such expressions as 'x is tall' or 'son of y'. Each variable employed in the language will accordingly be a name having as its intension, for some number n, the *nth variable intension:* that function whose value, at any index i, is that thing which is the nth term of the assignment coordinate of i. That thing is the extension, or value, of the variable at i. (Note that because there is more than one possible thing, the variable intensions are distinct: nothing is both the n_1th and the n_2th variable intension for two different numbers n_1 and n_2.) The extensions of 'x is tall' and 'son of y' depend on the assignment and world coordinates of indices just as the extensions of 'I am tall' and 'son of mine' depend on the speaker and world coordinates. Yet the assignment coordinate cannot naturally be included among features of context. One might claim that variables do not appear in sentences of natural languages; but even if this is so, it may be useful to employ variables in a categorial base. In any case, I seek sufficient generality to accommodate languages that do employ variables.

Perhaps other coordinates would be useful. (See the Appendix.) But let us stop here, even though the penalty for introducing a superfluous coordinate is mere clutter, while the penalty for omitting a needed one is inadequacy. Thus an *index* is tentatively any octuple of which the first coordinate is a possible world, the second coordinate is a moment of time, the third coordinate is a place, the fourth coordinate is a person (or other creature capable of being a speaker), the fifth coordinate is a set of persons (or other creatures capable of being an audience), the sixth coordinate is a set (possibly empty) of concrete things capable of being pointed at,

---

[10]Defended in "Counterpart Theory and Quantified Modal Logic," in this volume.

the seventh coordinate is a segment of discourse, and the eighth coordinate is an infinite sequence of things.

Intensions, our functions from indices to extensions, are designed to do part of what meanings do. Yet they are not meanings; for there are differences in meaning unaccompanied by differences in intension. It would be absurd to say that all tautologies have the same meaning, but they have the same intension: the constant function having at every index the value *truth*. Intensions are part of the way to meanings, however, and they are of interest in their own right. We shall consider later what must be added to an intension to obtain something that can do *all* of what a meaning does.

We may permit Carnapian intensions to be partial functions from indices, undefined at some indices. A name may not denote anything at a given possible world. 'Pegasus', for instance, denotes nothing at our world, so its intension may be taken as undefined at any index having our world as its world coordinate. A sentence that suffers from failure of presupposition is often thought to lack a truth-value.[11] If we adopt this treatment of presupposition, sentences susceptible to lack of truth-value should have intensions that are undefined at some indices. They might even have intensions that are undefined at *all* indices; a sentence with inconsistent presuppositions should have as its intension the empty function, defined at no index.

Hitherto I have spoken uncritically of 'things'. Things are name extensions and values of name intensions; sets of things are common-noun extensions and values of common-noun intensions; sequences of things are assignment coordinates of indices. Change the underlying set of things and we change the sets of extensions, indices, and Carnapian intensions. What, then, are things? Of course I want to say, once and for all: *everything* is a thing. But I must not say that. Not all sets of things can be things; else the set of things would be larger than itself. No Carnapian intension can be a thing (unless it is undefined at certain indices); else it would be a member of . . . a member of itself. We must understand the above definitions of extensions, indices, and Carnapian intensions (and the coming definitions of compositional intensions, meanings, and lexica) as tacitly relativized to a chosen set of things. Can we choose the set of things once and for all? Not quite; no matter what set we choose as the set of things, the system of intensions defined over that set will not provide intensions for certain terms—'intension', for instance—of the semantic metalanguage corresponding to that choice. Consider the language of this paper (minus this paragraph) with the extension of 'thing' somehow fixed; it is an adequate semantic metalanguage for some languages but not for itself. To do semantics for it, we must move to a second language in which 'thing' is taken more inclusively; to do semantics for that language we must move to a third language

---

[11]For instance in P. F. Strawson, "On Referring," *Mind* 59 (1950): 320–44; Edward Keenan, *A Logical Base for a Transformational Grammar of English;* James McCawley, "Semantic Representation," paper presented to a symposium on Cognitive Studies and Artificial Intelligence Research, University of Chicago Center for Continuing Education, March 1969.

in which 'thing' is taken more inclusively still; and so on. Any language can be treated in a metalanguage in which 'thing' is taken inclusively enough; but the generality of semantics is fundamentally limited by the fact that no language can be its own semantic metalanguage[12] and hence there can be no universal semantic metalanguage. But we can approach generality as closely as we like by taking 'thing' inclusively enough. For the remainder of this paper, let us proceed on the assumption that the set of things has been chosen, almost once and for all, as some very inclusive set: at least as the universe of some intended model of standard set theory with all the non-sets we want, actual or possible, included as individuals. Let us ignore the sequence of semantic metalanguages that still escape treatment.

In that case there is overlap between things, sets of things, and truth-values. (Not all sets of things can be things, but some should be.) Moreover, there is overlap between sets and truth-values if we adopt the common conventions of identifying the truth-values *truth* and *falsity* with the numbers 1 and 0 respectively, and of identifying each natural number with the set of its predecessors. Thus the appropriate extensions and intensions for sentences, names, and common nouns overlap. The same function that is the intension of all contradictions is also the intension of the name 'zero' and of the common noun 'round square'. Such overlap, however, is harmless. Whenever we want to get rid of it, we can replace intensions by ordered pairs of a category and an intension appropriate for that category.

IV. INTENSIONS FOR DERIVED CATEGORIES

Turning to derived categories, it is best to foresake extensions and Carnapian intensions in the interest of generality. Sometimes, for instance, a C/C—that is, an *adjective*—has an extension like that of a common noun: a set of things to which (at a given index) it applies. Probably 'married' is such an *extensional adjective*. But most adjectives do not have extensions. What is the set of things to which 'alleged' applies? An alleged Communist is not something which is, on the one hand, an alleged thing and, on the other hand, a Communist.

In general, an adjective takes a common noun to make a new, compound common noun; and the intension of the new common noun depends on the intension of the original common noun in a manner determined by the meaning of the adjective. A meaning for an adjective, therefore, is something that determines how one common-noun intension depends on another. Looking for an entity that does what a meaning does, we are led to say that an appropriate intension for an adjective is any function from common-noun intensions to common-noun intensions. In more detail: it is a function whose domain and range consist of functions from indices to sets. Thus the intension of 'alleged' is a function that, when given as argument

---

[12]Cf. Tarski, "Der Wahrheitsbegriff in den formalisierten Sprachen"; translated as 'The Concept of Truth in Formalized Languages,' in Tarski, *Logic, Semantics, Metamathematics*.

the intension of 'Communist', 'windshield', or 'chipmunk' yields as value the intension of the compound common noun 'alleged Communist', 'alleged windshield', or 'alleged chipmunk' respectively. Note that it would not work to use instead a function from common-noun extensions (sets) to common-noun extensions; for at certain indices 'Communist' and 'Maoist' have the same extension but 'alleged Communist' and 'alleged Maoist' do not—or, at other indices, vice versa.

More generally, let us say that an *appropriate intension for* a $(c/c_1, \ldots c_n)$, where $c, c_1, \ldots,$ and c_n are any categories, basic or derived, is any n-place function from c_1-intensions, $\ldots,$ and c_n-intensions to c-intensions. That is, it is any function (again in the most general set-theoretic sense) having as its range of values a set of c-intensions, having as its domain of first arguments the set of c_1-intensions, $\ldots,$ and having as its domain of nth arguments the set of c_n-intensions. A $(c/c_1 \ldots c_n)$ takes a c_1 and $\ldots$ and a c_n and makes a c by concatenation; correspondingly, a $(c/c_1 \ldots c_n)$-intension takes a c_1-intension and $\ldots$ and a c_n-intension as arguments and makes a c-intension as function value. We will call these intensions for derived categories *compositional intensions*.[13] The general form of the semantic projection rules for an interpreted categorial grammar is implicit in the nature of compositional intensions, just as the general form of the phase-structure rules is implicit in the nomenclature for derived categories. The result of concatenating a $(c/c_1 \ldots c_n)$ with intension ϕ_0, a c_1 with intension $\phi_1, \ldots,$ and a c_n with intension ϕ_n is a c with intension $\phi_0(\phi_1 \ldots \phi_n)$.

We have considered already the derived category *adjective* C/C. For another example, take the derived category *verb phrase,* S/N.

A verb phrase takes a name to make a sentence. (We rely on the transformational component to change the word order if necessary.) An appropriate intension for a verb phrase—an S/N-intension—is therefore a function from name intensions to sentence intensions. That is, it is a function from functions from indices to things to functions from indices to truth values. The intension of 'grunts', for instance, is that function ϕ whose value, given as argument any function ϕ_1 from indices to things, is that function ϕ_2 from indices to truth values such that, for any index i,

$$\phi_2(i) = \begin{cases} \textit{truth} \text{ if } \phi_1(i) \text{ is something which grunts at the world and time} \\ \text{given by the appropriate coordinates of } i \\ \textit{falsity} \text{ otherwise.} \end{cases}$$

Applying the projection rule, we find that the sentence 'Porky grunts' is true at just those indices i such that the thing named by 'Porky' at i grunts at the possible world that is the world coordinate of i at the time which is the time coordinate of

---

[13]Intensions resembling some of my compositional intensions are discussed in David Kaplan, *Foundations of Intensional Logic;* in Dana Scott, "Advice on Modal Logic"; and—as appropriate intensions for adjectives and other modifiers—in Terence Parsons, *A Semantics for English,* and in Richard Montague, "English as a Formal Language I." The latter discussion is due in part to J. A. W. Kamp.

i. (The appearance of circularity in this account is spurious; it comes of the fact that I am using English to specify the intension of a word of English.)

For another example, take the derived category *adverb* (of one sort), (S/N)/(S/N). An adverb of this sort takes a verb phrase to make a verb phrase; so an appropriate intension for such an adverb—an (S/N)/(S/N)-intension—is a function from verb-phrase intensions to verb-phrase intensions; or, in more detail, a function from functions from functions from indices to things to functions from indices to truth-values to functions from functions from indices to things to functions from indices to truth-values.

I promised simplicity; I deliver functions from functions from functions to functions to functions from functions to functions. And worse is in store if we consider the sort of adverb that modifies ordinary adverbs: the category ((S/N)/(S/N))/((S/N)/(S/N)). Yet I think no apology is called for. Intensions are complicated constructs, but the principles of their construction are extremely simple. The situation is common: look at any account of the set-theoretic construction of real numbers, yet recall that children often understand the real numbers rather well.

In some cases, it would be possible to find simpler intensions, but at an exorbitant cost: we would have to give up the uniform function-and-arguments form for semantic projection rules. We have noted already that some adjectives are extensional, though most are not. The extensional adjectives could be given sets as extensions and functions from indices to sets as Carnapian intensions. Similarly for verb phrases: we may call a verb phrase *extensional* if there is a function ϕ from indices to sets such that if ϕ_1 is the (compositional) intension of the verb phrase, ϕ_2 is any name intension, ϕ_3 is $\phi_1(\phi_2)$, and i is any index, then

$$\phi_3(i) = \begin{cases} \textit{truth} & \text{if } \phi_2(i) \text{ is a member of } \phi(i) \\ \textit{falsity} & \text{otherwise.} \end{cases}$$

If there is any such function ϕ, there is exactly one; we can call it the Carnapian intension of the verb phrase and we can call its value at any index i the extension of the verb phrase at i. 'Grunts', for instance, is an extensional verb phrase; its extension at an index i is the set of things that grunt at the world and the time given by the world coordinate and the time coordinate of the index i. Verb phrases, unlike adjectives, are ordinarily extensional; but Barbara Partee has pointed out that the verb phrase in 'The price of milk is rising' seems to be non-extensional.

There is no harm in noting that extensional adjectives and verb phrases have Carnapian intensions as well as compositional intensions. However, it is the compositional intension that should be used to determine the intension of an extensional-adjective-plus-common-noun or extensional-verb-phrase-plus-name combination. If we used the Carnapian intensions, we would have a miscellany of semantic projection rules rather than the uniform function-and-arguments rule. (Indeed, the best way to formulate projection rules using Carnapian intensions might be to combine a rule for reconstructing compositional intensions from Car-

napian intensions with the function-and-arguments rule for compositional intensions.) Moreover, we would sacrifice generality: non-extensional adjectives and verb
phrases would have to be treated separately from the extensional ones, or not at
all. This loss of generality would be serious in the case of adjectives; but not in the
case of verb phrases since there are few, if any, non-extensional verb phrases.

For the sake of generality, we might wish to take account of selection restrictions
by allowing a compositional intension to be undefined for some arguments of
appropriate type. If we thought that 'green idea' should lack an intension, for
instance, we might conclude that the intension of 'green' ought to be a partial
function from common-noun intensions to common-noun intensions, undefined for
such arguments as the intension of 'idea'. It proves more convenient, however,
never to let the intension be undefined but rather to let it take on a value called
the *null intension* (for the appropriate category). The null intension for the basic
categories will be the empty function; the null intension for any derived category
$(c/c_1 \ldots c_n)$ will be that $(c/c_1 \ldots c_n)$-intension whose value for any combination
of appropriate arguments is the null intension for c. Thus the intension of 'green',
given as argument the intension of 'idea', yields as value the null intension for the
category C. The intension of the adverb 'furiously', given as argument the intension
of 'sleeps', yields as value the null intension for the category S/N, and that in turn,
given as value any name intension, yields as value the null intension for the category
S. (I dislike this treatment of selection restrictions, but provide the option for those
who want it.)

It is worth mentioning that my account of intensions for derived categories, and
of the corresponding form for projection rules, is independent of my account of
intensions for basic categories. Whatever S-intensions and N-intensions may be—
even expressions of Markerese or ideas in someone's mind—it still is possible to
take S/N-intensions as functions from N-intensions to S-intensions and to obtain
the intension of 'Porky grunts' by applying the intension of 'grunts' as function to
the intension of 'Porky' as argument.

V. MEANINGS

We have already observed that intensions for sentences cannot be identified with
meanings since differences in meaning—for instance, between tautologies—may
not carry with them any difference in intension. The same goes for other categories,
basic or derived. Differences in intension, we may say, give us *coarse* differences in
meaning. For *fine* differences in meaning we must look to the analysis of a compound into consituents and to the intensions of the several constituents. For instance
'Snow is white or it isn't' differs finely in meaning from 'Grass is green or it isn't'
because of the difference in intension between the embedded sentences 'Snow is
white' and 'Grass is green'. For still finer differences in meaning we must look in
turn to the intensions of constituents of constituents, and so on. Only when we

come to non-compound, lexical constituents, can we take sameness of intension as a sufficient condition of synonymy.[14]

It is natural, therefore, to identify meanings with semantically interpreted phrase markers minus their terminal nodes: finite ordered trees having at each node a category and an appropriate intension. If we associate a meaning of this sort with an expression, we are given the category and intension of the expression; and if the expression is compound, we are given also the categories and intensions of its constituent parts, their constituent parts, and so on down.

Perhaps we would thereby cut meanings too finely. For instance, we will be unable to agree with someone who says that a double negation has the same meaning as the corresponding affirmative. But this difficulty does not worry me: we will have both intensions and what I call meanings, and sometimes one and sometimes the other will be preferable as an explication of our ordinary discourse about meanings. Perhaps some entities of intermediate fineness can also be found, but I doubt that there is any uniquely natural way to do so.

It may be disturbing that in our explication of meanings we have made arbitrary choices—for instance, of the order of coordinates in an index. Meanings are meanings—how can we *choose* to construct them in one way rather than another? The objection is a general objection to set-theoretic constructions,[15] so I will not reply to it here. But if it troubles you, you may prefer to say that *real* meanings are *sui generis* entities and that the constructs I call 'meanings' do duty for real meanings because there is a natural one-to-one correspondence between them and the real meanings.

It might also be disturbing that I have spoken of categories without hitherto saying what they are. This again is a matter of arbitrary choice; we might, for instance, take them as sets of expressions in some language, or as sets of intensions, or even as arbitrarily chosen code-numbers. It turns out to be most convenient, if slightly unnatural, to identify categories with their own names: expressions composed in the proper way out of the letters 'S', 'N', 'C' (and whatever others we may introduce later in considering revisions of the system) together with parentheses and diagonal slashes. This does not prevent our category-names from being names of categories: they name themselves. All definitions involving categories are to be understood in accordance with the identification of categories and category-names.

Some might even wish to know what a *tree* is. Very well: it is a function that assigns to each member of the set of nodes of the tree an object said to *occupy* or be *at* that node. The nodes themselves are finite sequences of positive numbers. A set of such sequences is the set of *nodes of* some tree iff, first, it is a finite set, and

[14]See Rudolf Carnap, *Meaning and Necessity,* sec. 14, on 'intensional isomorphism'; Clarence I. Lewis, "The Modes of Meaning," *Philosophy and Phenomenological Research* 4 (1944): 236–49, on 'analytic meaning'.

[15]See Paul Benacerraf, "What Numbers Could Not Be," *Philosophical Review* 74 (1965): 47–73.

second, whenever it contains a sequence $\langle b_1 \ldots b_k \rangle$ then it also contains every sequence that is an initial segment of $\langle b_1 \ldots b_k \rangle$ and every sequence $\langle b_1 \ldots b_{k-1} b'_k \rangle$ with $b'_k < b_k$. We regard $\langle \ \rangle$, the sequence of zero length, as the topmost node; $\langle b_1 \rangle$ as the b_1th node from the left immediately beneath $\langle \ \rangle$; $\langle b_1 b_2 \rangle$ as the b_2th node from the left immediately beneath $\langle b_1 \rangle$; and so on. We can easily define all the requisite notions of tree theory in terms of this construction.

Once we have identified meanings with semantically interpreted phrase markers, it becomes natural to reconstrue the phrase-structure rules of categorial grammar, together with the corresponding projection rules, as conditions of well-formedness for meanings.[16] Accordingly, we now define a *meaning* as a tree such that, first, each node is occupied by an ordered pair $\langle c \ \phi \rangle$ of a category and an appropriate intension for that category; and second, immediately beneath any non-terminal node occupied by such a pair $\langle c \ \phi \rangle$ are two or more nodes, and these are occupied by pairs $\langle c_0 \ \phi_0 \rangle$, $\langle c_1 \ \phi_1 \rangle$, $\ldots$, $\langle c_n \ \phi_n \rangle$ (in that order) such that c_0 is $(c/c_1 \ldots c_n)$ and ϕ is $\phi_0(\phi_1 \ldots \phi_n)$.

A meaning may be a tree with a single node; call such meanings *simple* and other meanings *compound*. Compound meanings are, as it were, built up from simple meanings by steps in which several meanings (simple or compound) are combined as sub-trees under a new node, analogously to the way in which expressions are built up by concatenating shorter expressions. We may call a meaning m' a *constituent of* a meaning m if m' is a subtree of m. We may say that a meaning m is *generated by* a set of simple meanings iff every simple constituent of m belongs to that set. More generally, m is *generated by* a set of meanings (simple or compound) iff every simple constituent of m is a constituent of some constituent of m, possibly itself, which belongs to that set.

We shall in many ways speak of meanings as though they were symbolic expressions generated by an interpreted categorial grammar, even though they are nothing of the sort. The *category of* a meaning is the category found as the first component of its topmost node. The *intension of* a meaning is the intension found as the second component of its topmost node. The *extension at* an index i *of* a sentence meaning, name meaning, or common-noun meaning is the value of the intension of the meaning for the argument i. A sentence meaning is *true* or *false* at i according as its extension at i is *truth* or *falsity;* a name meaning *names at* i that thing, if any, which is its extension at i; and a common-noun meaning *applies at* i to whatever things belong to its extension at i. As we have seen, extensions might also be provided for certain meanings in derived categories such as C/C or S/N, but this cannot be done in a non-artificial, general way.

Given as fundamental the definition of truth of a sentence meaning at an index, we can define many derivative truth relations. Coordinates of the index may be

---

[16]Cf. James McCawley, "Concerning the Base Component of a Transformational Grammar," *Foundations of Language* 4 (1968): 243–69.

made explicit, or may be determined by a context of utterance, or may be generalized over. Generalizing over all coordinates, we can say that a sentence meaning is *analytic* (in one sense) iff it is true at every index. Generalizing over the world and assignment coordinates and letting the remaining coordinates be determined by context, we can say that a sentence meaning is *analytic* (in another sense) *on* a given occasion iff it is true at every index *i* having as its time, place, speaker, audience, indicated-objects, and previous-discourse coordinates respectively the time, the place, the speaker, the audience, the set of objects pointed to, and the previous discourse on that occasion. Generalizing over the time and assignment coordinates and letting the others (including world) be determined by context, we define *eternal truth* of a sentence meaning *on* an occasion; generalizing over the assignment coordinate and letting all the rest be determined by context, we define simply *truth on* an occasion; and so on.

We also can define truth relations even stronger than truth at every index. Let us call a meaning m' a *semantic variant* of a meaning m iff m and m' have exactly the same nodes, with the same category but not necessarily the same intension at each node, and, whenever a common intension appears at two terminal nodes in m, a common intension also appears at those two nodes in m'. Let us call m' an *s-fixed semantic variant of m*, where *s* is a set of simple meanings, iff m and m' are semantic variants and every member of *s* which is a constituent of m is also a constituent, at the same place, of m'. Then we can call a sentence meaning *s-true* iff every *s*-fixed semantic variant of it (including itself) is true at every index. If *s* is the set of simple meanings whose bearers we would classify as logical vocabulary, then we may call *s*-true sentence meanings *logically true;* if *s* is the set of simple meanings whose bearers we would classify as mathematical (including logical) vocabulary, we may call *s*-true sentence meanings *mathematically true.* Analogously, we can define a relation of *s*-fixed semantic variance between sequences of meanings; and we can say that a sentence meaning m_0 is an *s-consequence* (for instance, a *logical consequence* or *mathematical consequence*) of sentence meanings $m_1, \ldots$ iff, for every *s*-fixed semantic variant $\langle m'_0\, m'_1 \ldots \rangle$ of the sequence $\langle m_0\, m_1. \ldots \rangle$ and every index *i* such that all of $m'_1, \ldots$ are true at *i*, m'_0 is true at *i*. (The premises $m_1, \ldots$ may be infinite in number. Their order is insignificant.) These definitions are adapted from definitions in terms of truth in all logically or mathematically standard interpretations of a given language. However, we have been able to avoid introducing the notion of alternative interpretations of a language, since so far we are dealing entirely with meanings.

VI. GRAMMARS RECONSTRUCTED

Our system of meanings may serve, in effect, as a universal base for categorially based transformational grammars. There is no need to repeat the phrase-structure rules of categorial well-formedness as a base component in each such grammar.

Instead, we take the meanings as given, and regard a grammar as specifying a way to encode meanings: a relation between certain meanings and certain expressions (sequences of sound-types or of mark-types) which we will call the *representing relation* determined by the grammar. We might just identify grammars with representing relations; but I prefer to take grammars as systems which determine representing relations in a certain way.

If we were concerned with nothing but transformation-free categorial grammars, we could take a grammar to consist of nothing but a *lexicon*: a finite set of triples of the form $\langle e \ c \ \phi \rangle$ where e is an expression, c is a category, and ϕ is an intension appropriate for that category. We may say that an expression e *represents* or *has* a meaning m *relative to* a lexicon L iff L contains items $\langle e_1 \ c_1 \ \phi_1 \rangle, \ldots , \langle e_n \ c_n \ \phi_n \rangle$ such that, first, e is the result of concatenating $e_1, \ldots , e_n$ (in that order), and second, the terminal nodes of m are occupied by $\langle c_1 \ \phi_1 \rangle, \ldots , \langle c_n \ \phi_n \rangle$ (in that order).

We could instead have proceeded in two steps. Let us define a *(categorial) phrase marker* as a tree having categories at its non-terminal nodes and expressions at its terminal nodes. Then a phrase marker p represents or *has* a meaning m *relative to* a lexicon L iff p is obtained from m as follows: given any terminal node of the meaning m occupied by a pair $\langle c \ \phi \rangle$, place below it another node occupied by an expression e such that the item $\langle e \ c \ \phi \rangle$ is contained in the lexicon; then remove the intensions, replacing the $\langle c \ \phi \rangle$ pair at each non-terminal node by its unaccompanied category c. Note that the set of meanings thus representable relative to a lexicon L comprises all and only those meanings that are generated by the set of simple meanings of the lexical items themselves; let us call it the set of meanings *generated by* the lexicon L.

Next, we define the *terminal string* of a phrase marker p as the expression obtained by concatenating, in order, the expressions at the terminal nodes of p. Thus we see that an expression e represents a meaning m relative to a lexicon L, according to the definition above, iff **e** is the terminal string of some phrase marker that represents m relative to L.

In the case of a categorially based transformational grammar, we have not two steps but three. Such a grammar consists of a lexicon L together with a *transformational component* T. The latter imposes finitely many constraints on finite sequences of phrase markers. A sequence $\langle p_1 \ldots p_n \rangle$ of phrase markers that satisfies the constraints imposed by T will be called a *(transformational) derivation of p_n from p_1 in* T. An expression e *represents* or *has* a meaning m in a grammar $\langle$ L T $\rangle$ iff there exists a derivation $\langle p_1 \ldots p_n \rangle$ in T such that e is the terminal string of p_n and p_1 represents m relative to the lexicon L. If so, we will also call e a *meaningful expression*, p_n a *surface structure of e*, p_{n-1} and ... and p_2 *intermediate structures of e*, p_1 a *base structure of e*, and m a *meaning of e* (all *relative to* the grammar $\langle$ L T $\rangle$). However, we will call any phrase marker p a *base structure* in $\langle$ L T $\rangle$ iff it represents a meaning relative to L, whether or not it is the base structure *of* any expression; thus we allow for base structures which are filtered out by not being the first term of any derivation in T.

The representing relation given by a grammar $\langle$ L T $\rangle$ is by no means a one-to-one correspondence between meanings and expressions. A given expression might be *ambiguous,* representing several different meanings. (If it represents several different but cointensive meanings, however, it might be inappropriate to call it ambiguous; for the common notion of meaning seems to hover between our technical notions of meaning and of intension.) On the other hand, several expressions might be *synonymous,* representing a single meaning. We might also call several expressions *completely synonymous* iff they share all their meanings; synonymy and complete synonymy coincide when we are dealing only with unambiguous expressions. If several expressions represent different but cointensive meanings, we may call them equivalent but not synonymous. If several expressions not only represent the same meaning but also have a single base structure, we may call them not only equivalent and synonymous but also *paraphrases* of one another.

Given a representing relation, all the semantic relations defined hitherto for meanings carry over to expressions having those meanings. (If we like, they may carry over also to the base, surface, and intermediate structures between the meanings and the expressions.) Thus we know what it means to speak, relative to a given grammar and qualified in cases of ambiguity by 'on a meaning' or 'on all meanings', of the category and intension of any meaningful expression; of the extension at a given index of any expression of appropriate category; of the thing named by a name; of the things to which a common noun applies; of the truth at an index, truth on an occasion, analyticity, logical truth, etc. of a sentence; and so on.

We should note an oddity in our treatment of logical truth. A synonym of a logically true sentence is itself a logical truth, since it represents the same logically true meaning as the original. Hence a descendant by synonym-substitution of a logical truth is itself a logical truth if the synonym-substitution is confined to single lexical items in the base structure; but not otherwise. 'All woodchucks are groundhogs' comes out logically true, whereas 'All squares are equilateral rectangles' comes out merely analytic (in the strongest sense).

A transformational component may constrain sequences of phrase markers in two ways. There is the local constraint that any two adjacent phrase markers in a derivation must stand in one of finitely many relations; these permitted relations between adjacent phrase markers are the *transformations.* There may also be global derivational constraints specifying relations between non-adjacent phrase markers or properties of the derivation as a whole. An example is the constraint requiring transformations to apply in some specified cyclic (or partly cyclic) order.

A transformation-free categorial grammar is a special case of a categorially based transformational grammar. It has a transformational component with no transformations or global constraints, so that the derivations therein are all and only those sequences $\langle p_1 \rangle$ consisting of a single phrase marker.

I will not attempt to say more exactly what a transformation or a transformational component is. Mathematically precise definitions have been given,[17] but to

---

[17]For instance in P. Stanley Peters and R. W. Ritchie, *On the Generative Power of Transformational Grammars* (Technical Report in Computer Science, University of Washington, Seattle, Wash., 1969).

choose among these would involve taking sides on disputed questions in syntactic theory. I prefer to maintain my neutrality, and I have no present need for a precise delineation of the class of transformational grammars. I have foremost in mind a sort of simplified *Aspects*-model grammar,[18] but I have said nothing to eliminate various alternatives.

I have said nothing to eliminate generative semantics. What I have chosen to call the 'lexicon' is the *initial* lexicon. Words not in that lexicon might be introduced transformationally on the way from base to surface, if that seems desirable. It might even be that none of the initial lexical items ever reach the surface, and that all surface lexical items (expressions found at terminal nodes of surface structures) are introduced transformationally within derivations. In that case it would be appropriate to use a standardized initial lexicon in all grammars, and to rechristen my base structures 'semantic representations'. In that case also there might or might not be a level between base and surface at which word-introducing transformations are done and other transformations have not yet begun.

I have also said nothing to eliminate surface semantics. This may seem strange, since I have indeed said that meanings are to be determined by base structures alone. However, I rely here on the observation[19] that surface-structure interpretation rules are indistinguishable from global derivational constraints relating three levels: base structures (regarded as semantic representations), deep structures (an *intermediate* level), and surface structures. Deep structures might be ambiguous; a transformational grammar with base-deep-surface constraints might permit two derivations

$$\langle p_B^1 \ldots p_D \ldots p_S^1 \rangle$$
$$\langle p_B^2 \ldots p_D \ldots p_S^2 \rangle$$

differing at the base and surface but not at the deep level, but it might rule out other derivations of the forms

$$\langle p_B^2 \ldots p_D \ldots p_S^1 \rangle$$
$$\langle p_B^1 \ldots p_D \ldots p_S^2 \rangle.$$

In such a case base structure (and hence meaning) would be determined by deep and surface structure together, but not by deep structure alone. Similarly, we might have constraints relating base structure not only to deep and surface structure but also to structure at various other intermediate levels.

I have said nothing to eliminate a non-trivial phonological component; but I would relocate it as part of the transformational component. The last few steps of a transformational derivation might go from the usual pre-phonological surface structure to a post-phonological surface structure whence the output expression can be obtained simply by concatenation of terminal nodes.

[18] Noam Chomsky, *Aspects of the Theory of Syntax* (Cambridge, Mass.: M.I.T. Press, 1965).

[19] George Lakoff, "On Generative Semantics," in *Semantics: An Interdisciplinary Reader in Philosophy, Linguistics, Anthropology and Psychology,* ed. by Danny Steinberg and Leon Jakobovits, (Cambridge: Cambridge University Press, 1970), sec. 3.

I have said nothing to eliminate an elaborate system of selection restrictions; but these will appear not as restrictions on the lexical insertions between meanings and base structures but as transformational filtering later on. There will be base structures representing the meanings of such questionable sentences as 'Seventeen eats beans' and 'He sang a pregnant toothbrush'. But these base structures need not be the first terms of any derivations, so these meanings may be unrepresented by sentences. If we like selection restrictions, we might match the lexicon to the transformational component in such a way as to filter out just those meanings that have the null intension.

I have not stipulated that only sentential meanings may be represented; that stipulation could be added if there is reason for it.

In fact, the *only* restriction I place on syntax is that transformational grammars should be categorially based. In other words: a transformational component should operate on a set of categorial phrase markers representing a set of meanings generated by some lexicon. But categorial bases are varied enough that this restriction is not at all severe. I claim that whatever familiar sort of base component you may favor on syntactic grounds, you can find a categorial base (i.e. a suitable part of the system of meanings, generated by a suitable chosen lexicon) that resembles the base you favor closely enough to share its attractive properties. Indeed, with a few preliminary rearranging transformations you can go from my categorial base structures to (notational variants of) more familiar base structures; then you can proceed exactly as before. I shall not marshall evidence for this claim; but I think that the following exploration of alternative categorial treatments of quantification will exhibit the close similarities between these categorial treatments and several alternative familiar base components. If it were necessary to choose between a categorial base that was convenient for semantics and a non-categorial base that was convenient for transformational syntax, I might still choose the the former. But I deny the need to choose.

This completes the exposition of my proposed system of categories, intensions, and meanings. Now I shall consider how this system—either as is or slightly revised—might be applied to two difficult areas: the semantics of quantification and the semantics of non-declaratives. The treatments following are intended only as illustrations, however; many further alternatives are possible, and might be more convenient for syntax.

VII. TREATMENT OF QUANTIFICATION AND NOUN PHRASES

Let us consider such expressions as 'a pig', 'most pigs', 'seventeen pigs', 'roughly seventeen pigs', 'some yellow pig', 'everything', 'nobody', and the like. We call these *quantifier phrases* (presupposing that they should belong to a common category). What category in our system is this? What sort of intensions do quantifier phrases have?

Quantifier phrases combine with verb phrases to make sentences: 'Some pig grunts', 'Nobody grunts', 'Roughly seventeen pigs grunt', and the like. Names do this, since the category *verb phrase* is the derived category S/N. But quantifier phrases cannot be names, under our semantic treatment of names, because they do not in general name anything. ('The pig' could be an exception at indices such that exactly one pig existed at the world and time given by the index.) The absurd consequences of treating 'nobody', as a name, for instance, are well known.[20] If a quantifier phrase combines with an S/N to make an S, and yet is not an N, it must therefore be an S/(S/N).

Except perhaps for one-word quantifier phrases—'nobody', 'everything', and such—quantifier phrases contain constituent common nouns. These may be either simple, as in 'some pig' or compound, as in 'every pink pig that wins a blue ribbon'. Indeed, we may regard common nouns simply as predicates used to restrict quantifiers.[21] The expressions 'a', 'the', 'some', 'every', 'no', 'most', 'seventeen', 'roughly seventeen', and so on which combine with common nouns (simple or compound) to make quantifier phrases and which are variously called *quantifiers, determiners,* or *articles* must therefore belong to the category (S/(S/N))/C. And modifiers of quantifiers like 'roughly', which combine with certain quantifiers to make quantifiers, must belong to the category ((S/(S/N))/C)/((S/(S/N))/C). Selection restrictions by means of transformational filtering could be used to dispose of quantifiers like 'roughly the'.

The intension of 'some pig' may be taken as that function ϕ from S/N-intensions to S-intensions such that if ϕ_1 is any S/N-intension, ϕ_2 is the S-intension $\phi(\phi_1)$, and i is any index, then

$$\phi_2(i) = \begin{cases} \textit{truth} \text{ if, for some N-intension } \phi_3, \phi_3(i) \text{ is a pig and if } \phi_4 \text{ is } \phi_1(\phi_3) \\ \quad \text{then } \phi_4(i) \text{ is truth} \\ \textit{falsity} \text{ otherwise.} \end{cases}$$

The intension of 'some' may be taken as that function ϕ from C-intensions to S/(S/N)-intensions such that if ϕ_1 is any C-intension, ϕ_2 is the S/(S/N)-intension $\phi(\phi_1)$, ϕ_3 is any S/N-intension, ϕ_4 is the S-intension $\phi_2(\phi_3)$, and i is any index, then

$$\phi_4(i) = \begin{cases} \textit{truth} \text{ if, for some N-intension } \phi_5, \phi_5(i) \text{ is a member of } \phi_1(i) \text{ and} \\ \quad \text{if } \phi_6 \text{ is } \phi_3(\phi_5) \text{ then } \phi_6(i) \text{ is } \textit{truth} \\ \textit{falsity} \text{ otherwise.} \end{cases}$$

I spare you the intension of 'roughly'.

Other intensions might be specified for 'some pig' and 'some' that would differ from these only when a quantifier phrase was applied to a non-extensional verb

[20]Charles L. Dodgson, *Through the Looking-Glass* (London, 1871).
[21]This suggestion derives from Richard Montague, "English as a Formal Language I."

phrase. If there are no non-extensional verb phrases in English, then the choice among these alternatives is arbitrary.

This treatment of quantifier phrases is motivated by a desire to handle simple sentences involving quantifier phrases as straightforwardly as possible, minimizing the use of transformations. But it raises problems. Quantifier phrases seemingly occur not only as subjects of sentences but also as objects of verbs or prepositions. And in all their roles—as subjects or as objects—they are interchangeable with names. That is why it is usual to have a category *noun phrase* comprising both quantifier phrases and names.

We might try the heroic course of doubling all our object-takers. We could have one word 'loves' which is an (S/N)/N and takes the object 'Petunia' to make the verb phrase 'loves Petunia'; and alongside it another 'loves' which is an (S/N)/(S/(S/N)) and takes the object 'some pig' to make the verb phrase 'loves some pig'. But we need not decide how much we mind such extravagant doubling, since it does not work anyway. It would give us one meaning for 'Every boy loves some girl': the weaker meaning, on which the sentence can be true even if each boy loves a different girl. But the sentence is ambiguous; where shall we get a stronger meaning, on which the sentence is true only if a certain girl—Zuleika, perhaps— is loved by all boys? (There are those who do not perceive this ambiguity; but we seek a treatment general enough to handle the idiolects of those who do.) The method of doubling object-takers is a blind alley; rather we must look to the method of variable binding, routinely used in the semantic analysis of standardly formulated symbolic logic.

The quantifiers of symbolic logic belong to the category S/NS, taking a name and a sentence to make a sentence. The name must be a variable; other combinations could be disposed of by transformational filtering. For instance, the logician's quantifier 'some' takes the variable 'x' and the sentence 'grunts x' to make a sentence translatable into English as 'something grunts'. The logician's 'some' has as its intension that function ϕ from N-intensions and S-intensions to S-intensions such that if ϕ_1 is the nth variable intension for any number n, ϕ_2 is any S-intension, ϕ_3 is $\phi(\phi_1\phi_2)$, and i is any index, then

$$\phi_3(i) = \begin{cases} \textit{truth} \text{ if, for some index } i' \text{ that is like } i \text{ except perhaps at the } n\text{th} \\ \quad \text{term of the assignment coordinate, } \phi_2(i') \text{ is } \textit{truth} \\ \textit{falsity} \text{ otherwise;} \end{cases}$$

and such that if ϕ_1 is any N-intension that is not a variable intension and ϕ_2 is any S-intension, then $\phi(\phi_1\phi_2)$ is the null intension. The intension of the logician's quantifier 'every' is specified similarly, with 'for every index i' . . .' replacing 'for some index i' . . .'.

It would be troublesome to employ logician's quantifiers in a grammar for English. In the first place, these quantifiers are unrestricted, ranging over everything. The base structure of 'Some pig grunts', for instance, would come out as

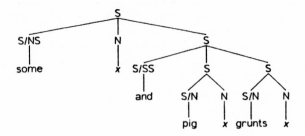

in which there is no constituent corresponding to 'some pig' and in which 'pig' and 'grunts' alike are put into the category S/N. (It was with structures like this in mind that Ajdukiewicz saw fit to omit the category C.) This attempt to dispense with quantifier phrases in favor of unrestricted quantifiers taking compound sentences is clumsy at best, and fails entirely for quantifiers such as 'most'.[22] In the second place, by having the quantifier itself do the binding of variables, we require there to be bound variables wherever there are quantifiers. We get the unnecessarily complicated base structure

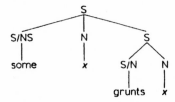

for 'Something grunts', whereas if we had employed quantifier phrases which take verb phrases and do not bind variables, we could have had

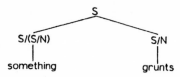

with three constituents instead of six and no work for the transformations to do.

It is not necessary, however, that the quantifier itself should bind variables. We can stick with verb-phrase-taking quantifier phrases of the category S/(S/N), restricted by constituent common nouns in most cases, and bind variables when necessary—but *only* when necessary—by means of a separate constituent called a *binder:* a certain sort of (S/N)/S that takes a sentence and makes an extensional verb phrase by binding a variable at all its free occurrences (if any) in the sentence.

[22]See John Wallace, "Sortal Predicates and Quantification," *Journal of Philosophy* 62 (1965): 8–13.

To every variable there corresponds a binder. Suppose 'x' is a variable; we may write its corresponding binder as '$\hat{x}$' and read it as 'is something x such that'. (But presumably binders may best be treated as base constituents that never reach the surface; so if the words 'is something x such that' ever appear in a meaningful expression, they will be derived not from an '$\hat{x}$' in base structure but in some other way.) For instance, the following base structure using a binder is equivalent to 'grunts' and might be read loosely as 'is something x such that x grunts'.

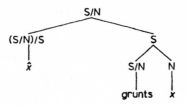

The following is a possible base structure for 'is loved by y'.

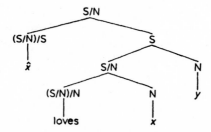

The following might be a base structure for 'Porky loves himself'.[23]

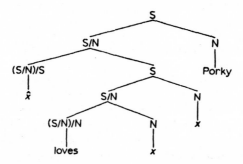

(Provided there is no ambiguity among our variables, we can use them in this way to keep track of coreferentiality, rather than subscripting the names in

[23]Cf. James McCawley, "Semantic Representation."

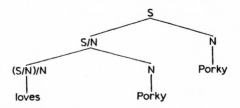

to indicate whether we are dealing with one Porky or two.)

If 'x' has the nth variable intension, then the corresponding binder '$\hat{x}$' has the nth *binder intension*: that function ϕ from S-intensions to S/N-intensions such that if ϕ_1 is any S-intension, ϕ_2 is the S/N-intension $\phi(\phi_1)$, ϕ_3 is any N-intension, ϕ_4 is the S-intension $\phi_2(\phi_3)$, i is any index, and i' is that index which has $\phi_3(i)$ as the nth term of its assignment coordinate and otherwise is like i, then $\phi_4(i) = \phi_1(i')$. It can be verified that this intension justifies the reading of '$\hat{x}$' as 'is something x such that'.

A finite supply of variables and binders, however large, would lead to the mistaken omission of some sentences. To provide an infinite supply by means of a finite lexicon, we must allow our variables and binders to be generated as compounds. We need only three lexical items: one simple variable having the first variable intension; an N/N having as intension a function whose value, given as argument the nth variable intension for any $n \geq 1$, is the $(n + 1)$th variable intension; and an ((S/N)/S)/N having as intension a function whose value, given as argument the nth variable intension for any $n \geq 1$, is the nth binder intension. The first item gives us a starting variable; the second, interated, manufactures the other variables; the third manufactures binders out of variables. However, we will continue to abbreviate base structures by writing variables and binders as if they were simple.

Variable-binding introduces a sort of spurious ambiguity called *alphabetic variance*. 'Porky loves himself' could have not only the structure shown but also others in which 'x' and '$\hat{x}$' are replaced by 'y' and '$\hat{y}$', or 'z' and '$\hat{z}$', etc. Since different variables may have different intensions, these structures correspond to infinitely many different cointensive meanings for 'Porky loves himself'. The simplest way to deal with this nuisance is to define an ordering of any such set of meanings and employ transformational filtering to dispose of all but the first meaning in the set (according to the ordering).

Binders have occasionally been discussed by logicians, under the name 'abstraction operators' or 'lambda operators'.[24]

[24]Alonzo Church, *The Calculi of Lambda Conversion* (Princeton: Princeton University Press, 1941); Rudolf Carnap, *Introduction to Symbolic Logic* (New York: Dover, 1958), sec. 33; Richmond Thomason and Robert Stalnaker, "Modality and Reference," *Noûs* 2 (1968): 359–72.

Now we are in a position to complete our account of the category S/(S/N) of verb-phrase-taking quantifier phrases, using binders as needed. The base structure for 'Every boy loves Zuleika' may be simply

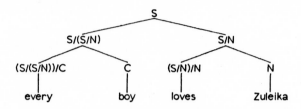

with no unnecessary variable-binding to make work for the transformational component. There is another base structure with variable-binding which we may read roughly as 'Every boy is something x such that x loves Zuleika'; it represents a different but equivalent meaning. We can either let these be another base structure and another (but equivalent) meaning for 'Every boy loves Zuleika' or get rid of them by transformational filtering. The base structure for 'Lothario loves some girl' is

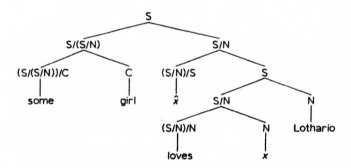

in which the quantifier phrase which is the surface object of 'loves' is treated as subject of a verb phrase obtained by binding the variable which is the base object of 'loves'. To reach an intermediate structure in which the quantifier phrase is relocated as the object of 'loves', we must have recourse to a transformation that moves the subject of a verb phrase made by variable binding into the place of one (the first?) occurrence of the bound variable and destroys the variable-binding apparatus. Note that, if desired, this transformation might apply *beneath* an intermediate level corresponding most closely to the ordinary level of deep structure. The two base structures for 'Every boy loves some girl' are

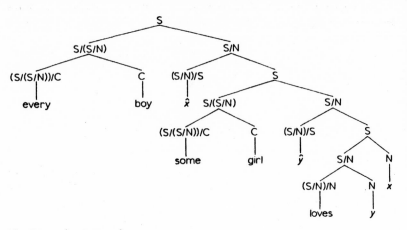

for the weak sense, and

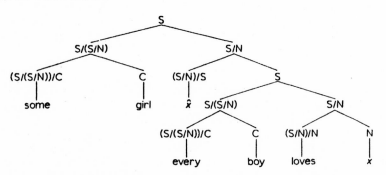

for the strong—Zuleika—sense.

It may be that quantifier-phrase objects should not be abandoned altogether. 'Lothario seeks a girl', in the sense in which it can be paraphrased as 'Lothario seeks a certain particular girl', can have the base structure

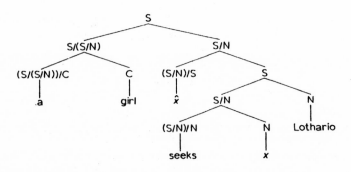

but what about the sense in which any old girl would do? We might give it the base structure

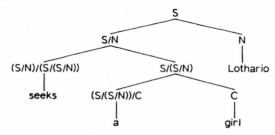

using a second 'seeks' that takes quantifier-phrase objects. The alternative is to let the word 'seeks' be introduced transformationally rather than lexically, as a transformational descendant of 'strives-to-find', so that the base structures would be

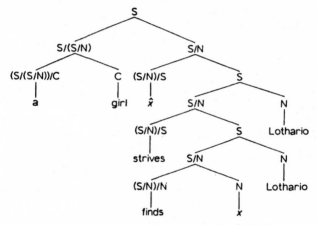

for the sense in which a certain particular girl is sought and

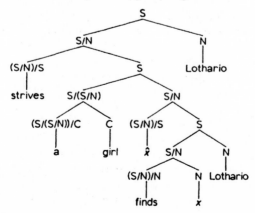

for the sense in which any old girl would do. But it is controversial whether we ought to let words be introduced transformationally in this way; and it is not clear how to apply this treatment to 'conceives of a tree'.[25] Perhaps conceiving-of is imagining-to-exist, but perhaps not.

This completes one treatment of quantifier phrases, carried out with no modification of the system I originally presented. It is straightforward from the semantic point of view; however, it might result in excessive complications to transformational syntax. Ordinary bases have a category *noun phrase* which combines quantifier phrases and names; and transformations seem to work well on bases of that sort. By dividng the category of noun phrases, I may require some transformations to be doubled (or quadrupled, etc.). Moreover, my structures involving variable-binding are complicated and remote from the surface, so by doing away with quantifier-phrase objects I make lots of work for the transformational component. It might be, therefore, that this treatment is too costly to syntax. Therefore let us see how we might reinstate the combined category *noun phrase*. There are two methods: we might try to assimilate names to quantifier phrases, or we might try to assimilate quantifier phrases to names.

The method of assimilating names to quantifier phrases proceeds as follows. For every name in our lexicon, for instance 'Porky', we add to our lexicon a corresponding *pseudo-name* in the category S/(S/N). If the intension of the original name 'Porky' is the N-intension ϕ_1, then the intension of the corresponding pseudo-name 'Porky*' should be that function ϕ from S/N-intensions to S-intensions such that for any S/N-intension ϕ_2, $\phi(\phi_2) = \phi_2(\phi_1)$. As a result, a sentence such as 'Porky grunts' can be given either of the base structures

and will have the same intension either way. The category S/(S/N) may now be renamed *noun phrase*. It contains our former quantifier phrases together with our new pseudo-names. It does not contain names themselves. Names are now unnecessary as subjects, but still needed as objects; so the next step is to replace all name-takers except verb phrases by noun-phrase-takers. For instance, the category (S/N)/N of transitive verbs is to be replaced by the category (S/N)/(S/(S/N)) of pseudo-transitive verbs. The intensions of the replacements are related to the intensions of the originals in a systematic way which I shall not bother to specify. Names now serve no further purpose, having been supplanted both as subjects and

[25]As remarked in Richard Montague, "Intensional Logic and Some of Its Connections with Ordinary Language," talk delivered to the Southern California Logic Colloquium, April 1969, and to the Association of Symbolic Logic meeting at Cleveland, Ohio, May 1969.

as objects by pseudo-names; so the next step is to remove names from the lexicon. The category N is left vacant.

Since we have provided for noun-phrase objects for the sake of the pseudo-names, we can also have quantifier-phrase objects and so cut down on variable-binding. For instance, we have

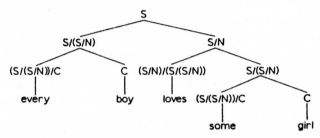

as the base structure for 'Every boy loves some girl' in the weak sense, leaving no work for the transformations. We cannot do away with variable-binding altogether, however. The base structure for 'Every boy loves some girl' in the strong—Zuleika—sense is now

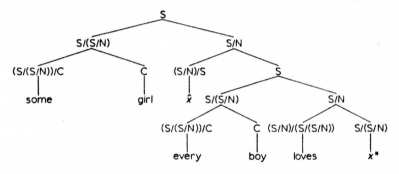

in which the seeming noun-phrase object 'some girl' is treated as subject of a verb phrase obtained by binding the pseudo-variable noun phrase 'x^*' which is the real object of 'loves'. Variables are names, of course, and therefore are replaced by pseudo-names just as any other names are; no change is made, however, in the corresponding binders.

So far we have not departed from the system I presented originally, and we *could* stop here. It is now advantageous, however, to take the step of eliminating the category N altogether and promoting the category *verb phrase* from a derived category S/N to a new basic category VP. Accordingly, the category of noun phrases becomes S/VP; the category of quantifiers becomes (S/VP)/C; the category of transitive verbs becomes VP/(S/VP); and the category which includes binders becomes VP/S.

We can also reopen the question of letting verb-phrase intensions be Carnapian rather than compositional. We rejected this simplification before, principally because it would require a projection rule which was not of our general function-and-arguments form; but that consideration no longer holds after names and verb-phrase-plus-name combinations are done away with. A lesser objection still applies: the simplification only works for extensional verb phrases. If any non-extensional verb phrases exist, they cannot go into our new basic category VP with Carnapian intensions. They will have to go into the category S/(S/VP) instead. The switch to Carnapian intensions for the now-basic verb phrases changes most other intensions in a systematic way which I need not stop to specify.

We turn last to the opposite method, in which quantifier phrases are assimilated to names to give an undivided category of noun phrases. This will require revising the extensions and intensions of names in a manner discussed by Mates[26] and Montague.[27]

In the dark ages of logic, a story something like this was told. The phrase 'some pig' names a strange thing we may call the *existentially generic pig* which has just those properties that some pig has. Since some pig is male, some pig (a different one) is female, some pig is pink (all over), and some pig is grey (all over), the existentially generic pig is simultaneously male, female, pink, and grey. Accordingly, he (she?) is in the extensions both of 'is male' and of 'is female', both of 'is pink all over' and of 'is grey all over'. The phrase 'every pig' names a different strange thing called the *universally generic pig* which has just those properties that every pig has. Since not every pig is pink, grey, or any other color the universally generic pig is not of any color. (Yet neither is he colorless, since not every—indeed not any—pig is colorless). Nor is he (?) male or female (or neuter), since not every pig is any one of these. He is, however, a pig and an animal, and he grunts; for every pig is a pig and an animal, and grunts. There are also the *negative universally generic pig* which has just those properties that no pig has (he is not a pig, but he is both a stone and a number), the *majority generic pig* which has just those properties that more than half of all pigs have, and many more. A sentence formed from a name and an extensional verb phrase is true (we may add: at an index *i*) if and only if the thing named by the name (at *i*) belongs to the extension of the verb phrase (at *i*); and this is so regardless of whether the name happens to be a name like 'Porky' of an ordinary thing or a name like 'some pig' of a generic thing.

This story is preposterous since nothing, however recondite, can possibly have more or less than one of a set of incompatible and jointly exhaustive properties. At least, nothing can have more or less than one of them *as its properties*. But something, a set, can have *any* combination of them *as its members*; there is no contradiction in that.

Let us define the *character* of a thing as the set of its properties. Porky's character

---

[26]Benson Mates, "Leibniz on Possible Worlds," in *Logic, Methodology, and Philosophy of Science III*, ed. by B. van Rootselaar and J. F. Staal, (Amsterdam: North-Holland Publ. Co., 1968).

[27]Richard Montague, "Intensional Logic and Some of Its Connections with Ordinary Language", "Universal Grammar," *Theoria* 36 (1970).

is that set which has as members just those properties that Porky has as properties. The various generic pigs do not, and could not possibly, exist; but their characters do. The character of the universally generic pig, for instance, is the set having as members just those properties that every pig has as properties.

A *character* is any set of properties. A character is *individual* iff it is a maximal compatible set of properties, so that something could possess all and only the properties contained in it; otherwise the character is *generic*.

Since no two things share all their properties (on a sufficiently inclusive conception of properties) things correspond one-to-one to their individual characters. We can exploit this correspondence to replace things by their characters whenever convenient. Some philosophers have even tried to eliminate things altogether in favor of their characters, saying that things are 'bundles of properties'.[28] We need not go so far. We will replace things by individual characters as extensions of names, and as members of extensions of common nouns. However, we may keep the things themselves as well, taking them to be related to their names via their characters. Having made this substitution, we are ready to assimilate quantifier phrases to names by letting them also take characters—in most cases, generic characters—as extensions. 'Porky' has as extension Porky's individual character; 'every pig' has as extension the generic character of the universally generic pig. Even 'nobody' has an extension: the set of just those properties that nobody has.

We revise the system of meanings as follows. Our basic categories are *sentence* (S), *noun phrase* (NP), and *common noun* (C). Appropriate extensions for sentences are truth values; appropriate extensions for noun phrases are characters, either individual or generic; appropriate extensions for common nouns are sets of individual characters. Intensions are as before: for basic categories, functions from some or all indices to appropriate extensions; for a derived category $(c/c_1 \ldots c_n)$, functions from c_1-intensions, . . . , and c_n-intensions to c-intensions. A *name* is an NP that never has a generic character as its extension at any index. The category of quantifiers becomes NP/C; the category of verb phrases becomes S/NP. Object-takers take NP objects which may or may not be names. Some variable-binding still is required; the two base structures for 'Every boy loves some girl' are

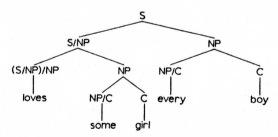

---

[28]Such a system is proposed as a formal reconstruction of Leibniz's doctrine of possible individuals in Benson Mates, "Leibniz on Possible Worlds," in *Logic, Methodology, and Philosophy of Science III*, ed. by van Rootselaar and Staal.

for the weak sense and

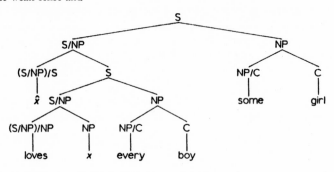

for the strong sense. Variables are names: the nth variable intension now becomes that NP-intension that assigns to every index i the character at the world coordinate of i of the thing that is the nth term of the assignment coordinate of i. The intensions of binders are revised to fit.

VIII. TREATMENT OF NON-DECLARATIVES

A meaning for a sentence, we said initially, was at least that which determines the conditions under which the sentence is true or false. But it is only declarative sentences that can be called true or false in any straightforward way. What of non-declarative sentences: commands, questions, and so on? If these do not have truth-values, as they are commonly supposed not to, we cannot very well say that their meanings determine their truth conditions.

One method of treating non-declaratives is to analyze all sentences, declarative or non-declarative, into two components: a *sentence radical* that specifies a state of affairs and a *mood* that determines whether the speaker is declaring that the state of affairs holds, commanding that it hold, asking whether it holds, or what.[29] We are to regard the sentences

> It is the case that you are late.
> Make it the case that you are late!
> Is it the case that you are late?

or more idiomatically

> You are late.
> Be late!
> Are you late?

---

[29] I adopt the terminology of Erik Stenius, "Mood and Language-Game," *Synthese* 17 (1967): 254–74, one recent exposition of such a view.

as having a common sentence-radical specifying the state of affairs consisting of your being late, but differing in their moods: declarative, imperative, and interrogative. They might be given the base structures

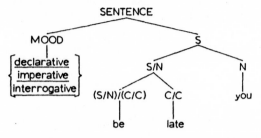

with S now understood as the category *sentence radical*. Different moods will induce different transformations of the sentence radical, leading to the different sentences above. The sentence radical is *not* a declarative sentence. If it is represented on the surface at all, it should be represented as the clause 'that you are late'. All that we have said about sentences should be taken as applying rather to sentence radicals. It is sentence radicals that have truth-values as extensions, functions from indices to truth-values as intensions, and meanings with the category S and an S-intension at the topmost node. We may grant that a declarative sentence is called true iff its sentence radical has the value *truth;* if we liked, we could also call an imperative or interrogative or other non-declarative sentence true iff its sentence radical has the value *truth,* but we customarily do not. Fundamentally, however, the entire apparatus of referential semantics (whether done on a categorial base as I propose, or otherwise) pertains to sentence radicals and constituents thereof. The semantics of mood is something entirely different. It consists of rules of language use such as these (adapted from Stenius[30]):

> Utter a sentence representing the combination of the mood *declarative* with an S-meaning *m* only if *m* is true on the occasion in question.
>
> React to a sentence representing the combination of the mood *imperative* with an S-meaning *m* (if addressed to you by a person in a suitable relation of authority over you) by acting in such a way as to make *m* true on the occasion in question.

In abstract semantics, as distinct from the theory of language use, a meaning for a sentence should simply be a *pair* of a mood and an S-meaning (moods being identified with some arbitrarily chosen entities).

The method of sentence radicals requires a substantial revision of my system. It works well for declaratives, imperatives, and yes-no questions. It is hard to see how

[30] *Ibid.*

it could be applied to other sorts of questions, or to sentences like 'Hurrah for Porky!'

I prefer an alternative method of treating non-declaratives that requires no revision whatever in my system of categories, intensions, and meanings. Let us once again regard S as the category *sentence,* without discrimination of mood. But let us pay special attention to those sentential meanings that are represented by base structures of roughly the following form.

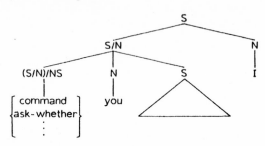

Such meanings can be represented by *performative sentences* such as these.[31]

> I command you to be late.
> I ask you whether you are late.

Such meanings might also be represented, after a more elaborate transformational derivation, by non-declaratives.

> Be late!
> Are you late?

I propose that these non-declaratives ought to be treated as paraphrases of the corresponding performatives, having the same base structure, meaning, intension, and truth-value at an index or on an occasion. And I propose that there is no difference in kind between the meanings of these performatives and non-declaratives and the meanings of the ordinary declarative sentences considered previously.

It is not clear whether we would classify the performative sentences as declarative. If not, then we can divide sentential meanings into declarative sentential meanings and non-declarative sentential meanings, the latter being represented both by performatives and by imperatives, questions, etc. But if, as I would prefer, we classify performatives as declarative, then the distinction between declarative and non-declarative sentences becomes a purely syntactic, surface distinction. The only distinction among meanings is the distinction between those sentential meanings that can only be represented by declarative sentences and those that can be represented either by suitable declarative sentences (performatives) or by non-

---

[31]See J. L. Austin, *How To Do Things with Words* (Cambridge, Mass.: Harvard University Press, 1962), for the standard account of performatives; but, as will be seen, I reject part of this account.

declarative paraphrases thereof. Let us call the latter *performative sentential meanings*. I need not delineate the class of performative sentential meanings precisely, since I am claiming that they do *not* need to be singled out for special semantic treatment.

The method of paraphrased performatives can easily be extended to those non-declaratives that resisted treatment by the method of sentence radicals. Not only yes-no questions but other questions as well correspond to performative sentences. The sentences below

> I ask who Sylvia is.
> Who is Sylvia?

for instance, might have a common meaning represented by a base structure something like this.

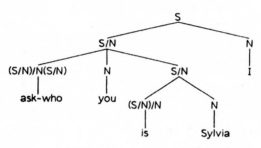

And the sentences

> I cheer Porky.
> Hurrah for Porky!

might have this base structure. (Thus the word 'Hurrah' would be introduced transformationally.)

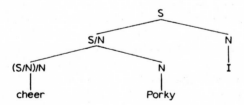

We may classify the sentential meanings represented by these base structures also as performative.

We noted at the outset that non-declaratives are commonly supposed to lack truth-values. The method of sentence radicals respects this common opinion by assigning truth-values fundamentally to sentence radicals rather than to whole sentences. We are under no compulsion to regard a non-declarative sentence as sharing the truth-value of its sentence radical, and we have chosen not to. The method of paraphrased performatives, on the other hand, does call for the assignment of truth-values to non-declarative sentences. The truth-value assigned is not that of the embedded sentence (corresponding to the sentence radical), however, but rather that of the paraphrased performative. If I say to you 'Be late!' and you are not late, the embedded sentence is false, but the paraphrased performative is true because I *do* command that you be late. I see no problem in letting non-declaratives have the truth-values of the performatives they paraphrase; after all, we need not ever mention their truth-values if we would rather not.

So far, I have assumed that performatives themselves do have truth-values, but that also has been denied.[32] I would wish to say that 'I bet you sixpence it will rain tomorrow' is true on an occasion of utterance iff the utterer *does* then bet his audience sixpence that it will rain on the following day; and, if the occasion is normal in certain respects, the utterer does so bet; therefore his utterance is true. Austin says it is obviously neither true nor false, apparently because to utter the sentence (in normal circumstances) is to bet. Granted; but why is that a reason to deny that the utterance is true? To utter 'I am speaking' is to speak, but it is also to speak the truth. This much can be said in Austin's defense: the truth-values (and truth conditions, that is intensions) of performatives and their paraphrases are easily ignored just because it is hard for a performative to be anything but true on an occasion of its utterance. Hard but possible: you can be play-acting, practicing elocution, or impersonating an officer and say 'I command that you be late' falsely, that is, say it without thereby commanding your audience to be late. I claim that those are the very circumstances in which you could falsely say 'Be late!'; otherwise it, like the performative, is truly uttered when and because it is uttered. It is no wonder if the truth-conditions of the sentences embedded in performatives and their non-declarative paraphrases tend to eclipse the truth conditions of the performatives and non-declaratives themselves.

This eclipsing is most visible in the case of performative sentences of the form 'I state that ————' or 'I declare that ————'. If someone says 'I declare that the Earth is flat' (sincerely, not play-acting etc.) I claim that he has spoken truly: he does indeed so declare. I claim this not only for the sake of my theory but as a point of common sense. Yet one might be tempted to say that he has spoken falsely, because the sentence embedded in his performative—the content of his declaration, the belief he avows—is false. Hence I do not propose to take ordinary declaratives as paraphrased performatives, as Ross has proposed,[33] because that would get their truth conditions wrong. If there are strong syntactic reasons for adopting Ross's proposal, I would regard it as semantically a version of the method

---

[32] J. L. Austin, *ibid.*, lecture one.

[33] John R. Ross, "On Declarative Sentences," *Readings in Transformational Grammar*, ed. by R. Jacobs and P. Rosenbaum, (Boston, Mass.: Blaisdell, 1970).

of sentence radicals, even if it employs base structures that look exactly like the base structures employed in the method of paraphrased performatives.

I provide only one meaning for the sentence 'I command you to be late'. Someone might well object that this sentence ought to come out ambiguous, because it can be used in two ways. It can be used to command; thus used, it can be paraphrased as 'Be late!', and it is true when uttered in normal circumstances just because it is uttered. It can be used instead to describe what I am doing; thus used, it cannot be paraphrased as an imperative, and it is likely to be false when uttered because it is difficult to issue a command and simultaneously say that I am doing so. (Difficult but possible: I might be doing the commanding by signing my name on a letter while describing what I am doing by talking.)

I agree that there are two alternative uses of this and other performative sentences: the genuinely performative use and the non-performative self-descriptive use. I agree also that the non-declarative paraphrase can occur only in the performative use. It still does not follow that there are two meanings. Compare the case of these two sentences.

I am talking in trochaic hexameter.
In hexameter trochaic am I talking.

The latter can be used to talk in trochaic hexameter and is true on any occasion of its correctly accented utterance. The former cannot be so used and is false on any occasion of its correctly accented utterance. Yet the two sentences are obviously paraphrases. Whether a sentence can be used to talk in trochaic hexameter is not a matter of its meaning. The distinction between using a sentence to talk in trochaic hexameter or not so using it is one sort of distinction; the distinction between using a performative sentence performatively and using it self-descriptively is quite another sort. Still I think the parallel is instructive. A distinction in uses need not involve a distinction in meanings of the sentences used. It can involve distinction in surface form; or distinction in conversational setting, intentions, and expectations; or distinction of some other sort. I see no decisive reason to insist that there is any distinction in meanings associated with the difference between performative and self-descriptive uses of performative sentences, if the contrary assumption is theoretically convenient.

We may ask to what extent the method of sentence radicals and the method of paraphrased performatives are compatible. In particular: given any sentence that can be analyzed into mood and sentence-radical, can we recover the mood and the sentence-radical intension from the meaning of the sentence according to the method of paraphrased performatives?

We almost can do this, but not quite. On the method of sentence radicals, the difference between the performative and self-descriptive uses of performative sentences *must* be treated as a difference of meanings. So given a performative sentence meaning, we will get two pairs of a mood and a sentence-radical intension corresponding to the two uses. Suppose we are given a performative sentential meaning represented by a base structure like this, for instance.

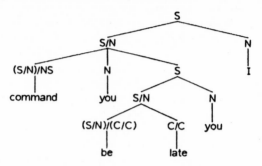

For the self-descriptive use, we do just what we would do for a non-performative sentence meaning: take the mood to be *declarative* and the sentence-radical intension to be the intension of the entire meaning. In this case, it would be the intension corresponding to the sentence radical 'that I command you to be late'. For the performative use, we take the mood to be determined by the $(S/N)/NS$-intension at node $\langle 1\ 1\rangle$, and the sentence-radical intension to be the S-intension at node $\langle 1\ 3\rangle$. In this case, these are respectively the intension of 'command', which determines that the mood is *imperative,* and the S-intension of the embedded sentence meaning, corresponding to the sentence radical 'that you are late'. Note here a second advantage, apart from fineness of individuation, of taking meanings as semantically interpreted phrase markers rather than as single intensions: we can recover the meanings of constituents from the meanings of their compounds.

APPENDIX: INDICES EXPANDED

Indices are supposed to be packages of everything but meaning that goes into determining extensions. Do we have everything? Let me speculate on several expansions of the indices that might prove useful.

First, consider the sentence '*This* is older than *this*'. I might say it pointing at a 1962 Volkswagen when I say the first 'this' and at a 1963 Volkswagen when I say the second 'this'. The sentence should be true on such an occasion; but how can it be? Using the intension of 'this', with its sensitivity to the indicated-objects coordinate, we obtain the intension of the whole sentence; then we take the value of that intension at an index with world and contextual coordinates determined by features of the occasion of utterance. (We generalize over indices alike except at the assignment coordinate; but we can consider any one of these, since the assignment coordinate is irrelevant to the sentence in question.) This procedure ignores the fact that the indicated object changes part-way through the occasion of utterance. So the sentence comes out false, as it should on any occasion when the indicated object stays the same.

On a more extensional approach to semantics, a solution would be easy. We could take the two extensions of 'this' on the two occasions of its utterance and use these, rather than the fixed intension of 'this', to determine the truth-value of the sentence. The intension and the occasion of utterance of the sentence as a whole would drop out. But since the extensions of compounds are not in general determined by the extensions of their constituents, this extensional solution would preclude a uniform treatment of semantic projection rules.

An acceptable solution has been suggested to me by David Kaplan, as follows. Let the indicated-objects coordinate be not just one set of objects capable of being pointed at but an infinite sequence of such sets. Let the indicated-objects coordinate determined by a given occasion of utterance of a sentence have as its nth term the set of things pointed to at the nth utterance of 'this' during the utterance of the sentence so long as n does not exceed the number of such utterances, and let it be the empty set when n does exceed that number. Let there be an infinite sequence of constituents 'this$_1$', 'this$_2$', . . . with intensions such that 'this$_n$' depends for its extension at an index on the nth term of the assignment coordinate. So that the lexicon will remain finite, let all but 'this$_1$' be compounds generated by iterated application of a suitable N/N to 'this$_1$'. Let all members of the sequence appear as 'this' in surface structure. Use transformational filtering to dispose of all base structures except those employing an initial segment of the 'this'-sequence so arranged that if the subscripts were carried to the surface, they would appear in numerical order without repetition. Thus the only base structure for 'This is older than this' will be

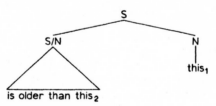

which will be true on occasions of the sort in question.

The solution must be modified to allow for the fact that 'this' is not the only demonstrative; I omit details. Similar difficulties arise, and similar solutions are possible, for other contextual coordinates: time, place, audience, and perhaps speaker.

Second, consider the sentence 'The door is open'. This does not mean that the one and only door that now exists is open; nor does it mean that the one and only door near the place of utterance, or pointed at, or mentioned in previous discourse, is open. Rather it means that the one and only door among the objects that are somehow prominent on the occasion is open. An object may be prominent because it is nearby, or pointed at, or mentioned; but none of these is a necessary condition of contextual prominence. So perhaps we need a *prominent-objects coordinate,* a new contextual coordinate independent of the others. It will be determined, on a given occasion of utterance of a sentence, by mental factors such as the speaker's expectations regarding the things he is likely to bring to the attention of his audience.

Third, consider the suggestion[34] that the extension of a personal name on a given occasion depends partly on the causal chain leading from the bestowal of that name on some person to the later use of that name by a speaker on the occasion in question. We might wish to accept this theory, and yet wish to deny that the intension or meaning of the name depends, on the occasion in question, upon the causal history of the speaker's use of it; for we might not wish to give up the common presumption that the meaning of an expression for a speaker depends only on mental factors within him. We might solve this dilemma[35] by including a *causal-history-of-acquisition-of-names coordinate* in our indices and letting the intensions of names for a speaker determine their extensions only relative to that coordinate.

Fourth, we have so far been ignoring the vagueness of natural language. Perhaps we are right to ignore it, or rather to deport it from semantics to the theory of language-use. We could say, as I do elsewhere,[36] that languages themselves are free of vagueness but that the linguistic conventions of a population, or the linguistic habits of a person, select not a point but a fuzzy region in the space of precise languages. However, it might prove better to treat vagueness within semantics, and we could do so as follows.[37]

Pretend first that the only vagueness is the vagueness of 'cool' and 'warm'; and suppose for simplicity that these are extensional adjectives. Let the indices contain a *delineation coordinate:* a positive real number, regarded as the boundary temperature between cool and warm things. Thus at an index i the extension of 'cool' is the set of things at the world and time coordinates of i having temperatures (in degrees Kelvin) less than or equal to the delineation coordinate of i; the extension of 'warm' is the set of such things having temperatures greater than the delineation coordinate. A vague sentence such as 'This is cool' is true, on a given occasion, at some but not all delineations; that is, at some but not all indices that are alike except in delineation and have the world and contextual coordinates determined by the occasion of utterance. But sentences with vague constituents are not necessarily vague: "This is cool or warm, but not both' is true at all delineations, on an

---

[34]David Kaplan, "Quantifying In," *Synthese* 19 (1968): 178–214; Keith Donnellan, "Proper Names and Identifying Descriptions," *Synthese* 21 (1970): 335–58.

[35]As I proposed in "Languages and Language," in this volume.

[36]*Convention: A Philosophical Study* (Cambridge, Mass.: Harvard University Press, 1969), chapter 5.

[37]A related treatment, developed independently, is to be found in J. A. Goguen, "The Logic of Inexact Concepts," *Synthese* 19 (1969): 325–73.

occasion on which there is a unique indicated object, even if the indicated object is lukewarm.

The delineation coordinate is non-contextual. It resembles the assignment coordinate, in that we will ordinarily generalize over it rather than hold it fixed. We may say that a sentence is *true over* a set *s* of delineations at an index *i*, iff, for any index *i'* that is like *i* except perhaps at the delineation coordinate, the sentence is true at *i'* if and only if the delineation coordinate of *i'* belongs to *s*. Given a normalized measure function over delineations, we can say that a sentence is *true to degree d* at *i* iff it is true at *i* over a set of delineations of measure *d*. Note that the degree of truth of a truth-functional compound of sentences is not a function of the degrees of truth of its constituent sentences: 'x is cool' and 'x is warm' may both be true to degree .5 at an index *i*, but 'x is cool or x is cool' is true at *i* to degree .5 whereas 'x is cool or x is warm' is true at *i* to degree 1.

Treating vagueness within semantics makes for simple specifications of the intensions of such expressions as 'in some sense', 'paradigmatic', '————ish', and '————er than'. The contemporary idiom 'in some sense', for instance, is an S/S related to the delineation coordinate just as the modal operator 'possibly' is related to the world coordinate. The intension of 'in some sense' is that function ϕ such that if ϕ_1 is any S-intension, ϕ_2 is $\phi(\phi_1)$, and *i* is any index, then

$$\phi_2(i) = \begin{cases} \textit{truth} \text{ if, for some index } i' \text{ that is like } i \text{ except perhaps at the delin-} \\ \text{eation coordinate, } \phi_1(i') \text{ is } \textit{truth} \\ \textit{falsity} \text{ otherwise.} \end{cases}$$

The comparative '————er than' is a ((C/C)/N)/(C/C) having an intension such that, for instance, 'x is cooler than y' is true at an index *i* iff the set of delineations over which 'y is cool' is true at *i* is a proper subset of the set of delineations over which 'x is cool' is true at *i*. It follows that the sun is not cooler than Sirius unless in some sense the sun is cool; but that conclusion seems correct, although I do not know whether to deny that the sun is cooler than Sirius or to agree that in some sense the sun is cool.[38]

More generally, the delineation coordinate must be a sequence of boundary-specifying numbers. Different vague expressions will depend for their extensions (or, if they are not extensional, for the extensions of their extensional compounds) on different terms of the delineation. More than one term of the delineation coordinate might be involved for a single expression. For instance, the intension of 'green' might involve one term regarded as delineating the blue-green boundary and another regarded as delineating the green-yellow boundary. The former but not the latter would be one of the two terms involved in the intension of 'blue'; and so on around the circle of hues.

[38] This analysis of comparatives was suggested to me by David Kaplan.

Postscripts to
"General Semantics"

A. INDEX AND CONTEXT[1]

An index is an *n*-tuple which serves as a package of the various features of context on which extensions may depend. But my packages were far too small. There are ever so many relevant features of context besides the ones I listed. For discussion of a few more of them, see "Scorekeeping in a Language Game" (in this volume).

We could wait for the end of linguistic inquiry, and define our indices then. But the less patient of us may prefer another solution. Let the features of context mostly be given implicitly. Once we have world, time, and speaker, what can be lacking? The place is the place where that speaker is at that time at that world; the appropriate resolutions of vagueness are (under)determined by the pragmatic forces present in the conversation that has been going on around that speaker just before that time at that world; and so on for other features of context, however numerous and however recondite.

So perhaps my packages were not too small after all, but rather were too big. Why not stop with world, time, and speaker? Or, as I would prefer, with all three in one: a world-bound time-slice of a (potential) speaker. Call this a *context*.[2]

A context gives us a world, time, and speaker that are suitably related: the speaker is present at that time at that world. If we take world-bound time-slices, the relatedness is automatic. If we take world-time-speaker triples, the relatedness is not automatic, but we must nevertheless demand it: without it, our method for recovering the other features of context makes no sense.

Then, sad to say, contexts cannot replace indices. For we must often consider an index whose world, time, and speaker are *not* suitably related, as witness the truth of "I was not here yesterday, and I might not have been here now". To evaluate this sentence as true, we must shift first time and then world in ways that destroy the relatedness. Likewise we may need to shift other coordinates in ways that destroy their relation to world, time, and speaker, as witness the truth of "No matter who you are, you'd better understand double indexing". It is a good ques-

---

[1] For a fuller discussion, see my "Index, Context, and Content," in Stig Kanger and Sven Öhman, eds., *Philosophy and Grammar* (Dordrecht: Reidel, 1981). I am much indebted to Robert Stalnaker, "Pragmatics," *Synthese* 22 (1970): 272–89, and to David Kaplan's unpublished study of demonstratives.

[2] It will not escape the reader of "Attitudes *De Dicto* and *De Se*" (in this volume) that these "contexts" are the same as the "subjects" that self-ascribe properties, and that sets of them are the self-ascribed properties. This agreement might well be exploited in the semantic analysis of *de se* attitude-sentences. Arnim von Stechow has put forward proposals to this effect in his contribution to a symposium held at Konstanz University in September 1981.

tion which, and how many, features of context are subject to such shifting. Certainly, far from all of them. I think it reasonable to hope for a short list of all the shiftable features of context, well before the end of inquiry.

Given that short list, the thing to do is to define an index so that its first coordinate is a context, and its remaining coordinates correspond not to all the relevant features of context but only to all the shiftable features. Then we must distinguish two sorts of indices: *Original indices,* in which the shiftable features are as determined by the context which appears as first coordinate; and *shifted indices,* in which that is not so. Truth in a context is truth at an original index, and this is the semantic notion that is directly relevant to truthful speech. Truth at indices generally is an auxiliary notion: truth of a sentence at an original index may be determined by the extensions of its constituents at shifted indices, and more generally by the structure of Carnapian and compositional intensions involving the full range of indices.

B. VARIABLES AND BINDING

I was able to make provision, within a purely categorial grammar and its system of intensions, for individual variables and for abstraction operators to bind them. But my method cannot be extended to provide variables and binders throughout the employed categories, lest we fall afoul of the *Fundierungsaxiom* of standard set theory. The utility of bound variables in many categories has been shewn in the work of M. J. Cresswell, so I now think it best to follow his example and invest in the means for variable-binding outside the categorial framework.[3]

C. INFINITIVES VERSUS CLAUSES

Although my framework did not require it, in several examples I went out of my way to transform surface infinitives into underlying sentential clauses. Thus "Lothario strives to find x" came out as (C) instead of (I).

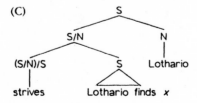

[3]See his *Logics and Languages* (London: Methuen, 1973).

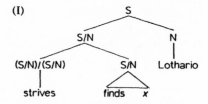

But (I) would have been better, for several reasons. (1) It is closer to surface structure. (2) It treats "strive to find x" as a genuine constituent. (3) It meshes with my proposal in "Attitudes *De Dicto* and *De Se*" that the objects of attitudes should be taken in general as properties rather than propositions. For instance, an appropriate object of (the attitudinal part of) striving would be a property such as the property of finding a certain individual x. (4) If Lothario does not realize that he himself is Lothario, striving that he himself find x might differ from striving that Lothario find x. If so, it is the former, rather than the latter, that we call "striving to find x".

Similarly, I would now prefer that the performative meaning underlying "Be late!" be taken as follows, so that it will include as a constituent the meaning of the transitive verb phrase "command to be late".

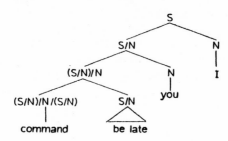

· T H I R T E E N ·

Scorekeeping in a Language Game

EXAMPLE 1: PRESUPPOSITION[1]

At any stage in a well-run conversation, a certain amount is presupposed. The parties to the conversation take it for granted; or at least they purport to, whether sincerely or just "for the sake of the argument." Presuppositions can be created or destroyed in the course of a conversation. This change is rule-governed, at least up

I am doubly grateful to Robert Stalnaker: first, for his treatment of presupposition, here summarized as Example 1, which I have taken as the prototype for parallel treatments of other topics; and second, for valuable comments on a previous version of this paper. I am also much indebted to Stephen Isard, who discusses many of the phenomena that I consider here in his "Changing the Context," in Edward L. Keenan, ed., *Formal Semantics of Natural Language* (Cambridge: Cambridge University Press, 1974). Proposals along somewhat the same lines as mine are to be found in Thomas T. Ballmer, "Einführung und Kontrolle von Diskurswelten," in Dieter Wunderlich, ed., *Linguistische Pragmatik* (Königstein, W. Germ.: Athenäum-Verlag, 1972), and Ballmer, *Logical Grammar: with Special Consideration of Topics in Context Change* (Amsterdam: North-Holland, 1978).

An early version of this paper was presented to the Vacation School in Logic at Victoria University of Wellington in August 1976; I thank the New Zealand–United States Educational Foundation for research support on that occasion. The paper also was presented at a workshop on pragmatics and conditionals at the University of Western Ontario in May 1978, and at a colloquium on semantics at Konstanz University in September 1978.

[1]This treatment of presupposition is taken from two papers of Robert Stalnaker: "Presuppositions," *Journal of Philosophical Logic* 2 (1973): 447–57, and "Pragmatic Presuppositions," in Milton K. Munitz and Peter K. Unger, eds., *Semantics and Philosophy* (New York: New York University Press, 1974).

to a point. The presuppositions at time t' depend, in a way about which at least some general principles can be laid down, on the presuppositions at an earlier time t and on the course of the conversation (and nearby events) between t and t'.

Some things that might be said require suitable presuppositions. They are acceptable if the required presuppositions are present; not otherwise. "The king of France is bald" requires the presupposition that France has one king, and one only; "Even George Lakoff could win" requires the presupposition that George is not a leading candidate; and so on.

We need not ask just what sort of unacceptability results when a required presupposition is lacking. Some say falsehood, some say lack of truth value, some just say that it's the kind of unacceptability that results when a required presupposition is lacking, and some say it might vary from case to case.

Be that as it may, it's not as easy as you might think to say something that will be unacceptable for lack of required presuppositions. Say something that requires a missing presupposition, and straightway that presupposition springs into existence, making what you said acceptable after all. (Or at least, that is what happens if your conversational partners tacitly acquiesce—if no one says "But France has *three* kings!" or "Whadda ya mean, '*even* George'?") That is why it is peculiar to say, out of the blue, "All Fred's children are asleep, and Fred has children." The first part requires and thereby creates a presupposition that Fred has children; so the second part adds nothing to what is already presupposed when it is said; so the second part has no conversational point. It would not have been peculiar to say instead "Fred has children, and all Fred's children are asleep."

I said that presupposition evolves in a more or less rule-governed way during a conversation. Now we can formulate one important governing rule: call it the *rule of accommodation for presupposition.*

> If a time t something is said that requires presupposition P to be acceptable, and if P is not presupposed just before t, then—*ceteris paribus* and within certain limits—presupposition P comes into existence at t.

This rule has not yet been very well stated, nor is it the only rule governing the kinematics of presupposition. But let us bear it in mind nevertheless, and move on to other things.

EXAMPLE 2: PERMISSIBILITY[2]

For some reason—coercion, deference, common purpose—two people are both willing that one of them should be under the control of the other. (At least within certain limits, in a certain sphere of action, so long as certain conditions prevail.) Call one the *slave,* the other the *master.* The control is exercised verbally, as follows.

[2]This treatment of permissibility is discussed more fully in my paper "A Problem about Permission," in Esa Saarinen *et al.*, eds., *Essays in Honour of Jaakko Hintikka* (Dordrecht: Reidel, 1979).

At any stage in the enslavement, there is a boundary between some courses of action for the slave that are permissible, and others that are not. The range of permissible conduct may expand or contract. The master shifts the boundary by saying things to the slave. Since the slave does his best to see to it that his course of action is a permissible one, the master can control the slave by controlling what is permissible.

Here is how the master shifts the boundary. From time to time he says to the slave that such-and-such courses of action are impermissible. Any such statement depends for its truth value on the boundary between what is permissible and what isn't. But if the master says that something is impermissible, and if that would be false if the boundary remained stationary, then straightway the boundary moves inward. The permissible range contracts so that what the master says is true after all. Thereby the master makes courses of action impermissible that used to be permissible. But from time to time also the master relents, and says to the slave that such-and-such courses of action are permissible. Or perhaps he says that some of such-and-such courses of action are permissible, but doesn't say just which ones. Then the boundary moves outward. The permissible range expands, if need be (and if possible), so that what the master says is true. Thereby the master makes courses of action permissible that used to be impermissible.

The truth of the master's statements about permissibility—one aspect of their acceptability—depends on the location of the boundary. The boundary shifts in a rule-governed way. The rule is as follows; call it the *rule of accommodation for permissibility*.

> If a time *t* something is said about permissibility by the master to the slave that requires for its truth the permissibility or impermissibility of certain courses of action, and if just before *t* the boundary is such as to make the master's statement false, then—*ceteris paribus* and within certain limits—the boundary shifts at *t* so as to make the master's statement true.

Again, this is not a very satisfactory formulation. For one thing, the limits and qualifications are left unspecified. But more important, the rule as stated does not say exactly how the boundary is to shift.

What if the master says that some of such-and-such courses of actions are permissible, when none of them were permissible before he spoke. By the rule, some of them must straightway become permissible. Some—but which ones? The ones that were closest to permissibility beforehand, perhaps. Well and good, but now we have a new problem. At every stage there is not only a boundary between the permissible and the impermissible, but also a relation of comparative near-permissibility between the courses of action on the impermissible side. Not only do we need rules governing the shifting boundary, but also we need rules to govern the changing relation of comparative near-permissibility. Not only must we say how this relation evolves when the master says something about absolute permissibility, but also we must say how it evolves when he says something—as he might—about comparative near-permissibility. He might say, for instance, that the most nearly permissible courses of action in a class A are those in a subclass A'; or that some courses of action in class B are more nearly permissible than any in class C. Again the rule is a rule of accommodation. The relation of comparative near-permissibility changes, if need be, so that what the master says to the slave is true. But again, to say that is not enough. It does not suffice to determine just what the change is.

Those were Examples 1 and 2. Examples of what? I'll say shortly; but first, a digression.

SCOREKEEPING IN A BASEBALL GAME

At any stage in a well-run baseball game, there is a septuple of numbers $\langle r_v, r_h, h, i, s, b, o \rangle$ which I shall call the *score* of that game at that stage. We recite the score as follows: the visiting team has r_v runs, the home team has r_h runs, it is the hth half (h being 1 or 2) of the ith inning; there are s strikes, b balls, and o outs. (In another terminology, the score is only the initial pair $\langle r_v, r_h \rangle$, but I need a word for the entire septuple.) A possible codification of the rules of baseball would consist of rules of four different sorts.

(1) *Specifications of the kinematics of score.* Initially, the score is $\langle 0, 0, 1, 1, 0, 0, 0 \rangle$. Thereafter, if at time t the score is s, and if between time t and t' the players behave in manner m, then at time t' the score is s', where s' is determined in a certain way by s and m.

(2) *Specifications of correct play.* If at time t the score is s, and if between time t and time t' the players behave in manner m, then the players have behaved incorrectly. (Correctness depends on score: what is correct play after two strikes differs from what is correct play after three.) What is not incorrect play according to these rules is correct.

(3) *Directive requiring correct play.* All players are to behave, throughout the game, in such a way that play is correct.

(4) *Directives concerning score.* Players are to strive to make the score evolve in certain directions. Members of the visiting team try to make r_v large and r_h small, members of the home team try to do the opposite.

(We could dispense with rules of sorts (2) and (3) by adding an eighth component to the score which, at any stage of the game, measures the amount of incorrect play up to that stage. Specifications of correct play are then included among the specifications of the kinematics of score, and the directive requiring correct play becomes one of the directives concerning score.)

Rules of sorts (1) and (2) are sometimes called *constitutive rules*. They are said to be akin to definitions, though they do not have the form of definitions. Rules of sorts (3) and (4) are called *regulative rules*. They are akin to the straightforward directives "No smoking!" or "Keep left!"

We could explain this more fully, as follows. Specifications of sorts (1) and (2) are not themselves definitions of "score" and "correct play." But they are consequences of reasonable definitions. Further, there is a systematic way to construct the definitions, given the specifications. Suppose we wish to define the *score function*: the function from game-stages to septuples of numbers that gives the score at every stage. The specifications of the kinematics of score, taken together, tell us that the score function evolves in such-and-such way. We may then simply define the score function as that function which evolves in such-and-such way. If the kinematics of score are well specified, then there is one function, and one only, that evolves in the proper way; and if so, then the score function evolves in the proper way if and only if the suggested definition of it is correct. Once we have defined the score function, we have thereby defined the score and all its components at any stage. There are two outs at a certain stage of a game, for instance, if and only if the score function assigns to that game-stage a septuple whose seventh component is the number 2.

Turn next to the specifications of correct play. Taken together, they tell us that correct play occurs at a game-stage if and only if the players' behavior at that stage bears such-and-such relation to score at that stage. This has the form of an explicit definition of correct play in terms of current score and current behavior. If current score has already been defined in terms of the history of the players' behavior up to now, in the way just suggested, then we have defined correct play in terms of current and previous behavior.

Once score and correct play are defined in terms of the players' behavior, then we may eliminate the defined terms in the directive requiring correct play and the directives concerning score. Thanks to the definitions constructed from the constitutive rules, the regulative rules become simply directives to strive to see to it that one's present behavior bears a certain rather complicated relation to the history of the players' behavior in previous stages of the game. A player might attempt to conform to such a directive for various reasons: contractual obligation, perhaps, or a conventional understanding with his fellow players based on their common interest in enjoying a proper game.

The rules of baseball could in principle be formulated as straightforward directives concerning behavior, without the aid of definable terms for score and its components. Or they could be formulated as explicit definitions of the score function, the components of score, and correct play, followed by directives in which the newly defined terms appear. It is easy to see why neither of these methods of formulation has found favor. The first method would pack the entire rulebook into each directive; the second would pack the entire rulebook into a single preliminary explicit definition. Understandably averse to very long sentences, we do better to proceed in our more devious way.

There is an alternative analysis—the baseball equivalent of operationalism or legal realism. Instead of appealing to constitutive rules, we might instead claim that the score is, by definition, whatever some scoreboard says it is. Which scoreboard? Various answers are defensible: maybe the visible scoreboard with its arrays of light bulbs, maybe the invisible scoreboard in the head umpire's head, maybe the many scoreboards in many heads to the extent that they agree. No matter. On any such view, the specifications of the kinematics of score have a changed status. No longer are they constitutive rules akin to definitions. Rather, they are empirical generalizations, subject to exceptions, about the ways in which the players' behavior tends to cause changes on the authoritative scoreboard. Under this analysis, it is impossible that this scoreboard fails to give the score. What is possible is that the score is in an abnormal and undesired relation to its causes, for which someone may perhaps be blamed.

I do not care to say which analysis is right for baseball as it is actually played. Perhaps the question has no determinate answer, or perhaps it has different answers for formal and informal baseball. I only wish to distinguish the two alternatives, noting that both are live options.

This ends the digression. Now I want to propose some general theses about language—theses that were examplified by Examples 1 and 2, and that will be exemplified also by several other examples.

CONVERSATIONAL SCORE

With any stage in a well-run conversation, or other process of linguistic interaction, there are associated many things analogous to the components of a baseball score. I shall therefore speak of them collectively as the *score* of that conversation at that stage. The points of analogy are as follows.

(1) Like the components of a baseball score, the components of a conversational score at a given stage are abstract entities. They may not be numbers, but they are other set-theoretic constructs: sets of presupposed propositions, boundaries between permissible and impermissible courses of action, or the like.

(2) What play is correct depends on the score. Sentences depend for their truth value, or for their acceptability in other respects, on the components of conversational score at the stage of conversation when they are uttered. Not only aspects of acceptability of an uttered sentence may depend on score. So may other semantic properties that play a role in determining aspects of acceptability. For instance, the constituents of an uttered sentence—subsentences, names, predicates, etc.—may depend on the score for their intension or extension.

(3) Score evolves in a more-or-less rule-governed way. There are rules that specify the kinematics of score:

> If at time t the conversational score is s, and if between time t and time t' the course of conversation is c, then at time t' the score is s', where s' is determined in a certain way by s and c.

Or at least:

> ... then at time t' the score is some member of the class S of possible scores, where S is determined in a certain way by s and c.

(4) The conversationalists may conform to directives, or may simply desire, that they strive to steer certain components of the conversational score in certain directions. Their efforts may be cooperative, as when all participants in a discussion try to increase the amount that all of them willingly presuppose. Or there may be conflict, as when each of two debaters tries to get his opponent to grant him—to join with him in presupposing—parts of his case, and to give away parts of the contrary case.

(5) To the extent that conversational score is determined, given the history of the conversation and the rules that specify its kinematics, these rules can be regarded as constitutive rules akin to definitions. Again, constitutive rules could be traded in for explicit definitions: the conversational score function could be defined as that function from conversation-stages to n-tuples of suitable entities that evolves in the specified way.

Alternatively, conversational score might be operationally defined in terms of mental scoreboards—some suitable attitudes—of the parties to the conversation. The rules specifying the kinematics of conversational score then become empirical generalizations, subject to exceptions, about the causal dependence of what the scoreboards register on the history of the conversation.

In the case of baseball score, either approach to the definition of score and the status of the rules seems satisfactory. In the case of conversational score, on the other hand, both approaches seem to meet with difficulties. If, as seems likely, the rules specifying the kinematics of conversational score are seriously incomplete, then often there may be many candidates for the score function, different but all evolving in the specified way. But also it seems difficult to say, without risk of circularity, what are the mental representations that comprise the conversationalists' scoreboards.

It may be best to adopt a third approach—a middle way, drawing on both the alternatives previously considered. Conversational score is, by definition, whatever the mental scoreboards say it is; but we refrain from trying to say just what the conversationalists' mental scoreboards are. We assume that some or other mental representations are present that play the role of a scoreboard, in the following sense: what they register depends on the history of the conversation in the way that score should according to the rules. The rules specifying the kinematics of score thereby specify the role of a scoreboard; the scoreboard is whatever best fills this role; and the score is whatever this scoreboard registers. The rules specifying the kinematics of score are to some extent constitutive, but on this third approach they enter only in a roundabout way into the definition of score. It is no harm if they underdetermine the evolution of score, and it is possible that score sometimes evolves in a way that violates the rules.

RULES OF ACCOMMODATION

There is one big difference between baseball score and conversational score. Suppose the batter walks to first base after only three balls. His behavior would be correct play if there were four balls rather than three. That's just too bad—his behavior does not at all make it the case that there *are* four balls and his behavior *is* correct. Baseball has no rule of accommodation to the effect that if a fourth ball is required to make correct the play that occurs, then that very fact suffices to change the score so that straightway there are four balls.

Language games are different. As I hope my examples will show, conversational score does tend to evolve in such a way as is required in order to make whatever occurs count as correct play. Granted, that is not invariable but only a tendency. Granted also, conversational score changes for other reasons as well. (As when something conspicuous happens at the scene of a conversation, and straightway it is presupposed that it happened.) Still, I suggest that many components of conversational score obey rules of accommodation, and that these rules figure prominently among the rules governing the kinematics of conversational score.

Recall our examples. Example 1: presupposition evolves according to a rule of accommodation specifying that any presuppositions that are required by what is said straightway come into existence, provided that nobody objects. Example 2: permissibility evolves according to a rule of accommodation specifying that the boundaries of the permissible range of conduct shift to make true whatever is said about them, provided that what is said is said by the master to the slave, and provided that there does exist some shift that would make what he says true. Here is a general scheme for rules of accommodation for conversational score.

> If at time t something is said that requires component s_n of conversational score to have a value in the range r if what is said is to be true, or otherwise acceptable; and if s_n does not have a value in the range r just before t; and if such-and-such further conditions hold; then at t the score-component s_n takes some value in the range r.

Once we have this scheme in mind, I think we will find many instances of it. In the rest of this paper I shall consider some further examples. I shall have little that is new to say about the individual examples. My interest is in the common pattern that they exhibit.

EXAMPLE 3: DEFINITE DESCRIPTIONS[3]

It is not true that a definite description "the F" denotes x if and only if x is the one and only F in existence. Neither is it true that "the F" denotes x if and only

[3]Definite descriptions governed by salience are discussed in my *Counterfactuals* (Oxford: Blackwell, 1973), pp. 111–17; and in James McCawley, "Presupposition and Discourse Structure," in David

if x is the one and only F in some contextually determined domain of discourse. For consider this sentence: "The pig is grunting, but the pig with floppy ears is not grunting" (Lewis). And this: "The dog got in a fight with another dog" (McCawley). They could be true. But for them to be true, "the pig" or "the dog" must denote one of two pigs or dogs, both of which belong to the domain of discourse.

The proper treatment of descriptions must be more like this: "the F" denotes x if and only if x is the most salient F in the domain of discourse, according to some contextually determined salience ranking. The first of our two sentences means that the most salient pig is grunting but the most salient pig with floppy ears is not. The second means that the most salient dog got in a fight with some less salient dog.

(I shall pass over some complications. Never mind what happens if two F's are tied for maximum salience, or if no F is at all salient. More important, I shall ignore the possibility that something might be highly salient in one of its guises, but less salient in another. Possibly we really need to appeal to a salience ranking not of individuals but rather of individuals-in-guises—that is, of individual concepts.)

There are various ways for something to gain salience. Some have to do with the course of conversation, others do not. Imagine yourself with me as I write these words. In the room is a cat, Bruce, who has been making himself very salient by dashing madly about. He is the only cat in the room, or in sight, or in earshot. I start to speak to you:

> The cat is in the carton. The cat will never meet our other cat, because our other cat lives in New Zealand. Our New Zealand cat lives with the Cresswells. And there he'll stay, because Miriam would be sad if the cat went away.

At first, "the cat" denotes Bruce, he being the most salient cat for reasons having nothing to do with the course of conversation. If I want to talk about Albert, our New Zealand cat, I have to say "our other cat" or "our New Zealand cat." But as I talk more and more about Albert, and not any more about Bruce, I raise Albert's salience by conversational means. Finally, in the last sentence of my monologue, I am in a position to say "the cat" and thereby denote not Bruce but rather the newly-most-salient cat Albert.

Dinneen and Choon-Kyu Oh, eds., *Syntax and Semantics* 11 (New York: Academic Press, 1979). A similar treatment of demonstratives is found in Isard, *op. cit.*

Manfred Pinkal, "How To Refer with Vague Descriptions" in *Semantics from Different Points of View*, ed. by R. Bäuerle *et al.*, (Berlin: Springer-Verlag, 1979). notes a further complication: if some highly salient things are borderline cases of *F*-hood, degree of *F*-hood and salience may trade off.

Indefinite descriptions that pave the way for referring expressions are discussed in Charles Chastain, "Reference and Context," *Minnesota Studies in the Philosophy of Science* 7 (1975): 194–269, and in Saul Kripke, "Speaker's Reference and Semantic Reference," *Midwest Studies in Philosophy* 2 (1977): 255–76.

The ranking of comparative salience, I take it, is another component of conversational score. Denotation of definite descriptions is score-dependent. Hence so is the truth of sentences containing such descriptions, which is one aspect of the acceptability of those sentences. Other aspects of acceptability in turn are score-dependent: non-triviality, for one, and possibility of warranted assertion, for another.

One rule, among others, that governs the kinematics of salience is a rule of accommodation. Suppose my monologue has left Albert more salient than Bruce; but the next thing I say is "The cat is going to pounce on you!" If Albert remains most salient and "the cat" denotes the most salient cat, then what I say is patently false: Albert cannot pounce all the way from New Zealand to Princeton. What I have said requires for its acceptability that "the cat" denote Bruce, and hence that Bruce be once again more salient than Albert. If what I say requires that, then straightway it is so. By saying what I did, I have made Bruce more salient than Albert. If next I say "The cat prefers moist food," that is true if Bruce prefers moist food, even if Albert doesn't.

The same thing would have happened if instead I had said "The cat is out of the carton" or "The cat has gone upstairs." Again what I say is unacceptable unless the salience ranking shifts so that Bruce rises above Albert, and hence so that "the cat" again denotes Bruce. The difference is in the type of unacceptability that would ensue without the shift. It is trivially true, hence not worth saying, that Albert is out of the carton. ("The carton" denotes the same carton as before; nothing has been done to raise the salience of any carton in New Zealand.) It may be true or it may be false that Albert has gone upstairs in the Cresswells' house in New Zealand. But I have no way of knowing, so I have no business saying that he has.

We can formulate a *rule of accommodation for comparative salience* more or less as follows. It is best to speak simply of unacceptability, since it may well be that the three sorts of unacceptability I have mentioned are not the only sorts that can give rise to a shift in salience.

> If a time *t* something is said that requires, if it is to be acceptable, that *x* be more salient than *y*; and if, just before *t*, *x* is no more salient than *y*; then— *ceteris paribus* and within certain limits—at *t*, *x* becomes more salient than *y*.

Although a rule of accommodation, such as this one, states that shifts of score take place when they are needed to preserve acceptability, we may note that the preservation is imperfect. It is not good conversational practice to rely too heavily on rules of accommodation. The monologue just considered illustrates this. Because "the cat" denotes first Bruce, then Albert, then Bruce again, what I say is to some extent confusing and hard to follow. But even if my monologue is not perfectly acceptable, its flaws are much less serious than the flaws that are averted by shifts of salience in accordance with our rule of accommodation. Confusing shifts of salience and reference are not as bad as falsity, trivial truth, or unwarranted assertion.

(It is worth mentioning another way to shift comparative salience by conversational means. I may say "A cat is on the lawn" under circumstances in which it is apparent to all parties to the conversation that there is some one particular cat that is responsible for the truth of what I say, and for my saying it. Perhaps I am looking out the window, and you rightly presume that I said what I did because I saw a cat; and further (since I spoke in the singular) that I saw only one. What I said was an existential quantification; hence, strictly speaking, it involves no reference to any particular cat. Nevertheless it raises the salience of the cat that made me say it. Hence this newly-most-salient cat may be denoted by brief definite descriptions, or by pronouns, in subsequent dialogue: "No, it's on the sidewalk." "Has Bruce noticed the cat?" As illustrated, this may happen even if the speaker contradicts my initial existential statement. Thus although indefinite descriptions—that is, idioms of existential quantification—are not themselves referring expressions, they may raise the salience of particular individuals in such a way as to pave the way for referring expressions that follow.)

EXAMPLE 4: COMING AND GOING[4]

Coming is movement toward a point of reference. Going is movement away from it. Sometimes the point of reference is fixed by the location of speaker and hearer, at the time of conversation or the time under discussion. But sometimes not. In third-person narrative, whether fact or fiction, the chosen point of reference may have nothing to do with the speaker's or the hearer's location.

One way to fix the point of reference at the beginning of a narrative, or to shift it later, is by means of a sentence that describes the direction of some movement both with respect to the point of reference and in some other way. "The beggars are coming to town" requires for its acceptability, and perhaps even for its truth, that the point of reference be in town. Else the beggars' townward movement is not properly called "coming." This sentence can be used to fix or to shift the point of reference. When it is said, straightway the point of reference is in town where it is required to be. Thereafter, unless something is done to shift it elsewhere, coming is movement toward town and going is movement away. If later we are told that when the soldiers came the beggars went, we know who ended up in town and who did not.

Thus the point of reference in narrative is a component of conversational score,

---

[4]See Charles Fillmore, "How To Know Whether You're Coming or Going," in Karl Hyldgaard-Jensen, ed., *Linguistik 1971* (Königstein, W. Germ.: Athenäum-Verlag, 1972), and "Pragmatics and the Description of Discourse," in Siegfried J. Schmidt, ed., *Pragmatik/Pragmatics II* (Wilhelm Fink Verlag, 1976).

governed by a rule of accommodation. Note that the rule must provide for two sorts of changes. The point of reference may simply go from one place to another, as is required by the following text:

> When the beggars came to town, the rich folk went to the shore. But soon the beggars came after them, so they went home.

But also the point of reference is usually not fully determinate in its location. It may become more or less determinate, as is required by the following:

> After the beggars came to town, they held a meeting. All of them came to the square. Afterwards they went to another part of town.

The first sentence puts the point of reference in town, but not in any determinate part of town. The second sentence increases its determinacy by putting it in the square. The initial fixing of the point of reference is likewise an increase in determinacy—the point of reference starts out completely indeterminate and becomes at least somewhat more definitely located.

EXAMPLE 5: VAGUENESS[5]

If Fred is a borderline case of baldness, the sentence "Fred is bald" may have no determinate truth value. Whether it is true depends on where you draw the line. Relative to some perfectly reasonable ways of drawing a precise boundary between bald and not-bald, the sentence is true. Relative to other delineations, no less reasonable, it is false. Nothing in our use of language makes one of these delineations right and all the others wrong. We cannot pick a delineation once and for all (not if we are interested in ordinary language), but must consider the entire range of reasonable delineations.

If a sentence is true over the entire range, true no matter how we draw the line, surely we are entitled to treat it simply as true. But also we treat a sentence more or less as if it is simply true, if it is true over a large enough part of the range of delineations of its vagueness. (For short: if it is *true enough*.) If a sentence is true enough (according to our beliefs) we are willing to assert it, assent to it without qualification, file it away among our stocks of beliefs, and so forth. Mostly we do not get into any trouble this way. (But sometimes we do, as witness the paradoxes that arise because truth-preserving reasoning does not always preserve the property of being true enough.)

When is a sentence true enough? Which are the "large enough" parts of the range of delineations of its vagueness? This is itself a vague matter. More important

[5]See the treatment of vagueness in my "General Semantics," in this volume. For arguments that hardly anything is flat or certain, see Peter Unger, *Ignorance* (Oxford University Press, 1975), pp. 65–68. For another example of accommodating shifts in resolution of vagueness, see the discussion of back-tracking counterfactuals in my "Counterfactual Dependence and Time's Arrow," in the sequel to this volume.

for our present purposes, it is something that depends on context. What is true enough on one occasion is not true enough on another. The standards of precision in force are different from one conversation to another, and may change in the course of a single conversation. Austin's "France is hexagonal" is a good example of a sentence that is true enough for many contexts, but not true enough for many others. Under low standards of precision it is acceptable. Raise the standards and it loses its acceptability.

Taking standards of precision as a component of conversational score, we once more find a rule of accommodation at work. One way to change the standards is to say something that would be unacceptable if the standards remained unchanged. If you say "Italy is boot-shaped" and get away with it, low standards are required and the standards fall if need be; thereafter "France is hexagonal" is true enough. But if you deny that Italy is boot-shaped, pointing out the differences, what you have said requires high standards under which "France is hexagonal" is far from true enough.

I take it that the rule of accommodation can go both ways. But for some reason raising of standards goes more smoothly than lowering. If the standards have been high, and something is said that is true enough only under lowered standards, and nobody objects, then indeed the standards are shifted down. But what is said, although true enough under the lowered standards, may still seem imperfectly acceptable. Raising of standards, on the other hand, manages to seem commendable even when we know that it interferes with our conversational purpose. Because of this asymmetry, a player of language games who is so inclined may get away with it if he tries to raise the standards of precision as high as possible—so high, perhaps, that no material object whatever is hexagonal.

Peter Unger has argued that hardly anything is flat. Take something you claim is flat; he will find something else and get you to agree that it is even flatter. You think the pavement is flat—but how can you deny that your desk is flatter? But "flat" is an *absolute term*: it is inconsistent to say that something is flatter than something that is flat. Having agreed that your desk is flatter than the pavement, you must concede that the pavement is not flat after all. Perhaps you now claim that your desk is flat; but doubtless Unger can think of something that you will agree is even flatter than your desk. And so it goes.

Some might dispute Unger's premise that "flat" is an absolute term; but on that score it seems to me that Unger is right. What he says is inconsistent does indeed sound that way. I take this to mean that on no delineation of the correlative vagueness of "flatter" and "flat" is it true that something is flatter than something that is flat.

The right response to Unger, I suggest, is that he is changing the score on you. When he says that the desk is flatter than the pavement, what he says is acceptable only under raised standards of precision. Under the original standards the bumps on the pavement were too small to be relevant either to the question whether the pavement is flat or to the question whether the pavement is flatter than the desk.

Since what he says requires raised standards, the standards accommodatingly rise. Then it is no longer true enough that the pavement is flat. That does not alter the fact that it *was* true enough *in its original context.* "The desk is flatter than the pavement" said under raised standards does not contradict "The pavement is flat" said under unraised standards, any more than "It is morning" said in the morning contradicts "It is afternoon" said in the afternoon. Nor has Unger shown in any way that the new context is more legitimate than the old one. He can indeed create an unusual context in which hardly anything can acceptably be called "flat," but he has not thereby cast any discredit on the more usual contexts in which lower standards of precision are in force.

In parallel fashion Unger observes, I think correctly, that "certain" is an absolute term; from this he argues that hardly ever is anyone certain of anything. A parallel response is in order. Indeed the rule of accommodation permits Unger to create a context in which all that he says is true, but that does not show that there is anything whatever wrong with the claims to certainty that we make in more ordinary contexts. It is no fault in a context that we can move out of it.

EXAMPLE 6: RELATIVE MODALITY[6]

The "can" and "must" of ordinary language do not often express absolute ("logical" or "metaphysical") possibility. Usually they express various relative modalities. Not all the possibilities there are enter into consideration. If we ignore those possibilities that violate laws of nature, we get the physical modalities; if we ignore those that are known not to obtain, we get the epistemic modalities; if we ignore those that ought not to obtain—doubtless including actuality—we get the deontic modalities; and so on. That suggests that "can" and "must" are ambiguous. But on that hypothesis, as Kratzer has convincingly argued, the alleged senses are altogether too numerous. We do better to think of our modal verbs as unambiguous but relative. Sometimes the relativity is made explicit. Modifying phrases like "in view of what is known" or "in view of what custom requires" may be present to indicate just which possibilities should be ignored.

But sometimes no such phrase is present. Then context must be our guide. The boundary between the relevant possibilities and the ignored ones (formally, the accessibility relation) is a component of conversational score, which enters into the truth conditions of sentences with "can" or "must" or other modal verbs. It may change in the course of conversation. A modifying phrase "in view of such-and-such" does not only affect the sentence in which it appears, but also remains in

[6]See Angelika Kratzer, "What 'Must' and 'Can' Must and Can Mean," *Linguistics and Philosophy* 1 (1977): 337–55. The accessibility semantics considered here is equivalent to a slightly restricted form of Kratzer's semantics for relative modality.

Knowledge and irrelevant possibilities of error are discussed in Alvin I. Goldman, "Discrimination and Perceptual Knowledge," *Journal of Philosophy* 73 (1976): 771–91.

force until further notice to govern the interpretation of modal verbs in subsequent sentences.

This boundary may also shift in accordance with a rule of accommodation. Suppose I am talking with some elected official about the ways he might deal with an embarassment. So far, we have been ignoring those possibilities that would be political suicide for him. He says: "You see, I must either destroy the evidence or else claim that I did it to stop Communism. What else can I do?" I rudely reply: "There is one other possibility—you can put the public interest first for once!" That would be false if the boundary between relevant and ignored possibilities remained stationary. But is is not false in its context, for hitherto ignored possibilities come into consideration and make it true. And the boundary, once shifted outward, stays shifted. If he protests "I can't do that," he is mistaken.

Take another example. The commonsensical epistemologist says: "I *know* the cat is in the carton—there he is before my eyes—I just *can't* be wrong about that!" The sceptic replies: "You might be the victim of a deceiving demon." Thereby he brings into consideration possibilities hitherto ignored, else what he says would be false. The boundary shifts outward so that what he says is true. Once the boundary is shifted, the commonsensical epistemologist must concede defeat. And yet he was not in any way wrong when he laid claim to infallible knowledge. What he said was true with respect to the score as it then was.

We get the impression that the sceptic, or the rude critic of the elected official, has the last word. Again this is because the rule of accommodation is not fully reversible. For some reason, I know not what, the boundary readily shifts outward if what is said requires it, but does not so readily shift inward if what is said requires that. Because of this asymmetry, we may think that what is true with respect to the outward-shifted boundary must be somehow more true than what is true with respect to the original boundary. I see no reason to respect this impression. Let us hope, by all means, that the advance toward truth is irreversible. That is no reason to think that just any change that resists reversal is an advance toward truth.

EXAMPLE 7: PERFORMATIVES[7]

Suppose we are unpersuaded by Austin's contention that explicit performatives have no truth value. Suppose also that we wish to respect the seeming parallelism of form between a performative like "I hereby name this ship the *Generalissimo*

---

[7]See J. L. Austin, "Performative Utterances," in his *Philosophical Papers* (Oxford University Press, 1961), for the original discussion of performatives. For treatments along the lines here preferred, see E. J. Lemmon, "On Sentences Verifiable by Their Use," *Analysis* 22 (1962): 86–89; Ingemar Hedenius, "Performatives," *Theoria* 29 (1963): 1–22; and Lennart Åqvist, *Performatives and Verifiability by the Use of Language* (Filosofiska Studier, Uppsala University, 1972). Isard *(op. cit.)* suggests as I do that performative utterances are akin to other utterances that "change the context."

Stalin" and such non-performative statements as "Fred thereby named that ship the *President Nixon*." Then we shall find it natural to treat the performative, like the non-performative, as a sentence with truth conditions. It is true, on a given occasion of its utterance, if and only if the speaker brings it about, by means of that very utterance, that the indicated ship begins to bear the name "Generalissimo Stalin." If the circumstances are felicitous, then the speaker does indeed bring it about, by means of his utterance, that the ship begins to bear the name. The performative sentence is therefore true on any occasion of its felicitious utterance. In Lemmon's phrase, it is a sentence verifiable by its (felicitous) use.

When the ship gets its name and the performative is verfied by its use, what happens may be described as a change in conversational score governed by a rule of accommodation. The relevant component of score is the relation that pairs ships with their names. The rule of accommodation is roughly as follows.

> If at time t something is said that requires for its truth that ship s bear name n; and if s does not bear n just before t; and if the form and circumstances of what is said satisfy certain conditions of felicity; then s begins at t to bear n.

Our performative sentence does indeed require for its truth that the indicated ship bear the name "Generalissimo Stalin" at the time of utterance. Therefore, when the sentence is felicitously uttered, straightway the ship bears the name.

The sentence has other necessary conditions of truth: the ship must not have borne the name beforehand, the speaker must bring it about that the ship begins to bear the name, and he must bring it about by uttering the sentence. On any felicitous occasion of utterance, these further conditions take care of themselves. Our rule of accommodation is enough to explain why the sentence is verified by its felicitous use, despite the fact that the rule deals only with part of what it takes to make the sentence true.

A similar treatment could be given of many other performatives. In some cases the proposal may seem surprising. "With this ring I thee wed" is verified by its felicitous use, since the marriage relation is a component of conversational score governed by a rule of accommodation. Is marriage then a *linguistic* phenomenon? Of course not, but that was not implied. The lesson of performatives, on any theory, is that use of language blends into other social practices. We should not assume that a change of conversational score has its impact only within, or by way of, the realm of language. Indeed, we have already seen another counterexample: the case of permissibility, considered as Example 2.

EXAMPLE 8: PLANNING

Suppose that you and I are making a plan—let us say, a plan to steal some plutonium from a reprocessing plant and make a bomb of it. As we talk, our plan evolves. Mostly it grows more and more complete. Sometimes, however, parts that had been definite are revised, or at least opened for reconsideration.

Much as some things said in ordinary conversation require suitable presuppositions, so some things we say in the course of our planning require, for their acceptability, that the plan contain suitable provisions. If I say "Then you drive the getaway car up to the side gate," that is acceptable only if the plan includes provision for a getaway car. That might or might not have been part of the plan already. If not, it may become part of the plan just because it is required by what I said. (As usual the process is defeasible. You can keep the getaway car out of the plan, for the time being at least, by saying "Wouldn't we do better with mopeds?") The plan is a component of conversational score. The rules governing its evolution parallel the rules governing the kinematics of presupposition, and they include a rule of accommodation.

So good is the parallel between plan and presupposition that we might well ask if our plan simply *is* part of what we presuppose. Call it that if you like, but there is a distinction to be made. We might take for granted, or purport to take for granted, that our plan will be carried out. Then we would both plan and presuppose that we are going to steal the plutonium. But we might not. We might be making our plan not in order to carry it out, but rather in order to show that the plant needs better security. Then plan and presupposition might well conflict. We plan to steal the plutonium, all the while presupposing that we will not. And indeed our planning may be interspersed with commentary that requires presuppositions contradicting the plan. "Then I'll shoot the guard (I'm glad I won't really do that) while you smash the floodlights." Unless we distinguish plan from presupposition (or distinguish two levels of presupposition) we must think of presuppositions as constantly disappearing and reappearing throughout such a conversation.

The distinction between plan and presupposition is not the distinction between what we purport to take for granted and what we really do. While planning that we will steal the plutonium and presupposing that we will not, we might take for granted neither that we will nor that we won't. Each of us might secretly hope to recruit the other to the terrorist cause and carry out the plan after all.

One and the same sentence may require, and if need be create, both provisions of the plan and presuppositions. "Then you drive the getaway car up to the side gate" requires both a getaway car and a side gate. The car is planned for. The gate is more likely presupposed.

· FOURTEEN ·

'Tensions

I have a problem for those who, like myself, admire intensional formal semantics and think it a key to understanding natural language. We can go to extremes of intensionality, if we like. Semantic rules can be stated entirely in terms of intensions, while extensions go unmentioned. But when we do, it seems for all the world as if we've gone purely *ex*tensional instead! Let me explain.

I. THE INTENSIONAL LANGUAGE L₁

I begin by describing an intensional language L_1. There are various categories of expressions.

S is the category of sentences. A sentence takes as its extension one of the two truth values, truth or falsehood. But the truth value of a sentence may depend on facts which vary from one possible world to another; on the time, place, speaker, and other features of context; on the values assigned to any free variables that may be present; on the resolutions of various sorts of vagueness; and perhaps on other things as well. So truth in L_1 is a three-place relation. A sentence has a truth value as its extension relative to an *index,* that being a package of a world, a time,. . ., and whatever else (apart from meaning) might be needed to determine an extension. Equivalently, for each sentence we have a function from indices to truth values. For any possible index, the function gives the truth value of the sentence at that index. This extension-determining function is the intension (in L_I) of the sentence.

N is the category of names. A name takes as its extension the thing named— perhaps a concrete material object, perhaps some other sort of entity. Again, the extension may vary; so for each name we have a function from indices that gives the extension of the name at any possible index. This function is the intension (in L_I) of the name.

For any two categories X and Y, we have a third category X/Y of expressions which can combine with expressions of category Y to form compound expressions of category X. Examples: an S/N is something that can combine with a name to make a sentence, so it is an intransitive verb. An (S/N)/N can combine with a name to make an intransitive verb, so it is a transitive verb. An (S/S)/S can combine with a sentence to make something that in turn can combine with a sentence to make a sentence, so it is a dyadic connective or operator. There are infinitely many of these functor categories, though only finitely many are employed in L_I. An X/Y has no extension. Its intension is a function from appropriate intensions for members of category Y to appropriate intensions for members of category X. All the compositional semantic rules of L_I are given by one simple schema, with various categories put in for X and Y:

> If α is an X/Y with intension A and β is a Y with intension B, then the result of combining α with β is an X with intension A(B), the value of the function A for the argument B.

"Combining" may simply be concatenation; or it may be some more complicated operation, perhaps different for different functor categories or even for different members of one category. Or it may be that structures built up by many successive combinations are subsequently transformed as a whole to give the "surface" expressions of L_I.

I described L_I as an intensional language. More precisely, (1) in any case of compounding, the intension of the compound is a function of the intensions of the constituents, but (2) the extension of the compound is not always a function of the extensions of the constituents. Part (1) follows from the given form for semantic rules; part (2) is an additional stipulation.

This completes a partial description of L_I, in a style that should be familiar nowadays.[1] It will be useful to give a shamelessly idealized reconstruction of the way that style evolved.

---

[1] I have followed the treatment in my "General Semantics," in this volume, stripped of such frills as many-place functors and a basic category of common nouns. The use of Ajdukiewicz's functor categories makes for brevity in stating the rules. But I could make my point just as well by discussing one of Richard Montague's well-known treatments of natural language. See his "The Proper Treatment of Quantification in Ordinary Language," in Hintikka, Moravcsik, and Suppes, eds., *Approaches to Natural Language* (Dordrecht: Reidel, 1972), or Barbara Partee's paper in Milton K. Munitz and Peter K. Unger, eds., *Semantics and Philosophy* (New York: New York University Press, 1974).

In the olden days, we knew only of extensions. We used semantic rules of this form:

(1S)   If α is an X with extension A, then the result of combining α with β is a Z with extension f(A).

with a special rule for each β; or, when generality was possible, of this form:

(1G)   If α is an X with extension A and β is a Y with extension B, then the result of combining α with β is a Z with extension f(A,B).

Then we began to pay attention to languages in which extensions could depend on features of context. We relativized to various sorts of indices, but still adhered to the old dogma that the extension of the compound is a function of the extensions of the constituents. We had special and general rules of these forms:

(2S)   If α is an X with extension A at index i, then the result of combining α with β is a Z with extension f(A,i) at index i.

(2G)   If α is an X with extension A at index i and β is a Y with extension B at index i, then the result of combining α with β is a Z with extension f(A,B,i) at index i.

But we knew that in a few cases, the extension of a compound at one index could depend on the extensions of the constituents not just at that index but at other indices as well. That was so for variable-binding quantifiers if we took the assignments of values to variables as indices; and for modal and tense operators, taking the indices as worlds or times. So we learned to tolerate a few special nonextensional rules of the form:

(3S)   If α is an X whose extension varies from index to index in manner A, then the result of combining α with β is a Z with extension f(A,i) at index i.

(For example: if α is a sentence which takes the truth value truth at all and only the worlds in a set A, then the result of prefixing $\square$ to α is a sentence that takes the value truth or falsehood at world i according as A does or does not contain all worlds possible relative to i.) Often the manner of variation did not even need to be explicitly mentioned as an entity, still less stigmatized as an intension. In the case of quantification, at least, such rules were not considered a significant breach of extensionality.

But these special rules proliferated in number when we considered languages with many different modalities; and in variety when we admitted intensional predicate modifiers or intensional sentential operators that could not be handled as modalities with relations of relative possibility. Generality requires quantification over appropriate entities. Once these are at hand, it is natural to identify them with intensions, since they carry all needed information about the meanings of the corresponding expressions. Thus we progressed to rules of the form:

(3G) If α is an X with intension A and β is a Y with intension B, then the result of combining α with β is a Z with extension f(A,B,i) at index i.

When a rule specifies the extension at every index, it thereby specifies the extension-determining function that we have called an intension. It is only a short step, therefore, to rules of the form:

(4G) If α is an X with intension A and β is a Y with intension B, then the result of combining α with β is a Z with intension f(A,B).

But this short step gives us a new freedom. For intension-specifying rules, unlike any sort of extension-specifying rules, can apply even when the resulting compound belongs to a category for which there are no appropriate extensions—for instance, when it is a compound modifier or quantifier or connective. In such cases, of course, the appropriate sort of intension can no longer be an extension-determining function from indices. We have seen already, in connection with the functor categories of L_I, what else it might be.

When an intensional rule is needed, an extensional rule will not work. But when an extensional rule will work, an intensional rule also will work. If we need some intensional rules, then we may gain uniformity by using intensional rules throughout, even where extensional rules would have sufficed. (It is a matter of taste whether this gain outweighs the waste of using needlessly intensional rules. For me it does.) At this point, our compositional semantic rules always specify how intensions of compounds depend on the intensions of their constituents. The extensions have faded away. We have come full circle, in a way: once again expressions are assigned semantic values on a single level, not two different levels. My description of L_I exemplifies this final, purely intensional, stage in the evolution of formal semantics.

II. THE EXTENSIONAL TRANSFORM L_E

Now I shall describe another language L_E; this time, an extensional language specified by purely extensional rules of the forms (1G) and (2S) above. L_E and L_I are obviously not identical, since one is an extensional language and the other is not. But they are closely related. All the structure of L_I is mirrored in L_E. Following Terence Parsons (more or less), I shall call L_E an *extensional transform* of L_I.

L_E has a category of names; but we do best to divide this into two subcategories according to the sort of thing that is named. S is the first category of names; an S-name takes as its extension—that is, it names—a function from indices to truth values. After all, any old entity is entitled to bear a name; nameability is not a special privilege of concrete particulars! N is the second subcategory of names; an N-name takes as its extension a function from indices to entities of any sort.

(Although S-names are not N-names, an appropriate extension for an S-name would also be an appropriate extension for an N-name). Names, in either subcategory, have their extensions rigidly. Their extensions do not vary from one index to another. We could say that the intension of an S-name or an N-name in L_E is the function which gives, for each index, the extension of the name at that index. (These are functions from indices whose values are themselves functions from indices.) But since these intensions are constant functions, they are scarcely worth mentioning.

L_E also has infinitely many functor categories: for any suitable categories X and Y, there is a third category X/Y of expressions which can combine with expressions of category Y to form compound expressions of category X. The "suitable categories" are the subcategories S and N of names, and also the functor categories themselves; but *not* the two further categories of L_E that we have not yet mentioned. The extension of an X/Y is a function from Y-extensions to X-extensions. All but one of the compositional semantic rules of L_E are given by this general, purely extensional schema:

> If α is an X/Y with extension A and β is a Y with extension B, then the result of combining α with β is an X with extension A(B), the value of the function A for the argument B.

Functors also have their extensions rigidly in L_E. We could take their intensions in L_E to be the constant functions from indices to their unvarying extensions. But why bother?

Such are the lexica of noncompound expressions in L_1 and L_E, and such are the combining operations associated with functors (alternatively, the transformational apparatus) in L_1 and L_E, that L_1 is related as follows to the fragment of L_E presented so far. Let us say that the categories S of L_1 and S of L_E are *namesakes*; also N of L_1 and N of L_E; also X/Y of L_1 and X/Y of L_E, whenever the X's are namesakes and the Y's are namesakes. Then for every pair of namesake categories of the two languages, exactly the same expressions belong to both. Further, whenever an expression α has A as its *in*tension in L_1, then also α has A as it *ex*tensions in L_E.

So far, L_E scarcely deserves to be called a language, for a language needs sentences. It would be quite wrong to think that S of L_E is the category of sentences. Tradition makes clear that the extensions of sentences are supposed to be truth values; whereas the extensions of members of S in L_E, we recall, are functions from indices to truth values. These are appropriate *in*tensions, but inappropriate *ex*tensions, for sentences. They are appropriate extensions only for names.

L_E does have a category of genuine sentences, however; and also a category of predicates for use in forming sentences. But there is only one predicate: $\mathbf{\mathfrak{s}}$. That is our metalinguistic name for it; actually, it is written as a blank space and pronounced as a pause. The remaining compositional semantic rule of L_E, again a purely extensional rule but special to the predicate $\mathbf{\mathfrak{s}}$, is as follows:

If α is an S with extension A, then the result of prefixing ⊀ to α is a sentence having as its extension at an index i the truth value A(i) given by the function A for the argument i.

So ⊀ is a sort of truth predicate; but a safe one, since there is no way in L_E to produce a paradoxical diagonalization.

We may note that whenever α is a sentence of L_I, then ⊀ α is a sentence of L_E with exactly the same truth conditions. There are no other sentences of L_E besides these images of the sentences of L_I.

This completes my description of L_E. It is an extensional language, as I said it would be. Inspection of the semantic rules confirms that the extension of a compound is always a function of the extensions of the constituents.

III. THE PARSONS TRANSFORM L_P

If we like, we can take the names and functors of L_E and trade them in for predicates and quantified variables. For instance, if we have

$$⊀((\alpha(\beta))(\gamma))$$

as a sentence of L_E, where β and γ are in the category N and α is in the category (S/N)/N, we can replace it by

$$\exists v \exists w \exists x \exists y \exists z (⊀ v \& Rvzw \& Rwyx \& \overline{\alpha}x \& \overline{\beta}y \& \overline{\gamma}z)$$

where R is a predicate meaning "—is the result of operating on the argument--by the function . . . " and $\overline{\alpha}, \overline{\beta}, \overline{\gamma}$ are monadic predicates uniquely satisfied by the entities that are the extensions in L_E of α, β, and γ, respectively. In this way we go from L_E to another extensional language L_P (if you consider quantifiers extensional). I shall call L_P the *Parsons transform* of our original language L_I, since when Terence Parsons speaks of an "extensional transform" he means a language like L_P.[2] But L_E is just as extensional as L_P. There is nothing anti-extensional about names and functors per se. Eliminating them is one enterprise, going extensional is another.

IV. THE PROBLEM

L_I can be a richly intensional language, whereas L_E is strictly extensional. An important difference, as we all were taught. But almost the only difference there is between the two!

[2] See Parsons, *A Semantics for English* (duplicated, 1968), and "Some Problems Concerning the Logic of Predicate Modifiers," *Synthese* 21 (1970): 327–29.

Two field linguists, I and E, fully equipped to perpetrate Cartesian deviltry, go to work on a certain tribe. They investigate the dispositions to verbal behavior under a wide range of deceptive stimulation, the beliefs and desires that would rationalize that behavior, and the neural hookup and laws that would explain it materialistically. They study these things until there is nothing more to know. Then I announce my conclusion: these tribesmen use the intensional language L_I. My colleague E, a keen extensionalist, disagrees. He thinks it gratuitous of me to ascribe to them a language that requires the notoriously obscure apparatus of intensional semantics. After all, a better explanation lies close at hand! His opinion is that they use the extensional language L_E. Dumbfounded by E's perversity, I know not what to say.

V. BAD REJOINDERS

I really don't know. I do know of several unsatisfactory arguments against E's opinion, and we had better clear those out of the way.

First, I might try arguing that E's account is worse than mine just because it is more complicated. He requires two more categories, one more lexical item, and one more rule. Besides, his extra rule departs from the standard form of his other rules.

But this argument is bad for two reasons. For one thing, extensionality itself is generally thought to be an important dimension of simplicity. E may say that it is cheap at the price. For another thing, I agree with E that a complete account should mention that speakers pause (and writers leave extra spaces) at the beginnings of their sentences. E has already covered this fact in his ascribed syntax and semantics. I have not, and I must find a place for it, at some cost in complexity, elsewhere in my total description of the tribe's use of language.

Second, I might try arguing that E's opinion goes against our paradigm cases of extension-bearing. "Boston" names Boston, for instance, and does not rather name some function from indices.

The paradigms, however, are cases of extension-bearing in certain particular languages: German, Polish, English, and some other familiar languages that can be translated into these by well-established procedures. We have no paradigm cases of extension-bearing in the language of these hitherto unstudied tribesmen.

Even if, in my opinion, their language does happen to be one of the familiar ones, still E cannot be expected to agree that the paradigms apply. For E and I disagree about which language is theirs.

Tarski's Convention T and its relatives will not help. Since the tribe's language is not—not uncontroversially, anyway—the same as our metalanguage for it, the only versions of these principles that apply are the ones stated in terms of translation. For instance, E and I may agree that a metalinguistic sentence of the form "———— names ———— in their language" (or "———— is a name having

————— as extension in their language") should be true whenever the first blank is filled with a name (in our language) of some name α in the tribe's language and the second blank is filled with a translation of α into our language. This gets us nowhere. Disagreeing as we do about what the names are and what their extensions are, E and I have no business agreeing about what the correct translations are.

Third, I might try arguing that their language cannot be an extensional language, as E claims, because certain inference patterns are invalid in it that are valid in any extensional language. For instance, I might point to inferences by Leibniz's Law, or by Existential Generalization, in which true premises yield false conclusions.

E should agree with me that Leibniz's Law (for example) preserves truth in any extensional language. He should also agree with me that truth is not preserved in the inferences I produce as counterexamples.[3] But he should not agree with me that those inferences are instances of Leibniz's Law. An inference by Leibniz's Law needs an identity premise, and how do we identify those? Not by looking for a stack of two or three or four horizontal lines! Semantically, an expression with two gaps expresses identity iff (1) the result of inserting names in the gaps is a sentence, and (2) the sentence so formed is true if the inserted names are coextensive, otherwise false. An identity premise is a sentence formed by thus inserting names in the gaps of an expression that expresses identity. Since E and I disagree about which are the coextensive names, we will disagree also about which are the expressions that express identity, which sentences are identity premises, and which inferences are genuine instances of Leibniz's Law. If E identifies instances of Leibniz's Law correctly according to his opinions about names and their extensions, the inferences he selects will indeed preserve truth.

Fourth, I might try arguing ad hominem that E has not really managed to escape intensionality, since the things he takes for extensions are intensional entities. Functions from indices to truth values are commonly identified with propositions (especially if the indices consist of possible worlds and little else). Functions from indices to things in general are likewise identified with individual concepts. How can *in*tensional entities be *ex*tensions?

But this is confusion. Intensionhood is relational. Intensions are things that play a certain characteristic role in semantics, not things of a special sort. E and I agree that in a suitable language (whether or not it happens in the language of this tribe) the very same thing that is the intension of one expression is also the extension of another. For instance, speaking in a fragment of technical English suited for use as the metametalanguage of a smaller fragment of English, we agree that one and the same thing is both the intension of the object-language expression "my hat" and

---

[3] I am here ignoring our disagreement about whether an S must be preceded by ⚡ to make a sentence. Strictly speaking, if $\alpha, \beta, /\therefore \gamma$ is a non-truth-preserving inference in L_1, then ⚡α, ⚡$\beta, /\therefore$ ⚡γ is a non-truth-preserving inference in L_E. The original ⚡-less version is not any sort of inference in L_E, since its "premises" and "conclusion" are S-names rather than sentences.

the extension of the metalanguage expression "the intension of 'my hat'." In itself, this thing is neither an intension nor an extension.

What is true is that some things can serve only as extensions, while other things—functions from indices, for instance—can serve either as extensions or as intensions. But there is no kind of thing that is ineligible by its nature to be an extension.

Fifth, I might try arguing that E's opinion ascribes an extravagant ontology to the tribesmen. When I say that a certain word of their language names a certain concrete, material hill, E says that it names something rather more esoteric: a set-theoretic object built up from a domain of individuals that contains unactualized possibilia.

E and I, if we are consistent, believe in these esoteric entities ourselves. We do not doubt that we can have names for them. Then on what grounds can I deny E's claim that the tribesmen also have names for them? In fact, we both agree that they have names for other entities far more suspect, to wit certain far-fetched gods (according to me) or functions from indices to such gods (according to E).

I might do better to argue that the ontology ascribed by E is bad not because certain esoteric things are present in it but rather because certain unesoteric things are missing from it. Saul Kripke has suggested (in conversation, 1972) that it is wrong to ascribe to someone an ontology that contains sets without their members, functions without their arguments and values, or the like.

A plausible principle. But has E really violated it in ascribing the use of L_E, a language in which all the names are names of functions from indices and none are names of the concrete, commonplace things that are among the values of those functions? I think not. The ascribed ontology is not the same thing as the ascribed set of name-bearers. If there is an ontology associated with our language, for instance, it includes all the real numbers; not just the countable minority of them that bear names. It is of no significance that the set of name-bearers violates Kripke's closure principle, unless it can be shown to be the whole of the ascribed ontology. But it is hard to say what ontology, if any, is ascribed in ascribing the use of L_E. One looks for the domain of quantification. But L_E has no quantifiers! Quantifiers are sentence-makers; but the only sentence-maker in L_E is $\mathbf{\mathfrak{S}}$, and that is no quantifier. So L_E does not have a domain of quantification in any straight-forward sense, either one that satisfies the closure principle or one that does not.

Unlike L_E, the Parsons transform L_P does have a natural domain. More precisely, there is a set D such that we get the intended truth conditions for those sentences of L_P that are transforms of sentences of L_1 iff D is included in the range of the quantified variables. (This assumes that the predicates of L_P have their intended interpretations.) The set D, which is the same as the set of extensions of expressions in L_E, does violate Kripke's closure principle and so is unsuitable to be ascribed as someone's ontology. If some extensionalist claimed that our tribesmen used L_P, disguised by transformations, I think we would have a promising line of attack against him. But how does that affect E, whose claim is different? Perhaps there is some way to show that if it is bad to ascribe the use of L_P, then it is just as bad to ascribe the use of L_E. But so far, this looks to me like nothing better than guilt by association.

VI. COMMON GROUND

So I have no way to argue against E's absurd opinion. But though we certainly disagree about something, the extent of our differences should not be exaggerated. In some sense, we have given equivalent descriptions of the phenomena. (That is just what makes it so hard to build a case for one description against the other.) More precisely, if we treat our semantic jargon as theoretical vocabulary and eliminate it by Ramsey's method of existential quantification, then our disagreement will vanish. Our two accounts are equivalent in the sense that they have a common Ramsification.

We can agree on the following description in neutral terms. There is a system of categories: call them just S, N, and X/Y whenever X and Y are categories in the system. There are three relations of expressions to things: call them the 1-'tension, 2-'tension, and 3-'tension relations. The 1-'tension of an expression, but not the 2-'tension or 3-'tension, may vary from one index to another. The 1-'tension of an S at an index is a truth value; the 1-'tension of an N at an index may be anything; an expression in one of the other categories has no 1-'tension. The 2-'tension of an S or an N is the function from indices that gives the proper 1-'tension at each index. The 2-'tension of an X/Y is a function from appropriate 2-'tensions for members of Y to appropriate 2-'tensions for members of X; if α is an X/Y with 2-'tension A and β is a Y with 2-'tension B, then the result of combining α with β is an X with 2-'tension A(B). The 3-'tension of any expression is the constant function from indices to the unvarying 2-'tension. Finally, a tribesman speaks the truth in his language just when he utters an S preceded by a pause, and the 1-'tension of that S at the index (or set of indices) determined by the occasion of utterance is truth.

So far, so good. To complete my account, I need only add a gloss: the 1-'tensions are the extensions, the 2-'tensions are the intensions, the 3-'tensions are neither, and S is the category of sentences. To complete his contrary account, E need only add his contrary gloss: the 2-'tensions are the extensions, the 3-'tensions are the intensions, the 1-'tensions are neither, and S is a subcategory of names.

But these disputed additions do not add much. No matter which way we apply our traditional semantic vocabulary of extension, intension, naming, and sentencehood, the facts of the matter are already covered by the unglossed neutral description which is the common Ramsification of both our opinions. That is all we would need, for instance, in giving an account of the tribe's use of language as a rational activity for imparting information, or as a physical phenomenon. The questions under dispute are, so far as I can see, idle. If they are not, their import should give us a way to settle them.

VII. MORALS

This story has an abundance of morals. But most of them are available only if you recklessly conclude that because I have not been able to solve my problem, therefore it must be insoluble. Actually I believe nothing of the sort. Probably there is some perfectly good reason why L_1 and not L_E is the tribe's language, and I have just overlooked it. Still, what if the problem were insoluble?

First moral: we would have another good example of Quine's inscrutability of reference. Different assignments of extensions would account equally well for the solid facts of the matter, and there would be nothing to choose between them. But at the same time the indeterminacy would be made to seem less formidable than we might have thought. In view of the common Ramsifications, it seems that even the semantic facts are not in dispute. E and I disagree about the proper way to describe those facts in our traditional semantic jargon. That is only a localized indeterminacy in one small region of our language. Can Quine's other alarming indeterminacies be disarmed in the same way?

Second moral: intension and extension would be correlative concepts. Neither would make sense except by contrast with the other. In a two-level semantic analysis, where expressions are assigned certain entities that are functions and other entities that are the values of those functions at particular indices, clearly the functions are intensions vis-à-vis the values and the values are extensions vis-à-vis the functions. But in a one-level analysis, whether we approach it by getting more and more intensional or less and less, there is no more contrast and the correlative terms might therfore be out of place.

Our *final moral* is unconditional. It stands whether or not my problem can be solved. So elusive is the difference between using an intensional language and using an extensional language that it can scarcely matter much which we do use. Those who value the superior clarity of extensional languages as such[4] are misguided. There are differences that do matter. There is the difference between languages that can be analyzed by the methods of formal semantics and ones that (so far as we know) cannot. For any sort of ontic purist, there is the difference between languages that can be analyzed without recourse to suspect entities and ones that cannot. And there is the difference between standard first-order predicate calculus and all less familiar and less well-investigated languages. But none of these real differences between better and worse languages coincides with the difference between extensional and intensional.[5]

---

[4]For instance, David Lewis when he wrote the opening lines of "Counterpart Theory and Quantified Modal Logic," in this volume, as follows: "We can conduct formalized discourse about most topics perfectly well by means of our all-purpose extensional logic. . . . Then we introduce modal operators to create a special-purpose, nonextensional logic. Why this departure from our custom?" He proceeded to put the departure right; but his views might just as well have been presented as an extensional semantic analysis of an intensional language.

[5]I am grateful to Graham Nerlich and Max Cresswell for the conversations in which this paper had its origins, and to the National Science Foundation for research support.

· F I F T E E N ·

Truth in Fiction

We can truly say that Sherlock Holmes lived in Baker Street, and that he liked to show off his mental powers. We cannot truly say that he was a devoted family man, or that he worked in close cooperation with the police.

It would be nice if we could take such descriptions of fictional characters at their face value, ascribing to them the same subject-predicate form as parallel descriptions of real-life characters. Then the sentences "Holmes wears a silk top hat" and "Nixon wears a silk top hat" would both be false because the referent of the subject term—fictional Holmes or real-life Nixon, as the case may be—lacks the property, expressed by the predicate, of wearing a silk top hat. The only difference would be that the subject terms "Holmes" and "Nixon" have referents of radically different sorts: one a fictional character, the other a real-life person of flesh and blood.

I don't question that a treatment along these Meinongian lines could be made to work. Terence Parsons has done it.[1] But it is no simple matter to overcome the difficulties that arise. For one thing, is there not some perfectly good sense in which Holmes, like Nixon, *is* a real-life person of flesh and blood? There are stories about the exploits of super-heroes from other planets, hobbits, fires and storms, vaporous

I thank the many friends and colleagues who have given me helpful comments on a previous version of this paper, and I thank the American Council of Learned Societies for research support. Special thanks are due to John G. Bennett and Saul Kripke for valuable discussions.

[1] In "A Prolegomenon to Meinongian Semantics," *Journal of Philosophy* 71 (1974): 561–80, and in "A Meinongian Analysis of Fictional Objects," *Grazer Philosophische Studien* 1 (1975): 73–86.

intelligences, and other non-persons. But what a mistake it would be to class the Holmes stories with these! Unlike Clark Kent *et al.*, Sherlock Holmes is just a person—a person of flesh and blood, a being in the very same category as Nixon.

Consider also the problem of the chorus. We can truly say that Sir Joseph Porter, K.C.B., is attended by a chorus of his sisters and his cousins and his aunts. To make this true, it seems that the domain of fictional characters must contain not only Sir Joseph himself, but also plenty of fictional sisters and counsins and aunts. But how many—five dozen, perhaps? No, for we cannot truly say that the chorus numbers five dozen exactly. We cannot truly say anything exact about its size. Then do we perhaps have a fictional chorus, but no fictional members of this chorus and hence no number of members? No, for we can truly say some things about the size. We are told that the sisters and cousins, even without the aunts, number in dozens.

The Meinongian should not suppose that the quantifiers in descriptions of fictional characters range over all the things he thinks there are, both fictional and non-fictional; but he may not find it easy to say just how the ranges of quantification are to be restricted. Consider whether we can truly say that Holmes was more intelligent than anyone else, before or since. It is certainly appropriate to compare him with some fictional characters, such as Mycroft and Watson; but not with others, such as Poirot or "Slipstick" Libby. It may be appropriate to compare him with some non-fictional characters, such as Newton and Darwin; but probably not with others, such as Conan Doyle or Frank Ramsey. "More intelligent than anyone else" meant something like "more intelligent than anyone else in the world of Sherlock Holmes." The inhabitants of this "world" are drawn partly from the fictional side of the Meinongian domain and partly from the non-fictional side, exhausting neither.

Finally, the Meinongian must tell us why truths about fictional characters are cut off, sometimes though not always, from the consequences they ought to imply. We can truly say that Holmes lived at 221B Baker Street. I have been told[2] that the only building at 221B Baker Street, then or now, was a bank. It does not follow, and certainly is not true, that Holmes lived in a bank.

The way of the Meinongian is hard, and in this paper I shall explore a simpler alternative. Let us not take our descriptions of fictional characters at face value, but instead let us regard them as abbreviations for longer sentences beginning with an operator "In such-and-such fiction. . . ." Such a phrase is an intensional operator that may be prefixed to a sentence ϕ to form a new sentence. But then the prefixed operator may be dropped by way of abbreviation, leaving us with what sounds like the original sentence ϕ but differs from it in sense.

Thus if I say that Holmes liked to show off, you will take it that I have asserted an abbreviated version of the true sentence "In the Sherlock Holmes stories, Holmes liked to show off." As for the embedded sentence "Holmes liked to show off," taken by itself with the prefixed operator neither explicitly present nor tacitly

---

[2] I have also been told that there has never been any building at that address. It doesn't matter which is correct.

understood, we may abandon it to the common fate of subject-predicate sentences with denotationless subject terms: automatic falsity or lack of truth value, according to taste.

Many things we might say about Holmes are potentially ambiguous. They may or may not be taken as abbreviations for sentences carrying the prefix "In the Sherlock Holmes stories . . . ." Context, content, and common sense will usually resolve the ambiguity in practice. Consider these sentences:

> Holmes lived in Baker Street.
> Holmes lived nearer to Paddington Station than to Waterloo Station.
> Holmes was just a person—a person of flesh and blood.
> Holmes really existed.
> Someone lived for many years at 221B Baker Street.
> London's greatest detective in 1900 used cocaine.

All of them are false if taken as unprefixed, simply because Holmes did not actually exist. (Or perhaps at least some of them lack truth value.) All are true if taken as abbreviations for prefixed sentences. The first three would probably be taken in the latter way, hence they seem true. The rest would probably be taken in the former way, hence they seem false. The sentence

> No detective ever solved almost all his cases.

would probably be taken as unprefixed and hence true, though it would be false if taken as prefixed. The sentence

> Holmes and Watson are identical.

is sure to be taken as prefixed and hence false, but that is no refutation of systems of free logic[3] which would count it as true if taken as unprefixed.

(I hasten to concede that some truths about Holmes are not abbreviations of prefixed sentences, and also are not true just because "Holmes" is denotationless. For instance these:

> Holmes is a fictional character.
> Holmes was killed off by Conan Doyle, but later resurrected.
> Holmes has acquired a cultish following.
> Holmes symbolizes mankind's ceaseless striving for truth.
> Holmes would not have needed tapes to get the goods on Nixon.
> Holmes could have solved the A.B.C. murders sooner than Poirot.

I shall have nothing to say here about the proper treatment of these sentences. If the Meinongian can handle them with no special dodges, that is an advantage of his approach over mine.)

The ambiguity of prefixing explains why truths about fictional characters are

---

[3]For instance, the system given in Dana Scott, "Existence and Description in Formal Logic," in *Bertrand Russell: Philosopher of the Century,* ed. by Ralph Schoenman (London: Allen & Unwin, 1967).

sometimes cut off from their seeming consequences. Suppose we have an argument (with zero or more premises) which is valid in the modal sense that it is impossible for the premises all to be true and the conclusion false.

$$\frac{\psi_1, \ldots, \psi_n}{\therefore \phi}$$

Then it seems clear that we obtain another valid argument if we prefix an operator "In the fiction f . . ." uniformly to each premiss and to the conclusion of the original argument. Truth in a given fiction is closed under implication.

$$\frac{\text{In } f, \psi_1, \ldots, \text{In } f, \psi_n}{\therefore \text{ In } f, \phi}$$

But if we prefix the operator "In the fiction f . . ." to some of the original premises and not to others, or if we take some but not all of the premises as tacitly prefixed, then in general neither the original conclusion ϕ nor the prefixed conclusion "In the fiction f, ϕ" will follow. In the inference we considered earlier there were two premises. The premiss that Holmes lived at 221B Baker Street was true only if taken as prefixed. The premiss that the only building at 221B Baker Street was a bank, on the other hand, was true only if taken as unprefixed; for in the stories there was no bank there but rather a rooming house. Taking the premises as we naturally would in the ways that make them true, nothing follows: neither the unprefixed conclusion that Holmes lived in a bank nor the prefixed conclusion that in the stories he lived in a bank. Taking both premises as unprefixed, the unprefixed conclusion follows but the first premiss is false. Taking both premises as prefixed, the prefixed conclusion follows but the second premiss is false.[4]

Our remaining task is to see what may be said about the analysis of the operators "In such-and-such fiction . . . ." I have already noted that truth in a given fiction is closed under implication. Such closure is the earmark of an operator of relative necessity, an intensional operator that may be analyzed as a restricted universal quantifier over possible worlds. So we might proceed as follows: a prefixed sentence "In fiction f, ϕ" is true (or, as we shall also say, ϕ is true in the fiction f) iff ϕ is true at every possible world in a certain set, this set being somehow determined by the fiction f.

As a first approximation, we might consider exactly those worlds where the plot of the fiction is enacted, where a course of events takes place that matches the story. What is true in the Sherlock Holmes stories would then be what is true at all of those possible worlds where there are characters who have the attributes, stand in the relations, and do the deeds that are ascribed in the stories to Holmes, Watson, and the rest. (Whether these characters would then *be* Holmes, Watson, and the rest is a vexed question that we must soon consider.)

[4]Thus far, the account I have given closely follows that of John Heintz, "Reference and Inference in Fiction." *Poetics* 8 (1979).

I think this proposal is not quite right. For one thing, there is a threat of circularity. Even the Holmes stories, not to mention fiction written in less explicit styles, are by no means in the form of straightforward chronicles. An intelligent and informed reader can indeed discover the plot, and could write it down in the form of a fully explicit chronicle if he liked. But this extraction of plot from text is no trivial or automatic task. Perhaps the reader accomplishes it only by figuring out what is true in the stories—that is, only by exercising his tacit mastery of the very concept of truth in fiction that we are now investigating. If so, then an analysis that starts by making uncritical use of the concept of the plot of a fiction might be rather uninformative, even if correct so far as it goes.

A second problem arises out of an observation by Saul Kripke.[5] Let us assume that Conan Doyle indeed wrote the stories as pure fiction. He just made them up. He had no knowledge of anyone who did the deeds he ascribed to Holmes, nor had he even picked up any garbled information originating in any such person. It may nevertheless be, purely by coincidence, that our own world is one of the worlds where the plot of the stories is enacted. Maybe there was a man whom Conan Doyle never heard of whose actual adventures chanced to fit the stories in every detail. Maybe he even was named "Sherlock Holmes." Improbable, incredible, but surely possible! Now consider the name "Sherlock Holmes," *as used in the stories.* Does the name, so used, refer to the man whom Conan Doyle never heard of? Surely not! It is irrelevant that a homonymous name is used by some people, not including Conan Doyle, to refer to this man. We must distinguish between the homonyms, just as we would distinguish the name of London (England) from the homonymous name of London (Ontario). It is false at our world that the name, "Sherlock Holmes," as used in the stories, refers to someone. Yet it is true in the stories that this name, as used in the stories, refers to someone. So we have found something that is true in the stories but false (under our improbable supposition) at one of the worlds where the plot of the stories is enacted.

In order to avoid this difficulty, it will be helpful if we do not think of a fiction in the abstract, as a string of sentences or something of that sort. Rather, a fiction is a story told by a storyteller on a particular occasion. He may tell his tales around the campfire or he may type a manuscript and send it to his publisher, but in either case there is an act of storytelling. Different acts of storytelling, different fictions. When Pierre Menard re-tells *Don Quixote,* that is not the same fiction as Cervantes' *Don Quixote*—not even if they are in the same language and match word for word.[6]

---

[5]Briefly stated in his addenda to "Naming and Necessity," in *Semantics of Natural Language,* ed. by Gilbert Harman and Donald Davidson (Dordrecht: Reidel, 1972); and discussed at greater length in an unpublished lecture given at a conference held at the University of Western Ontario in 1973 and on other occasions. My views and Kripke's overlap to some extent. He also stresses what I have called the ambiguity of prefixing and regards the storyteller as engaged in pretence. The conclusions he draws from the present observation, however, differ greatly from mine.

[6]Jorge Luis Borges, "Pierre Menard, Author of the *Quixote*" in *Ficciones* (Buenos Aires, 1944; English translation, New York: Grove, 1962).

(It would have been different if Menard had copied Cervantes' fiction from memory, however; that would not have been what I call an act of storytelling at all.) One act of storytelling might, however, be the telling of two different fictions: one a harmless fantasy told to the children and the censors, the other a subversive allegory simultaneously told to the *cognoscenti*.

Storytelling is pretence. The storyteller purports to be telling the truth about matters whereof he has knowledge. He purports to be talking about characters who are known to him, and whom he refers to, typically, by means of their ordinary proper names. But if his story is fiction, he is not really doing these things. Usually his pretence has not the slightest tendency to deceive anyone, nor has he the slightest intent to deceive. Nevertheless he plays a false part, goes through a form of telling known fact when he is not doing so. This is most apparent when the fiction is told in the first person. Conan Doyle pretended to be a doctor named Watson, engaged in publishing truthful memoirs of events he himself had witnessed. But the case of third-person narrative is not essentially different. The author purports to be telling the truth about matters he has somehow come to know about, though how he has found out about them is left unsaid. That is why there is a pragmatic paradox akin to contradiction in a third-person narrative that ends ". . .and so none were left to tell the tale."

The worlds we should consider, I suggest, are the worlds where the fiction is told, but as known fact rather than fiction. The act of storytelling occurs, just as it does here at our world; but there it *is* what here it falsely purports to be: truth-telling about matters whereof the teller has knowledge.[7] Our own world cannot be such a world; for if it is really a fiction that we are dealing with, then the act of storytelling at our world was not what it purported to be. It does not matter if, unbeknownst to the author, our world is one where his plot is enacted. The real-life Sherlock Holmes would not have made Conan Doyle any less of a pretender, if Conan Doyle had never heard of him. (This real-life Holmes might have had his real-life Watson who told true stories about the adventures he had witnessed. But even if his memoirs matched Conan Doyle's fiction word for word they would not be the same stories, any more than Cervantes' *Don Quixote* is the same story as Menard's. So our world would still not be one where the Holmes stories—the *same*

---

[7]There are exceptions. Sometimes the storyteller purports to be uttering a mixture of truth and lies about matters whereof he has knowledge, or ravings giving a distorted reflection of the events, or the like. Tolkien explicitly purports to be the translator and editor of the Red Book of Westmarch, an ancient book that has somehow come into his possession and that he somehow knows to be a reliable record of the events. He does not purport to be its author, else he would not write in English. (Indeed, the composition of the Red Book by several hobbits is recorded in the Red Book itself.) I should say the same about a first-person historical novel written in English in which the narrator is an ancient Greek. The author does not pretend to be the truthful narrator himself, but rather pretends to be someone of our time who somehow has obtained the Greek narrator's story, knows it to be true, and passes it on to us in translation. In these exceptional cases also, the thing to do is to consider those worlds where the act of storytelling really is whatever it purports to be—ravings, reliable translation of a reliable source, or whatever—here at our world. I shall omit mention of these exceptional cases in the remainder of this paper.

Holmes stories that Conan Doyle told as fiction—were told as known fact.) On the other hand, any world where the story is told as known fact rather than fiction must be among the worlds where the plot of the story is enacted. Else its enactment could be neither known nor truly told of.

I rely on a notion of trans-world identity for stories; this is partly a matter of word-for-word match and partly a matter of trans-world identity (or perhaps a counterpart relation) for acts of storytelling. Here at our world we have a fiction f, told in an act a of storytelling; at some other world we have an act a' of telling the truth about known matters of fact; the stories told in a and a' match word for word, and the words have the same meaning. Does that mean that the other world is one where f is told as known fact rather than fiction? Not necessarily, as the case of Menard shows. It is also required that a and a' be the same act of storytelling (or at least counterparts). How bad is this? Surely you would like to know more about the criteria of trans-world identity (or the counterpart relation) for acts of storytelling, and so indeed would I. But I think we have enough of a grip to make it worthwhile going on. I see no threat of circularity here, since I see no way of using the concept of truth in fiction to help with the analysis of trans-world identity of acts of storytelling.

Suppose a fiction employs such names as "Sherlock Holmes." At those worlds where the same story is told as known fact rather than fiction, those names really are what they here purport to be: ordinary proper names of existing characters known to the storyteller. Here at our world, the storyteller only pretends that "Sherlock Holmes" has the semantic character of an ordinary proper name. We have no reason at all to suppose that the name, as used here at our world, really does have that character. As we use it, it may be very unlike an ordinary proper name. Indeed, it may have a highly non-rigid sense, governed largely by the descriptions of Holmes and his deeds that are found in the stories. That is what I suggest: the sense of "Sherlock Holmes" as we use it is such that, for any world w where the Holmes stories are told as known fact rather than fiction, the name denotes at w whichever inhabitant of w it is who there plays the role of Holmes. Part of that role, of course, is to bear the ordinary proper name "Sherlock Holmes." But that only goes to show that "Sherlock Holmes" is used at w as an ordinary proper name, not that it is so used here.[8,9]

---

[8] A rather similar treatment of fictional names, different from mine in that it allows the actual and purported meanings of "Sherlock Holmes" to be the same, is given in Robert Stalnaker, "Assertion" in *Syntax and Semantics* 9, ed. by Peter Cole, (New York: Academic Press, 1978).

[9] Many of us have never read the stories, could not produce the descriptions that largely govern the non-rigid sense of "Sherlock Holmes," yet use this name in just the same sense as the most expert Baker Street Irregular. There is no problem here. Kripke's causal picture of the contagion of meaning, in "Naming and Necessity," *(op. cit.)*, will do as well for non-rigid senses, as for rigid ones. The ignoramus uses "Sherlock Holmes" in its standard non-rigid sense if he has picked it up (in the right way) from someone who knew the governing descriptions, or who picked it up from someone else who knew them, or . . . . Kripke's doctrines of rigidity could not be defended without the aid of his doctrine of contagion of meaning; contagion without rigidity, on the other hand, seems unproblematic.

I also suggest, less confidently, that whenever a world w is not one of the worlds just considered, the sense of "Sherlock Holmes" as we use it is such as to assign it no denotation at w. That is so even if the plot of the fiction is enacted by inhabitants of w. If we are right that Conan Doyle told the Holmes stories as fiction, then it follows that "Sherlock Holmes" is denotationless here at our world. It does not denote the real-life Sherlock Holmes whom Conan Doyle never heard of, if such there be.

We have reached a proposal I shall call Analysis 0: *A sentence of the form "In fiction f, φ" is true iff φ is true at every world where f is told as known fact rather than fiction.*

Is that right? There are some who never tire of telling us not to read anything into a fiction that is not there explicitly, and Analysis 0 will serve to capture the usage of those who hold this view in its most extreme form. I do not believe, however, that such a usage is at all common. Most of us are content to read a fiction against a background of well-known fact, "reading into" the fiction content that is not there explicitly but that comes jointly from the explicit content and the factual background. Analysis 0 disregards the background. Thereby it brings too many possible worlds into consideration, so not enough comes out true in the fiction.

For example, I claim that in the Holmes stories, Holmes lives nearer to Paddington Station than to Waterloo Station. A glance at the map will show you that his address in Baker Street is much nearer to Paddington. Yet the map is not part of the stories; and so far as I know it is never stated or implied in the stories themselves that Holmes lives nearer to Paddington. There are possible worlds where the Holmes stories are told as known fact rather than fiction which differ in all sorts of ways from ours. Among these are worlds where Holmes lives in a London arranged very differently from the London of our world, a London where Holmes's address in Baker Street is much closer to Waterloo Station than to Paddington.

(I do not suppose that such a distortion of geography need prevent the otherworldly places there called "London," "Paddington Station," . . . from being the same as, or counterparts of, their actual namesakes. But if I am wrong, that still does not challenge my claim that there are worlds where the stories are told as known fact but where it is true that Holmes lives closer to Waterloo than to Paddington. For it is open to us to regard the place-names, as used in the stories, as fictional names with non-rigid senses like the non-rigid sense I have already ascribed to "Sherlock Holmes." That would mean, incidentally, that "Paddington Station," as used in the stories, does not denote the actual station of that name.)

Similarly, I claim that it is true, though not explicit, in the stories that Holmes does not have a third nostril; that he never had a case in which the murderer turned out to be a purple gnome; that he solved his cases without the aid of divine revelation; that he never visited the moons of Saturn; and that he wears underpants. There are bizarre worlds where the Holmes stories are told as known fact but where all of these things are false.

Strictly speaking, it is fallacious to reason from a mixture of truth in fact and truth in fiction to conclusions about truth in fiction. From a mixture of prefixed and unprefixed premises, nothing follows. But in practice the fallacy is often not so bad. The factual premises in mixed reasoning may be part of the background against which we read the fiction. They may carry over into the fiction, not because there is anything explicit in the fiction to make them true, but rather because there is nothing to make them false. There is nothing in the Holmes stories, for instance, that gives us any reason to bracket our background knowledge of the broad outlines of London geography. Only a few details need changing—principally details having to do with 221B Baker Street. To move the stations around, or even to regard their locations as an open question, would be uncalled for. What's true in fact about their locations is true also in the stories. Then it is no error to reason from such facts to conclusions about what else is true in the stories.

You've heard it all before. Reasoning about truth in fiction is very like counterfactual reasoning. We make a supposition contrary to fact—what if this match had been struck? In reasoning about what would have happened in that counterfactual situation, we use factual premises. The match was dry, there was oxygen about, and so forth. But we do not use factual premises altogether freely, since some of them would fall victim to the change that takes us from actuality to the envisaged counterfactual situation. We do not use the factual premiss that the match was inside the matchbox at the time in question, or that it was at room temperature a second later. We depart from actuality as far as we must to reach a possible world where the counterfactual supposition comes true (and that might be quite far if the supposition is a fantastic one). But we do not make gratuitous changes. We hold fixed the features of actuality that do not have to be changed as part of the least disruptive way of making the supposition true. We can safely reason from the part of our factual background that is thus held fixed.

By now, several authors have treated counterfactual conditionals along the lines just sketched. Differences of detail between these treatments are unimportant for our present purposes. My own version[10] runs as follows. A counterfactual of the form "If it were that ϕ, then it would be that ψ" is non-vacuously true iff some possible world where both ϕ and ψ are true differs less from our actual world, on balance, then does any world where ϕ is true but ψ is not true. It is vacuously true iff ϕ is true at no possible worlds. (I omit accessibility restrictions for simplicity.)

Getting back to truth in fiction, recall that the trouble with Analysis 0 was that it ignored background, and thereby brought into consideration bizarre worlds that differed gratuitously from our actual world. A fiction will in general require some departures from actuality, the more so if it is a fantastic fiction. But we need to keep the departures from actuality under control. It is wrong, or at least eccentric, to read the Holmes stories as if they might for all we know be taking place at a world where three-nostrilled detectives pursue purple gnomes. The remedy is, roughly speaking, to analyze statements of truth in fiction as counterfactuals. What

[10]Given in *Counterfactuals* (Oxford: Blackwell, 1973).

is true in the Sherlock Holmes stories is what would be true if those stories were told as known fact rather than fiction.

Spelling this out according to my treatment of counterfactuals, we have ANALYSIS I: *A sentence of the form "In the fiction f, φ" is non-vacuously true iff some world where f is told as known fact and φ is true differs less from our actual world, on balance, than does any world where f is told as known fact and φ is not true. It is vacuously true iff there are no possible worlds where f is told as known fact.* (I postpone consideration of the vacuous case.)

We sometimes speak of *the* world of a fiction. What is true in the Holmes stories is what is true, as we say, "in the world of Sherlock Holmes." That we speak this way should suggest that it is right to consider less than all the worlds where the plot of the stories is enacted, and less even than all the worlds where the stories are told as known fact. "In the world of Sherlock Holmes," as in actuality, Baker Street is closer to Paddington Station than to Waterloo Station and there are no purple gnomes. But it will not do to follow ordinary language to the extent of supposing that we can somehow single out a single one of the worlds where the stories are told as known fact. Is the world of Sherlock Holmes a world where Holmes has an even or an odd number of hairs on his head at the moment when he first meets Watson? What is Inspector Lestrade's blood type? It is absurd to suppose that these questions about the world of Sherlock Holmes have answers. The best explanation of that is that the worlds of Sherlock Holmes are plural, and the questions have different answers at different ones. If we may assume that some of the worlds where the stories are told as known fact differ least from our world, then these are the worlds of Sherlock Homes. What is true throughout them is true in the stories; what is false throughout them is false in the stories; what is true at some and false at others is neither true nor false in the stories. Any answer to the silly questions just asked would doubtless fall in the last category. It is for the same reason that the chorus of Sir Joseph Porter's sisters and cousins and aunts has no determinate size: it has different sizes at different ones of the worlds of *H.M.S. Pinafore*.[11]

Under Analysis I, truth in a given fiction depends on matters of contingent fact. I am not thinking of the remote possibility that accidental properties of the fiction might somehow enter into determining which are the worlds where that fiction is told as known fact. Rather, it is a contingent matter which of those worlds differ more from ours and which less, and which (if any) differ least. That is because it is a contingent fact—indeed it is *the* contingent fact on which all others depend— which possible world is our actual world. To the extent that the character of our world carries over into the worlds of Sherlock Holmes, what is true in the stories depends on what our world is like. If the stations of London had been differently located, it might have been true in the stories (and not because the stories would

---

[11]Heintz (*op. cit.*) disagrees; he supposes that for each fiction there is a single world to be considered, but a world that is in some respects indeterminate. I do not know what to make of an indeterminate world, unless I regard it as a superposition of all possible ways of resolving the indeterminacy—or, in plainer language, as a set of determinate worlds that differ in the respects in question.

then have been different) that Holmes lived nearer to Waterloo Station than to Paddington Station.

This contingency is all very well when truth in fiction depends on well-known contingent facts about our world, as it does in the examples I have so far given to motivate Analysis 1. It is more disturbing if truth in fiction turns out to depend on contingent facts that are not well known. In an article setting forth little-known facts about the movement of snakes, Carl Gans has argued as follows:

> In "The Adventure of the Speckled Band" Sherlock Holmes solves a murder mystery by showing that the victim has been killed by a Russell's viper that has climbed up a bell-rope. What Holmes did not realize was that Russell's viper is not a constrictor. The snake is therefore incapable of concertina movement and could not have climbed the rope. Either the snake reached its victim some other way or the case remains open.[12]

We may well look askance at this reasoning. But if Analysis 1 is correct then so is Gans's argument. The story never quite says that Holmes was right that the snake climbed the rope. Hence there are worlds where the Holmes stories are told as known fact, where the snake reached the victim some other way, and where Holmes therefore bungled. Presumably some of these worlds differ less from ours than their rivals where Holmes was right and where Russell's viper is capable of concertina movement up a rope. Holmes's infallibility, of course, is not a countervailing resemblance to actuality; our world contains no infallible Holmes.

Psychoanalysis of fictional characters provides a more important example. The critic uses (what he believes to be) little-known facts of human psychology as premisses, and reasons to conclusions that are far from obvious about the childhood or the adult mental state of the fictional character. Under Analysis 1 his procedure is justified. Unless countervailing considerations can be found, to consider worlds where the little-known fact of psychology does not hold would be to depart gratuitously from actuality.

The psychoanalysis of fictional characters has aroused vigorous objections. So would Gans's argument, if anyone cared. I shall keep neutral in these quarrels, and try to provide for the needs of both sides. Analysis 1, or something close to it, should capture the usage of Gans and the literary psychoanalysts. Let us find an alternative analysis to capture the conflicting usage of their opponents. I shall not try to say which usage is more conducive to appreciation of fiction and critical insight.

Suppose we decide, *contra* Gans and the literary psychoanalysts, that little-known or unknown facts about our world are irrelevant to truth in fiction. But let us not fall back to Analysis 0; it is not our only alternative. Let us still recognize that it is perfectly legitimate to reason to truth in fiction from a background of well-known facts.

[12]Carl Gans, "How Snakes Move," *Scientific American*, 222 (1970): 93.

Must they really be facts? It seems that if little-known or unknown facts are irrelevant, then so are little-known or unknown errors in the body of shared opinion that is generally taken for fact. We think we all know that there are no purple gnomes, but what if there really are a few, unknown to anyone except themselves, living in a secluded cabin near Loch Ness? Once we set aside the usage given by Analysis 1, it seems clear that whatever purple gnomes may be hidden in odd corners of our actual world, there are still none of them in the worlds of Sherlock Holmes. We have shifted to viewing truth in fiction as the joint product of explicit content and a background of generally prevalent beliefs.

Our own beliefs? I think not. That would mean that what is true in a fiction is constantly changing. Gans might not be right yet, but he would eventually become right about Holmes's error if enough people read his article and learned that Russell's viper could not climb a rope. When the map of Victorian London was finally forgotten, it would cease to be true that Holmes lived nearer to Paddington than to Waterloo. Strange to say, the historical scholar would be in no better position to know what was true in the fictions of his period than the ignorant layman. That cannot be right. What was true in a fiction when it was first told is true in it forevermore. It is our knowledge of what is true in the fiction that may wax or wane.

The proper background, then, consists of the beliefs that generally prevailed in the community where the fiction originated: the beliefs of the author and his intended audience. And indeed the factual premisses that seemed to us acceptable in reasoning about Sherlock Holmes were generally believed in the community of origin of the stories. Everyone knew roughly where the principal stations of London were, everyone disbelieved in purple gnomes, and so forth.

One last complication. Suppose Conan Doyle was a secret believer in purple gnomes; thinking that his belief in them was not shared by anyone else he kept it carefully to himself for fear of ridicule. In particular, he left no trace of this belief in his stories. Suppose also that some of his original readers likewise were secret believers in purple gnomes. Suppose, in fact, that everyone alive at the time was a secret believer in purple gnomes, each thinking that his own belief was not shared by anyone else. Then it is clear (to the extent that anything is clear about such a strange situation) that the belief in purple gnomes does not "generally prevail" in quite the right way, and there are still no purple gnomes in the worlds of Sherlock Holmes. Call a belief *overt* in a community at a time iff more or less everyone shares it, more or less everyone thinks that more or less everyone else shares it, and so on.[13] The proper background, we may conclude, comprises the beliefs that are overt in the community of origin of the fiction.

[13]A better definition of overt belief, under the name of "common knowledge," may be found in my *Convention* (Cambridge, Mass.: Harvard University Press, 1969), pp. 52–60. That name was unfortunate, since there is no assurance that it will be knowledge, or even that it will be true. See also the discussion of "mutual knowledge*" in Stephen Schiffer, *Meaning* (Oxford: Oxford University Press, 1972), pp. 30–42.

Assume, by way of idealization, that the beliefs overt in the community are each possible and jointly compossible. Then we can assign to the community a set of possible worlds, called the *collective belief worlds* of the community, comprising exactly those worlds where the overt beliefs all come true. Only if the community is uncommonly lucky will the actual world belong to this set. Indeed, the actual world determines the collective belief worlds of the community of origin of the fiction and then drops out of the analysis. (It is of course a contingent matter what that community is and what is overtly believed there.) We are left with two sets of worlds: the worlds where the fiction is told as known fact, and the collective belief worlds of the community of origin. The first set gives the content of the fiction; the second gives the background of prevalent beliefs.

It would be a mistake simply to consider the worlds that belong to both sets. Fictions usually contravene at least some of the community's overt beliefs. I can certainly tell a story in which there are purple gnomes, though there are none at our collective belief worlds. Further, it will usually be overtly believed in the community of origin of a fiction that the story is not told as known fact—storytellers seldom deceive—so none of the worlds where the fiction is told as known fact can be a collective belief world of the community. Even if the two sets do overlap (the fiction is plausible and the author palms it off as fact) the worlds that belong to both sets are apt to be special in ways having nothing to do with what is true in the fiction. Suppose the story tells of a bungled burglary in recent times, and suppose it ends just as the police reach the scene. Any collective belief world of ours where this story is told as known fact is a world where the burglary was successfully covered up; for it is an overt belief among us that no such burglary ever hit the news. That does not make it true in the story that the burglary was covered up.

What we need is something like Analysis 1, but applied from the standpoint of the collective belief worlds rather than the actual world. What is true in the Sherlock Holmes stories is what would be true, according to the overt beliefs of the community of origin, if those stories were told as known fact rather than fiction.

Spelling this out, we have ANALYSIS 2: *A sentence of the form "In the fiction f, φ" is non-vacuously true iff, whenever w is one of the collective belief worlds of the community of origin of f, then some world where f is told as known fact and φ is true differs less from the world w, on balance, than does any world where f is told as known fact and φ is not true. It is vacuously true iff there are no possible worlds where f is told as known fact.* It is Analysis 2, or something close to it, that I offer to opponents of Gans and the literary psychoanalysts.

I shall briefly consider two remaining areas of difficulty and sketch strategies for dealing with them. I shall not propose improved analyses, however; partly because I am not quite sure what changes to make, and partly because Analysis 2 is quite complicated enough already.

I have said that truth in fiction is the joint product of two sources: the explicit content of the fiction, and a background consisting either of the facts about our world (Analysis 1) or of the beliefs overt in the community of origin (Analysis 2).

Perhaps there is a third source which also contributes: carry-over from other truth in fiction. There are two cases: intra-fictional and inter-fictional.

In the *Threepenny Opera,* the principal characters are a treacherous crew. They constantly betray one another, for gain or to escape danger. There is also a street-singer. He shows up, sings the ballad of Mack the Knife, and goes about his business without betraying anyone. Is he also a treacherous fellow? The explicit content does not make him so. Real people are not so very treacherous, and even in Weimar Germany it was not overtly believed that they were, so background does not make him so either. Yet there is a moderately good reason to say that he is treacherous: in the *Threepenny Opera,* that's how people are. In the worlds of the *Threepenny Opera,* everyone put to the test proves treacherous, the streetsinger is there along with the rest, so doubtless he too would turn out to be treacherous if we saw more of him. His treacherous nature is an intra-fictional carry-over from the treacherous natures in the story of Macheath, Polly, Tiger Brown, and the rest.

Suppose I write a story about the dragon Scrulch, a beautiful princess, a bold knight, and what not. It is a perfectly typical instance of its stylized genre, except that I never say that Scrulch breathes fire. Does he nevertheless breathe fire in my story? Perhaps so, because dragons in that sort of story do breathe fire. But the explicit content does not make him breathe fire. Neither does background, since in actuality and according to our beliefs there are no animals that breathe fire. (It just might be analytic that nothing is a dragon unless it breathes fire. But suppose I never *called* Scrulch a dragon; I merely endowed him with all the standard drag-only attributes except fire-breathing.) If Scrulch does breathe fire in my story, it is by inter-fictional carry-over from what is true of dragons in other stories.

I have spoken of Conan Doyle's Holmes stories; but many other authors also have written Holmes stories. These would have little point without inter-fictional carry-over. Surely many things are true in these satellite stories not because of the explicit content of the satellite story itself, and not because they are part of the background, but rather because they carry over from Conan Doyle's original Holmes stories. Similarly, if instead of asking what is true in the entire corpus of Conan Doyle's Holmes stories we ask what is true in "The Hound of the Basker-villes," we will doubtless find many things that are true in that story only by virtue of carry-over from Conan Doyle's other Holmes stories.

I turn finally to vacuous truth in impossible fictions. Let us call a fiction *impossible* iff there is no world where it is told as known fact rather than fiction. That might happen in either of two ways. First, the plot might be impossible. Second, a possible plot might imply that there could be nobody in a position to know or tell of the events in question. If a fiction is impossible in the second way, then to tell it as known fact would be to know its truth and tell truly something that implies that its truth could not be known; which is impossible.

According to all three of my analyses, anything whatever is vacuously true in an impossible fiction. That seems entirely satisfactory if the impossibility is blatant: if we are dealing with a fantasy about the troubles of the man who squared the circle, or with the worst sort of incoherent time-travel story. We should not expect to have a non-trivial concept of truth in blatantly impossible fiction, or perhaps we should expect to have one only under the pretence—not to be taken too seriously—that there are impossible possible worlds as well as the possible possible worlds.

But what should we do with a fiction that is not blatantly impossible, but impossible only because the author has been forgetful? I have spoken of truth in the Sherlock Holmes stories. Strictly speaking, these (taken together) are an impossible fiction. Conan Doyle contradicted himself from one story to another about the location of Watson's old war wound. Still, I do not want to say that just anything is true in the Holmes stories!

I suppose that we might proceed in two steps to say what is true in a venially impossible fiction such as the Holmes stories. First, go from the original impossible fiction to the several possible revised versions that stay closest to the original. Then say that what is true in the original is what is true, according to one of our analyses of non-vacuous truth in fiction, in all of these revised versions. Then nothing definite will be true in the Holmes stories about the location of Watson's wound. Since Conan Doyle put it in different places, the different revised versions will differ. But at least it will be true in the stories that Watson was wounded elsewhere than in the left big toe. Conan Doyle put the wound in various places, but never there. So no revised version will put the wound in the left big toe, since that would change the story more than consistency demands.

The revised versions, like the original fiction, will be associated with acts of storytelling. The revised versions, unlike the original, will not actually be told either as fiction or as known fact. But there are worlds where they are told as fiction, and worlds where they are told as known fact.

Even when the original fiction is not quite impossible, there may be cases in which it would be better to consider not truth in the original fiction but rather truth in all suitably revised versions. We have a three-volume novel set in 1878. We learn in the first volume that the hero had lunch in Glasgow on a certain day. In the third volume, it turns out that he showed up in London that same afternoon. In no other way does this novel purport to be a fantasy of rapid transit. The author was just careless. We could without vacuity apply our analyses directly to the novel as written. Since the closest worlds where it is told as known fact are worlds with remarkable means of travel, the results would astonish anyone—for instance, our forgetful author—who had not troubled to work out a careful timetable of the hero's movements. It would be more charitable to apply the analyses not to the original story but instead to the minimally revised versions that make the hero's movements feasible by the means of travel that were available in 1878. At least, that would be best if there were ways to set the times right without major changes in the plot. There might not be, and in that case perhaps truth in the original version—surprising though some of it may be—is the best we can do.

Postscripts to

"Truth in Fiction"

A. MAKE-BELIEVE TELLING, MAKE-BELIEVE LEARNING

The storyteller purports—normally, if not invariably—to be telling the truth about matters whereof he has knowledge. I take the actual telling of the story, in effect, as part of the story itself; or in other words, I subsume the pretended truth of the story under the pretence of truthful telling. Thus I dodge Kripke's objection that the story might come true by accident, yet be as fictional as ever. For the part about the deeds of Holmes might come true by accident, but not the part about the historical origins of the stories we were told.

I thought this an artificial dodge to meet a technical difficulty. But Kendall Walton's papers on fiction[1] have persuaded me, first, that it is not at all artificial; and second, that the storyteller's pretence of truth and knowledge is only the tip of the iceberg. There is a cooperative game of make-believe, governed by conventional understandings, with players in (at least) two roles. The storytellers pretend to pass on historical information to their audience; the audience pretends to learn from their words, and to respond accordingly.

Attention to this broader game of make-believe ties up some of the loose ends. The audience may make-believedly learn their history from several different storytellers. They make-believedly do what real students of history really do: they combine information from several sources. Consider the worlds where all our accumulated make-believe learning about the doings of dragons is honest history: in the closest of these, Scrulch the dragon breathes fire. (Or better, some where he does are closer than any where he doesn't.) It doesn't matter how much about fire-breathing we get from the tale of Scrulch, how much from other stories in the same game. Likewise, take the worlds where we learn the true history of famous mysteries partly from Conan Doyle and Christie, and partly from the newspapers. (The fact that we really do trust the newspapers need not stop us from putting them to use in this game.) In the closest of these worlds, arguably, Holmes could have solved the A.B.C. murders sooner than Poirot, and he would not have needed tapes to get the goods on Nixon.

---

[1] In particular, his "On Fearing Fictions," *Journal of Philosophy* 75 (1978): 5–27, and others cited therein.

B. IMPOSSIBLE FICTIONS

An inconsistent fiction is not to be treated directly, else everything comes out true in it indiscriminately. But where we have an inconsistent fiction, there also we have several consistent fictions that may be extracted from it. (Perhaps not in the very hardest cases—but I think those cases are *meant* to defy our efforts to figure out what's true in the story.) I spoke of the consistent corrections of the original fiction. But perhaps it will be enough to consider *fragments*: corrections by deletion, with nothing written in to replace the deleted bits.

Perhaps we should take the maximal consistent fragments, obtained by deleting the bare minimum that will give us consistency. But I think it might be better to respect the salient divisions of the story into parts, even if that means taking less-than-maximal consistent fragments. I believe that Isaac Asimov's *The End of Eternity*[2] falls into inconsistency by changing its conception of time travel part way through. If so, perhaps the book less its final chapters would make a salient consistent fragment, even if we leave out scattered bits from the final chapters that could consistently have been left in.

Be that as it may, what do we do with our several consistent fragments (or corrections) when we have them? See what is true in each according to my analysis of non-vacuous truth in fiction (in whichever version seems called for). Then what?

I suggested this *method of intersection*: ϕ is true in the original fiction iff ϕ is true in every fragment. Now I would favor instead this *method of union*: ϕ is true in the original fiction iff ϕ is true in some fragment. (Not that we need choose once and for all—we can have both methods, distinguishing two senses of truth in inconsistent fiction.)

Intersection is the conservative method. Even if the fiction was inconsistent, what's true in it will still comprise a consistent theory, fully closed under implication. (I mean, to speak redundantly, *classical* implication.) But we pay a price: some of what's explicit in the fiction gets lost. That price now seems to me too high.

The method of union gives us all the truth in inconsistent fiction that the method of intersection does, and more besides. What's explicit will not get lost, for presumably it will be true in its own fragment. But we lose consistency and we lose closure under implication. Suppose two fragments disagree: ϕ is true in one, not-ϕ in the other. Then ϕ and not-ϕ both are true in the fiction as a whole. But their inconsistent conjunction is not, though they jointly imply it. Likewise many other things are not true in the fiction, though every one of them is implied jointly by two premises both true in the fiction.

All this is as it should be. If we deny that contradictory pairs are true in inconsistent fiction, we deny its distinctive peculiarity. Then we must not close under

[2](New York: Fawcett, 1955).

implication, on pain of obliterating the distinction between what's true in the story and what isn't. We should not even close under the most obvious and uncontroversial sort of implication: the inference from conjuncts to conjunction. (Here is where the relevantists go wrong, seduced by their hope that truth in inconsistent fiction might after all be closed under some relation that might colorably bear the name of implication.) It is true in the Holmes stories that Watson was wounded in the shoulder; it is true in the stories that he was wounded in the leg. It is simply not true in the stories that he was wounded in the shoulder and the leg both—he had only *one* wound, despite the discrepancy over its location.[3]

C. FICTION IN THE SERVICE OF TRUTH

There are some who value fiction mostly as a means for the discovery of truth, or for the communication of truth. "Truth in Fiction" had nothing to say about fiction as a means to truth. But the topics can indeed be connected.

Most simply, there may be an understanding between the author and his readers to the effect that what is true in his fiction, on general questions if not on particulars, is not to depart from what he takes to be the truth. (Indeed, such an understanding might extend to particular matters as well. Imagine a scandalous political exposé, by an insider, with characters called "Nicksen," "Hague," "Wagoner," "Bondsman,". . . .) Then the audience, if they know that the author is well informed, could learn the truth by figuring out what is true in his fictions. Further, the author might discover some truth in the course of trying to keep his side of the bargain.—Doubtless this is not quite what people have in mind when they speak of the cognitive value of literature! Let us find something a bit loftier for them to mean.

Fiction might serve as a means for discovery of modal truth. I find it very hard to tell whether there could possibly be such a thing as a dignified beggar. If there could be, a story could prove it. The author of a story in which it is true that there is a dignified beggar would both discover and demonstrate that there does exist such a possibility. An actor or a painter might accomplish the same. Here the fiction serves the same purpose as an example in philosophy, though it will not work unless the story of the dignified beggar is more fully worked out than our usual examples. Conversely, note that the philosophical example is just a concise bit of fiction.

More importantly, fiction can offer us contingent truths about this world. It cannot take the place of nonfictional evidence, to be sure. But sometimes evidence

[3]The method of union goes back to Stanisław Jaśkowski, "Propositional Calculus for Contradictory Deductive Systems," *Studia Logica* 24 (1969): 143–57, and has been revived in several recent discussions of how to tolerate inconsistency. See my "Logic for Equivocators," *Noûs* 16 (1982): 431–441, and works there cited.

is not lacking. We who have lived in the world for a while have plenty of evidence, but we may not have learned as much from it as we could have done. This evidence bears on a certain proposition. If only that proposition is formulated, straightway it will be apparent that we have very good evidence for it. If not, we will continue not to know it. Here, fiction can help us. If we are given a fiction such that the proposition is obviously true in it, we are led to ask: and is it also true *simpliciter*? And sometimes, when we have plenty of unappreciated evidence, to ask the question is to know the answer. Then the author of the fiction has made a discovery, and he gives his readers the means to make that same discovery for themselves.

Sometimes the proposition learned may be one that we could formulate, once we have it in mind, without reference to the fiction that drew our attention to it. Not so in general. Sometimes reference to a fiction is the only way we have, in practice if not in principle, to formulate the truths that the fiction has called to our attention. A schlemiel is someone such that what is true of him strikingly resembles what is true in a certain fiction of a certain character therein, Schlemiel by name. Temporarily or permanently, first for those who know the story and then for others (like myself) who don't, the word "schlemiel" is indispensable in stating various truths.

So fiction can indeed serve truth. But we must beware, for also it can spread error. (1) Whatever understandings to the contrary might prevail, what is true in an author's fiction might not be true, either because the author is mistaken or because he wishes to deceive those who rely on the supposed understanding. (2) Under the method of union, several things might be true together in a fiction, but not really compossible. Then the fiction might persuade us of a modal falsehood, leading us to believe in a possibility that doesn't really exist. (3) If we have plenty of misleading evidence stored up, there may well be falsehoods that need only be stated to be believed.

D. THE PUZZLE OF THE FLASH STOCKMAN

The singer sings this song.

> I'm a stockman to my trade, and they call me Ugly Dave.
> I'm old and grey and only got one eye.
> In a yard I'm good, of course, but just put me on a horse,
> And I'll go where lots of young-'uns daren't try.

The boasting gets ever steeper: riding, whipping, branding, shearing, ...

> In fact, I'm duke of every blasted thing.

Plainly, this is fiction. What is true in it?

The answer should be that in the fiction a stockman called Ugly Dave tells a boastful pack of lies.[4] And that is indeed the answer we get if we take the closest worlds where the storyteller really is doing what he here pretends to be doing. For this is one of those exceptional cases, covered briefly in my footnote 7, in which the storyteller does not pretend to be telling the truth about matters whereof he has knowledge. The singer makes believe that he is Ugly Dave telling boastful lies.

There is a fiction in the fiction: Ugly Dave's lies are themselves a fiction, and his boasting is make-believe truthtelling. In the fiction in the fiction, he really is duke of everything. In the outer fiction he is not, but only claims to be. This iteration, in itself, is not a problem.

But there is a real problem nearby, and I have no solution to offer. Why doesn't the iteration collapse? When the singer pretends to be Ugly Dave pretending to tell the truth about himself, how does this differ from pretending to be Ugly Dave *really* telling the truth about himself? It must be the former, not the latter; else we should conclude that there is no inner fiction and that what is true in the outer fiction—now the only fiction—is that Ugly Dave is duke of everything and tells us so. That would be to miss the point entirely. We must distinguish pretending to pretend from really pretending. Intuitively it seems that we can make this distinction, but how is it to be analyzed?

---

[4] Or, at least, it is not true in the fiction that he is telling the truth. Even that would be enough to serve my purpose here. But it is simpler, and credible enough, to stick with the stronger answer.

Index

Printed in the United Kingdom
by Lightning Source UK Ltd.
107008UKS00001B/3

9 780195 032048